D1275977

TRACING THE PAST

TRACING THE PAST

WRITINGS OF
HENRY P. HEDGES
1817–1911

RELATING TO THE

History of the East End

———

Including East Hampton, Southampton,
Sag Harbor, Bridgehampton, and Southold
in Suffolk County, New York

———

EDITED BY
TOM TWOMEY

NEWMARKET PRESS   NEW YORK

All of the proceeds from the sale of this book will be
dedicated to enhancing, preserving, and building The Long
Island Collection at the East Hampton Library.

⸺◦◦◦⸺

FIRST EDITION
1   3   5   7   9   10   8   6   4   2

Library of Congress Cataloging-in-Publication Data is available upon request.

ISBN 1-55704-424-4

QUANTITY PURCHASES
Companies, professional groups, clubs, and other organizations may
qualify for special terms when ordering quantities of this title. For information,
write Special Sales Department, Newmarket Press, 18 East 48th Street,
New York, NY 10017; call (212) 832-3575; fax (212) 832-3629;
or email newmktprs@aol.com.

www.newmarketpress.com

Illustration of Henry P. Hedges on page ii reprinted
from *History of East Hampton, N.Y.*, by Henry P. Hedges
(Sag Harbor, NY: J. H. Hunt, 1897), courtesy of
The Long Island Collection at the East Hampton Library.

Book design by M.J. DiMassi

Manufactured in the United States of America

THE PUBLICATION OF THIS BOOK
WAS MADE POSSIBLE THROUGH MAJOR UNDERWRITING BY
TWOMEY, LATHAM, SHEA & KELLEY
Attorneys at Law
AND
JOHN R. KENNEDY

WITH SIGNIFICANT UNDERWRITING FROM
ALEXANDRA & ROBERT GOELET
JOAN & JOSEPH F. CULLMAN, III
KENNETH LIPPER
BICKY & GEORGE KELLNER
FRANCI & JOE RICE

Acknowledgments

THIS BOOK WOULD NOT have been possible without the extraordinary efforts of Janice Olsen, who meticulously typed and proofread the manuscript, and Stacey Schweitzer, who painstakingly created the voluminous index. Also, Dorothy King, Librarian at The Long Island Collection of the East Hampton Library, and Sheryl Foster, former East Hampton Village Historian, reviewed the early drafts and improved the book considerably. Esther Margolis of Amagansett and her staff at Newmarket Press in New York deserve special thanks for the wonderful end result.

Special attention was given to the spelling and style of the original documents with only obvious misspellings corrected in this edition of the works.

Contents

Introduction

‒‒‒‒⟨⟨⟨⟩‒‒‒‒

HENRY HEDGES died in 1911 at the age of 93. Born on a farm in Wainscott in the Town of East Hampton, he entered Clinton Academy and later became a student in Yale College. He practiced law in Sag Harbor and Bridgehampton. He was elected to the Assembly on the Whig ticket and, later, was District Attorney of Suffolk County and for many years a County Judge.

But what separated him from his fellow public servants was his abiding life long interest in local history. His first major lecture was in 1849 at the age of 32 when he delivered the Oration at the celebration of the Bicentennial Anniversary of East Hampton Town. Little about the history of East Hampton had seen its way into print prior to 1849. It was a time when books were leather-bound and somewhat scarce. Hedges broke new ground in providing historical facts and figures to residents in the community who cared about local history. His orations were printed in pamphlet form or printed in local newspapers for wide dissemination to the public. While, at times, Hedges' prose becomes florid, it was delivered at a time when oratory was one of the main entertainments of a small community. There were no movies, TV, or magazines.

What Hedges provided in lecture after lecture was a level of primary-source research using Town and Trustee records not used in prior histories. He was systematically providing access to local history in a style and language local people enjoyed—something unique until then on the East End.

xi

The sixteen lectures in this book were delivered over a 62-year period from 1849 to 1911. They have never before been collected into one, indexed, chronological volume. These works represent all of his extant historical writings. No doubt he delivered scores of other speeches and lectures which have not survived to the present.

What spurred Hedges' interest in East End local history? What relevance did he and his audiences see in learning about the early settlers of the area? Why was local history so important to Hedges and his neighbors that he spent so much time reading, thinking, and writing about what occurred on the East End two hundred years earlier?

The writer Lewis Mumford liked to point out that the main subject of history is the drama of a community's life—that is, in what manner and to what purpose did people live: what did they eat, how did they dress, at what did they work, what kind of houses had they to shelter their heads, what ideas and beliefs had they to fill their heads? Perhaps Hedges intuitively understood that to know the world, one needed to know one's community. He may have realized that all history begins in a place and eventually connects with a region, with a nation, then with the world. It all starts someplace.

At the time Hedges first began his writing, the United States was still an infant in the world of nations. Regionalism had set in dividing the north from the south. The west was being opened at a rapid pace. Change was occurring at an exponential rate—railroads and telegraphs were shrinking distances and blurring community boundaries. After the Civil War, the nation needed time to heal. Communities needed time to think about the terrible tragedy that had occurred and why communities were so different one from the other.

Perhaps, Hedges understood that his mission was to trace the past and tell stories which were little known or understood in the communities in which he lived. To help his neighbors understand who they were and from where they had come. To build their confidence. To instill some pride that they were living in a special place—a very special place. For the most part, he satisfied himself with writing solely about the East End and about the communities where he was born, raised a family and practiced law—East Hampton, Sag Harbor, Bridgehampton. He wrote no histories of Long Island or New York State—only of the East End.

In this age of instant electronic information, it may be thought of as quaint to reprint a set of writings by a man whose influence never reached beyond his local community. But as we become more world wide in our commerce and communications, there is a deep yearning for belonging to a real local community—not simply a virtual one—a place where friends greet us on the street, invite us to their homes, and talk about local issues. Issues that tangibly affect our family, our friends, and us. Issues that we feel personally.

As a result, many successful and thoughtful people yearn to participate in shaping their local community. And a community is more than a physical location with boundary lines on a map. A community can be a few people, a small neighborhood, or a whole Town. It is a place where we feel welcome—where we have participated. A place where we have invested part of ourselves. Where we have given to others, not just taken.

Whether we were born here and learned local history at our parents' knee or we chose this community as a place to live, much of what makes the East End a special place to live is its sense of community flowing from a connection to a history that began more than 350 years ago. Mumford made the interesting observation that the more history lies in back of a community, the more confident the community is that more history will lie ahead. In other words, we humans intuitively believe, right or wrong, that a good past is the guarantee of a good future.

And a good portion of what we now know or can know about the East End, what our community feels about its collective historical roots, can be traced to Henry Hedges who began quixotically talking to everyone he could find about the wonders of our local history—about the special qualities of the area. In doing so, he helped define the community we now call the East End.

All of us who love this special place owe Henry Hedges more than we can imagine.

TOM TWOMEY
East Hampton Town Historian
President, East Hampton Library
November 1999

THE LIFE OF
HENRY P. HEDGES

1817-1911

THE DETAILS OF Henry Hedges life can be found in two items which were published near the turn of the century.The first is *Portrait an Biographical Record of Suffolk County* published in 1896.The second is an interview in *The Brooklyn Eagle* published on April 10,1910.

Excerpt from *Portrait and Biographical Record of Suffolk County:*
The family of Hedges is an old and prominent one in the East, and its members, in different generations, have, in one way or another, become quite well known. Judge Hedges, who is a representative of one branch of this family, is a lawyer of more than ordinary ability. Strong individuality and force of character have made for him an enviable reputation, which marks him as one of the most striking figures at the Suffolk County Bar. A love of his fellow-men, which finds expression in a genial and kindly disposition toward every worthy man and every worthy movement, has made him one of the most popular citizens of Bridgehampton.

On the paternal side, Judge Hedges is of English descent. The first of the name to come hither was William Hedges, who emigrated from England in 1639, and purchased a tract of land in East Hampton, L.I., where he passed the remainder of his days. His son, Stephen, and grandson, Daniel, and great-grandson, Daniel, Jr., were born on Long Island, as was also the son of the latter, David, our subject's grandfather, whose birth occurred in 1744.

A man of prominence and influence, David Hedges was for fifty years a Deacon in the Presbyterian Church. He was a member of the Colonial Congress that convened at Kingston, and was a member of the convention of the state of New York which ratified the Constitution of the United States. For twenty-two years he was Supervisor, which is a longer period than any other man has ever held that office in the town of Southampton. For seven or eight sessions he was a member of the Assembly of the state of New York. By occupation he was a farmer, and in that occupation, as in public affairs, was noted for his great executive capacity. In 1777, when Sag Harbor was occupied by the British, he was coerced to furnish a large supply of hay for the army. In Meig's expedition, all these stores were burned by the American forces, who came over from Guilford, Conn., in whale-boats. The promise to pay for the supplies was not kept by the British in consequence of their loss, and Deacon Hedges was a sufferer thereby.

The father of our subject, Zephaniah Hedges, was born in Suffolk County, in December, 1768. Subsequently, he removed from the town of Southampton, his birthplace, and settled in East Hampton, where the remainder of his life was passed. He was a man of decision of character, unswerving rectitude and unerring judgment, which enabled him to achieve success. By his first marriage, which united him with Miss Susan Miller, he had an only child, Thomas S., who died in infancy. December 13, 1809, he married Miss Phebe P. Osborn, who was born October 12, 1781. He passed away September 16, 1847, and his wife died March 12, 1864, when eighty-two years old.

The children of the parental family were as follows: Thomas S., born February 22, 1810; Edwin, December 29, 1811; Maria P., August 13, 1815; Henry P., October 13, 1817; Jeremiah O., August 29, 1819; and Phoebe P., August 23, 1822.

It has been said that the farm is the training ground that produces men of physical and intellectual strength. From it have gone forth men now eminent in every profession, business and calling; men of brawn as well as brain, who have been changed into living forces, as crude gold is transmuted into current money. Thus it has been with Judge Hedges. He was born on his father's farm in Suffolk County, and there obtained those habits of self-reliance and perseverance which have been the stepping-stones to his success.

Not satisfied with the education received in the common schools, our subject entered the Clinton Academy at East Hampton when fourteen years old, and three years later became a student in Yale College, from which he was graduated with the Class of '38. The following year was spent at home, after which he spent a year in the law school at

New Haven, Conn. Entering the office of David S. Seymour, of Troy, N.Y., he continued the study of law from May until September, and then studied with Judge Miller, of Riverhead, until April, 1842. From there he went to New York City, and was in the office of J.C. Albertson for some time.

After his admission to the Bar, our subject went to Ohio, with a view to locating, but six months later returned home, and September 27, 1843, began practicing his profession at Sag Harbor. March 16, 1854, he removed from that village to Bridgehampton, where he has since remained, although he continued his practice in Sag Harbor until 1893. In the fall of 1851, he was elected to the Assembly on the Whig ticket, and later was District Attorney of Suffolk County. This was in 1861, and he was re-elected to that position in 1864. His fearless loyalty to his honest convictions, his sturdy opposition to misrule in municipal affairs, and his deep insight into men and their motives led to his election to the office of County Judge in 1865, and that position he held for four years. In 1873 he was re-elected, and was the incumbent of the office six years more. Since 1869 he has been President of the Sag Harbor Savings Bank. He has been executor for many estates, is himself the owner of one hundred acres of fine land, and has other interests in the county.

Politically the Judge was first a Whig, being a Free-Soiler, and was one of the founders of the Republican party in 1856, since which time he has always exercised a potential influence in the party in Long Island and the state. During the Civil War he did all in his power to aid the Union cause. As a citizen, lawyer, jurist or public officer, he has endeared himself to his many friends, whose regard he has gained by his probity of character, broad intellectual attainments and grace of manners.

May 9, 1843, Judge Hedges married Glorianna, daughter of Samuel and Mary Ann (Smith) Osborn. To them were born three children, namely: Samuel O., who is a farmer in Bridgehampton; Edwin, who graduated from Yale College in 1869, was admitted to the Bar, and practiced for some years, but died in 1881; and William, a graduate of Yale College, Class of '74, now a minister of the Congregational Church in Harwinton, Litchfield County, Conn. Mrs. Glorianna Hedges died February 1, 1891, and the Judge married Mary G. Hildreth, February 23, 1892.

The Judge is a speaker of unusual force and ability, and has delivered many addresses in the county. He is deeply interested in local history, and has completed a book relating to the town. At this time he is working on a history of his native town, East Hampton, that will soon be published. Since the fall of 1841 he has been a member of the Presbyterian Church, and has been an Elder for many years.

Excepts from an interview published in *The Brooklyn Eagle* on April 10, 1910.

"I suppose I am related to all the Parsons in this part of the country. My grandmother on my mother's side was a Parsons. My mother was an Osborne. My grandmother on my father's side was a Howell. I am kin to all the Daytons, Bakers and many more old families of Long Island descent. I was born October 13, 1817, in Wainscott, town of East Hampton, Suffolk County, N.Y. I graduated from Yale in 1838. The first minister of Southampton was Abraham Pierson and his son was the first President of Yale College. Alphonso Taft, father of our President, was my tutor in Latin, and I remember him as one of the finest men I have ever known. A great, big, grand man with a big voice—just the man to have such a son as our present President of these United States—for I am a Republican, and have been from the very start.

"I was admitted to the bar of the State of New York in May, 1842. I practiced law in Sag Harbor from 1843 to 1845. In 1852, I was elected member of the Assembly. I removed from Sag Harbor to Bridgehampton in March, 1854. Here I have resided and I ran a large farm until within the last ten years. I was district attorney of the county of Suffolk from January 1, 1862 to January 1, 1866; county judge from 1866 to 1870, and from 1874 to 1880, was also surrogate. I was president of the Sag Harbor Savings Bank from 1868 to 1898. I have been largely a student of local history, and have delivered many centennial, bi-centennial and semi-centennial addresses, which have been published as histories of Bridgehampton and Sag Harbor.

"My largest published work was the history of the Town of Easthampton. It was published in 1897. Of the many addresses I have delivered, one circumstance was very remarkable. In 1849, on the occasion of the two hundredth anniversary of the settlement of the town of Easthampton, I delivered the address, and in 1899 I was again the speaker, at the two hundred and fiftieth anniversary of the settlement of the same town.

"My long life and health I attribute to the fact that I am a total abstainer from all intoxicants as a beverage. I have not been a pessimist, but an optimist, an observer of the Sabbath and a church member attending regularly the services of the church, and since 1847 have been a Presbyterian elder. I have found that tranquility, peace of mind and hope all tend to longevity; that temperance in eating and drinking are absolutely necessary. I contend that when good bread and butter cease to taste good, it is time to stop eating.

"I have always been a hard worker. I believe in it—manual, moral and intellectual. The only way to be happy is to be useful. God gave man the Sabbath as a day of rest. You cannot really rest until you first get tired. So I work for six days and then I rest. Of course, I have had my relaxation from arduous labor, and have found the greatest enjoyment in fishing. I have fished in fresh water for all the small fish, eels included, and for all the big fish, whales included, in salt water. In 1838 I was in one of two boats off the shore of Easthampton when we killed a whale. In the vernacular of fisherfolk, 'I was in the boat that killed the whale.' It was a good-sized whale, too. We got 30 barrels of oil from it and three barrelfuls just from the tongue alone. In my fishing experiences, I found that a man could stand more exposure and do more work without strong drink than he could with it. Long life and temperance go together and result in happiness.

"In 1883 was celebrated the two hundredth anniversary of this county. I was one of the speakers on that occasion, and the published history of the county contains my picture, a steel engraving, as a frontispiece. I am now busy at work, historically, getting ready for the two hundred and fiftieth anniversary of Bridgehampton, which is to be celebrated on the 4th of next July. We are to have a great celebration, and one of the main features will be the dedication of a monument which has cost $2,500 and which will be in memory of the many famous people who have gone out from this modest island and become known as great among men. An invitation has been sent to Colonel Roosevelt, and we are hoping that he will be among the many guests expected. I am taking a very deep interest in preparing an address for the occasion."

Henry P. Hedges died at his residence in the Town of Southampton on September 26, 1911. He left a widow Mary G. Hedges, residing at Bridgehampton; a son Samuel Q. Hedges, residing at Bridgehampton; and a son William Hedges, residing at Colebrook, Connecticut.

TRACING THE PAST

for Patti

January 2000

CHAPTER I

THE CELEBRATION OF THE BI-CENTENNIAL ANNIVERSARY OF EAST HAMPTON

Delivered in 1849 at the age of 32

FELLOW TOWNSMEN OF EAST-HAMPTON:

WE MEET TO-DAY as natives of the same neighborhood, having enjoyed the same blessings, entertained the same early associations, indulged the same recollections, being bound together by the same social ties, and descended from the same common ancestry, to celebrate the Second Centennial Anniversary of the settlement of this Town.

We are not unwilling to acknowledge our origins—we delight to honor the memory of our heroic fathers, "Our pious ancestry," who "first planted religion, civilization and refinement upon these shores." Degenerate and base indeed were we, enjoying as we do the fruits of their toils and sacrifices, never to turn in grateful remembrance and pay the tribute of filial affection to those who so dearly purchased them for their descendants. It is a high and holy sentiment of our nature which prompts us, amid all our wanderings, to re-visit the home of our childhood, and look upon the graves of our fathers. Travel far as we may from the smiling abode of our infancy; remain, as we may, for many long years absent, and still this sentiment clings to us in our wanderings. It travels with us to the remotest lands. It swells our bosom on the ocean wave. It triumphs over time and space. One after another the associations and early remembrances of our youth come gushing upon the memory. We are overwhelmed by the tender recollections of our native land, and—subdued by the emotions which our memory brings—we are irresistibly prompted to turn our footsteps to the

1

home of our infancy and the land of our fathers. There, where we drew our first faint breath, we would breathe our last: and where our fathers are buried we desire our lifeless bodies to repose.

It is a kindred, social sentiment which prompts us to inquire into our origin, to trace our ancestry, to commune in imagination with the spirits of our fathers, to recount their deeds, to celebrate their valor, honor their memory, and profit by their example and experience. Such considerations, we trust, brought us together to this, our home, the land of our venerated fathers.

History we know is over instructive in its lessons. The future to us is unknown and uncertain; but the past is forever fixed and unchangeable. We may speculate upon the future; each for himself may plan and arrange and build his superstructure according to his visionary anticipations. But whether that future shall rise in the shape and fair proportions of his visions or not, who can tell? But the past admits no change. Its realities remain unaffected by the present, unaltered by images of the future. There we rest upon the solid basis of experience, not upon the illusions of the imagination. But history becomes doubly interesting to us when it relates the experience of our individual ancestors; of those whose blood flows in our veins; who reared the successive generations that lived and died until they at length gave to us that life which had been transmitted to them.

Under such revelations of history we feel our souls thrilling with interest in the relation of every incident of the past. We sympathize with our fathers. We feel the cold blast that sent its shivering power upon their venerable, unsheltered heads. We feel the burning sun that poured its fierce, relentless rays upon them. We tremble for them amid their dangers. We triumph with them in success. We hope with them in their anticipations. We lose our consciousness of the present. We seem to feel the spirits of the departed animating our own bosoms; and as we live in their experience almost say, "The souls of our fathers live in us."

Our ancestors were the Puritans of England. We cannot doubt as to their character, their purposes, or their motives. England had just awoke from her religious slumbers. The principles of civil and religious liberty were forcing their way upon the mind of the nation. The royal houses of Plantagenet and Tudor, of York and Lancaster, had passed away. Kings were seen to be mortal. Their right to prescribe a religion for the people began to be denied. Their Divine right to govern began to be doubted. Resistance to arbitrary imposition and authority was openly proclaimed. The right of the people to a constant representation in the government was asserted; and civil war rolled over the fair field of their native England.

Amid the strife of battle and the din of murderous conflict our fathers left their country—sought this unexplored, unsettled Western World,—trusting here to hold unmolested their religion and their liberties, and transmit them to a peaceful, happy posterity in the wilds of their new abode. They left in the age of John Hampden and Milton, and soon after their arrival came the news of the Royal overthrow. The same year that saw the triumph of liberty in Great Britain, and consigned Charles Stuart, its monarch, to the block, saw the settlement of this, our native town.

This town was purchased as far eastward as Montauk in 1648 by Theophilus Eaton, Governor of the Colony of New Haven, and Edward Hopkins, Governor of the Colony of Connecticut, for the benefit of the original settlers, and was assigned to them by Eaton and Hopkins in the spring of 1651, in consideration of the sum of £30, 4s, 8d sterling.

Gardiner's Island had been purchased and was settled by Lion Gardiner in 1639. Southampton and Southold were settled in 1640.

At what precise date the first inhabitants of this town planted themselves upon the soil is not known. It was probably in the spring or summer of 1649. The earliest instrument I find on record indicating their residence here is a letter of attorney from John Hand in relation to some lands in Stanstede, in Kent, England; it bears date Oct. 1st, 1649.

As many of the inhabitants came from Maidstone, in the County of Kent, in England, they first called their plantation by that name. As early as 1650, and within a year from the first settlement it is mentioned on the Records by its present name.

At the time of the first occupation of this new territory the Indians were numerous, and situated on every side. On the East, at Montaukett, the Royal Wyandanch swayed the scepter. On the North, at Shelter Island, his brother, Poggatacut, ruled the tribe of Manhassets, and a third brother, by the name of Nowedinah presided over the destinies of the Shinnecock tribe. Little or no intercourse was held between East Hampton and Southampton through the unbroken wilderness which intervened.

What a bold and daring step was that: to leave behind the comforts, the convenience and the joys of their native land; leave far, and perhaps forever, their friends so dear to them. Forsake their homes and their firesides, and, arrived at Salem, at Boston, or Lynn, to leave still behind those flourishing towns and bend their steps hitherward. And here, in the dark and gloomy wilderness, in silence unbroken save by the Indian war-whoop, by the hideous cry of the wild beast, or the solemn and majestic roar of Father Ocean, take up their final earthly resting-place and home.

Interesting to us would it be did we know more of the character and circumstances of those first few families. We should like to paint them as they were, in life and being—what undaunted resolution— what firm religious trust spoke upon their countenances and told of the soul within. What high purposes, what sublime hopes lighted up their eyes and swelled their bosoms—what intellectual cultivation sat upon their brows? We should like to set before you their stalwart forms and iron frames, but their bones have long since reposed in the cemetery of their own selection, and no painter's canvass secures their earthly form.

The first settlers of East Hampton were

JOHN HAND,	JOHN STRATTON, SEN'R,
THOMAS TALMAGE, JR.	ROBERT BOND,
DANIEL HOWE,	ROBERT ROSE,
THOMAS THOMSON,	JOSHUA BARNES,
JOHN MULFORD.	

The following became very early their associates:

THOMAS OSBORN,	NATHANIEL BISHOP,
WILLIAM HEDGES,	WILLIAM BARNES,
RALPH DAYTON,	LION GARDINER,
THOMAS CHATFIELD,	JOHN OSBORNE,
THOMAS OSBORN, JR.,	JEREMIAH VEALE,
WILLIAM FITHIAN,	JOHN MILLER,
RICHARD BROOKES,	CHARLES BARNES,
WILLIAM SIMONDS,	STEPHEN HAND,
SAMUEL BELKNAP,	THOMAS BAKER,
SAMUEL PARSONS,	ANANIAS CONKLIN,
JOSHUA GARLICKE,	RICHARD SHAW,
FULKE DAVIS,	JEREMIAH MEACHAM.

The first six of the original nine settlers came from Lynn, Massachusetts, to this place. The father of Talmage was a large proprietor of Lynn and was made a freeman of that town previous to 1638. Howe had been a sea captain and had lived in Salem, Massachusetts; in 1650 he sold his possessions in East Hampton to Thomas Baker, and removed to England. Hand was from the hamlet of Stanstede, in the County of Kent, England. Thomson came here from New London. Barnes and Mulford arrived at Salem, from England, but a short time previous, it is said.

It has, however, been a tradition in the Mulford family that he came to East Hampton from Southampton. Perhaps he made but a short stay in Southampton. Ralph Dayton came from England to Boston and thence here. Thomas Baker came from Milford, Connecticut, in 1650; he was an inhabitant of that town as early as 1639. Thomas James and his father came to Charlestown, in Massachusetts, in 1632; they afterwards went to New-Haven, Connecticut, and Thomas James removed from thence to East-Hampton as early as 1651; and became their first Minister of the Gospel. The father of Charles Barnes resided in Eastwinch, in the County of Norfolk, in England; he died in 1663, leaving property to his son. Charles Barnes was the first schoolmaster. Joshua Garlicke was the miller. The family of Fithian have a tradition that their first ancestor in this town came from Southampton.

The family of Schellenger are mentioned in the Town Records as early as 1657. Thomas Edwards is mentioned as early as 1651. Lion Gardiner removed from Gardiner's Island to this town in 1653.

Few facts in relation to the family history of our early ancestors remain. The hand of time has moved on with sure, resistless progress, and left on record but few memorials of the dead.

It is said that of the first settlers:

Ralph Dayton died in	1657.
John Hand and Lion Gardiner in	1663.
Robert Rose, who was the father of Thomas Rose	
of Southampton, must have died previous to	1665.
as appears by the record of conveyance of his lands,	
by his son, Thomas, to George Miller, dated 19th Dec., 1665.	
William Hedges died about	1674.

Many of our ancestors, however, lived to a very great age. Their simple habits, correct life, and perhaps an originally strong constitution lengthened out their days far beyond the ordinary life of man.

Richard Stratton died	June 7th, 1698.
William Barnes, Sen'r	Dec'r 1st, 1698.
Joshua Garlicke, aged about 100 years	March 7th, 1700.
Richard Shaw	Oct'r 18th, 1708.
Thomas Osborne, aged 90 years	Sept. 12th, 1712.
Robert Dayton, a son of Ralph Dayton,	
aged 84 years	April 16th, 1712.
Samuel Parsons, aged 84 years	July 6th, 1714.
Steven Hedges, a son of William Hedges,	
lacking 6 months of 100 years old	July 7th, 1734.

He must have been familiar with the origin of this town, and with its history for at least 85 years.

Joseph Osborn, (a son of Thomas Osborn, one of the first settlers,) died here, in this Temple of our fathers, while worshiping, a little more than one hundred years since. The following is a literal copy of the record of his death as contained in the Records of the Rev. Nathaniel Huntting, the then minister of the town:

> "Oct. 2nd, 1743:—Joseph Osborn, son of Tho's Osborn deceased, sunk down and died in ye Meeting House just after morning prayer was begun, a quarter after ten, aged almost 83 years. He never spake a word but expired at once."

The first inhabitants of this town settled in the Southern part of the main street and on each side of what is now Town Pond. At that time however there was no collection of water, and a swamp or marsh covered the center of the street. A small rivulet or drain communicated with and ran into the swamp from the North.

The following are the names of those who lived upon the East side of the street, commencing with the Southern extremity and succeeding in the following order:

WILLIAM HEDGES,   BENJAMIN PRICE,
JEREMIAH MEACHAM,   WILLIAM EDWARDS,
GEORGE MILLER,   JOHN EDWARDS,
THOMAS JAMES,   NATHAN BIRDSALL,
LION GARDINER,   SAMUEL PARSONS,
THOMAS CHATFIELD,   WILLIAM BARNES,
ROBERT DAYTON,   NATHANIEL BISHOP.
JOHN OSBORN,

The following are a few of those who lived upon the West side, without any reference to order, it being difficult to locate them.

JEREMIAH DAILY,   JOSHUA GARLICKE,
ANDREW MILLER,   RICHARD BROOKE,
JOHN HAND,   THOMAS TALMAGE,
JOHN STRATTON,   STEPHEN HAND,
ROBERT BOND,   JOHN MULFORD,
THOMAS BAKER,   RICHARD STRATTON,
WILLIAM FITHIAN,   STEPHEN OSBORN.

The church stood near the old burying-ground or on its site, on the east side of the street. A highway ran from near where the church now stands, over the swamp east, and afterwards was the travelled road to the village of Amagansett.

Their houses were small, with thatched roofs. The Church was of similar dimensions—thatched roof and boarded sides.

The original allotments of land were thirty-four in number. The lots were from eight to twelve acres each, laid out between the street and Hook Pond, and the Swamp East and what was then common land West, (*probably now the highway*.) The Mill stood at the south end of the town and gave the name to the lane which leads to the beach. It was then called "Mill-Lane."*

Thomas Baker kept the Tavern or Ordinary. Before the Church was erected the meetings were held at his house, for which he was to have "the sum of £0 1s. 6d. each Sabbath."

The licensing of Baker to keep Tavern in 1654 is thus concisely expressed upon the Records:

"June 29th, 1654.—It is ordered that Thomas Baker shall keep the Ordinary."—Town Records, book 2, p. 33.

Perhaps nothing is more conspicuous in the character of our forefathers than their untiring energy, activity and enterprize. Having arrived at the chosen place of their residence they set themselves at work with ceaseless industry and perseverance until their object had been accomplished. While they were busied in laying the foundations of government, education and morals they were equally active in their daily toil and occupation.

As early as 1653 they allotted and improved the Northwest and Acabonac meadows. They soon subdued a great extent of wilderness and brought it under cultivation. As early as 1653 nearly all the arable land in the Eastern and Western Plains, a circuit of two miles, was under some degree of cultivation.

The first settlers, (although undoubtedly well educated men, as their records and laws most equivocally prove,) were chiefly farmers. They suffered many inconveniences for the want of mechanics. They sent to Southold for a weaver; to Huntington for a blacksmith, and to Wethersfield for a carpenter. The invitation to the weaver is on record in the following words:

---

*This Mill was driven by cattle.

"February 2nd, 1653.—It is Ordered yt there shall bee an invitation sent to Goodman Morgan of Southold, if hee will come and live here and weave all the Townswork, hee shall come in free from all former charges and the Town will give him 5 and break him up 2 ackres of Land."—See Town Records, book 2, p. 31.

The country afforded a wide range and abundant pasture for cattle, and hence large flocks were kept. The first stock consisted of goats; afterwards large herds of cows and horses were maintained. They were driven out in the morning by the shepherd and back at night. The whole town's-herd were pastured together, and each one took his turn in succession in tending them.

Among their other pursuits was that of whaling. They very early made this a source of profit as well as amusement. Doubtless it was congenial to their bold and adventurous spirits. I find the following early reference to that business.

"November the 6th, 1651.—It was Ordered that Goodman Mulford shall call out ye Town by succession to loke out for whale."—Book No. 2, page 20.

Their difficulties were oftentimes occasioned by conflicting claims to shares of the whales taken by them. In 1652 upon a difficulty of that kind they "Ordered that the share of whale now in controversie between the Widow Talmage and Thomas Talmage shall be divided between them as the lot is."—Book No. 2, p. 30.

Even in our day we have heard the old and venerable fathers speak, with the enthusiasm and fire of other days, of the sports and perils of the whale chase and of their success. And tradition still informs us that Abigail Baker, who was married in 1702 to Daniel Hedges, the first settler of the name in Sagg, in her day in riding from East-Hampton to Bridgehampton, saw thirteen whales on the shore at that time between the two places. Whaling suffered sad misfortunes in that day:

"Feb. 24, 1719.—This day a whale-boat being alone the men struck a whale and she coming under ye boat in part staved it, and tho ye men were not hurt with the whale yet, before any help came to them four men were tired and chilled and fell off ye boat and oars to which they hung and were drowned, viz: Henry Parsons, William Schellinger, Junior,

Lewis Mulford, Jeremiah Conkling, Junr."—Records of Rev. Nathaniel Huntting.

We may discover the wisdom and foresight of our ancestors in establishing a free and popular Government for themselves—in laying deep and broad the foundations of their little commonwealth upon the basis of education and good morals.

The Government of the town was vested in the People. They, assembled at their Town Meetings, had all power and all authority. They elected officers; constituted courts; allotted lands; made laws, tried difficult and important causes, and from their decision there was no appeal. This Town Meeting, or "General Court," as it was sometimes called, probably met once a month. Every freeholder was required to be present at its meetings and take upon himself a part in the burdens of government; all delinquents were fined 12*d.* for non attendance at each meeting. It is almost impossible to specify the numerous and diverse acts of authority and orders made and done by this assembly. It provided school teachers and made regulations for the education of the youth. It hired the minister; assessed his salary by tax upon the property of individuals.* It built churches, and provided for the payment of building in the same manner. It admitted or excluded inhabitants or proposed settlers from its society and privileges. No person was allowed to buy or sell lands without the license and consent of the town. Hired laborers were liable to be excluded from the bounds and hospitality of the town. Their laws were made not only for the purpose of establishing order and securing justice, but they everywhere breathe a deep solicitude to prevent disputes and difficulty. The following is an illustration.

> "19th April, 1659.—It is Ordered that every man shall sett the two letters for his name at each end of his fence, in large letters, on the inside of the Post, above the upper Raile, upon penalty," &c.—Book No. 2, p. 33.

The only other Court constituted by the original inhabitants was a Court of Three Justices, sometimes called the "Court of the Three Men."

---

*The salary of Mr. James, the first minister, was £50 per annum, and afterwards £60; besides many very valuable privileges, and an exemption from taxation.

The salary of the Schoolmaster was £33 per annum.

The first three Justices who composed this Court were John Mulford, Thomas Baker, and Robert Bond. Thomas Talmage Jr. was the first Recorder or Secretary.

This Court met "at eight o'clock in the morning on the 2nd day of the 1st week in every month." It had cognizance of affairs of minor importance, and in cases of danger had power to call a special Meeting of the Town. It tried cases where the matter in controversy did not exceed five pounds. It remitted fines under that amount. An appeal might be had from the decision of this Court to the General Court or Town Meeting, as appears from the following order:

> "Oct'r 1652. Ordered if any man be aggrieved by anything that is done by the men in authority that he shall have libertie to make his appeal to the next General Court, or when the men are assembled together on the public occasions."

An illustration at once of their tender regard for their rights and their distrust of any authority irresponsible to the people. No set of men ever knew better than they that authority should never be delegated by the people "upon the presumption that it will not be abused."

Besides these three Judges their only officers were a Secretary or Recorder and a Constable. The Constable was the executive officer. He held an important station—was generally a man of some consequence. He presided as moderator in their Town Meetings.

The Records of this Court still remain. They are written in a very singular hand, by a skilful penman; but those antique hieroglyphics defy the curiosity of any but the most patient and persevering investigator.

The reports or records of adjudged cases are perhaps the best illustrations of the habits, character and severe morals of our fathers that any where exist. They gave all a hearing. The Indian or foreigner, citizen or stranger, rich or poor were admitted to their courts and received at their hands the same equal justice.

In the year 1658 Wyandanch, Sachem of Montaukett, Plaintiff, prosecuted Jeremy Daily, Defendant, for an injury done to his "*great cannow.*" The case was tried by the "three men," and the Jury in the cause rendered a verdict of ten shillings as damages for the plaintiff.

At the same time that the people provided for an appeal to themselves from the decision of the Special Court of the three men, they nobly sustained their magistrates in the discharge of their duty. They gave them repeated tokens of their confidence; often conferred upon them important trusts, and protected them from insult and injury. As early as 1651 they passed the following order:

> "Nov. 17th, 1651. The 3 men chosen for Town Officers are ordered to sett out the place for a Meeting-House, and they shall have power to marrie during the year."

The General Court upon another occasion when an individual had derided and insulted their magistrates, passed the following order:

> Oct'r 3d 1655. It is ordered that William Simons for his provoking speeches to the 3 men in authoritie, being a disturbance to them in their proceedings, that he shall forthwith pay 5 shillings, which is to be disposed of to make a paire of stocks."—Book 2, p. 39.

While our ancestors admitted the equal rights of all within their community, they deemed themselves as having also a perfect right to exclude any from their number who were loose in their morals and dangerous to the well being of the young. Nothing can exceed the tender solicitude with which they watched over the moral and spiritual interests of their rising village. In 1651 they ordered:

> "That Goodman Meggs' lot shall not be laid out for James Still to go to work on, and that he shall not stay here."
> —Book 2, p. 21.

And again—

> "East Hampton. April 7th, 1657.—It is agreed by the voate of the town that the bargain yt Goodman Davis, made with Goodman Birdsall in selling of his lands is annulified and not to stand."—Book 2, p. 44.

At the same time they designed to take no undue advantage over others in the exercise of their authority. On the decease of Nathaniel Foster, a son of Christopher Foster of Southampton, they passed the following:

> "The beginning of October 1660.—At our Meeting, upon Goodman Foster's request, he was accepted to possess as an

inhabitant, his sonne Nathaniel's lott, to live upon it himselfe or put in such an inhabitant as the town should accept
of, and hee to defray all charges."—Book 2, p. 85.

This town at first took its laws from the Colony of Connecticut, se-
lecting such as it deemed applicable to its peculiar circumstances, and
moulding them to suit its wants. The laws were chosen by them, not
forced or imposed upon them by any superior. They therefore exhibit
the living, breathing spirit of the people; the uninfluenced and sponta-
neous choice of their own minds—clothed in the quaint language, and
in some measure partaking of the spirit of the times.

They provided in 1656 that slander should be punished "by a fine
not above £5 as the men in authoritie see meet."—Book 2, p. 45.

At the same period they enacted a law against personal violence in
the following words:

"It is ordered yt whosoever shal rise up in anger against his
neighbor and strike him, he shall forthwith pay ten shillings
to ye town and stand to the censure of the Court and if in
smiting he shall hurt or wound another he shall pay for the
cure, and also for his time that he is thereby hindered."
—Book 2, p. 45.

It would seem that they felt deeply and most solemnly the obligation of an oath, and detested and despised perjury as an abominable
crime, richly meriting the most severe punishment. They enacted the
following law against the crime:

"Februarie 12th, 1656.—It is ordered yt whosoever shall
rise up as a false witness against any man to testifie yt which
is wrong, there shall be done to him as he had thought to
have done unto his neighbour, whether it be to the taking
away of Life, Limbe, or Goods."—Book 2, p.45.

Another striking fact to be borne in mind—speaking volumes for
the good principles of our forefathers, and their dealings with others—
is that they never had any serious difficulty with the Indians. Doubtless
this was partly owing to the friendly regard of Wyandanch, the mighty
Sachem of the Island. That he used his great name as a shield for the
prevention of difficulty and bloodshed is well known. He had acted an
important part in assisting, as an ally, the early settlers of New England

in their war against the Pequots, and acquired a hard and well earned fame by his martial achievements in that deadly contest.

Worthy was the barbarian Chieftain of an immortal fame! Worthy rival of his white compeers in the generous and kindly impulses that ennoble and adorn the human soul.*

The powerful intercession of Lion Gardiner, (*that sterling Puritan,*) no doubt often had its influence in averting threatened and impending difficulties with the Indians.

But, be it ever remembered, that every foot of soil which their labors redeemed from nature's wildness, and made to smile with the luxuriant harvest, was fairly purchased by our ancestors of the Aborigines of the forest. The stipulated price was honestly paid. The Indians themselves bore the highest testimonials of their kindness and hospitality, and gratefully acknowledged it in some of their conveyances to the whites.

After the tribe had been almost exterminated in the fatal battle on Block Island; they came about the year 1660, from Montauk and resided upon the parsonage at the south end of the Town Street, under the immediate protection of the whites. Their burying ground, made in the parsonage at that time, within a few years might have been seen.

Truth, however, demands the acknowledgment that there was once a time when much danger was apprehended from the Indians. In the year 1653 the Narraghansetts and other tribes had endeavored to form an alliance of all their forces against the whites. They attempted to seduce Wyandanch from his friendship to them. With his tribe they partly succeeded. A murder was committed by the Indians at Southampton, and they assumed a hostile attitude.

The records of this period show that our ancestors shrank not from the crisis. They never dreamed of deserting their post. Providence, as they thought, had led them to this spot as their home. Wild and savage as it was, they had planted their feet upon its soil—erected their rude habitations—begun their struggle in subduing the wilderness; and, where providence had led them, there, under God, they would remain and abide like men the destiny that awaited them. They were not regardless of the danger. They set a watch of two by night and one by day. They gave power to the "three men" to call a Town Meeting at a half hour's notice. They sent to Connecticut River for "a firkin of power and shot equivalent," as their order expressed it. They never

---

*Wyandanch died about 1659.

thought however of abandoning the Sanctuary. Their worship must not cease. The Sabbath morning breaks. The sun casts his rays upon the scene. The primeval forest rises in majesty, unruffled by the breeze. The virgin fields smile with the harvest. From many a habitation the curling smoke ascends. How quiet, how peaceful that Sabbath morn appears, as it illuminates the little village. The morning prayer has been offered under every roof,—but still no sound of busy life or labor breaks upon the ear. The hours pass on—higher the sun ascends. At length the sound of the warlike drum rises from the front of their little church; it sends farther and farther its pealing notes,—it is the summons to prepare for the services of the Sanctuary. An hour elapses and again at the drum's beat the villagers pour from their dwellings,—infancy, manhood, and tottering age—matron and maiden, all throng to the Church. The sun flashes upon the armor they bear. Thomas James, their Pastor, follows—small in stature, sprightly and undaunted in step and bearing—and takes his seat to minister the word of Life. There sit our ancestors, solemn, anxious, hopeful, and praise and worship the Most High, with their arms and warlike equipments by their side. We see them in their devotions. We hear them say—"We are troubled on every side, yet not distressed—we are perplexed, but not in despair—persecuted, but not forsaken—cast down, but not destroyed."

When, ye spirits of our sires; when shall we see the like again?—such wisdom in the council?—such valor in the field?

This, however, was only an alarm, although its aspect was for a time so serious. And it is believed, and to the honor of all be it said, that Indians and whites never drew from each other a drop of blood in murderous contest, from the date of the earliest settlement to our present peaceful times.

It was under the influence of such energy of character, purity of morals, wise precaution and forethought for the future, that this little settlement, under providence, prospered and grew on every side. It spread with great rapidity. Adjoining villages soon rose up, almost in rivalry of their more venerable and early home.

It was but a short period after the first settlement of the town before some families colonized the villages of Wainscott and Amagansett. As early as 1670 John Osborn exchanged his lands here, with the town and with individuals, and procured a tract of land bounded "South by the Ocean and East by Wainscott Pond." It is probable that about this time Wainscott and Amagansett were settled. And it is said that as early as 1700 those villages had attained nearly if not quite their present size.

Wainscott was originally settled by the families of Hand, Hopping and Osborn. Amagansett is said to have been settled originally by the families of Hand, Conkling, Schellenger and Barnes.

This Town existed as an Independent Settlement or Plantation until 1657, a period of eight years. In that year it united with the Colony of Connecticut in an alliance for the purpose of counsel and defence. Southampton had joined the same confederacy. Southold was attached to the colony of New-Haven.

Our fathers often sought counsel and advice of these neighbouring towns in difficult cases. Their attachment to New-England was exceedingly strong. With the Dutch inhabitants of New-York they had less affinity and intercourse. When the Dutch, in 1664, surrendered their Colony of New-York to the English, the whole Island was claimed by the Duke of York as included in his grant and under this Jurisdiction. And after unavailing remonstrances against it, in despite of their entreaties they came under the Duke's Government and formed a part of his colony. From that time they remained under the jurisdiction of the Government of the Colony of New-York.

After the revolution of these American States, Gardiner's Island, which until then had remained an independent manor or Lordship, was annexed to and has since remained a part of the Town of East Hampton.

The limits of an address forbid my dwelling as minutely upon the minor traits of character and the habits of our ancestors as might otherwise be desirable.

It will now be my chief object as I trace the history of the Town to bring more vividly before the mind the ardent love of liberty and devotion to their religion, which our forefathers have ever manifested.

For the first few years it does not appear that our ancestors had any written Constitution or compact as a foundation for their Government. They probably lived together under the tacit and implied contract of a people bound only by the great principles of natural equity, justice and reason, aided by their knowledge of divine revelation.

In 1654, however, and on the 18th of September, they passed the following resolve:

"It is ordered that there shall be a copie of the Connecticut Combination drawn forth as is convenient for us, and yt all men shall set to their hands."—Book 2, p. 32.

Their constitution was copied accordingly from the preamble of their model. They added to the original, however, the last quarter, referring to the obligations of conscience, and the covenant to stand by their officers. The following was their covenant or constitution.

East-Hampton, October 24, 1654.

> Forasmuch as it has Pleased the Almighty God by the wise dispensation of his providence, so to Order and Dispose of things that we, the Inhabitants of East Hampton are now dwelling together; the word of God requires that to maintain the Peace and Union of such a people there should be an Orderly and Decent Government established according to God—to Order and Dispose as Occasion shall require:— We Do therefore associate and conjoin ourselves to be one Town or Corporation; and Do for ourselves and successors, and such as shall be adjoined to us at any time hereafter, enter into combination and confederation together to maintain and preserve the Purity of the Gospel of our Lord Jesus Christ, which we now possess, as also the Discipline of the Church, which, according to the Truth of said Gospel, is now practised among us. As also in our civil affairs to be guided and Governed by such Laws and Orders as shall be made according to God, and which by vote of the Major Part shall be in force among us. [Furthermore we do engage ourselves that in all votes for choosing Officers or making Orders that it be according to Conscience and our best Light. And Also we do engage ourselves by this combination to stand to and maintain the authority of the several Officers of the Town in their Determination and actions according to their Orders and Laws that either are or shall be made, not swerving therefrom.*] In Witness whereof, each accepted Inhabitant set our hand."

Their recognition of the "Providence" of "Almighty God," and acknowledgment of their obligation to obey the requisitions of his work, are too conspicuous to demand our notice. Their determination to be governed by such Laws and Orders as were passed by vote of "the Major Part" "among us," bespeak as clearly their understanding of the superior right of the majority of the people; and their engagement that "in all votes for choosing officers or making orders" "it be according to

---

*The lines inclosed in brackets are the part added.

conscience and our best light," reflects as from a mirror, the high sense of moral obligation which pervaded them.

The pursuits of public and of private life—the affairs of utmost or ordinary importance were to be conducted according to "CON-SCIENCE." What a lesson to the people of our day did they leave on record two centuries ago. When will their descendants enter into the affairs of government and of public life, discharging their duties according to "Conscience"—when disown the principle that a Christian cannot discharge his high duties as a citizen and elector in a free country, without contamination from the pervading corruption? Why slumbers the spirit of our fathers amid our fathers' home?

Their religion was free, coparatively, from the errors and superstition of the day. In the year 1657 complaint was made to the magistrates of the Town that "Goodwife Garlicke" had practised witchcraft. An investigation of the charge was had, but the people finally concluded to send her to Hartford for trial. Perhaps they were distrustful of their skill and knowledge of Witchcraft. Enough appears upon the records to show that the "Goodwife" had many and powerful friends. Lion Gardiner strenuously maintained her innocence—Whether any further order was made in her case does not appear. It is highly creditable to them that amid the prevalent belief and superstitions of the day, entertained alike by the ignorant and the learned—the King and the People—this was the only case of accusation for Witchcraft. It is probable nothing further was ever done on the complaint than as above stated.*

It has already been seen that as early as 1651 they took measures for erecting a church. That church was enlarged in 167__; and again, after some difference of opinion, it was enlarged in 1698. The present church was erected in 1717; was remodeled and repaired in 1822.

The illustrious succession of Ministers who flourished for the first 150 years in this town, are too widely known, and too familiar to us all to require enlargement here.

The historian has already recorded the genius, originality, and resolution that lived in the character of Thomas James, the first semi-centenarian Pastor of this town. The learning, ability, and devotion of Nathaniel Huntting, the second semi-centenarian Pastor.

The *third Pastor*, for a like period, the Rev'd Samuel Buell, D.D., was probably the cause and author of the erection of Clinton Academy.

---

*The conduct of Goodwife Garlicke was not such as to disarm and quiet suspicion. Upon her examination it was, among other things, proved that she had used various herbs to bewitch with; that she had said that she had no objection to be thought a witch, and had said she "had as good please the Devil as anger him."

He lives upon the historians' pages,—lives in the remembrances of his venerable survivors. His sound judgment, clear perception, vivid fancy, impressive power and manner, have left their influence behind him.

The *fourth Pastor*, the Rev'd Lyman Beecher, D.D., is known by fame in every land. We send up our prayers that this venerable spiritual warrior may yet be able, for many a long year, to wear and wield the armor of his manhood's prime, so well and often proved.

We shrink from our honoured position, as speaker of the day, when we remember that forty-four years since he stood up here in the maturity of his genius, and the fire of his eloquence, and drew, in living lines, the character and history of our forefathers. Happy alike in the achievements they had won and in him who spoke their praise.

The *fifth Pastor*, the Rev'd Ebenezer Philips has passed from this earthly stage. His solemn, deliberate, clear address, replete with truth and doctrine, are among the remembrances of our boyhood days.

The *sixth Pastor*, the Rev'd Joseph D. Condit, mild, tender, and pathetic, is also deceased. His child-like spirit fled to the children's home on high.

The *seventh Pastor*, the Rev'd Samuel R. Ely, *supplied* this pulpit for about nine years. He removed some years since on account of declining health.

The *ninth Pastor*, the Rev'd Samuel Huntting, stood up here for a little while to minister to this People, at that altar where a hundred and fifty years before, his honored ancestor had kindled and fed the holy altar's flame. He rose, and, quickly struck by the fatal arrow, fell, and his spirit joined in high communion with his ascended fathers.*

---

*The following list of Ministers, with the time of settlement in East-Hampton, time of removal, decease, and age, is as complete as I have been able to compile.

	SETTLED	REMOVED	DIED	AGED
1. Thomas James,	1659	——	1696	——
2. Nathaniel Huntting,	1696	——	1753	78 years.
3. Samuel Buell, D.D.,	1746	——	1798	82 years.
4. Lymam Beecher, D.D.,	1799	1810	——	now living
5. Ebenezer Phillips,	1811	1830	1840	——
6. Joseph D. Condit,	1830	1835	1847	——
7. Samuel R. Ely,	1836	1846	——	——
8. Alexander Bullions,	1846	1848	——	——
9. Samuel Huntting,	1848	——	1849	27 years.

The three years intervening between the decease of Mr. James and the settlement of Mr. Huntting, were supplied by a Mr. Jones.

We now call your attention to the patriotism of our ancestors; to their adherence to free institutions, and the resolute, unflinching tenacity with which they maintained their rights.

As their religion was free, in a great degree, from superstition and bigotry, so their principles of politics and government were, comparatively, free from persecution and untolerance.

When their country demanded their assistance, feeble and exposed as they were, they generously proffered it. They say—

"June 29th, 1654.

"Having considered the Letters that came from Keneticut, wherein we are required to assist the power of England, against the Dutch: we Doe think ourselves called to assist the sd Power."

Subsequently, throughout their whole history, it does not appear that their country ever raised the cry for her sons to arm for battle, unheard by them.

The Colony of New-Haven adopted a Covenant or Constitution excluding all who were not members of the Church from the privileges of Electors. Our fathers, disliking this narrow and exclusive spirit, joined the confederacy of Connecticut, consisting of Hartford, Windsor, and Wethersfield, which admitted all their citizens to equal rights and privileges.

The Royal Duke of York, by his deputized Governors, swayed the sceptre of government over the Colony of New-York, with arbitrary power.

They oftentimes excluded the people altogether from choosing Representatives of their own to pass laws in a General Assembly. Sometimes, after yielding to the popular demand, they disobeyed the Assembly which they had chosen of their own arbitrary will. Hence the sympathy of our fathers with their early friends of Connecticut, and their attachment to the free and chartered Government of that Colony. Hence their earnest appeal in 1664 to that colony to continue them under their government and jurisdiction. Hence, in the same year, their determination not to pay their taxes to the Government of New-York.

It was in June, 1682, at a General Training of the Militia, that they drew up and signed their petition to Anthony Brockholst, the then Governor of New-York. In this memorable petition they recite their

---

The Rev'd Samuel R. Ely was never settled here, but officiated as a stated supply.

grant and charter from Governor Nicolls, in 1666. They refer to the promises of Freedom of Liberty, then made to them when they received that Patent. And they go on to say—"But, may it Please your Honour to understand that since this time wee are deprived and prohibited of our Birthright, Freedoms, and Privileges to which both wee and our ancestors were borne; although we have neither forfeited them by any misconduct of ours, nor have we at any time been forbidden the due use and exercise of them, by command of our Gratious King, that we now of. And as yet neither we nor the rest of his Majesty's subjects upon this Island have been at any time admitted since then, to enjoy a general and free Assembly of our Representatives, as others of his Majestie's subjects have had the privilege of. But Lawes and Orders have been imposed uppon us from time to time without our consent, (and therein we are totally deprived of a fundamental privilege of our English Nation,) together with the obstruction of Trafficke and Negotiation with others of his Majestie's subjects, so that we are become very unlike other of his Majestie's subjects in all other colonies here in America, and cannot but much resent our grievances in this Respect, and Remain discouraged with Respect to the Settlement of ourselves and posteritie after us."

They then go on to recite the *payment* of their *taxes* as a further reason why they were entitled to the privileges of a free assembly, which they declared to be one of the "Fundamentall Lawes of England," and they conclude with the [word?] determination that if the Governor refused them their rights they would present to the throne itself their petition for redress.

Thus, more than ninety years before the Declaration of American Independence, they proclaimed the free principles upon which it was based.

It is believed that no people in this country saw farther, or earlier than they, the correct principles of a Free Representative Government. None placed them upon the records before them. We wonder! We admire the wisdom of our fathers.

In 1683 Governor Dongan, who succeeded Anthony Brockholst as Governor, landed on the east end of Long-Island. Upon his first arrival we are told he heard the language of discontent and dissatisfaction. Perhaps he saw then, good reason to conclude as he declared in his report to the committee of Trade, of 22nd February, 1687, that "most part of the people of that Island, especially towards the east end, are of the same stamp with those of New-England. Refractory and very loath to have any commerce with this Place to the great Detr'm't of his Ma'tys

Revenue and ruin of our merchants."—Vide Doc. His. N.Y., p. 166.

In Page 151 of the same report he urges that Connecticut should be annexed to New-York, and says, "Wee found by experience, if that Place bee not annexed to that Government, it will bee impossible to make any thing considerable of his Ma'tys Customs and Revenues in Long-Island; they carry away with't entering all our Oyles, which is the greatest part of what wee have to make returns of from this Place."

These loud petitions of the people procured temporary relief. The General Assembly of the Representatives met in 1683, 1684, and 1685, when the Assembly was discontinued by the despotic mandate of Gov'r Dongan.

In the year 1686 the present Town Patent was granted by Gov'r Dongan, confirming that of Gov'r Nicolls, and giving authority to the Trustees of the Town to purchase the yet unpurchased part of Montauk, which was effected of the Indians, and a conveyance given by them, dated July 25th, 1687. This conveyance covers all the land east of Fort-Pond, extending to the Point. Thus, by various purchases, the Indian title to the lands was extinguished, and a final conveyance was taken from them in 1702-3, when a lease, not transferable, was executed to them, vesting in them the limited enjoyments of a certain part of their ancient inheritance, on which the few remaining families of the tribe now reside.

The subsequent history of the town cannot be more clearly exhibited than by reference to the life of the celebrated Samuel Mulford.

Samuel Mulford was the eldest son of John Mulford—was born in 1645; and for a period of twenty years, from 1700 to 1720, represented this County in the Provincial Assembly. From his father he inherited the strong, reflecting mind; the stern principles and unyielding determination of the early Puritans. He was attached to the Government of Connecticut, and remonstrated against the annexation of the town to New York. That Colony was then in the hands of the High-Church Episcopalians and upon them alone the patronage of Government bestowed its offices and honors. He watched the abuses of Government with a jealous eye, and no combatant ever maintained his post more unflinchingly than he.

In the year 1716, the Assembly, subservient to the wishes of Gov'r Hunter, ordered a speech of Mulford's to be put into the hands of the Speaker. Mulford boldly published his speech and circulated it. It denounced the corruption and governmental misrule of the finances—the usurpations in collecting the revenue, and its disbursement. The Governor commenced an oppressive and harrassing lawsuit against him in the Supreme court, whose judges he himself had appointed. Mulford was a farmer and not possessed of a large property. He had gained his estate and support by his daily toil; and the House, in sympathy for him, on the 21st August, with their Speaker, attended the Governor, and presented to him a resolve which they had passed, soliciting the discharge of Mulford from the suit. The suit was suspended, and Mulford was permitted to return home. On his return here he resolved to petition the King in person, for redress.

Among other grievances the towns of East Hampton and Southampton complained bitterly of a duty of one-tenth on whale oil, exacted from them by the Governors of the Colony. Whaling was to them an important interest, and Mulford desired to procure a bounty for its encouragement.

He concealed his departure lest he should be arrested by the Governor—landed at Newport—walked to Boston, and embarked for the Court of St. James. He presented his memorial, which, it is said, attracted much attention, and was read by him to the House of Commons. The tax on oil was "ordered to be discontinued," and Mulford returned home, triumphant, at the age of 71 years.*

Picture to yourself the homely apparel; the simple manners; the stern bearing; the lofty, unquailing appearance of that self taught, high minded man, and you have a noble exhibition of what our ancestors were.

Capt'n Mulford returned, took his seat in the House of Representatives, and again the old question of his speech was called up. Perhaps the Governor was stung by the success of Mulford, and his bold exposition in England, of his cupidity and injustice. The war was renewed with fiercer feeling than before. The compliant House called upon him to give the reasons for printing his speech. He gave them, and withdrew,—a motion having been made and carried to that effect. Mulford had the honour of being expelled from the House. A new election was held to supply the vacancy, and the people, true to themselves, notwithstanding all the influence of power, patronage, and wealth, again elected Mulford as their representative,—an act worthy of themselves and the champion of their cause. They were not to be bought, deceived, or terrified.

---

*Songs and rejoicings took place among the whalemen of Suffolk County upon his arrival, on account of his having succeeded in getting the King's share given up.—MSS of J. Lyon Gardiner, dec'd.

In the autumn of 1717 he again took his seat in the House; and again, alone waged the unequal contest in defence of the people. What was there in pride, pomp, power, pretension or station, that should deter him from exposing fraud or corruption wherever he found it?

In 1720 Governor Burnet succeeded Gov'r Hunter. And the bold denunciations of Capt'n Mulford, again drew down upon him the censure of the officers of Government. On the 26th October, 1720 having refused to act with the old Assembly, then in session, upon the ground that a new one should have been chosen, and that the acting Assembly was unconstitutional, he was again expelled from the House.

Thus, 50 years before the time of Wilkes, Capt'n Mulford ran the same career in America, with purer motives, and had been as nobly sustained by his constituents.

Thus ended Capt'n Mulford's public life. His great age deterred him from farther services. He died August 21st, 1725, aged almost 81 years.

The very grievances which Mulford complained of were afterwards redressed by the King, and the people finally triumphed. Why sleeps his memory, unrecorded on the historians' page?

In the war ending in the conquest of Canada, in 1760 Captains Elias Hand and Jonathan Baker of this town were engaged, commanding companies raised by them in their vicinity. They were both at the attack of Ticonderoga, by General Abercrombie; and were present, under General Amherst, at the capture of Crown Point. At the close of the war they returned to their homes.

At the very commencement of difficulty between Great Britain and these United States, this town sent her pledge to abide by the cause and interests of their countrymen. The Boston Port Bill was passed in March 1774, interdicting all commerce with that port. With reference to that we find the following proceeding:

"At a meeting of the Inhabitants of East-Hampton, legally warned by the Trustees, June 17, '74; Eleazar Miller, Esq., Moderator.

1st. *Voted,* That we will, to the utmost of our abilities, assert, and in a lawful manner, defend the liberties and immunities of British America. That we will co-operate with our Brethren in this Colony in such measures as shall appear best adapted to save us from the burdens we fear, and in a measure already feel, from the principles adopted by the British Parliament, respecting the Town of Boston in Particular, and the British Colonies in North America in General.

2nd. *Voted*, That a non-importation agreement through the Colonies is the most likely means to save us from the present and future troubles.

3d. *Voted*, That John Chatfield, Esq., Col. Abm. Gardiner, Burnett Miller, Stephen Hedges, Tho's Wickham, Esq., John Gardiner, Esq., and David Mulford be a Standing Committee for keeping up a correspondence with the City of N.Y., and the Towns of this Colony, and if there is occasion, with other Colonies; and that they transmit a copy of these votes to the committee of Correspondence for the City of N.Y.

Voted, *Unanimously, not one dissenting voice.*

BURNET MILLER,
Town Clerk."

Some of the first and heaviest blows struck in the war of our Independence, fell upon this Town.

"Whilst the British were at Boston their vessels occasionally carried off stock from Suffolk County."

The Journals of the Provincial Congress contain the following:

"July 5th, '75.—The people of E. and S. Hampton pray Congress that Capt'n Hulbert's company, now raising for Schuyler's army, may remain to guard the Stock on the common Lands of Montauk, (2,000 cattle and 3 or 4,000 sheep,) from the ravages of the enemy." — "Jour. 75."

"July 31st, '75.—Congress allow Griffin and Hulbert's companies to remain to guard Stock." — "Jour: 95."

It appears from the Journal and correspondence of Capt'n Hulbert, that his Company was stationed at Shagwonnack; that they were supplied with arms, ammunition, and provisions, by the people of the town, through Burnet Miller and Stephen Hedges, their committee. And that on the 7th, September, '75, the company marched off of Montauk, and Hulbert and his men were supplied with guns and ammunition; and were afterwards stationed at Fort Constitution.

"In consideration of the defenceless state of E. part of Suffolk Co., the 3 companies raised for Continental service were continued there." —Ap. 3, "'76."

The return of Col. Smith's Regiment, May 30, '76, shows Ezekiel Mulford, Captain of a Company of 40 privates, "complete in arms." Another account is as follows:

> "12th Comp., Capt. Ezekiel Mulford; 1st Lt., Saye; 2d Lt., Nath'l Hand; Serg'ts, M. Mulford, Pierson, Domini; Corp's, Henry Sherrel, Benj. Crook, Ludlam Parsons."

As early as the Spring of 1776, an invasion of the British forces upon New-York City had been anticipated. The fate of Long Island was readily seen to be linked with that of the City. Remote, exposed, defenceless, save by their own strong arms, but few volunteers could have been expected from this neighborhood. Yet East-Hampton had her full proportion of minute men in the field.

The battle of Long Island was fought August 27, 1776, and its whole extent came under the control of the British forces. Those forces, in part, made the east end of the Island their winter quarters, and levied supplies upon the country. There are now, even a few venerable, living veterans, who remember the sufferings, the scenes of robbery, and violence which were perpetrated by the enemy, and indured by the inhabitants,—remember how the pulse beat high and joyful at the news of Burgoyne's defeat,—remember the lively, heartfelt sympathy with their brethren in the field.

It was not until the 25th of November, 1783, that the British troops evacuated New-York City. During all this seven years the Island groaned under the oppressive occupation of their soil by the hostile Invader.

Their circumstances exposed them, however, to sufferings and outrages from both parties. Their forced submission to the Royal Army, (their misfortune, not their fault,) caused them to be viewed with suspicion of their brethren upon the continent; and often invited parties of plunder from that quarter. Multitudes fled for shelter and protection, to the shores of Connecticut.

I find this memorandum in 1776:

> "Sept. 15.—Wharves at Sag-Harbor crowded with emigrants."

> "Dr. Buell writes from E. Hampton, Sept'r 22, '76, that the People are as a torch on fire at both ends, which will speedily be consumed, for the Cont. Whigs carry off their stock and produce, and the British punish them for allowing it to

go,—hopes the Whigs will not *oppress the oppressed*, but
let the stock alone."

The history of that seven years' suffering will never be told. Philosophy has no adequate remedy for silent, unknown, unpitied suffering.
Man may brave danger and endure every evil, perhaps, if human sympathy be ministered to him in life, and human immortality and applause crown his tomb. But the display of passive virtues is a sublimer
field—a spiritual elevation above our sphere. It rises into being only
when upheld by the Divinity; and His aid withdrawn, we fall.

Throughout this period, it is not known that a single Tory lived in
the bounds of the town.

Left to the tender mercies of the foe; plundered by country-man
and stranger, of their property and ripened harvest; robbed of the
stores which they had reaped and garnered; slandered by suspicious
brethren; taunted and scoffed at by the mercenary victors, they never
wavered. Their hearts were in their country's cause; and in the memorable language of their great compatriot, "Sink or swim, live or die, survive or perish," they were true to their country, unterrified, unalterable,
devoted Americans.

The events of that memorable struggle are fast becoming matters
of tradition only. But tradition has still her unrecorded events. We might
instance many a feat of personal prowess. We might tell how, often and
again our fathers, pressed, insulted, attacked by the presumptuous foe,
felt their blood boil within them, and enduring until human nature
could endure no more, turned with club or pitchfork upon the sword
of the invader, and drove him from their sight.

In their difficulties Dr. Buell, their minister, did not abandon them.
His talents, ingenuity, wit and mingled prudence and firmness, often
averted threatened perils, and rendered important service to his people.

Tradition has however handed down no name more illustrious
than that of Capt. John Dayton, a lineal descendant of Ralph, the first
settler of that name.

Capt. Dayton was one of nature's uneducated heroes; reckless, daring, shrewd, sanguine, he often succeeded when others dared not
hope. His lonely dwelling, two miles west from the centre of town, was
an inviting location for the miscreant and coward to attack or plunder.
His house was several times beset. It was once attacked in the night by
the enemy, and while he was in the act of lighting a candle, a musket
was discharged at him. This was no time for hesitation; the ball missed

him and passed in the beam of his weaver's loom. Putting his little son, (Josiah,) out of the back door, in the midst of a deep snow, and directing him to flee for shelter and safety, he snatched the long, famous, deadly *carabine* of his from its resting place, sallied out of the house, returned the enemy's fire, and withdrew in the house. He immediately began to call all imaginary names, as if he had a regiment of assistance sleeping in his chamber—loudly daring the British, meanwhile, to come on. The shot or the deception, or perhaps both, were successful. The enemy retired and left the marks of blood behind them.

The next day the Captain, while in the yard was visited by the officer of the regiment. The officer leaped his horse astride him—brandished his cutlass—loaded the Captain with abuse, and threatened to slay him for killing one of his men. To use the Captain's own language, as in after years he related it, "His blood boiled within him, and his hair stood on end." Discovering a pitchfork near, he sprang for it, faced his adversary, brandished his rustic weapon, and ordered him to "be off." It needed no second command. The horse bounded with his rider over the pickets, and left the hero master of the field.

We cannot forbear relating one other incident equally characteristic. During the revolution a British fleet anchored off Montauk. It was supposed by the inhabitants that they were about to land there and seize the hordes of cattle and sheep which then as now were there depastured and fatted.

The Captain thought he could prevent their landing, and save the cattle. He offered to lead forty of his neighbors, if so many would go, and save their flocks. Forty volunteered to accompany the Captain, and they marched on to Montauk. He selected a hill, marched over it at the head of his company—descended into a hollow, where he was out of sight from the fleet. Shifting the position of his men, and *each* exchanging his coat, he again led them back, through a hollow, unobserved by the fleet, to the starting place and over the hill; and thus the company continued their march over and around the hill. The manouvre was calculated to produce the impression upon the fleet that a large army were marching and encamping in the vale below. Whether this strategem was the cause or not, the result was that the British did not land and the flocks were saved.

The bold artifice reflects equal credit upon the warrior's courage and fertile brain.

This venerable chieftain and mighty hunter died in 1825, aged 98 years.

The war of the Revolution left our town like the rest of the country, worse in morals; wasted in property; burdened with national debts, and groaning under taxes. Agriculture had declined; commerce had been ruined; estates swept away; and when the first thrilling, triumphant transports of a free, victorious people were over, they wept at the surrounding desolation.

But the spirit that had stood the test of war and conquest was not the spirit to fail in the arts of peace. By degrees prosperity returned; commerce and agriculture flourished; education revived, and within a year after the British troops evacuated New-York, Clinton Academy was erected. It was incorporated by the authorities, and received under the patronage of the Government, being the first chartered Academy in the State.

We feel that we are trespassing upon your time and patience; that however pleasing it might have been to continue them, we must now break off these reminiscences of the past. Even in the relation of our early history, we have been compelled to omit much that is interesting, much that is essential to a thorough knowledge of the character of our ancestors.

We could not describe, even briefly, the Maidstone they left, and the river Medway, upon the grassy banks of which they had sported. We had intended to relate more minutely the origin and nature of the early controversies of the Puritans in their own native country. We had designed to vindicate their laws from the slanders of many a prejudiced historian and writer—to have shown more fully with what wisdom they laid the foundations of a free and equitable jurisprudence. How many of us think you, unskilled in the practice and unstudied in the law, would in our day frame a better or wiser code than they? We had intended to have shown how, (imperfect as they were,) they stood upon an intellectual eminence head and shoulders above the rest of the world in the knowledge of the principles of a free government.

The question is not whether their laws and simple machinery of government is applicable to us. Was it a wise system for them? We doubt whether up to their day in this world's history any community had ever enacted laws more appropriate or established a government better suited to their wants, wishes and welfare, then were heirs to them. We doubt whether any courts ever worked better or dispensed more impartial justice, or rendered more suitable redress than theirs.

We have heard of "illiberality," of "canting hypocrisy," of "narrow-minded bigotry," of "blue laws," and "Salem witchcraft," and a thousand other flings and sneers at the honest old Puritans of this country, until by the constant repetition of some faults which the Puritans shared in common with their opponents of that day, and by the imputation of many which they never had, many a weak minded man has been ashamed of those worthy ancestors who founded the institutions which secure us our political and religious freedom.*

Let England thank God that the Puritans lived—thank the Puritans under God for many of the free principles which were engrafted in her constitution.

Let America own them as the fathers of education, piety and freedom.

We might have told from time immemorial until within the last half century the simple manners of the early planters of this colony remained unimpaired the manners and customs of their descendants.

We might have told how regularly Monday morning was devoted by the matrons to washing, and how with equal regularity Monday afternoon was devoted to social visits. And if it was so, is there any thing particularly sinful or ludicrous in their order and method. I have yet to learn that there is any better day of the week for that purpose than the one they chose.

We are well aware that there is a sickly silly sentimentality afloat, which looks with conceited contempt upon every thing connected with Puritanism. We well know how much wiser some of their descendants feel themselves to be than their Puritan ancestors were.

It may have been that their broad backs and stiff knees bent with less grace and pliancy than ours to the mandate of human custom. It may have been that they felt constrained by their understanding of revealed truth to adopt a more strict and faithful parental control than we. Perhaps their coats were more for use and less for show; perhaps they were broader in some places, and coarser and plainer than ours.

But those same queer old men and women in their antique apparel built America. They cleared her forests; exterminated her wild beasts; founded schools and colleges; fought the Revolution; established the Republic; framed the best Government under Heaven for a free people, and transmitted those immunities and institutions unsullied and unimpaired to their descendants.

As we are bound to maintain and defend our institutions and privileges, our invaluable inheritance; so are we bound to honour and defend whatever was high and manly in their character, and cherish with a filial tenderness their fame and memory.

---

*The wilful and superlative mendacity of Peter's History of Connecticut is fully exposed in the Historical Discourses of Prof. Kingsley and Leonard Bacon of New-Haven, Ct.

Standing amid the graves of our ancestors, collected in their ancient temple of worship, what thrilling recollections rush along the
memory. While we are reminded by the crumbled dust of former generations, that we hold our existence by the frailest tenure, and that we
too shall soon pass away from this stage of living action, and our departed dust will mingle with theirs; we are also reminded of the proper
objects and purposes of life; we are incited to act faithfully our part in
the several spheres in which we move:

> *"In the world's broad field of battle,*
> *In the bivouac of life,*
> *Be not like dumb driven cattle,*
> *Be a hero in the strife."*

Where shall the spiritual aspirations of our nature rise if not upon
the graves of our sires? Where if not there shall the high resolve and
noble purpose of the soul be formed? Well may we lay the passions, the
prejudices and the selfishness of our nature by the tomb of our ancestors. We may there learn the lessons of a high and holy patriotism of a
purer and more elevated piety.

We feel our souls kindle in generous emulation of their example.
We feel above the limited recollections and interests of every days pursuit. We break through the present objects of sight and sense. We feel
our relation to the venerable past, to the pious dead. We contemplate
our connection as one of the links that stretch along the chain of the
boundless future.

Our ancestors; who has fully comprehended the meaning of those
words?

They lived when this world's bright but transient morn began.
They lived when sin began its reign.

> *"Earth felt the wound, and Nature from her seat,*
> *Sighing through all her works gave signs of woe*
> *That all was lost."*

In that long night of wretchedness which followed, they lived.
They lived when Heaven sent its Saviour down to earth. When Caesar
stormed the Northern Isles they met him like heroes on the very
shore. They fought at Hastings when the invaders wrenched their dear-
est liberties and rights.—Through all past time they lived.

Our posterity; they will extend through all coming time. Another centennial anniversary of the planting of this little commonwealth, you and I shall never see. But our children that rise up after us we trust will rejoice at its return and pay the tribute of respectful gratitude to our memory and the memory of those who have now long since passed away. Changes will come—kingdoms and nations be overturned—and yet the waves of successive generations will rise and roll onward, far onward until the winding up this world's affairs.

We are not severed fragments—broken remnants of a disjointed race—but connected, closely, intimately connected with all that is past—with all in this world yet to come.

Matrons and maidens of my native town:—Worthy were your mothers of their noble partners in the vicissitudes and perils of their earthly career—meet helps in laying the foundations of learning, liberty and morals—fit in rearing the finished and tasteful superstructure. We admire their courage, their constancy, their devotion. Tradition has told us of their simple habits, their pure desires. Despise not ye their bright example. What though the fashion of their day has passed away—what though we smile at the antiquated equipage and costume of their time. The fashion and the paraphernalia of our day will also soon be past forever. The attire of the living will be put off, and the habiliments of the dead will enclose our dust; and in your turn ye will be the departed mothers of future generations. So live that the graces and simple habits and worthy pursuits of the early mothers of our village shall survive and adorn the life of our descendants.

And now, ye fellow townsmen, ye have looked upon the graves of your departed sires. We have recounted their deeds—we have lived in the historic remembrances of the past—we have traced the origin of its early settlement—we have seen the deep foundations of permanency, prosperity and peace, in the life and habits of the Pilgrim band. That ardent, patriotic fire burned in as bright a flame the first three half centuries in the breasts of their descendants. That spirit assisted in rearing the imposing edifice of our National Liberty. It built our Academic Hall,—illustrious in its name—illustrious as the first that flourished with a chartered life within the confines of our state,—proud and thrice happy in the annual cohorts that it dismissed with its parting blessing, to adorn the land. That spirit reared the venerable temple of the living God.

Still longer do we love to linger around the remembrances of the past. Are our fathers dead? Do we look at all that remains of them when we survey their departed dust? No! ah! no! Their memory lives! Their deeds survive! Their labours speak their fame. Their institutions, founded in toil and built in sacrifice, are the inheritance of their descendants.

They live.—They, the spirits of the just, perchance to-day look down upon us from their high abode—blest in the inheritance of the Saints! Blest in the welcome of the Highest! Blest in the homage of the Living!

They speak to us to-day—

"For you we did maintain our birthright and our liberties. For you we raised the Hall of science and of learning; enlarge its walls; adorn its portals; fill its alcoves. For you we reared a holy Church to our High King—that church, that dear, blest Church, maintain. Fulfill your mission on the earth; live for the world as we have lived; live for the boundless future. Beyond this day, this present fleeting day, will generations rise; they feel your impress; they are moulded by your character; they are destined to move onward as your impulses have directed them. Live then as men, as patriots, and as Christians. Leave the impress and the memory of your noble efforts with your posterity, and join us in His good time, this side the swelling Jordan, in our promised, everlasting Home."

CHAPTER II

AGRICULTURE IN SUFFOLK COUNTY

Delivered on September 30, 1866, at the age of 48

MR. PRESIDENT AND GENTLEMEN OF THIS SOCIETY:

LONG DEVOTED to the cares of professional life, it has been a pleasing relief at intervals to forget them in the bracing, congenial pursuit of agriculture. Although born on a farm, and I descended from seven generations of farmers, you know that I am but *half* a farmer. That lingering, clinging, growing love of farm life prompts me to meet you with the greatest pleasure, to confer in an hour's talk upon farming; not upon foreign or fanciful farming, not upon the literature or poetry of farming, but of practical farming, right here on our own Long Island, and within this scouted Suffolk County, upon our supposed unproductive soil, and by our supposed unprogressive farmers.

It was most fitting that the display of the manufacturer's excellence, the craftsman's handiwork, and the artist's skill, should crown with beauty yonder tents. All industrial achievement is allied. All depend upon each other, and all are sustained by the products of mother earth. Yet, although thus reminded that this is not a purely agricultural exhibition, it is chiefly so; and, as such, demands our chief regard. This audience can, at their leisure, speculate regarding "Eden's bowers," and follow Adam dressing and keeping his garden. Their flights of fancy might attain to higher, wider realms of beauty than any to which the speaker could conduct, and they will pardon him for such omission. Commencing, then, at a somewhat later period in the history of the race, many of us can remember when the ungainly wooden plow, armed with iron hoops and old wagon tire, inverted the sod to the

33

depth of four inches. Our hands have wielded the sickle in the waving grain, progressing at the rate of half an acre a day. We have threshed with a hickory flail, and winnowed with a wooden shovel; mowed with a scythe in a crooked snath, spread and raked hay with a white-oak rake; and, panting, pitched it with an enormous iron-tined oak-handled fork. We have made holes for planting corn with a heavy iron hoe, that the most untutored native of the Emerald Isle would now kick aside. We have carried in a corn basket the manure to fertilize the hills of corn; and, as farmers, reading the Inspired Record, when we came to the Patriarchal sentence and prophecy, "Issachar is a strong ass, couching between two burdens," we thought if there were *more* "burdens," *that means us.*

But the "old ark" of a plow has descended "to that bourne from whence no plow returns." The sickle is antique, or is not. The flail "has dissolved and gone to" Asia, or elsewhere. The fanning-mill superseding the wooden shovel, is itself being superseded. Machinery mows the meadow, and reaps the grain. Revolvers rake the hay, and only ask to *"go ahead."* The horse begins to ask the man for the job of pitching, and corn-planters only ask to have the rows marked, and the corn drops itself. The farmer rides out, sometimes "mowing," sometimes "raking," sometimes "hoeing," and looking from the abandoned, unregretted past, upon the living, moving present, says, "If I was and am *'strong,'* my name is not *'Issachar,'* and I am not—*the other thing."*

We know that in a comparatively old country like ours, we are colonizing new States and Territories, including the central and western part of our own State. That our young men are behind counters in cities, and carrying the flag of the nation on every sea under heaven. The elements of strength, and power, and enterprise, have been largely drawn from us. The aged, feeble, inefficient remain. What are they doing? In the march of progressive agriculture where is Suffolk County? And what is she achieving? Can she compare her agriculture with other counties? Can she enter the lists of competition within the Empire State and not hide her head in humiliation at the result? Our position is secluded, and we seem to others to be a remote district, little known, and, so far as known, to derive little honor or credit therefrom. We have been so much accustomed to their unfavorable consideration, that we assume it as a matter of course that we shall be (and deservedly) lightly esteemed. If, now, I proposed to institute a comparison between our agricultural condition and that of this State generally, I presume three-fifths of this audience would say (if they spoke as they thought), "I wish you would not do it." But that comparison is just the thing I propose, and was, in truth, the chief motive in view in inducing me to consent to deliver this address, in the place of one of your own citizens widely and favorably known, whom illness prevented from standing this evening here before you. I now invite your attention to a few dry, hard, but incontestable and interesting figures, showing the relative agricultural position of Suffolk County. The State census of 1865 reports:

Improved acres in Suffolk County	148,661
" New York State	14,827,437
Unimproved acres in Suffolk County	230,556-1/2
" New York State	10,411,863

Thus it appears Suffolk County has a trifle less than one-hundredth of all the improved lands, and over one fiftieth of all the unimproved lands found in this State. Our extensive beaches and woodlands forming and accounting for the greater proportion of unimproved lands, what use do we make of the improved land, and how do we cultivate it? Further figures from the census report:

	ACRES PLOWED.	BUSHEL HARVESTED.	BUSHELS. AVERAGE.
		CORN	
Suffolk County	16,460-1/4	580,015	35
N.Y. State	632,213-1/4	17,987,763-1/4	28
		WHEAT.	
Suffolk County	10,563-1/41	99,941-1/4 (short)	19
N.Y. State	399,918-3/4	5,432,282-1/2	14
		OATS.	
Suffolk County	10,945	289,575 (over)	26
N.Y. State	1,109,910	19,052,833-1/4 (over)	17
		RYE.	
Suffolk County	5,353	61,555-1/2 (over)	17
N.Y. State	234,689	2,575,384-3/4 (short)	11
		TURNIPS.	
Suffolk County	689-1/4	160,457 (over)	232
N.Y. State	8,123-7/8	1,282,338 (over)	457
		BARLEY.	
Suffolk County	498	14,095(over)	28
N.Y. State	189,029-3/4	3,075,052-3/4 (over)	16
		POTATOES.	
Suffolk County	3,439-1/2	292,738(over)	85
N.Y. State	232,058-1/4	23,236,687-3/4 (over)	98

Although these figures show the averages on all the great staples of grains and roots, and show that this County, averaging 13 bushels of potatoes less per acre than were produced in the entire State, averaged per acre, in the harvest of 1864, more on all else, being in excess in corn, 7 bushels; wheat, 5; oats, 9; rye, 8; barley, 12; and turnips 75 bushels per acre, it further appears that this County raised nearly one-thirtieth of all the corn in the State; and more than one-thirtieth of all the wheat; over one-seventieth of the oats; and nearly one-fortieth of the rye; and over one-eighth of all the turnips; and nearly one-eightieth of all the potatoes. There were produced in the State of New York, 131,455 bushels of carrots, and of these Suffolk County raised 15,408, or nearly one-eighth of the total crop. The grasslands show the hay cut, as follows:

	ACRES.	TONS CUT.
Suffolk County	34,577-3/4	34,758
New York State	4,237,085-3/4	3,897,914-1/8

that is, Suffolk County averaged over one ton to the acre. The whole State fell short; and the figures show Suffolk County to be among the twenty-one counties which produced over the ton.

The neat cattle in the whole State were	1,824,221
In Suffolk County	18,792

so that in stock we had more than our fair one-hundredth proportion upon the same proportion of improved lands. If this record proceeded no farther, it would be manifest that the agriculture of this County could bear a comparison with that of the whole State, at least without an unfavorable result. We have shown that this County produced from its improved acres its proportionate part of the total products, and, at the same time, sustained its relative number of neat cattle. But of the products, where did the corn and oats go? How do we farm it? Are we skinning our farms? Let us see. There were slaughtered in 1865, in

	LBS.	AVG. LBS.
N.Y. State, 706,716 hogs, producing	128,462,487	181
Suffolk Co., 13,942 " "	3,060,602	219

Thus, this County produced nearly one-fortieth of the total pork. Nineteen counties slaughtered more hogs, and eleven only made more pork, and our hogs averaged 38 pounds over the State average. Neither is this people without the implements and improved machinery for facilitating agricultural operations. The value thereof in this State in 1865 is given at $21,181,099-3/4. In Suffolk County 407,257 that is, tilling one-hundredth of the improved land in the State, we, of this County, held about one-fiftieth of the whole value. Nor, in addition to all the fertilizing material applied from the waters upon the soil, did the farmers of this County stop there. The total value of fertilizers which Suffolk County purchased in 1865 was $294,429.40. The total value purchased in the State was $383,907.52. Suffolk County, therefore, purchased more than one-third of all the fertilizers in the State, and more than was purchased by any other ten counties in the same. Tested by these figures, the relative position of Suffolk County agriculture is in no respect unfavorable, but wholly creditable to our farmers, showing no relative lack of skill in the art of producing herbage, fruits, roots, or grains from the soil, no deficiency in the equipments and apparatus that facilitate agricultural operations, no "skinning process" that makes good land poor, and poor land poorer; but a high, healthy, generous culture of the soil, constantly improving in productions, and in the capacity to produce. The corn, oats, and roots and grass were fed to domestic animals, and the elements of increased and increasing fertility restored to the soil. "There is that scattereth and yet increaseth, and there is that withholdeth more than is meet, and it tendeth to poverty."

Not unmindful of the harmonious utterances of that voice which speaks the like wisdom in the beauties of Nature and Revelation, the tillers of *this* soil have demonstrated in the records of agricultural achievement that they have acted no inglorious part in the triumphant advance of their chosen pursuit.

The census furnishes no competent material from which can be deduced the facts regarding the production, number, weight, and value of cattle sold, including those slaughtered here and driven elsewhere. There were, in 1864,

Slaughtered for beef in New York State 221,481-1/4
"   "   Suffolk County   2,447

showing over one-hundredth slaughtered in this County. But of the great number driven to the New York market and transported to the New England markets, no record remains. That number must be large, and, I think, nearly equal, if not greater, than the number slaughtered here. One of several drivers in the Hamptons has annually, for twenty-four years, driven cattle therefrom averaging $12,000 in value.

You will indulge me in a still further notice of the recorded statistics bearing on this subject. The value of the poultry owned in 1865, and of poultry and eggs respectively sold in 1864, in twelve counties, is stated as follows:

	VALUE IN 1865.	SOLD IN 1864.	EGGS SOLD IN 1864.
Albany	$52,466.30	$31,016.40	$34,957.61
Cayuga	52,911.75	41,696.50	44,772.00
Columbia	59,816.00	31,199.05	33,125.14
Dutchess	77,194.00	76,326.50	52,059.50
Monroe	53,977.33	38,706.05	33,743.98
Onondaga	49,251.05	34,607.28	45,978.84
Orange	63,410.00	32,101.24	36,858.36
Queens	79,597.00	80,035.00	45,960.00
Saratoga	52,576.53	36,500.81	45,082.91
Ulster	55,292.12	29,277.20	36,601.30
Westchester	75,643.75	45,068.46	41,346.53
Suffolk	47,708.75	47,120.00	57,003.13

Suffolk County, owning less in 1865 than either of the eleven other counties, sold more poultry in 1864 than any, except the counties of Queens and Duchess. But Suffolk beat all the counties in eggs, and Queens beat all except Duchess and Onondaga. Although *crowing* is as unpleasing to the *crowee* as it is delightful to the *crower*, and hence not usually a judicious exercise, we submit that if it were proper in this case, we are entitled to raise a *long, loud, wide crow*, that may be heard from the beating waves of Montauk Point, to the far-off falling waters of Niagara.

Washington, traveling on Long Island in 1790, made memoranda in his journal, showing the average yield of

Corn	25	bushels,
Wheat	15	"
Rye	12	"
Oats	15	"

What progress we have made the figures cited tell.

If what has been said shall tend to remove undue depreciation of the relative agricultural position of this County, shall lessen the tendency of young men to undervalue the importance and merits of that occupation, shall simply *put us to right* before ourselves and the world, the desire and aim of the speaker will be accomplished. No vain boasting, no undue elation, no invidious comparison, is desired. But, in all candor and fairness, can facts be shown, proving agricultural inferiority the rightful position of this County? Is not such view the result of prejudice, of overweening self-esteem, or of the limited range of the railroad traveler, who superficially supposes that seeing the central and untilled pinelands of the County, and unconscious of the bright verdure and surpassing loveliness that spread around its shores, insists that he has seen the whole? As if the central wilds were all, and "the fertile vales and dewy meads," the charming landscapes, the clustered hamlet, and the thriving village (like gems in the circumference of her diadem) were nothing. Traveler! eyesore and weary with the wilderness of the center, will you pronounce judgment now, or will you not rather view the contrast that shines and attracts in the surrounding shores? Thus seeing, we seek not to elude your sentence. Thus neglecting and judging, you will excuse us if we suggest the application of that incident in the life of Alfred the Great, who (tradition tells us) once corrected an old priest, who had, in the Latin prayers, ignorantly used the word "*mumpsimus*" for "*sumpsimus*;" and for answer could only obtain for his pains, "Your Majesty may be right, but I can't give up my old *mumpsimus* for your new *sumpsimus*."

If then our agriculture is *not*, as Rev. Dr. Vinton once said (speaking in Connecticut), "*agritorture*," if something has been attained not unworthy of regard, that attainment should be but the harbinger of the future; a partial should lead to a more perfect excellence. This height gained is but a step toward another elevation. This knowledge should incite to further search and enlightenment. This power secured, should be the lever to higher power. Standing where we are, it is our proposition to use the past as a means of greater and future achievement. This exhibition of the products of our soil and all similar efforts are designed to write upon our agriculture, and all over our fields, the word *progress! progress!!*

When I speak of a more thorough and deeper tillage, of a more generous application of fertilizers, of a wiser economy of force in the application of improved utensils and machinery, I know that I shall be met with the inevitable query, "Does it pay?" No matter what the proposition, whether political, agricultural, or moral, somebody will inquire, "Does it pay?" And now in this light, unproductive, porous soil of ours, will high farming pay? There have been gray-haired, stiff-jointed, hard-headed, weasel-faced farmers peering around your Fair Grounds, squinting at long carrots, large potatoes, larger beets, and the innumerable specimens of roots, grains, animals, &c., and every squint seemed to blink the shrewd question, "Does it pay?" May I personate? "Them carrots, them potatoes, them beets, them cattle—wonder how much manure it took, how much labor, how much more it cost to raise all them, than they'd fetch in market? Rich men can buy guano and all such stuff, and raise big water-melons" (excuse me, "water millions"); "I can do it; but *does it pay?*"

Admitting the pertinency of the query, not denying that there may have been specimens on exhibition that have cost more than their value, I maintain that high farming does pay. Not stopping to inquire whether "poor farming pays," which is just as pertinent, please recall a few recited figures. Our averages exceeded the State average per acre, as follows:

	ACRES.	TOTAL.	PRICE PER BUSHEL.	TOTAL VALUE.
Corn, 7 bush	16,460-1/4	115,221-3/4	$1.00	$115,221.75
Wheat, 5 bush	10,563-1/4	52,816-1/4	2.60	137,322.25
Oats, 9 bush	10,945	98,505	.80	78,804.00
Rye, 8 bush	5,353	42,824	1.10	47,106.40
Barley, 12 bush	498	5,976	1.10	6,573.60
Turnips, 75 bush	689	51,675	.40	20,670.00

Total value of excess of County average $405,698.00

	ACRES.	TOTAL.	PRICE PER BUSHEL.	
Potatoes, 13 bush	3,439-1/2	44,713-1/2	$ .80	35,770.80

Deducting our loss in the average on potatoes,
we still have an excess of   369,927.20

After the value of fertilizers purchased ($294,429.40) has been deducted from the value of the average excess, the sum of $75,497.80 remains. So that, at the cost of fertilizers (and allowing that our land averaged just as the State averages), our County excess of production per acre paid the cost, and left the sum of nearly $76,000 surplus. Whether our soil is a better average than that of the State generally may well be doubted; but, if not, whence comes the excess of average production, unless from the application of fertilizers purchased? and, if thence, that purchase pays. And high farming to *that extent* pays. It pays in larger production alone, both principal and interest, and it leaves the soil improved and not impoverished in condition. It pays in cash. It pays in the gratifying consciousness of successful achievements; in the addition to earth's products, and its people's comforts; in the richer, greener, gladder view that strikes the eye. In all that addresses the lower or higher emotions of mind and heart, it pays.

There are precepts to be observed, there are errors to be shunned, or success in agriculture can not be obtained. *Agriculture is a business.* It demands the entire dedication of body, heart, and mind. No pursuit calls for more wise forethought, unwearied diligence, ceaseless attention. A half-farmer will succeed no better than a half-sailor, half-mechanic, or half-merchant. Nor is it probable, because the sailor, mechanic, or merchant have profitably pursued their varied concerns, *therefore* each or any can farm well. I know that farmers sometimes think they could excel others in their trade or art. I know that artists and merchants often suppose they could excel the farmer at his business. And I know that generally *ignorance*, and not knowledge, is the foundation of such supposed superiority. It is wholly a mistake to suppose success if one secures success in another direction.

Let all discard the notion that farming can be made a profitable *amusement.* Wealthy sea-captains, accomplished merchants, fortunate note-shavers in the cities, have retired to the serenity of rural life, reared splendid houses, barns, and fixtures, purchased fast horses, blooded stock, at fabulous prices, applied expensive fertilizers, and aimed to teach successful and *progressive* agriculture. In nine cases out of ten they have learned and confessed that "this farming is a considerably expensive *amusement.*" This amusing, poetic life may have its charms, but it pays, if at all, *poetically*, not *pecuniarily*.

Farming will afford much comfort. It can feed little pride, it can sustain little display. To him who, like Agur, seeks the Divine Father "neither poverty nor riches," it bestows a bounteous and sufficient, rather than fatally and richly destructive return.

And now observe, I do *not* say that individuals have relinquished "life on the ocean wave," in the busy store, or "thronging, crowded mart," for the purer, sweeter toils of the husbandman, and *always failed.* One of the best farmers I ever knew had been a weaver, another a carpenter, a third a shoemaker, another a merchant, and others sailors. But I *do say* that gathered all their forces, and brought *heart, soul, mind,* and *strength* to bear with irresistible energy and precision upon their business. Every blow added impetus to another. Thought accelerated thought. Like that fabled giant who, touching his mother earth, redoubled strength, and baffled, rose the mightier, their very errors taught the lessons of triumphant victory. All success is the result of patient, enduring, concentrated effort. The records of science, art, and industrial achievement contain the high, undying names that, whispered, lift our hearts in admiring wonder. But protracted weary toil preceded and taught them all the results that now blaze out to the world. Just as surely as the ball and cartridge were put in the cannon before its flash and crash awoke us to its destructive power, just so surely thought, diligence, strength, and wise absorbing effort and direction were put back of all achievement. Farming must not be an amusement. Success therein is attainable by no process that does not apply to success elsewhere. Point me to an accomplished, successful farmer, who has made his fields bring forth a richly remunerative return, and you will show me one who is *entirely* and *wholly* a farmer, and who with heart and hand pursues it *as a business*. Thus, and thus only, do the conditions promise fortune.

Again, agriculture should not reject *science*.

I am aware that it is dangerous and debatable ground that the relations of science to agriculture are so undefined, that the agricultural judgment has so universally condemned what is called "book-farming," "fancy farming," "scientific farming," and so often with justice, that small allowance is given to discriminating toleration. We must not forget that science has given us the mower, reaper, rake, and thresher, to cut, gather, and thresh the harvest; that now, our tribute and gratitude and praise to mechanical science should be full and unreserved; nor reject the possibility, nay, *probability*, that science may yet contribute more magnificent and richer endowments to lighten and elevate the farmer's life. Knowing that seamanship is an art, that study, without practice, can never confer it, that a philosopher, *as such*, can not sail a ship, but must learn, as any sailor learned, by experience, to do it, we yet confess the claims of nautical science, teaching the mariner how, from the orbs of heaven, to track his way with precision over pathless sea and ocean, what laws govern forces of wind and wave, what curves present the least impediment to waters; and how, against wind and wave, steam propels the sailless boat. Every where, by land and sea, the monuments and marks of scientific achievement demand our gratitude. But if a philosopher, *as such*, can not sail a ship, or conduct a farm, that neither proves that sailor or farmer has dispensed, or can afford to dispense with philosophy and science. It is possible for others to know more of horses and less of *my* horse than myself; more of agriculture generally, and less of *my* farm than myself. You watch and are quick to judge, by his appearance and action, when and how to feed *your* horse in the best manner, and can learn by practice only. But, knowing your horse in some respects better, feeding him and driving him better, do you know more of the anatomy, physiology, and science of horses than a horse professor? Cultivating your farm with skill and profit, and, in the practical operations of farming, perhaps far excelling the most learned doctors of science, knowing more of *your farm* and how to till it, do you know more of *farms*, of *soils*, of elementary substances, of the constituents of plants, grains, and fertilizers, than he does? Just as true as that there is a round of practical operations wherein you excel, so true is it that there is a deeper, wider, more recondite field wherein, though both are children, you are a mere infant.

Observe, I do not say you should accept all or any thing that science is supposed to teach. Philosophers may be, and have often been mistaken. I have heard of an eminent chemist who supposed he could mix in small quantities a chemical fertilizer that would, by variation in compounding, produce corn, wheat, oats, beans, &c., in an unheard of abundance. He cultivated a farm on that theory, applied the ingredients, and in eighteen months sunk eighteen hundred dollars, and made a splendid failure as a farming experiment. He knows that bath of chemistry won't work like good barn-yard manure, and we know the same. Farming is, and must be, chiefly learned by experience; you and I can, and should experiment on a small scale. I *do* say that you should be open to conviction and the acceptance of scientific teaching; that, receiving with caution such teaching, it is your privilege and place to prove, by actual experiment, and illustrate the truth or error thereof. Thus, step by step, true science and practical agriculture, joining hands in mutual amity, give, receive, and prove the mutual lessons of each. When science whispers a hint, let the farmer experiment. If she measures the value of soils and fertilizers, you measure too. She measures in the scales of an imperfect chemistry, by imperfect rules: you, in the sure laboratory of the Almighty. Chemistry told us that a bag of yellowish sneezing powder would fertilize an acre; wondrous as it is, the farmer, applying the Guano, *proved* it so. She may, and she will reveal to us yet other wonders. Be it ours to listen with candor to her utterances.

WORK ON SYSTEM.

There is a great deal of what may be called irregular, aimless farming. Plowing *about* so much, hoeing *about* so much, or rather *about so little*; fertilizing as it happens; keeping about so much stock. This loose, inaccurate, unmethodical manner of farming will not accomplish the most attainable results. What we need is accuracy. Not *about*, but *just* how many acres are to be cultivated. A nice adaption of laboring force to the proposed work. A clear-cut plan of tillage, fertilizing, and cropping, covering the whole farm, and a round of operations thereon. You know what I mean, and you know when you see a farm brought up to a high, uniform producing capacity, well and symmetrically subdivided, fenced, tilled, and fertilized, that a *plan* has governed and wrought out these results. The farm spells it, and tells it to the farmer's eye, as clearly as the words themselves. The fields, fences, buildings, all tell it.

Wherein does horticulture differ from agriculture? Thus: I select a small warm, rich spot; fertilize abundantly; plow or spade deeply; hoe and till thoroughly; and there is *my garden*. That small spot furnishes a surprising amount of vegetables, and pays better for the liberal expenditure of labor, manure, seed, and fencing than my farm averages. Supply plant-food, comminute the soil, and till year after year, and it yields its fullness with yet more bounteous returns. Change your garden, and let the grass grow on the garden-spot, and year after year *that place* abounds in herbage, and for a score of years shows that something has been done *there* that never has been done elsewhere. The *old garden-spot* is a landmark of luxuriant growth all your days.

What made it so? Extra fertilization, thorough tilth, deeper tillage. How many farmers say, "I wish my farm was *all like* that garden." Did you make your garden? Yes! Then transfer that system (or just as much of it as is possible) to the farm, and reap like results. The law that governs one square rod, governs miles. Horticulture teaches agriculture. It is impracticable to make the expenditure at once. Then aim at it. Strive for it. Keep doing a little better, and, above all, as an attainable object, *plow deeper*; working up not so much dead bottom soil as to choke the breath out of what you had already, but an inch now and half an inch afterward, and let the air permeate, sun warm, and frosts pulverize it, and, by the wonderful elemental forces of creation, turn that yellow, useless mass into living, producing soil, *"dirt cheap."* Work for yourself, and let Nature help you. You and I know that the plow *bears down* by just so much as there is top pressure. Where it runs there is a plow-floor, packed, pressed, and partially impervious. Roots reaching there, generally reach no deeper; spading makes no floor: that is one difference wherein spade-husbandry has thus far contended strenuously, and not altogether without claims, for the victory. Just in proportion as I deepen my soil, let down that *plow-floor*, I gain toward the excellence of horticulture. What we need is *more land underneath, and less on top.*

FERTILIZE LIBERALLY.

I have heard and somewhere read of a gentleman who applied an hundred dollars' worth of barn-yard manure to an acre of land (remember this was when dollars meant *gold*), and who said he thought that application paid him as well as any he ever made for such purposes. Successful farmers succeed more generally from an extra liberal fertilization than from any other cause. The soil is just in its returns: it pays for what it receives, and if it pays *generously* at all, it is to the generous giver. A poor farm scraped and skinned tends to poverty. Its owner must continue the exhausting process to keep body and soul together, until farm and farmer both *"go to the dogs."*

TILL THOROUGHLY.

Courteous hearer! I am not disposed to weary your patience. What I am saying has often been said, "line upon line, and precept upon precept," in addresses, newspapers, and by the wayside. It is common talk. And it is introduced here, not for enlargement, but as a maxim not to be forgotten, and a rounding off of my six points, otherwise incomplete.

Now recall the positions, or, as lawyers say, the points made.

Agriculture is, and must be made a business, not an amusement; scientific teachings should be received with caution; work on a system; plow deep; fertilize liberally; till thoroughly.

Count them on the fingers. The *thumb* is shorter, stronger, perhaps less symmetrical than the fingers; but with it I can touch any finger. It can *bear on all.* It means business. Just so the proposition that farming is a *business*, bears on all my points, pervades all farm operations. The *first* is the index finger, pointing the way, and it fitly represents my second point—that the farmer should look and learn where science points. The *second* is the longest, strongest finger, and it aptly represents my third point—that the farmer should work *on a plan;* plan and forethought is the longest, strongest finger and point in the agricultural hand. The *third* finger adds augmented force to the thumb and other two, and represents my fourth point—*plow deep.* The little finger completes the hand in its wonderful and symmetrical proportions, and represents my *fifth* point—*fertilize liberally.* But did you not give us a sixth point? I did. You have done counting points on the fingers then? Yes! But now shut the thumb and fingers, and that is symbolical of *crushing* the lumps and clods, and of *thorough tillage*, which is my last point: all of which you carry *on the tips* of thumb and fingers and in the *closed hand.* The simplicity of the illustration you will excuse, remembering it is not what you hear, but what you take with you, that instructs; and that it is the speaker's aim to so present and enforce, not what you do *not*, but what you *do now*, so that you must carry it from hence, resolved to practice it.

Such diversity of soil as Long Island shows, is rarely seen crowded in as narrow compass. Here clear sand, there stiff clay; here light loam, there lighter gravel; here hard marl, there heavy loam—a mosaic plain of all textures and colors. What ample experience can compass and comprehend all. What complex knowledge turn each and all to their best account? Therefore it is that agriculture here demands a more varied, wider range of observation and experience than elsewhere. Soil, climate, tillage, fertilizers, crops, must vary. Here corn, there buckwheat; here oats, there rye; here roots, there grains flourish most favorably. This soil lacks lime, that bone-dust, another something else; and all lack that vegetable food which barn-yard manure supplies. Sometimes fertilizers produce greater effects on heavy loams as top-dressing; on lighter, warmer soils, plowed under. On one section, corn flourishes best when manured in the hill; on another, by its application under the furrow. Here on heavy cold sand, you must plant and sow early; there on lighter, warmer soil, late. The varieties of soil, the application of improved machinery, the system of mixed farming, demand more thorough, comprehensive knowledge of the farm than formerly, and demand no less here than elsewhere. The days when American-Yankee laborers can be procured are past. Then we could trust the field operations to men who could whittle, hew, splice, drive nails, or drive a team. All days, wet or dry; all seasons, hot or cold; they were at home. They could hang an ax or scythe, mend a cradle or rig a ship. They inquired *what* to do, and not *how* to do it. They have gone, some to the Arctic Ocean after whales; some to Kansas or Oregon, to farm on larger fields and sit in Legislative halls; some to California, and some here conduct and manage their own acres. In their place, step before you, with that peculiar tip of the beaver and unequaling assurance and betraying brogue, those gentlemen, who tell you with an air that seems to defy doubt: "Sure an' its meself can do farm work as good as any man." We concede that they handle the shovel, spade, and shilalah with equal ease, grace, and dexterity; but when put to the test, find their range of acquaintance with labor limited. Doing some things well, they must acquire the practice of doing others. And the farmer requiring knowledge of soils, fertilizers, animals, mechanical powers, and implements, finds that he must add to that patience which "waits for the early and latter rain," the patience and skill to train, direct, watch, and teach others.

Speakers have often expressed the belief that much of the central forest plains in our County will yet be redeemed from its wild state and subjected to a profitable tillage. Some have claimed that it can *now* be done profitably. It is my belief that it will be done. Land will pay to clear and till at certain prices, and this is a question to be determined, and achieved when it is demonstrated that *it will pay*. Perhaps it *will pay* now. If not, when population thickens, capital increases, and the long cleared and cultivated fields bring twice their present value in the market, it will be cheaper to carve out a farm there than to purchase elsewhere. That day will come, and sooner, perhaps, than we are aware. The soil is not destitute of good qualities, it is not barren, it is easily tilled, quick to respond to fertilizers, adaptable to a great variety of crops, and much more than usually productive in fruits, berries, and roots. Perhaps the desire may have been indulged in, if not uttered, that some earthquake would engulf the whole. But this island seems to be planted upon no reeling or unstable foundations. And when the future shall reveal the time of its redemption, clad in beauty and in the green of earth's own mantle, what is now the regret and reproach of the present, will rejoice the eyes and hearts of our sons. Till then, waiting with patience, and in the hope that becometh the husbandman, let us endure serenely the flings at our poverty, assured, at last, that we may be cheered with the coming transformation.

SUGGESTIONS.

If my suggestions grow out of my own experience and mode of farming, perhaps they will not be any less deserving of consideration. I was early impressed with the proverb: "where no oxen are, the crib is clean; but much increase is by the strength of the ox." Having purchased a farm, long neglected and unproductive, it became necessary for profitable farming to make, save, procure, and apply, with the utmost economy, largely fertilizing materials; to feed chiefly the products to domestic animals, sell little except beef, pork, wheat, and potatoes. I think no grain crop pays so well for care, labor, and fertilizers, as corn; and doubt whether from the tip-end of Montauk Point, to its western extremity, any crop is better suited to Long Island soil. It is more sure, ore natural, and less exhausting than other grains. Aiming to produce this with the same fertilizers, the crop has steadily increased from an average of seventy-five bushels, at first, to one hundred, and then to one hundred and twenty-five bushels of ears, per acre; and twice has averaged (including this year) as high as one hundred and forty-five bushels. I plant from twelve to fifteen acres yearly; manure in the hill on a part, plow under some coarse manure, put fish or fishscrap on the remainder of the ground; plant in four feet hills as early as convenient; till thoroughly, first east and west with the cultivator, then north and south with the plow, in ridges in the middle of the rows, and keep all weeds down; continue cultivating and hoeing, and, whatever comes, cultivate finally during the commencement of the mowing season, which last saves much hoeing. My plan is to cut and clear from two to five acres of corn yearly, sowing wheat to succeed corn. On the remaining land, put oats, barley, and potatoes, and lay all down to grass with wheat, applying barn-yard manure, and a dressing of bone-dust, sowing on it clover seed. Mow from four to five years, and pasture, one or two, if convenient, before another breaking up, and breaking up generally where the grass crop has failed most; keeping full stocked, feeding all the corn and grass grown on the farm, and turning it chiefly into beef and pork. Thus, the more we raise and feed, the more we can raise. It is just as sure as that a snow ball will grow larger with rolling. The more grass, the more cattle; the more cattle, the more manure; and the more manure, the more hay and cattle again. This is the *slow* method of farming. It takes a shorter time to get a rick farm, it takes longer to get a full purse; but if the capital is not in cash, it is in the land and stock, and can be soon skinned out and sold, stock and all, if the owner wants to sell, and that is frequently done, preparatory to a sale.

What the turnip crop has done in keeping and fattening stock in England, under our drier skies must be chiefly done with corn.

I must hasten to a close; and now suggest that it pays: 1st. To have and preserve, in a definite *place*, all the slops, soap-suds, old bones, dead fowl, animals, and whatever else may serve for valuable fertilizers. That place should be a sort of *onium-gatherum*, and, it is economy to have it, if it is economy to purchase fertilizers. 2d. A small patch or turnips and other roots *pays* to feed domestic animals in winter, in change of diet, forming flesh and milk, and is so much more fodder. 3d. A like patch of corn sowed for fodder, perhaps, where otherwise weeds would grow, will kill the weeds or swamp them; is convenient for feeding the team at noon; and, when pasture is short, will help it out; *that pays.* 4th. One evening, at each Annual Exhibition of this Society, set apart for the farmers to talk over their experience, exchange views, and make short, spicy speeches, would develop and extend intelligence, teach the difference between theory and practice *in speaking;* and *that would pay.* 5th. As an illustration, my farming on heavy, wet loam is no criterion or guide for the best mode on another kind of soil, and with the intent to other productions; a varied experience can only supply varied instruction. 6th. The aim of the farmer should be to produce the utmost possible paying product upon his farm. I do not say he *can attain it.* If he could, he would demonstrate what science is now trying to do. Who can say *how much* his fields can be made to produce profitably? What crop or what series of crops is most suitable to his soil? What specific fertilizer is cheapest? What lacking element, supplied, would promote fertility? Science labors, and labors in vain. Experimental agriculture gropes in the dark. Now and then a spark is struck from the laboratory or the agricultural experiment. Let us walk in its light, assured that God has given us this land for *something*, and that if perfection is not attainable, it is ours to aim and attain to higher excellence and more transcendent merit.

Mr. President, for myself, and for the farmers of this County, I desire to express our grateful appreciation of the services of yourself and your co-laborers in reviving this Agricultural Society. It opens a new avenue of delight and instruction; it affords occasion for mutual interchange of views; it might result in some organization to facilitate the exchange of products without the necessity of passing through the hands of many middlemen. All trades and arts have organization. Farmers, requiring it most, have it least.

I have been informed that the great outlay here, made to erect suitable and permanent fixtures, will require greater contributions or loans to meet it. Until facts demonstrate the truth, I cannot doubt that this Agricultural community will, with wise, nay, generous liberality, respond to such call.

I find in an old Almanac of 1774, "Hutchin's Improved," "a list of Fairs to be held in the Province of New York, by virtue of acts of General Assembly," as follows: "For Suffolk County—the first at Southampton, the First Tuesday in July; the second at Southold, the second Tuesday in September, each to continue four days." In 1775, the like appointment was made. It is incredible that we cannot now maintain the half that was done one hundred years gone by.

We have our local attachments to the scenes whereon our delighted eyes first opened, the sounds to which our ears first listened, the trees on which we first climbed, the greens where first we played, the fields where first we roved, the houses where first the light dawned upon us, the church where, in mute reverence, we were taught to worship, the spot wherein repose the crumbling, consecrated dust of loved and long lost ones,—these thronging memories cling to us, and they return with a freshness and thrilling power, which, if unwilling (as we dare not be), we cannot resist. Aye! every sight of that *old homestead* where we were born, the trees we knew and loved, the hills we used to climb—every spot and every object there is vocal to us of days and moods, of short-lived pain, of lingering pleasure, of voices now hushed, of affections no longer received. *The homestead of our fathers*, to us, is hallowed ground. Beneath our own roof-tree let us so lovingly surround the shrubs, the plants, the flowers, in our own homes, so furnish the innocent attractions of intellectual, physical, emotional enjoyment, that, in the coming years, other hearts may yearn toward the houses we have reared, and the homesteads we have adorned.

Our country! historic in age!! venerable and full in tradition!!! What clustering memories and legends cling to its streams and lakes, float over its harbors and bays, glide around its headlands, hover in its hills and valleys, bind us to its hearthstones! Envying no other climate or soil, not least of all our mercies, we thank the bounteous Giver of all for our *home*, and *for it here*. "The surging billows' roar" first strikes our ears in the wakening morn; last lulls to sleep on wearied eve. Its anthem will sound in expiring breath, and over our final rest.

And now, with you looking out upon those seas which begirt our island home, fanned by the gales that sweep across their bosom; gathering inspiration as we have gathered health from those waves whose counterparts are rolling on other continents; purified by the remembrance of that azure ocean, which, in its solemn depths, is like the azure vault; reminded around, beneath, above, of Him who bestowed upon us and our fathers this charming inheritance; grateful that the hopes of opening spring and smiling summer have been filled with the golden treasures of bounteous autumn; reverently, yet gladly, it most of all becomes the husbandman to raise the song of thanksgiving and of joy. Not inaptly has the Quaker bard of New England's soil selected and sung the theme we accept as beautifully expressive and appropriate to ourselves:

THE CORN SONG.

Heap high the farmer's wintry hoard!
Heap high the golden corn!
No richer gift has autumn poured
From out her lavish horn!
Let other lands exulting glean
The apple from the pine,
The orange from its glossy green,
The cluster from the vine.
We better love the hardy gifts
Our rugged vales bestow,
To cheer us when the storm shall drift
Our harvest-fields with snow.

Through vales of grass and meads of flowers
Our plows their furrows made,
While on the hills the sun and showers
Of changeful April played.
We dropp'd the seed o'er hill and plain
Beneath the sun of May;
And frighten'd from our sprouting grain
The robber crows away.
All through the long, bright days of June
Its leaves grew green and fair,
And waved in hot midsummer noon
Its soft and yellow hair.
And now with autumn's moonlit eves
Its harvest time has come,
We pluck away the frosted leaves
And bear the treasure home.
There, richer than the fabled gifts
Apollo showered of old,
Fair hands the broken grain shall sift,
And knead its meal of gold.
Let vapid idlers loll in silk
Around their costly board;
Give us the bowl of samp and milk
By homespun beauty poured.
Where'er the wide old kitchen hearth
Sends up its smoky curls,
Who will not thank the kindly earth,
And bless our farmer girls?
Then shame on all the proud and vain,
Whose folly laughs to scorn
The blessings of our hardy grain,
Our wealth of golden corn!

Let earth withhold her goodly root,
Let mildew blight the rye,
Give to the worm the orchard's fruit,
The wheat-field to the fly.
But let the good old crop adorn
The hills our fathers trod;
Still let us for His golden corn,
Send up our thanks to God!

CHAPTER III

THE SETTLEMENT OF BRIDGE-HAMPTON, L.I.

Delivered on July 4, 1876, at the age of 58

AT WHAT PRECISE date Bridge-Hampton was settled, is uncertain. The monument at the grave of Anthony Ludlam, in Mecox burying ground, records the fact that he died March 17, 1681, in the 31st year of his age. That proves a previous settlement, and I have no doubt it was in fact settled both at Sagg and Mecox as early as 1676, and probably previously.

It is not therefore inappropriate, in celebrating this Centennial, to commemorate also this as the two hundredth year of the settlement of Bridge-Hampton. More than twenty years previous the fertile lands in Sagg have been allotted and the like to a considerable extent had been done with those in Mecox.

An entry in page 149, 1st book of Southampton Town Records, and under date of September 21st, 1658, contains some indication that Mr. Stanboro, having goods and chattels at Sagaponack, may have then resided there, because an amount equal to 130£ was to be appraised in behalf of the children of the deceased Thomas Wheeler.

Josiah Stanborough's will is dated July 6th, 1661, and proved September 3d, 1661,—see Town Records, p. 12. It recites the fact that he was sick, and continues: "I give my soul to Almighty God, and my body to bee buried at Sag-aponack by my former wife." That proves a previous settlement and a previous death in that family. The Town Records show that Anthony Ludlam and Arthur Howell, hired Indians to whale in 1671; that Ellis Cook lived in Mecox in 1671, and John Beswick at that date sells a house, &c. to Isaac Mills; that Wm. Bower had a home lot in Sagg in 1672; records (see p. 95,) that John Lupton and John Cook had houses in Mecox in 1681, p. 147; that in 1686 Obadiah Rogers had the privilege of setting a fulling mill on Sagg stream, p. 168; that Joseph Wickham, "Tanner," obtained the privilege of land on the west side of Sagg pond or swamp, north of the path going over said swamp; in 1686, p. 171. That Henry Pierson, James Hildreth and Theophilus Howell had the grant for 12 years of Sagg stream, for a grist mill, about April 6th, 1697—see page 220. That there was "granted to Captn. Theophilus Howell, Elisha Howell, Lemuel Howell and Jeremiah Halsey, liberty to build a windmill at Mecox, upon ye triangle commons not prejudicing highways." April 2d, 1706, p. 229; that the 20 acres parsonage at the corner, now the premises of William H. H. Rogers, was laid out in 1712. p. 266.

Some writers say Thomas Topping settled in Sagg in 1649; others that an act passed the Assembly for building a Meeting House in the precincts of Sagaponack and Mecox in 1669. I know no foundation for the former assertion and have not been able to verify the latter.

The Records of both East-Hampton and Southampton contain ample evidence that for over half a century after the first settlement whaling formed an important branch of business, and aside from Agriculture was the chief reliance of the inhabitants. All their settlements in the two towns on the South shore were located with regard to convenience in this business, including Sagg and Mecox. It is therefore probable that when the villages became inhabited, a number sufficiently large to man whale boats, soon located there, and as a fact the locations chosen were near the ocean, and grew by enlarged numbers, Northward from it. The hardy pioneers who felled the forest and hunted its wild beasts to extermination, with equal alacrity responded to the summons for chasing whales.

In 1715 Samuel Mulford of East-Hampton, was engaged in a memorable controversy with the Governor and Courts of this Colony, resisting the imposition of a license and an export duty on oil,—himself an old whaleman, he states in his defence "that it hath been a custom for above 60 years," &c., "to go out upon the seas adjacent to their lands, six men in a small boat, to take and kill whales and other fish," &c; "that Capt. Theophilus Howell's company, in Bridge-Hampton, had a license from the Governor to go and kill whales, obliging themselves to pay the 20th part," and then recites the fact of the whale drifting 40 miles west, where Floyd found it; and made it into oil for them, and was afterwards prosecuted therefor.

The sentiments characterizing a Puritan settlement belonged to the settlers here; a profound regard for the education and morals of the youth; a deep and abiding reverence for religion and its ordinances; and abhorence of any disregard of the sanctity of the Sabbath; a thorough consciousness of the individual responsibility of each soul directly to his God; a distinct acknowledgement of each and all to maintain the ministry and institutions of their church as a sacred duty, and therein to suffer, and do, and dare, as if inspired to emulate the example of the primitive saints and martyrs, whose heroic devotion to the cause of their great master, impelled to withhold nothing as too great to do or give to the eternal leader and King.

As a consequence, the history of these settlements is so closely identified with the history of the Church, that its changes and condition, and relation to the community, give the key to its progress so much so that it would not be inappropriate to mark as epochs, the history of Bridge-Hampton, previous to its first church—previous to its second, and to the erection of its third church, as proper divisions for the record of its career.

With this view, let me refer to the brief notices of the town records, marking two of these epochs in the precise language of the original.

"At a meeting of the Inhabitants of the Town of Southampton, July 22, 1686. It was agreed and granted unto Isaac Willman that hee shall have twelve acres of land laid out unto him where it may be most convenient to him upon ye comons not prejudicial to ye Town at ye discretion of ye Layers out of Land which is granted upon this condition that the Said Isaac Willman shall allow and make over to the Town four pole wide of his Land butting to Sagaponack pond all the whole length thereof for a high way and allow so much Land more as will contain a Meeting House lying to the said Highway to be about four poles square" Liber A, Book No. 2, p. 140 Town records.

"It is also concluded at ye aforesaid meeting by the major vote that the Towne in a general Town Rate including ye whole Town shall pay toward the building of a Bridge over Sagaponack pond fifty pounds in pay to the inhabitants of Sagaponack and Mecox to make and maintain the said bridge forever at their own charge: and they are to make and maintaine the said Bridge sufficient for either men horses or Cartes to pass over it." Liber A, No. 2, p. 141.

"June 22nd 1691. It is also granted by generale vote of the Town that there shall be laid out forthwith, by the Layers out sixty acres of Land in some convenient place where it can be had to be layd out to the neighbors of Sagaponac and Mecox which is given and granted to them upon this account to be improved for a parsonage there forever and for no other end and purpose: but if it shall so happen that at any time hereafter, it shall not be so improved as aforesaid then the said sixty acres shall be laid open to the common use until it shall be so improved again." P. 162 and 3, Liber A, No. 2.

These records demonstrate, that the colonies on either side of Sagg Pond had so far multiplied, that when met for worship no private house would furnish sufficient room, and that their wants required a separate church building. That the Eastern colony in Sagg were so numerous that the town voted for the bridge an appropriation of fifty pounds in addition to the sixty acre parsonage. And when minister White settled here, he located in Sagg. All circumstances showing that the tradition, that in early days the inhabitants of Sagg outnumbered those in Mecox, may have been true; and is said to be the fact even down to a period later than the revolution.

In 1695 minister White was settled. The meeting house was constructed near Sagg Pond, on its Western shore, in a valley just North of the highway thrown out by Isaac Willman, and on his land, being the same premises sold lately by John A. Sanford to Silas Tuthill, Josiah Rogers and John White. The Bridge started at the East from the end of Bridge Lane, on the Sagg side of the pond, and was constructed over it just South of the present structure erected by said Tuthill, Rogers and White, and, perhaps, not over forty feet South thereof.

Previous to this time the inhabitants attended church at Southampton, traveling over the beach when the bay was not running in the Ocean, and when it was, over the wading place at the foot of Ludlow's neck.

Now they have a church. A spectator standing on the hill, just west of its location, could almost reproduce the view. Looking South, he would see the Pond sweeping to the beach, that shifting, yet eternal barrier of Ocean, which spread illimitable beyond. On the banks at Mecox and at Sagg were the wigwams where the whalers watched for the monsters of the deep—near them were the stage poles which they climbed to get a better look for a long sweep over the watery waste, or make a "weft" when whale were seen. Close at hand were the boats, resting on elevated poles, with all the craft at hand, ready to be launched. Looking East, he would see the church at his feet, with its chimney rising from the roof, (for this church had a fire-place,) the bridge cut the pond below him; and on the level, fertile plain wherein the early settlers of Sagg planted themselves, he could locate the houses by the curling smoke rising from chimney top, and the pole hanging at its peculiar angle over the well. Looking North, the stream meandered through a swampy, woody valley, until lost in the majesty of the forest that extended far as the eye could reach. Looking West he saw the table land whereon he stood, dotted with dwellings; here was Hildreth, and Mills, and Howell, and Cooper, and Sanford, and Willman; and on further the old horse-mill at the mouth of Horse-Mill Lane, and further still, Lupton and Ellis Cook, and Anthony Ludlam, all mighty hunters on forest or ocean wild. It was a lovely view. A mile or so of land, adjoining the Ocean only, was cleared and rescued from the wilderness that extended Northwardly far as the eye could see. But this redeemed inheritance abounded in green pastures; yielded a luxuriant growth of corn, and oats, and rye, and flax; flocks of wild ducks and geese hovered over the bay and pond, and around the creeks, and within them, delightful fish sported and cut the wave. But ocean —ocean heaving its vast billows, uttering its dread and solemn roar; emblem of all that is vast in nature; ocean, resistless in the wildness and recklessness of its wrath and tempest; that moody element now so low and soft of its mournful note; now so thundering and lofty its tone— the monument and the music of its God. This fair, dread scene opened to the eye of the onlooker; then as now, two centuries later, when time has changed all except what steadfast landmarks of nature resist all change. If to the soul of the Puritan of that day the voice of ocean suggested mighty thoughts and "spoke a prophet's word" as it does to the Puritan of this day; who shall say that its voice failed to lift the soul nearer to its mighty maker, or that the speech of nature and the strains of inspiration blending in sweet accord, tended not to make our fathers, as they tend to make us, more reverential to the great Father and maker of all.

What in all the ages of its history had bound the hearts of all Long Islanders, wherever else wandering, to their loved and native soil. What turns the thoughts of its far off sons and daughters in remotest territories and states back to the spot that gave them birth. Sweeter fruits may invite the taste; milder skies warm the frame; more fertile plains gratify the desire; and yet, who can forget the breeze that blows strength from the ocean to the dweller on its shores; who tire of its wondrous and varied anthem.

> *"Thou little spot where light first on me shone,*
> *Where my first pang, my earliest joy I knew,*
> *What tho' remote, unnoticed and unknown,*
> *Yet shall my heart to thee be ever true."*

"May ye first 1712. Voated that Sagaponac and Meacocks shall have Twenty acres of Land Layed out for a parsonage for a Prisbeterian minister or other wise to return to ye Town again." Liber A, No. 2, p. 75.

"Southampton April ye 5th day 1737. At an election Meeting to choose Town officers according to the Tenor of our pattent. Voated by ye Town yt the people of Bridge Hampton shall have liberty to build a Meeting House upon ye knowle on ye south side of Henry Wicks Land between Abraham Howells house and Joshua Hallworth and it was a cleane voate." Liber B, p. 138.

"Southampton April 2nd 1751. Whereas there having been a major vote of the Towne passed in the Public Meeting on the election day that Bridge Hampton Parish should have all that piece of Land upland swampland and meadow Land lying Northward of the Road &c All which said Land as it is above specified and bounded being by the Town given to the above said Parish to be and remain forever for the use of the ministry and for no other use whatsoever commonly called Parsonage Land. Wherefore we the Trustees being legally warned and assembled together at the School House do as Trustees ratify confirm and establish the above written vote of the Town that the Land therein mentioned as it is therein specified by its situation and bounds shall be to that said Parish and remain to them and their successors forever for the use therein mentioned and for no other use service or usage whatsoever than the use of a Gospel minister only always and provided that the said Parish shall leave common two acres of their Parsonage at Meacocks near their windmill for the Towns use witness our hands" Nathan Rogers and eleven others. Liber B, page 218.

All persons familiar with the history of Bridge-Hampton know that the sixty acres, voted for a parsonage in 1691, is what was called the Eastern Parsonage, now the farm of John S. Osborn.

The twenty acres voted for a like purpose in 1712, is the tract comprising the homestead of the late Rev. Amzi Francis, and extending West and North of that corner, including most of the home lots of L.D. Wright, M.D., and that of Wm. L. Jones, deceased.

The parsonage voted in 1751, included all the lot now owned by Jeremiah O. Hedges, all the West part of the homestead of Silvanus T. Ludlow, who occupies the old Woolworth homestead, and fourteen acres of swamp land, now owned by Capt. Benjamin H. Halsey.

By the record it appears that a knoll on Henry Wicks' land was selected in 1737 as a site for a church, which was the second church erected in Bridge-Hampton, about three fourths of a mile North by a few points West of the former one. This land is now owned by Edmund

A. Hildreth, and the site of the church, partly in the street and on the knoll, as described in the record, is plainly visible.

The site of this church, located probably with reference to the center of the village, geographically, and by population, shows the progress of population North and West. As early as "Jan. 16th 1719, John Wicks died in the 59th yr. of his age," and was buried in the lot formerly the Gray homestead, now land of Wm. Gardiner Esq., where his monument, solitary and singular, as he himself is said to have been, may be seen. He lived in or near what is now called Bull's Head, at the four corners. He was reputed to possess magic and wizardly powers. There is a tradition that the whalemen on the ocean's shore declared that at his death they saw and heard his soul winging in spiritual and unearthly flight over their heads, his dark and lonely way across the waste of waters.

He was said to have been a large land holder and a man of substantial means; sometimes a magistrate; and it is probable the Henry Wicks, on whose land the second church was erected, derived title from this John.

Just here let me observe, in all the records of an early date, Sagg and Mecox are mentioned as distinct and separate settlements. It is so in the votes of 1686, 1691, and 1712. Whereas, in the votes of 1737 and 1751 they are called "the people of Bridge-Hampton," and "Bridge-Hampton Parish." Why Bridge-Hampton? Undoubtedly that Bridge, built in 1686, binding together these localities, thereby practically making them one, gave to all the territory thereby connected the name Bridge-Hampton, and the gifts of parsonages recited, and of the home lot to minister White, so far endowed the society with means and property to aid in sustaining the minister and church, that the name, Parish of Bridge-Hampton, became an appropriate term whereby these descendants of Englishmen, accustomed to that term, denoted the bounds and locality of the people forming a religious society.

There is extant a list of the inhabitants of the town of Southampton, made in 1698, numbering, slaves included, 821, and excluded, 738, and summing up all the male freemen at 389. Howell, in the History of Southampton, quoting that history, says, all the names after No. 270 are those of residents of Mecox, Sagg, and Bridge-Hampton; and if so, out of 387, 119 males is the number of inhabitants therefor, comprising about one third of all the people of the town. I find there occurring the names of

BARBOUR,	HALEY,	LUDLOW,	SAYRE,
BURNETT,	HILDRETH,	LUPTON,	STANBOROUGH,
COOPER,	HAND,	LOOME,S	TRICKLING,
COOK,	HERICK,	NORRIS,	TARBILL,
DIAMOND,	HAINES,	NUTTON,	TOPPING,
FLINT,	HUSE,	PETTY,	WADE,
FOSTER,	MITCHELL,	RESCO,	WILMOT,
FORDHAM,	MASEN,	PERSON,	WOOD,
HALSEY,	MILLS,	ROGERS,	WICKHAM,
HASEY,	MORE,	ROSE,	WHITE,
HOWELL,	MOREHOUSE,	SANFORD,	

By the year 1712, or near that time, Edward Howell, great grand father of Esq. Hervey Howell, had settled in Poxabogue—had built the house which still stands there, and in which his great grand son resides. Wick had built at Bull's Head.

Scuttle Hole and the Hay Ground were settled, and the parish had attained a considerable size and population. The houses of Wick and Howell were probably the farthest north at that time, and Howell's is said to have been. This Howell was a merchant; is said to have opened what is called Merchant's path. I conjecture that his goods were landed at North West, instead of Sag-Harbor, which was then unsettled, and brought up from North West by that road.

In the wars that prevailed with the Dutch, and with the Indians, I find no record or tradition relating to this village. During the French and Indian war of 1756, soldiers and officers served from Bridge-Hampton.

I read some memoranda from the records of the Colonial Congress and Continental Congress. Bridge-Hampton.

"Company 3, Capt. David Pierson*, 1st Lieut. Daniel Hedges*, 2d Lieut. David Sayre*, Ensign Theophilus Pierson*.

"Company 9, Capt. John Stanford*, 1st Lieut. Edward Topping*, 2d Lieut. Phillip Howell*, Ensign John Hildreth*." Onderdonk's Rev. Incidents, &c. p. 20.

NOTE. *David Pierson was grand father of the late David Pierson, of Sagg. Daniel Hedges was brother of Deacon David Hedges. David Sayre was great grand father of the present Steven Sayre. Theophilus Pierson is supposed to have been a brother of Capt. David Pierson. John Sanford, of the Mecox family of Sanfords. Edward Topping was grand father of Alanson Topping, Esq. Phillip Howell was grand father of Matthew Hildreth's wife, and John Hildreth was grand father of Matthew Hildreth, who has the Commission issued to his grand father, which reads as follows:

I understand that anciently two companies of militia were formed in Bridge-Hampton, one at Sagg and one at Meacox, the former being the larger. Company 3 was the Sagg, and 9 the Mecox company.

This record, undated, must have been a statement of the companies as existing before 1776, and probably as made up in 1775.

Maltby Gelston certifies the election of David Pierson, Capt.; John Foster, Jr., 1st Lieut.; Abm. Rose, 2d Lieut., and Edward Topping, Ensign of another Company of Minute Men in Southampton. Onderdonk, &c. p. 25.

This was a Bridge-Hampton Company.

"List of officers of Col. Smith's Regiment. 1st Company, Capt. Reph. Rogers, 1st Lieut. Edward Topping, 2d Lieut. Paul Jones, Sergts. Hugh Gelston*, Tim. Halsey*, David Lupton; Corporals, Jehiel Howell, Silas Pierson, Jona Cook.

"Col. Abm. Gardiner administered the oath of allegiance to the people of East and South Hampton. He surrounded the house of Col. Hedges, at Sagg, and of Col. Mulford, at East-Hampton, and forced them to take the oath. The cattle on Montauk were driven in to Erskine. Tories enlisting at Coram before Sept. 7, '76." Onderdonk, p. 49.

"Septr. 15th. Wharves at Sag-Harbor crowded with emigrants."

"Buell writes from East-Hampton, Sept. 22d, '76, That the people are as a torch on fire at both ends, which will be speedily consumed, for the Continental Whigs carry off their stock and produce, and the

---

In Committee of Safety for the Colony of New-York,
the thirteenth day of September, 1775.

To John Hildreth, Gentleman, Greeting:

By Virtue of the Authority reposed in us by the Pronvincial Congress of the said Colony,—We do hereby nominate, authorize, consitute and appoint you, the said John Hildreth, Ensign of the ninth Company, in the second Regiment, in Suffolk County, hereby requiring you, before you enter into the Exercise of your said Office, to make in Writing, and subscribe in Presence of the Chairman of the Committee of the City, Town, District, or Precinct wherein you reside, the Declaration appointed and directed by the Eleventh Section of the Seventh Resolve contained in the Rules and Orders for regulating the Militia of the Colony of New-York, recommended by the Provincial Congress, on the 22d day of August, 1775, and authorizing you fully to execute all the Powers belonging to your said Office, by Virtue of the said Rules and Orders, and the said Declaration: And we do hereby rquire all Persons under your Command, to pay due Obedience to you, according to the said Rules and Orders as shall be made and recommended for the Militia of this Colony, by the present, or any future Continental Congress, or Provincial Congress of this Colony. By Order of the Committee.

Attest, John Haring, Chairman.
Rob't. Benson, Sec'y.

NOTE. *Hugh Gelston was brother of Tom Gelston. Tim Halsey was grand father of the present Oliver Halsey, and David Lupton was father of the late John Lupton.

British punish them for allowing it to go. Hopes the Whigs will not oppress the oppressed, but let the stock alone." Onderdonk, p. 48.

After the Battle of Long Island, many who had been active in advocating the independence of the Colonies, fled to Connecticut for safety. David Pierson, John Gelston, Maltby Gelston, David Sayre, Abram Rose, Dan'l Haines, Ezekiel and Daniel Howell, and Silas Norris petition Gov. Trumbull to remove flax, wool, stock &c. from Long Island to Connecticut, Feb. 27. Onderdonk, p. 70.

July 3d, '77. Oba. Jones, John Hurlbut and Thos. Dering, gave permits to refugees going to Long Island. *Ib.* p. 70.

New London, Aug. 14th, '78. We hear 1,000 troops from New-York, were at the East End of Long Island, a few days ago collecting provisions for the British army. *Ib.* p. 75.

At different times we find and locate David Pierson, †Ezekiel Sanford, David Sayre, John Hurlbut, Theophilus Halsey, Maltby Gelston, Uriah Rogers, and Benj. Sayre,* at East-Haddam, Jas. Sayre, at Saybrook, David and Silvanus Howell and Dr. Silas Halsey, at Killingworth, Jos. Topping, in Middletown, Thomas Topping, tanner and shoemaker, in Westfield.

Nov. '79. Hugh and Wm. Gelston petition to winter their horses on Long Island.

Nov. 16th, '79. Thos. Topping obtained permit to bring off from Long Island, some flour and grain, produce of his land.

Decr. 3, '79. Hugh Gelston allowed to go to Long Island for 300 bushels of salt, without carrying goods, produce or money. Onderdonk.

Copy of a blank order left with the inhabitants of Suffolk County, Long Island, Sept. 1776:

"You are hereby ordered to preserve, for the King's use—loads of hay,—bushels of wheat,—of oats,—of rye,—of barley,— of Indian corn, and all your wheat and rye straw, and not to dispose of the same, but to my order, in writing, as you will answer the contrary at your peril." Onderdonk, p. 55.

The battle of Long Island occurred August 27th and 28th, 1776. On the night of the 29th, Washington made the ever memorable retreat of his entire army, under cover of the fog and darkness, to New-York.

Thenceforth, from that date until Nov. 25th, 1783, (Evacuation day,) the whole Island remained in the possession of the British Forces— seven long years.

NOTE: †Ezekiel Sanford was grand father of the present James L. Sanford, and Ben. Sayre was grand father of the present Horatio G. Sayre.

The genial and gentlemanly Erskine sometimes protected the Americans from the brutalities of the soldiery. But Cochran, Major in the British Army, was often and long at Sagg, as his head quarters. And no man more vile; no man more brutal; no memory more execrated has passed down in the traditions of these towns, concerning that period, than his. After the Revolution this whole country was rife with anecdotes of his inhumanity. Howell has recorded the incident of his causing to be whipped William Russell. When at Sagg he took a young boy, had him shot, or pretended to shoot at him as a mark. The mother, in her distress, sent an old servant to ask for the boy. Cochran released the boy, and ordered the slave to be tied in the same place, calling him "a black limping devil," and actually continued to shoot at him at intervals through the afternoon.

What soldiers from here fought through the Revolution after that battle, is somewhat uncertain. It is known that many, somehow, reached the continental army, and joined in giving the blows that won independence. Whether the regiment commanded by Col. Josiah Smith, marching to engage in the battle of Long Island, reached the spot in time, is at least doubtful, and whether they joined the American army in the retreat, is improbable. The weight of evidence is that their march was intercepted by the British forces. That defeat occurred before their arrival. That in the confusion of that disaster, they were disbanded, and fled, some to their homes, some to the continent, and some to the continental army.

It is said that Steven Halsey, grand father of Hugh, was a Surgeon in the Revolutionary army. Abram and Thomas Halsey, brothers of Ethan Halsey, are said to have served in fort Ticonderoga. Silvanus Halsey was a pensioner, as a Revolutionary soldier. Phillip Halsey, as also in the Revolutionary army. John White, grand father of the present John, of Sagg, was in the Revolutionary army, and one of the soldiers engaged in the gallant and successful expedition of Col. Meigs, at Sag-Harbor, in 1777. John Gelston fled to Connecticut; also Daniel Hedges of Sagg. David Gelston, son of Maltby, it is believed, fled to Connecticut. He had been elected to the second, third, and fourth Provincial Congress; was, afterwards, member of Congress, in 1789, and became Collector of the port of New-York.

David Hand started to go in the expedition with Montgomery; became sick at Albany, and returned. He afterwards followed the seas in privateers; was taken prisoner by the British five times; was impressed in service, and escaped; was in the Sugar House, at the Wallabout, and in the prison ships. A man of indomitable courage and spirit. He it was who, when robbed and plundered of clothing, and denied his wages, by the commander of a British vessel, indignantly said to the Captain, "All I ask now is to begin at your taffrail rail and fight the whole ship's crew forward, and die like a man."

During these years, 1776-1783, the condition of this Island was most deplorable. At heart, thorough patriots, (one village name, only, has descended to posterity, in the traditions of the past, as that of Tory); cut off from their fellow countrymen; suspected and plundered by both friend and enemy; the very necessities of life ruthlessly taken by the foe, or ravaged by their countrymen for fear they would be seized to feed the foe; harrassed, insulted, starved, abandoned of friends; what years of darkness, and depression, and desolation rolled over this fair heritage; the fields tilled in the hope of finding sustenance; the cattle, and sheep, and harvests wrenched from them by both invader countrymen, and invader foe.

At the first, Buell's burning soul prompted the utterance: "The people are as a torch on fire at both ends, which will be speedily consumed," for the Continental Whigs carry off their stock and produce, and the British punish them for allowing it to go—hopes the Whigs will not oppress the oppressed, but let the stock alone." Onderdonk, p. 48.

Remember, this was at the commencement of the dark days that "tried men's souls." What then can measure the depth of misery attained by descending years. When peace was proclaimed, farms were impoverished; buildings and fences dilapidated; fortunes wasted; comforts fled. But liberty, worth more than all, was gained. When the last British soldier stepped off this soil; when the defeated army embarked from New-York harbor; when the British fleet passed through Long Island Sound and vanished from our shores; when the last momento of hostile power fled and faded away before the light of freedom: no heavier burthen was lifted from any part of these United Colonies than from this. From none ascended more triumphant cheers. One long accordant shout from bursting hearts went up from these shores as if to rend the Heavens in glad acclaim:

> *"Another breeze is on the sea,*
> *Another wave is there,*
> *And floats abroad triumphantly*
> *A banner bright and fair.*
> *And peaceful hands and happy hearts*
> *And gallant spirits keep*
> *Each star that decks it, pure and bright,*
> *Above the rolling deep."*

And now commences another era, which can be stated by the covenant between the people of the parish and Dr. Woolworth—speaking for itself.

Sag-Harbor was unquestionably so called because it was the Harbor of Sagg, and, in fact, it was part of the Hamptons. When these Hamptons were settled, and had been for four score years, Sag-Harbor was, as such, unknown. Before the war of 1812 some offshoots from the old families of Sagg and Bridge-Hampton, removed to their Harbor, including the Hands, Gardiners, Howells, Hedges, Gelstons, Piersons, Halseys, Squires, Hildreth, Strong, Topping, Mitchell.

The present Long Wharf was constructed about 1795, chiefly by labor and capital furnished from the Hamptons. The garrison stationed there, in the war of 1812, was largely composed of Bridge-Hampton men. David Hedges was Captain, Rufus Rose was Surgeon; Col. Levi Howell held some office; David Haines, afterwards Col. and father of Alderman Haines, held some office. At the first news of the arrival of the British fleet, in Gardiner's Bay, Gen. Rose requested the Assembly, gathered for worship on the Sabbath, to remain after service, and addressed the audience from the Church door, urging them to volunteer in defence of the country; a call unanimously welcomed and largely responded to. Again the contest comes:

> *"Hark! a bugle's echo comes,*
> *Hark! a fife is singing,*
> *Hark! the roll of far off drums*
> *Through the air is ringing.*
>
> *Nearer the bugle's echo comes,*
> *Nearer the fife is singing,*
> *Nearer and nearer the roll of drums*
> *Throughout, the air is ringing.*
>
> *War, it is thy music proud,*
> *Wakening the brave hearted;*
> *Memories, hopes, a glorious crowd*
> *At its call have started.*
>
> *Memories of our sires of old,*
> *Who oppression driven,*
> *High their rainbow flag unfolded*
> *To the Sun and Sky of Heaven,*

Memories of the true and brave,
Who at honors bidding,
Stepped, their country's life to save,
To war as to their wedding.

Hopes that the children of their prayers
With them in valor vying,
May do as noble deeds as theirs
In living and in dying.

And make for children yet to come,
The Land of their bequeathing;
The imperial and the peerless home
Of happiest beings breathing.

No history of Bridge-Hampton could be complete unless some sketch of noted characters were drawn.

There is a tradition that Daniel and David Hedges, brothers, started with their effects, after the Island was surrendered, to the British, in '76, intending to embark for Connecticut. Daniel went on; David when on the hill where Robert Hedges now lives, changed his mind, wheeled his ox cart south, and remained through the Rebellion.

Brown, the Minister, resigned in 1775, March 27th, and the church remained twelve years without a minister. Deacon Stephen Rose writes "during the desolating scenes of the Revolutionary war, when the church had no pastor, and his brother Deacons only returned to die and be buried among the people, Deacon Hedges never deserted his post. He kept up pubic worship, officiated in the absence of the minister, read sermons, and prayed. He loved the hill of Zion, and whether it was to hear preaching, or to take the lead in the service of the sanctuary himself, he was constantly seen on the Sabbath morning, coming up to worship in her courts. He was emphatically a man of large and deep feeling. On some occasions, when he was pouring out his soul in language as solemn and appropriate as a mortal could use, the tears were seen coursing down his cheeks. Not only in the church, but at prayer meetings and funerals, and other occasions, his prayers were solemn and edifying." He died Nov. 8th, 1817, aged 73 years. He was a member of the convention for deliberating on the adoption of the Constitution of the United States, assembled at Poughkeepsie, June 17, 1788, and a member of Assembly in 1786-87-88-89-1804-6-8. He lost largely by the Revolutionary war. The British compelled him to cart large quantities of hay and other products, (he being a larger farmer,) to Sag-Harbor; the writer's father, then a boy, carting with his father. All these stores were burned by Meigs' expedition, and no compensation made by the British to those from whom they were levied.

Nathan Sanford, son of Thomas Sanford, was born in Bridgehampton in 1777. In 1803 he was appointed District Attorney of the United States for the Southern District of New-York, holding the office for 12 years. In 1811 was Speaker of the Assembly, being the last who presided in a cocked hat, according to ancient custom. In 1815 he became a senator of the United States. From 1823 to 1826 he was Chancellor of the State of New-York, and was, in the latter year, again elected Senator of the United States. He died at Fushing [sic], L.I., in 1838. He is said to have been a finished scholar, and master of the Latin, Italian, French, and Spanish tongues.

Jonathan Rogers, grand father of the present Benjamin F. Rogers, was for some time one of the Judges of the Court of Common Pleas, in and for this County; a long time Justice of the Peace, well known as a man of great intelligence, rare natural gifts of intellect, and wise in counsel and judgment.

Tom. Gelston was the joker and wag of Bridge-Hampton. He never lost an opportunity of a witticism, and never lacked the inspiration.

It is related that on one occasion "Uncle Tom," as he was familiarly called, was driving at a furious rate from Sag-Harbor, and when abreast of the Old Farm, some one called him to stop. "Oh, I can't stop, can't stop," said he, "I've got my wife's bonnet in the wagon—afraid it will be out of fashion before I get home-get up," and drove on.

Uncle Tom once took a grind-stone to Ithuriel Hill, the stone cutter, at Sag-Harbor, to have the surface rounded. Hill, who was also a wag, asked six shillings for the job. Uncle Tom said he could not afford it, and left it to be rounded four shillings worth. When he called for it he found Hill had smoothed two third, and left the remaining third rough, when he gave up beat, and agreed to pay Hill to finish it.

Job Pierson, son of Samuel, born in Sagg, removed to Rensselaer Country, wherein he was Surrogate 1835-1840. Representative in Congress 1831-1835, and died there some 15 years since.

It is a singular coincidence that in succession three Presidential Electors were chosen from this village. Gen. Abraham Rose in 1840, Hugh Halsey in 1844, and Abraham T. Rose in 1848; each voting for the successful candidate.

Abraham T. Rose, son of Doctor Samuel H. Rose, was born in Bridge-Hampton in 1792, died April 29th, 1857. He graduated at Yale College in

1814; became a practising lawyer, residing always in his native village. He was County Judge and Surrogate of this County from July 1847 to January 1852, and from January 1856, until his resignation in the month wherein he died. In 1848 he was one of the Presidential Electors.

A man of varied genius; generous and kindly impulse; poetic temperament, and magnetic eloquence. Turning to any subject, and by intuition becoming master of all literature-all mechanics-all science, and even all music. How many aradent friends admired and loved him. How large audiences always gathered to hear him speak. How invariably his eloquence carried court and jury, spectators and parties, his own way, none so well as younger lawyers, like myself, could then know. At the end he professed his undoubting faith in Jesus Christ; was received into this church, at his own residence on the Sabbath shortly before his death; received the holy communion at the hands of the elders; expressed his regret and repentance for past errors, and his hope in the Redeemer, and when the power of utterance in him, so attractive and wonderful, became obstructed, commenced to us the 116th psalm, as expressive of his experience and hope. May the memory of his vision, in the dark and shadowy valley, lead and light the footsteps of those who knew and loved him before.

That curtain closes,
Which shall rise no more."

Hugh Halsey, son of Dr. Stephen Halsey, was born in Mecox, June 26th, 1794, died May 29th, 1858; graduated at Yale in 1814. He represented this County in the Assembly in the session of 1823-1824. Was Surrogate from 1827 to 1840, and first Judge from 1833 to 1847; a Presidential Elector in 1844, and Secretary of the electoral body; Surveyor General from 1845-1848; Member of the Senate from 1854-1855.

A thoroughly upright, clear headed, well balanced, judicious counsellor; learned in the law; diligent in its study; never litigious; always calm and clear in judgment; a promoter of peace; an ardent advocate of temperance; a devout believer in Jesus Christ; a pillar in the church. What streams of pure and happy influences flowing by and from his efforts, purified and blessed this village. His record is on high.

It would be both appropriate and pleasant to dwell upon the names of those who were, in their day, men of mark, and might, and high position in this village. The Piersons, Howells, Halseys, Toppings, Rose—Gen. Abraham, Deacon Stephen, Doctors Rufus and Samuel, and Col. Edwin—all born and bred in Bridge-Hampton. All according to their day and time, in church and state, according to their gifts, working for the elevation of their race, the enfranchisement of the nation, the maintenance of freedom, the birth and defence of the Union. But time fails. All honor to their memory. All praise for the good they wrought. All forgiveness for their errors.

The first Methodist Church in Bridge-Hampton, was erected about 1820. It stood just North and East of the present house of Wm. H.H. Rogers, Esq., near the Francis corner, and in 1833, July 2d, the premises and church being "seven poles more or less," bounded West by the Parsonage, North and South by Rev. Amzi Francis, and East by the Highway, were conveyed to William Corwithe, who reconveyed to Rev. Amzi Francis.

In the latter year a new and commodious church was erected on a site on the Main street, now owned by David Hallock and John W. Hull, who purchased the land in 1870, when the edifice was removed to its present location, enlarged and constructed as it now stands.

In the war for the maintenance of the Union of these United States, this village was eminently patriotic and by an overwhelming public sentiment; by generous donations and large numbers of Volunteers gave aid to the armies of the Nation, in crushing the Great Rebellion. One contribution in the winter of 1863-4 for the relief of the sick and wounded Union soldiers under the auspices of the Sanitary Commission amounted to nearly One Thousand dollars. The Volunteers from the Northern School District outnumbered the dwelling houses therein. Edwin Rose, a graduate at West Point, was for a time Colonel of the 127th Regiment, N.Y. Volunteers, and his genial nature and well known fitness for command, attracted large numbers of our inhabitants to the standard of their eminent fellow citizen. Of our soldiers in this war, some were killed in Battle; some died in Rebel Prisons; some fell victims to the malarial influence of Southern swamps; some breathed their last in Hospitals; some shattered in constitution returned home to suffer awhile and die. We decorate the graves where rest their remains; we keep sweet and green their memory; we honor their heroic devotion to the cause and the land they loved.

An hundred years and more ago, John Wicks kept tavern near the four corners. A Gardiner family kept tavern at Poxabogue, on the Mott corner. Stores were kept down Mecox, in Sagg and Poxabogue, dealing out Rum in destructive profusion. Doctors and Ministers, Justices and Deacons, church and anti-church, men of all grades, all occupations, all professions, unthinkingly joining in one universal tippling, followed by shipwreck in life, in fortune, in morals, in happiness; corrupted and corrupting the succeeding generations to follow, in like dark career. Now no place and no practice of tippling can be found within the bounds of this parish. It remains for posterity but to—"Hold the Fort."

And now I stand here, at this point, where my father and grand father might have stood an hundred years ago. I see, as they might have seen, a fair sight from this central point. Three miles North, the hills rise whereon the forest crowns the heights. Three miles South, ocean rolls. Three miles East the town and parish limits run. Three miles West the bay and pond mark the bounds nature has made to divide this from the mother plantation. If they could see fair fields, I can see them yet more beautiful and more bountiful. If they could see comfortable dwellings, I can see them with an added grace and beauty. If they could see the old church on the knoll of Henry Wick's lot; no steeple, no bell, no tower, no spire, I see a church on a grander elevation, symmetrical in architectural proportions, ample in dimensions, crowned and complete in massive tower, and music bell, and lofty spire. In dim vision they hoped for coming freedom. In full fruition we enjoy its rich inheritance. Cloud, and darkness, and battle carnage, and captivity hid their eyes, ere the flag that now floats over us, floated triumphantly over them.

And now my neighbors, my countrymen! of the same blood, the same fathers, and soil, we have reviewed, in swift retrospection, two centuries. We have communed with the eight past generations. We have stood over the graves that cover their crumbling, consecrated dust. They are gone, human eye will look on them no more forever. Yet still they live—live in the bright example they bequeathed—live in the patriotic purpose they formed—live in the glorious principles they proclaimed; undoubting, undaunted, unterrified Americans. I hear the melodies of the past. I catch the notes of the far off years. Sounding through the ages come the utterances of the long time ago. Truth, and principle, and right, can never die. White still preaches to this generation as he preached in the old thatched roof church, by the shores of Sagg Pond. Brown still expounds God's holy word, as he expounded it in the Church on the knoll. Woolworth still thunders, as he thundered in the high raised pulpit, under the sounding board, on the old Church. Francis still breathes out the gospel of Jesus Christ, as in measured and scholarly accents he uttered them fifty years ago. Tom Gelston cracks his jokes in the tongues of this generation, as by his own, seventy-five years past. Rose and Halsey fire the heart by the remembrance of a logic and eloquence which let in light on the generations gone. The Revolutionary Gelstons, and Halseys, and Howells, and Piersons, and

Toppings, and Cooks, still breathe indignant defiance to tyrants; still hail independance, in the lips of this generations, as by their own, an hundred years gone by.

God of the heaving Ocean and the steadfast land. God of the earth below and skies above. God of the summer's breeze and whirlwind storm. God of the mountain height and lowland vale. God of the roaming beast, and winged bird, and blossoming flower. God of nations. God of war. God of our beloved land. Our fathers' God, to whom belong the eternal years. As to them thou gavest the selectest influence, so now, to their descendants, to remotest time, bestow thy spirit. Make them divinely strong in righteousness. Make them divinely pure in heart. Make them divinely fruitful and beautiful in goodness. When the fleeting years of mortal life are ended, receive them to "an inheritance incorruptible and undefiled, and that fadeth not away."

I.

"Our fathers' God! from out whose hand
The Centuries fall like grains of sand,
We meet to day, united, free,
And loyal to our land and Thee,
To thank Thee for the era done,
And trust Thee for the opening one.

VI.

Oh make Thou us through centuries long,
In peace secure, in justice strong;
Around our gift of freedom draw
The safeguards of Thy righteous law;
And cast in some diviner mold
Let the new cycle shame the old!"

NOTE.—Since the delivery of the Centennial Address at Bridge-Hampton, July 4th, 1876, I have become satisfied that Col. Josiah Smith's Regiment of Minute Men, or many of them, were engaged in the battle of Long Island. Certain soldiers and officers were selected from the Militia, who were bound to take their arms with them in the field at work and wherever they went, and to march at a moment's notice to an assigned rendezvous, hence their name, "Minute Men." Their organization appears from the Public Records. Josiah Smith was their Colonel. The fact that some of them were in action at Brooklyn has been published and was proved by affidavits of old soldiers applying for Revolutionary pensions. One of them, living to be an old man, then frequently described his standing as guard when Washington's forces retreated from New-York city.   H.P.H.

CHAPTER IV

DEVELOPMENT OF AGRICULTURE IN SUFFOLK COUNTY

Delivered on November 18, 1883,
at the age of 66

IN THESE CENTENNIAL exercises the subject assigned to me was "The Development of Agriculture." Agriculture, new and old, what it was two hundred years gone by, and what is now in Suffolk County. From 1639, when Lyon Gardiner made the first English settlement in the County of Suffolk, and within the present bounds of the State of New York, other colonies were founded at Southampton and Southold in 1640; in East-Hampton in 1649, and extending to Shelter Island, Setauket, Smithtown and Huntington, soon thereafter covered by charter the territory of the county of Suffolk. At the organization of the county in 1683, forty-four years had passed since Gardiner came to his island. This county comprised about two-thirds of the territory of Long Island. The census of 1875 gives the area thus:

	IMPROVED,	WOODLAND,	OTHER,	TOTAL,
Kings county, acres,	9,110	600	1,174	11,090
Queens county, "	117,686	29,736	24,561	171,983
Suffolk county, "	156,760	102,550	129,135	388,445

TOTAL AREA, 571,518

One-third is 190,506

Area of Kings and Queens is 183,073

Area of Suffolk over one-third is—acres 7,433

The precise population of the State or county in 1683, I have not ascertained. There was a partial statement in 1693, and the apportionment of militia to each county, thus:

City and county of New York,	477
Queens county,	580
Suffolk "	533
Kings "	319
Albany "	359
Ulster county and Dutchess,	277
Westchester county,	283
Richmond "	104
	Total, 2,932

Suffolk was the third county in the colony in the Quotas. I 1698, 1703 and 1723, the population is thus given:

	1698.	1703.	1723.
New York,	4,937,	4,436,	7,248.
Queens county,	3,565,	4,392,	7,191.
Suffolk "	2,679,	3,346,	6,241.
Kings "	2,017,	1,915,	2,218.
Albany "	1,476,	2,273,	6,501.
Ulster " } Dutchess " }	1,384,	1,669,	1,083.
Richmond,	727,	504,	1,506.
Orange,	————	268,	1,244.
Westchester,	1,063,	1,946,	4,409.
Total,	17,848	20,749	40,564

These results show that Suffolk County in population was the third in the State in 1693 and 1703, and the fourth county in 1723. A similar comparison will show that by the census in 1731 and 1737 this county held the same rank. In 1746 and 1749 it was the third; in 1756 the fifth, and in 1771 the sixth county of the State in numbers. In these periods reaching over almost one hundred and forty years, when the State was largely agricultural, the population of this county, chiefly so sustained, was nearly one-sixth of that in the entire State. In 1790 it was the eighth county, and contained 16,440 out of 340,120 in the State—a little under one-twentieth of the whole amount. On the 17th day of May, 1683, the tax of the province of New York was fixed at £2556 4s. 0d., and was apportioned thus:

	£	s.	d.
The city and county of New York to pay	434	10	00
County of Westchester, "	185	15	00
City and county of Albany, "	240	00	00
County of Richmond, "	185	15	00
County of Ulster, "	408	00	00
Kings County, "	308	08	00
Queens County, "	308	08	00
County of Suffolk, "	434	10	00
*Dukes County, "	40	00	00
County of Orange "	10	00	00

*The County of Dukes comprised Nantucket, Martha's Vineyard and the Eizabeth Islands.

Thus at the organization of the county its farmers were taxed to pay over one-sixth of all the taxes paid in the then ten counties of the province of New York, and as much as the city and county of New York, and more than any other county that alone excepted. Unless the county of Suffolk was then a productive territory, agriculturally, the tax was unequal, oppressive and unjust. Assuming its equality, it is given as an evidence that even then agriculture had so far progressed that in wealth, in substantial comfort, in ministry to the necessities of mankind, this county as an agricultural county stood even with the then commercial metropolis of the province, and second to none in the province. In 1693 Queens County furnished the highest number of militia men by 47, Suffolk County the next highest number by fifty-six over the number assigned to New York, which latter county came then third on the list of Quotas.

In the Journal of the Legislative Council of New York, under date of September 28, 1691, I find a memorandum of the Address of the House of Representatives, setting forth their sense of the displeasure of Almighty God for their manifold sins "by the blasting of their corn," etc., and an order that the first Wednesday of every month, until the month of June following, be observed and kept *a fast day*, and that proclamation be issued through the government to enjoin the strict observation thereof, and that all persons be inhibited any servile labor on the said days. Thus the uncertainties of unfavorable seasons, sometimes occurring now, clearly prevailed widely at that early day.

In the Journals of the same Council, under date of October 16, 1738, among the bills read before the Council is one entitled "An act to encourage the destroying of wild cats in Kings County, Queens County

and Suffolk County." By an act of February 16, 1771, a like provision applied to Suffolk County, and later, up to the first constitution of the
State and acts passed under it, similar provision was made, until the
matter was, after the Revolution, devolved, by statute passed March
7th, 1788, upon the several towns in the State. Thus, for nearly one hundred and fifty years, the agriculture of the county, from its infancy, contended against the depredations of wild animals, as well as the blights
and mildews of adverse seasons.

Through all this period it encountered a greater obstruction in the
method of conducting it. In all early settlements, when the axe clears
the forest and the plow inverts the virgin soil, where ages of repose
have stored up treasures of fertility, those treasures appear for years unexhausted and inexhaustible. It so seemed to the first settlers on the
Mohawk Flats, in the Genesee Valley, in the vales of Ohio, on the prairies
of the far West—and it so seemed to our ancestors on the shores of
Long Island. They cropped field after field with little, and oftener no
manure; they fenced large farms; they plowed, and raising more oats,
and little wheat, and more rye, left the land unseeded with grass for
eight, ten or fifteen years, hoping that rest would restore the exhaustion of cropping. Up to the time, and long after the Revolution this
skinning process went on all over this county and Island. What manure
was made, and that was small in quantity and poorly cared for, was applied on the few acres of mow land, and was thought to be wasted if
put on pasture. The vast old pasture lot, comprising often one-half the
area of the whole farm, impoverished and skinned, produced a few
wild bayberry bushes, such few weeds as worn out land could grow,
and everlasting five-fingers and briers. Nine pasture lots in ten were
blackberry lots in my early days. This skinning process, that run down
the averages of wheat per acre on the Mohawk flats, in the Genesee
Valley, and through Ohio, to twelve or thirteen bushels, was perpetuated here for nearly two hundred years. The pasture where I, when a
child, was sent to bring home the cows, was such a vast waste that
often in a fog I was lost for a time and could find neither cows nor the
way to them or to my home. With all the abundance of fish in the waters, I find no evidence that they were caught and applied as a fertilizer
to any noticeable extent until after the Revolution. The application of
fish, ashes, bone dust and other fertilizers, to any considerable extent,
upon the farms of this county, with few exceptions, dates within the
last sixty years. Within that time the production of grass, grain and root
crops in the county, I think, must have been more than doubled by the
increased and increasing application to fertilizers.

So little change occurred in the modes of farming and farm life that the farm and farmer of 1683 might well stand as a picture for those of 1783—the same tools, the same methods, the same surroundings. Grass was cut with the scythe, raked by a hand-rake, pitched by the old heavy iron fork; grain was reaped with the sickle, threshed with the flail and winnowed with a riddle; land was plowed with a heavy wooden framed plough, pointed with wrought iron, whose mole board was protected by odd bits of old cart wheel tire; harrows were mostly with wooden teeth; corn hills were dug with the hoe; the manure for the hill was dropped in heaps, carried by hand in a basket and separately put in each hill. The farmer raised flax and generally a few sheep. Threshing lasted well into the winter, and then out came the crackle and swingle, knife and board. The flax was dressed, wool carded, and the wheel sung its song to the linen and woolen spun in every house. The looms dreary pound gave evidence that home manufacture clad the household. From his feet to his head the farmer stood in vestment produced on his own farm. The leather of his shoes came from the hides of his own cattle. The linen and woolen that he wore were products that he raised. The farmer's wife or daughter braided and sewed the straw-hat on his head. His fur cap was made from the skin of a fox he shot. The feathers of wild fowl in the bed whereon he rested his weary frame by night, were the results acquired in his shooting. The pillow-cases, sheets and blankets, the comfortables, quilts and counterpanes, the towels and table cloth, were home made. His harness and lines he cut from hides grown on his farm. Everything about his ox yoke except staple and ring he made. His whip, his ox gad, his flail, axe, hoe and fork-handle, were his own work. How little he bought, and how much he contrived to supply his wants by home manufacture would astonish this generation.

The typical farm house of 1683 and 1783, were much alike. It was a single house unpainted, the front two, and the sloping rear roof made that one story. Four Lombardy poplars, tall, slim and prim, its sole ornament in front. The well pole, a few feet in the rear of the kitchen, pointed 45 degrees towards mid heaven—underneath swung the bucket,

"The old oaken bucket,"

immortal in song. Two small windows, of 6x8 glass, dimly lighted his front room. A large beam ran across its upper wall. Houses then were built to stay. The floor was uncarpeted. The chimney and fire-places

were capacious masses of masonry, looking with contempt upon the
Lilliputian proportions of like structures of these modern times. The
mass of chimney and oven and fire-places contracted into an entry
what would otherwise be a hall. The front stairs zig-zagged and turned,
and wound and squirmed towards the upper rooms. Over the fire-
place hung the old King's Arm, with flint-lock wherewith he had
brought down deer and wild ducks, and brant, and geese in no small
numbers. Outside hung his eel spear, clam and oyster tongs. Close at
hand was the upright hollow log that was his samp mortar. The barn-
yard was near, and in view of the kitchen, and on the farther side his
small barn. One roof sloped down low in the yard, and on that in the
cold winter's day he spread his sheaves of flax to dry for crackling. All
day he labored in the fields. In the long autumn and winter evenings he
husked corn and shelled the ears over the edge of his spade. No horse-
rake; no corn sheller, no horse pitch-fork; no horsemower or reaper—
the life of the farmer was literally a battle against the forces of nature
for little more than the actual necessities of subsistence, and with the
most rude and unwieldy supply of weapons for the war. The monotony
of his life was relieved by hunting and fishing in their season. The
farmer raised rye and corn, rarely wheat, for bread. He ate fresh pork
while it lasted, and salt pork while that lasted. Corn was pounded into
samp; ground into hominy and meal; baked or boiled into johnny-cake,
Indian bread, griddle-cakes, pudding, or what the Dutch called "sup-
pawn" and the Yankee "hasty pudding;" and in a variety of ways eaten
with or without milk. In some shape corn was a chief article of diet.
Rye bread, the chief bread, and wheat bread a rare luxury. Oysters,
clams, eels and other fish, with game of the forest or fowl of the air,
helped out the supply of food in the olden time. The statistics of ancient agriculture, if to be found at all, are not accessible to me. I turn to
the State census reports of 1865 and find:

Improved acres in New York State,	14,827,437
" " " Suffolk County,	148,661
Unimproved acres in New York State,	10,411,863
" " " Suffolk County,	230,556 1-2

Showing that Suffolk County contains a trifle less than one-hundredth part of all the improved lands in the State, and over one-fiftieth
of all its unimproved lands. The extensive beaches and woodlands of
the county constitute its unimproved lands.

The same census reports thus:

	CORN.	BUSHELS HARVESTED.	BUSHELS AVERAGE.
New York State acres plowed	632,213 1-4	17,987,763 1-4	28
Suffolk County, " "	16,460 1-4	580,015	35
	WHEAT.		
N.Y. State, " "	399,918 3-4	5,432,282 1-2	14
Suffolk County, " "	10,563 1-	199,941 1-4 short	19
	OATS.		
N.Y. State, " "	1,109,910	19,052,833 1-4 over	17
Suffolk County, " "	10,945	289,575 over	26
	RYE.		
N.Y. State, " "	234,689	2,575,348-304 short	11
Suffolk County, " "	5,353	61,555 1-2 over	17
	BARLEY.		
N.Y. State, " "	189,029 3-4	3,075,052 3-4 over	16
	CORN.		
Suffolk County, " "	498	14,095 over	28
	TURNIPS.		
N.Y. State, " "	8,123 7-8	1,282,338 over	157
Suffolk County, " "	689 1-4	160,457	232
	POTATOES.		
N.Y. State, " "	235,058 1-4	23,236,687 3-4 over	98
Suffolk County, " "	3,439 1-2	292,738 over	85

	ACRES OF GRASS CUT	TONS CUT.
N.Y. State,	4,237,085 3-4	3,897,914 1-8 short 1 ton.
Suffolk County,	34,577 3-4	34,758 over "
New York State, neat cattle,	1,824,221	
Suffolk County, "	18,792	

	HOGS SLAUGHTERED	LBS.	AVERAGE.
New York State,	706,716	128,462,487	181
Suffolk County,	13,942	3,060,602	219

CATTLE SLAUGHTERED FOR BEEF.

New York State, 221,481 1-4.   Suffolk County, 2447

VALUE OF FARM IMPLEMENTS AND MACHINERY.

New York State, $21,189,099.75.   Suffolk County, $407,257.

FERTILIZERS PURCHASED.

New York State, $838,907.52.   Suffolk County, $294,429.40

The value of poultry owned in 1865, and of poultry and eggs sold in 1864, in twelve counties, is thus:

	VALUE.	POULTRY SOLD IN 1864.	EGGS SOLD IN 1864.
Albany,	$52,466.30	31,016.40	34,957.61
Cayuga,	52,911.75	41,696.50	44,772.00
Columbia,	59,816.00	31,195.05	33,125.14
Dutchess,	77,194.00	76,326.50	52,059.50
Monroe,	53,977.33	38,706.05	33,743.98
Onondaga,	49,251.05	34,607.28	45,978.84
Orange,	63,410.00	32,101.24	36,858.36
Queens,	79,597.00	80,035.00	45,960.00
Saratoga,	52,576.53	36,500.81	45,082.91
Ulster,	55,292.12	29,277.20	36,601.30
Westchester,	75,643.75	45,068.46	41,346.53
Suffolk,	47,708.75	47,120.00	57,003.13

The results of these figures make this showing a fraction less than one-hundredth part of all the improved lands in the State lie in the county of Suffolk. If that county produces one-hundredth part of all the aggregate product of the crops in the State that shows, other things being equal, that the farmers of Suffolk County understand their business at least as well as the average farmer. If the land of our country be reckoned poorer than the average in the State, that fact will not lessen the force of the figures, or detract from the greater credit due to Suffolk County farming, provided that production comes up to the average State production. At the outset it appears that of all the tools and machinery used in farming in the State, Suffolk County held in value about one-fiftieth part—showing that the Suffolk County farmer was up to the average twice over in the value of mechanical appliances in his business.

Suffolk County purchased over one-third of all the fertilizers in the State, and more than any other ten counties. Suffolk County kept over one-hundredth of all the neat cattle in the State, and slaughtered over that proportion of all the cattle slaughtered therein, showing that her system of agriculture returned to the soil very largely the products, and was no skinning process; that the corn, oats, roots and grass were fed to domestic animals, and thereby the elements of fertility were restored to the soil.

Although these figures show an *average* for the county per acre of 13 bushels of potatoes less than the State average, they show more on all other productions. The average of the county over the State is, per acre in corn, 7 bushels; wheat, 5; oats, 9; rye, 8; barley, 12; and turnips 75 bushels. This county raised nearly one-thirtieth of all the corn raised in the State more than one-thirtieth of all the wheat, over one-seventieth of all the oats, nearly one-fortieth of all the rye, over one-eighth of all the turnips, and nearly one-eightieth of all the potatoes. It produced nearly one-fortieth of the total pork, and our average weight of hogs exceeded that of the State by 38 pounds. Suffolk County is credited with less poultry in 1865 than any of the twelve counties I have named, but sold more in 1864 than any counties in the State except Queens and Dutchess. Suffolk County beat all other counties in the State on eggs, and sold nearly $5,000 more than Dutchess County, which is the next highest on the list.

The census of 1875 gives these figures.

Improved lands in the State, acres,	15,875,552
Unimproved lands in the State, acres,	9,783,714
Suffolk County, improved lands,	156,760
" " unimproved lands,	332,685

The relative proportion of lands in the State and county remained nearly as in 1865:

Value of all stock in the State,	$146,497,154
" " " " " " County,	1,879,073
" " tools and implements in the State,	44,228,263
" " " " " " Suffolk County,	541,158

Value of all farm buildings other than dwellings,
In the State, $148,715,775.   In Suffolk County, $2,161,675

Value of all fertilizers purchased in the State,	$1,767,352
" " " " " " Suffolk County,	316,737
Area mown in the States—acres,	4,796,739
" " " Suffolk County,	38,744
Hay produced in the State, tons	5,440,612
" " " Suffolk County	41,980

CORN.—The State produced 20,294,800 bushels; Suffolk County produced 582,690.

OATS.—The State produced 37,968,429 bushels; Suffolk County produced 280,566.

WINTER WHEAT.—The State produced 9,017,737 bushels; Suffolk County produced 182,867.

POTATOES.—The State produced 36,639,601 bushels; Suffolk County produced 405,237.

Number of cattle slaughtered in the State,   85,571
"   "   "   "   " Suffolk County,   889
"   " hogs   "   in the State,   521,490
"   "   "   "   " Suffolk County,   11,585
Pork made in the State, lbs.,   121,184,622
"   "   " Suffolk County, lbs.   2,708,759
Gross sales of farm produce in the State, $121,187,467
"   "   "   "   "   " Suffolk County, 1,019,617
Apples produced in the State, bushels   23,118,230
"   "   " Suffolk County, bushels   308,315
Poultry sold in the State, value $1,772,084
"   "   " Suffolk County, value $65,572
Eggs sold in the State, value   2,513,144
"   "   " Suffolk County, value   118,049

Two counties sold more poultry, and two only, viz.:

Dutchess County sold $77,188; Queens County sold $88,403.

Onondaga sold eggs in value next to Suffolk, and to the amount of $91,818.

A careful comparison of these tables show results not unfavorable to the agriculture of Suffolk County, and the average of crops of the State and county are these:

AVERAGES OF STATE AND COUNTY PRODUCTION COMPARED.

		BUSHELS PER ACRE.		BUSHELS. PER ACRE.
Corn,	New York State,	32.	Suffolk County,	35.
Barley,	" "	22.	"	25.
Oats,	" "	28.	"	28.
Rye,	" "	11.	"	12.
Potatoes,	" "	102.	"	96.
Hay,	" "	1 ton.	"	1 ton.
Hogs,	" "	223 lbs.	"	233 lbs.

All fractions are rejected in the foregoing figures.

Suffolk County contained in value one-seventieth of all the farm buildings, exclusive of dwellings in the State of New York. Its farmers owned in round numbers one-eightieth of all the farm tools and machinery in the State. They purchased one-sixth of all the fertilizers purchased in the State. The value of the stock in the county was over one-eightieth part of all owned in this State. The acres mown to feed that stock was less than one-hundredth of all mown in the State, and the average cut of hay was within a fraction of the State average per acre. The number of cattle slaughtered in the county was over one-hundredth of all slaughtered in the State. The pork made in the county was over one-fiftieth of all made in the State, and the average weight of hogs in the county beat the State average ten pounds. Of all the corn raised in this State, Suffolk County produced over one-fortieth; of winter wheat over one-fiftieth, and of potatoes about one-ninetieth. The proportion of oats raised in the county was about one hundred and thirty-fifth of the State production. It was thought Suffolk County would be a poor county for the production of fruit, and yet the apple crop of the county was over one-eightieth of the whole State production. In the amount of poultry sold Suffolk County stands third in the list of counties in New York State. In the value of eggs sold this county stands first, beating every county, and beating Onondaga by over $26,000.

The results of the oat crop of the county as reported in the tables were a disappointment to me. I knew that in 1865 our average and aggregate product put this county among the foremost. Why in 1875 it was among the hindmost seemed unaccountable. The census of 1875 reports the product of 1874. Consulting my record of 1874, I found that I had ten acres in oats. I remembered that the crop never promised better for from 50 to 60 bushels per acre than then. I threshed 50 bushels, and the army worm threshed the rest. That clears the mystery. The loss on oats that year in the best oat region of the county on the south shore was ten times more than the amount harvested. Generally in my section none were threshed. In round numbers 10,000 acres were sown in the county. I estimate the loss by the army worm to be not less than 100,000 bushels, of the value of 55 cents per bushel, and in the aggregate $55,000. This loss should be credited to the county in any fair calculation of averages with other counties not so ravaged. This is pre-eminently the age of criticism. Moses and the Pentateuch are questioned. All the old foundations are pried up to see if they have good corner-stones. Men build capitols, and monuments, and bridges, and hotels by the job, covering up vast frauds. Practical men, and literary men, and mechanics, and the professions, believe nothing until it is demonstrated. The whole earth is a war of question and denial and call for proof. I anticipate this question: If Suffolk County is the purchaser of one-third of all the fertilizers sold in the State in 1865, and one-sixth in 1875, it must be a poor county; if not, why not? Other counties purchase little or none, while Suffolk is so poor it must purchase to produce, and unless the production is increased so as to pay the cost of fertilizers, Suffolk County is still in arrears. All that may be said regarding the necessity of restoring fertilizers to a soil long abused by the skinning process in this old county and the like necessity that will come to other counties will avail nothing. All that may be said showing that feeding produce to animals on the farm while in the main good farming lessens the amount of sales and apparent profit, will avail nothing. More largely than in other counties Suffolk fed on the farm the hay, corn, oats and roots, and sold proportionately more meat, lessening not really but apparently her farming profits. All this is apparent, but still the demand comes and must be met or avoided.

The excess and value of county over State averages may be thus stated for 1865:

	ACRES.	TOTAL.	PRICE PER BUSH.	VALUE.
Corn, 7 bushels	16,460 1-4	115,221 3-4	$1 00	$115,221 75
Wheat, 5 "	10,563 1-4	52,816 1-4	2 60	137,322 25
Oats, 9 "	10,945	98,505	0 80	78,804 00
Rye, 8 "	5,353	42,824	1 10	47,106 40
Barley, 12 "	498	5,976	1 10	6,573 60
Turnips, 75 "	689	51,675	0 40	20,670 00

The like excess for 1875.

	ACRES.	TOTAL.	PRICE PER BUSH.	VALUE.
Corn, 3 bushels	16,304	48,932	$1 00	$48,932 00
Wheat, 3 "	9,388	28,164	1 25	35,205 00
Barley, 3 "	186	568	1 00	568 00
Rye, 1 "	4,333	4,333	1 00	4,333 00
Apples 1 "trees	130,406	130,406	0 50	65,203 00
Loss on oat crop by army worm,				55,000 00

Total value of county excess,	$614,939 00
Add for permanent improvement of land by fertilizers,	100,000 00

Total,	$714,939 00

Deduct for less county average.

	ACRES.	TOTAL.	PRICE.	
1865. Potatoes 13 bu.	3,439 1-2	44,713 1-2	$0 80	$35,770 80
1875. " 6 "	4,208	25,248	0 50	12,624 00

Total to deduct,	$48,394 80
Balance of county over State production,	$666,545 20

Cost of fertilizers in 1865, $294,429 40
" " " " 1875, 316,737 00

Amounting to	611,266 40

Balance credit to the county over the State average after deducting cost of all fertilizers,	$55,278 80

In this calculation I have disregarded the item of fertilizers purchased by other counties and have under-estimated the amount of permanent improvement which I believe the land derived from the large application of fertilizers. No account is made of any extra straw or stalks thereby grown, and none of the extra market value of Long Island potatoes. All these items in the statement would make it still more favorable to the county, and would add force to he demonstration that Suffolk County can afford to purchase, and actually profits by the large application of fertilizers. It is usually the farmer who purchases judiciously the most manure who makes the most profit.

J.H. Wardle, Esq., has kindly sent in advance sheets of the census of 1880, from which I give these figures:

No. of farms in the State of New York,	241,058
" " " " Suffolk County,	3,379
" " acres improved in the State,	17,717,862
" " " " " " County,	156,223
" " " unimproved in the State,	6,062,892
" " " " " " County,	152,694
" " " woodland in the State,	5,195,795
" " " " " " County,	134,836
Value of farms in the State,	$1,056,176,741
" " " " " County,	17,079,652
" " farm tools and machinery in the State,	42,592,741
" " " " " " " " County,	563,225
" " live stock in State,	117,868,283
" " " " " County,	1,359,047
" " fertilizers purchased in State,	2,715,477
" " " " " County,	272,134
" " farm productions in State,	178,025,695
" " " " " County,	2,198,079

	BUSHELS.	ACRES.
Barley, in the State,	7,792,062	356,629
" " " County,	5,459	199
	BUSHELS.	ACRES.
Indian corn, in the State,	779,272	25,690,156
" " " " County,	18,097	624,407
Oats, in the State,	1,261,171	37,575,506
" " " County,	9,556	311,581
Rye, in the State,	244,923	2,634,690
" " " County,	3,931	47,471
Wheat, in the State,	736,611	11,587,766
" " " County,	5,660	182,537

	AREA MOWN ACRES.	CROP,TONS.
Hay, State,	4,644,452	5,255,642
" County,	33,197	40,111

NUMBERS POULTRY.

6,448,886,	Eggs Produced, in the State,dozens	31,958,739
160,173,	" " " Suffolk County,"	910,848
214,595,	" " " Erie " "	1,116,191
194,950,	" " " Cayuga " "	932,947
183,395,	" " "Oneida " "	1,008,330
204,295,	" " "Onondaga " "	972,206
199,840,	" " "St. Lawrence Co."	1,073,385
217,826,	" " "Steuben Co. "	1,037,509

	BUSHELS.	ACRES.
Irish potatoes, State	340,536	33,644,807
" " County,	3,796	493,078
Orchard Products value, State		$3,409,794
" " " County		17,248
Market garden products sold, State value		4,211,642
" " " " Co. "		118,293

Amount of cord-wood cut.

State, 4,187,942.   County, 34,228.

Value of fruit products sold.

State, $8,759,901.   County, $127,960.

The results of the figures of the census of 1880, are these:

The area of farms in the State averages over acres,	73
" " " " " " County " " "	45

measured by the acres of improved lands.

Less than one-hundredth of all the improved lands in the State lie in Suffolk County, yet the county has nearly one-seventieth in number of all the farms, showing thereby a more general distribution of land among the masses of people. Suffolk County contains about one-fortieth part of all the unimproved lands in the State, and a fraction over that proportion of all the woodlands. The farms of this county in value aggregate over one sixty-second part of the whole State valuation.

Suffolk County owns over one-eightieth part of the farm tools and machinery in the State, and over one-eightieth in value of all live stock in the State. Suffolk County purchased over one-tenth of all the fertilizers purchased in the State. The aggregate farm production of the county was over one-eightieth of all produced in the State. This county raised over one-fortieth of all the corn raised in the State, nearly one-hundredth part of all the oats; over one-sixtieth of all the rye, and over one sixty-fourth of all the wheat. Suffolk County mowed less than one-hundred and fortieth of all the acres mown in the State. It produced nearly the one-hundred and thirty-first of all the hay crop cut.The State average per acre was a little over one and one-tenth tons, and the county average per acre a little over one and two-tenths tons. Suffolk County produced nearly one-thirty-fifth of all the eggs in the State, from less than one-fortieth of all the poultry, ranking the seventh in product of eggs, and holding in number of poultry by over twenty thousand less than any of the six counties which produced more eggs. In acreage Suffolk County had of potatoes a fraction less than one-ninetieth contained in the State, and produced therefrom a fraction over one-seventieth of all the bushels produced. In value of orchard product the county, compared with the State, fails to come up to anything which might in former results have been reported.

In value of market garden products sold, the county sales were over one thirty-fifth of all sales made in the State. Suffolk County cut less than the one hundred and twenty-second part of all the wood cut in cords in the State, but sold in products of the forest over one-seventieth of all sold in the State.

The State and county averages compare thus per acre:

		BUSHELS.		BUSHELS.
Barley,	State,	21.85	County,	27 3-10
Indian corn,	"	32.97	"	34 4-10
Oats,	"	20.79	"	32 6-10
Rye,	"	10.76	"	12
Wheat,	"	15.73	"	18 8-10
Potatoes,	"	98 6-10	"	129 8-10

In all these products the county, rejecting fractions, exceeded the State averages thus: Per acre, on barley, 6 bushels; on corn, oats and rye, two bushels each; on wheat, three; and potatoes, twenty-one bushels. The deficiency of the county in potatoes in the years 1865 and 1875, is more than offset by its surplus per acre in 1880.The former surplus reported for the State in oats, in 1875, when our county suffered by the army worm, does not continue in 1880. In the great staples of corn and winter wheat the surplus average of this county continues through all these years, to the credit of the county. It will be observed that while Suffolk County purchased in 1865 one-third, in 1875 one-sixth, and in 1880 one-tenth of all the fertilizers purchased in the State, other counties were increasing their proportion of fertilizers after her example, and following more closely her methods. I introduce this account to show that such purchase pays:

The whole farm products of the State in value are	$178,025,695
" " " " " " County, " "	2,198,079
The county owns less than 1-100 of all the improved lands of the State, and measured thereby, 1-100 of the products is,	1,780,256
Credit of surplus product to the county is	$417,823
Cost of fertilizers purchased in the county is	272,134
Excess product,	$145,689

These figures add force to all former statements favorable to the quality of land or purchase of fertilizers to make farming pay in the county or State. The variety of soil in Suffolk County is seldom found elsewhere. For corn, no land on the continent is better suited. Midway between the cold blasts of a northern climate and the extreme heat of a southern, it is peculiarly adapted to the growth of that crop. In the production of wheat its conditions are favorable. The low, moist lands of the southern sea coast are well suited to raise oats. For vegetable growth and root crops, both the variety of its soil and temperature of its climate are favorable. The hardier fruits, like apples and pears, flourish here. The cauliflower and strawberry are so extensively cultivated that for the transportation of both crops extra railroad trains are specially run, and for the latter steamers from Greenport to Boston. The tables of the census demonstrate much of these remarks. But those of 1875 were compiled before the culture of these crops had reached their present very large proportions, or become a largely developed industry and been proved to be so profitable in pecuniary results. It is a matter of regret that no records exist whereby the precise extent of production in these crops can be ascertained. Yet it is significant that as New York city has judged the flavor of Long Island potatoes to be so superior as to command a premium in her markets, so Boston seeks in preference the strawberry that grew in Suffolk County. How this old county from the acorn grew in wealth and comfort to the solid oak; what changes occurred from its primitive government, jurisprudence and the administration of justice; how the light of education, intelligence and literary culture shone from its early dawn to the brightness of the present day; what progress it has made reaching for the wisdom that comes from above; how its commerce, navigation and fisheries were pursued by its adventurous citizens. All these are subjects assigned to other speakers and prohibited to me. Of that glad acclaim which echoed from the shores of this county in exultation to Heaven, when in 1783 the last British soldier evacuated forever its soil—even to speak of this is to tread on ground dedicated to another. But in all these historic events the farmer of Suffolk County was the central figure, and the tillers of the soil the prominent actors. The first settlers derived their subsistence chiefly from the farms they cleared in the wilderness. The early primeval government organized was instituted, and perpetuated, and developed by farmers. The diffusion of the light of education, intelligence and literary culture was mainly due to the farmer. If true devotion spoke anywhere to the power on high, it spoke at the hearthstone and fireside of the farmer. If commerce and navigation carried adventurous enterprise to the remotest sea, the sons of the farmer manned and sailed the ship. If fisheries were followed on stream or bay, on harbor, or sound, through strait or ocean, his hardy sons cast the net, threw the line or harpoon with the foremost pioneers. In colonial conflicts with the Indians or with the French, or both, the yeomanry of this county contended side by side with their compeers of other counties. The numbers they armed and the tax they paid were often among the largest contributed by any county in the State. In the long Revolutionary war, from the first, the farmers of Suffolk County were solid in resisting the oppressions of the Crown. In the disastrous battle of Long Island her sons bled in defence of the country. The seven dark years of captivity and desolation that followed, what historian can record! what pencil can paint! Abandoned by countrymen, oppressed by foe, plundered and derided by both, this county suffered its long hours of agony, upheld by the hope that the power that rules the universe would bring deliverance to them. From its household altars ascended in devotion the thought in a later day beautifully embodied thus:

> *"If for the age to come, this hour*
> *Of trial hath vicarious power;*
> *And blest by thee our present pain*
> *Be Liberty's eternal gain—*
> *Thy will be done!*
> *Strike; Thou the Master, we thy keys,*
> *The anthem of the destinies!*
> *The union of thy loftier strain;*
> *Our hearts shall breathe the old refrain,*
> *Thy will be done!*

In every line of the record of the historic past; in every great crisis of the colony or State, the farmers of Suffolk County have imperishably recorded their names with the illustrious dead. Go to the Declaration of Independence, and with the signers to that indestructible landmark of the Nation is written the name of William Floyd, a farmer of Suffolk County! Look for the consecrated dust of those who fell martyrs in the Revolutionary struggle, and within the limits of this county find buried one of her farmers over whose memory broods unceasing regret, and over whose name burns the undying fire of patriotism. Monuments may perish; age may obscure; yet after monuments have vanished, after ages have passed the name and memory of General Nathaniel Wood-hull will remain in the minds of his countrymen linked forever with the remembrance of that great contest in which he fell.

For the farmers of Suffolk County I might and I must say more. But for them there had been no Suffolk County as it now is. The bed rock of Agriculture underlies all other occupations; is the mother of all arts, of all manufactures, of all navigation, subsisting on the products of the prolific earth, all these may flourish. Thereby manufactures may expand; the mechanic arts make progress, and commerce be carried, for exchange of products over every ocean. But for Agriculture there had been no planting of colonies on these shores; no commerce over her waters; no United States on this Continent. The farmer made all this possible. Mainly by his strong arm; the feeble colonies grew in numbers and power, into States, and fought successfully the great Revolution that made them free and independent of all other nations. All honor to the farmer! all praise to agriculture! Not least of all to the agriculture and the farmer of Suffolk County. The mariners who from this county traversed every sea; the mechanics who wrought in all the arts of industry; the professions which shone as lights in theology, in medicine, in jurisprudence; the Legislators who sat in the halls of the State or Nation, were born and reared on the farms of Suffolk County. Therefrom came her Senators in both. Thenceforth marched that wondrous tide of emigration from colonial days to other counties of this great State, north and west, and to east and west Jerseys, as then known; and through after ages to the expanding West and the remotest Pacific coast. That mighty tide, enlarging, enriching, augmenting the population and power of other counties and States and territories, diminished the growth of this county while it enlarged theirs.

The proximity of Suffolk County to the large cities of the continent attracted visitors from the earliest days. The invalid and wayworn found its ocean breeze *bracing* in summer and mild in winter. The sportsman found game running in its forests, swimming in its abounding waters, and flying in its air. The lover of quiet and repose found it here. The good cheer and substantial comfort of its old taverns and farm houses were widely and well known. From the tip ends of Orient and Montauk Points to its western limits, in early, and increasing in later days, Suffolk County was the resort of hundreds now grown to thronging thousands. Dominy's and Sammis' hotels were almost as well known as the Astor House and Delmonico's; yet Fire Island and Bay Shore were but two, out of scores of other resorts where, on both shores of the county, and extending eastward, then and now the interior and the cities pour their residents on the sea coast of this county. The products of its soil were largely consumed by boarders in farm houses, and hence the returns of those products foot up relatively less for this than other counties in the census reports.

If elsewhere the farmer communes with nature and comes nearer her gates than other industrial classes; if elsewhere the contest to overcome the obstacles nature interposes to impede the fruition of his desire, is waging; if elsewhere the study of her laws and mysteries awakes close observation, minute search and absorbing thought; if elsewhere conformity to her laws by the requirement of success in the battle of wrestling from the soil its products; if elsewhere the vastness of her range, the uniformity of her constitutions, the precision of her methods, the inexorable power of her elements, the evidences of design in her arrangements, reveal the hand and mind of a mighty Maker. In all these surroundings the Suffolk County farmer lives within a field as vast, as varied, as full of all that animates observation, impels to study, excites to wonder or elevates to devotion as his brother farmer in other locations, here the fields of green grass or waving grain are varied with the growth of the forest. Here the parching droughts of summer's long day are relieved by the munificent dews of the evening. Here the oppressive heat of winds from north and west is overcome by the breeze of ocean. The glimmer of stream and creek, of harbor and bay and Sound, add to the charm of rural landscape—and over all the sound of ocean's wave.

Since 1683, when under Governor Thomas Dongan, Suffolk County as a county was organized; six generations of its farmers have passed away. The simple funeral rites of those times strangely contrast with the pomp, display and pageantry of the present.

"The Power incens'd the pageant will desert." On the bier on the shoulders of the living the dead were reverently carried to their final rest. The stars of heaven shine upon their graves as they shone then;

the blue vault that o'er arches us, hung over them; the anthem of ocean
that sung their funeral dirge, age after age, rolls on, and will sound in
our expiring breath and over our crumbling dust.

Celebrating this day that great event that two hundred years gone
by organized the then living generation in one compact body as a
county; paying our tribute to them and their descendants; honoring
their virtues and their patriotism; blessed with the results of their toils,
their fortitude and their courage, as if standing beside their opened
graves, we bear our unworthy offering to their memory and their solid
worth. They built this time-honored county and made it what it is; sire
and son, after each other, transmitted to coming posterity the fruits of
their industry, the immunities they gained, the free institutions they
formed possessing this fair inheritance from them, let our thanks be
given from age to age, constant as the lights or the voices that Nature
gives. In this let us not fail, as these never fail.

> *"The harp, at Nature's advent strung,*
> *Has never ceased to play;*
> *The song the stars of mourning sung*
> *Has never died away;*
> *And prayer is made, and praise is given*
> *By all things near and far;*
> *The ocean looketh up to heaven*
> *And mirrors every star.*
> *Its waves are kneeling on the strand*
> *As kneels the human knee;*
> *Their white locks bowing to the sand,*
> *The Priesthood of the sea.*
> *The winds with hymns of praise are loud,*
> *Or low with sobs of pain;*
> *The thunder organ of the cloud,*
> *The dropping tears of rain.*
> *The blue sky is the temple's arch;*
> *Its transept earth and air;*
> *The music of its starry March*
> *The chorus of a prayer.*
> *So Nature keeps her reverent frame*
> *With which her years began,*
> *And all her signs and voices shame*
> *The prayerless heart of man."*

CHAPTER V

BI-CENTENNIAL OF THE BRIDGE-HAMPTON PRESBYTERIAN CHURCH

Delivered in 1886 at the age of 69

FRIENDS OF BRIDGE-HAMPTON:

THE LARGEST of all the pioneer waves that rolled over this Continent was the Puritan, striking Plymouth Rock; it swelled in majestic momentum, moving to all points until movement became part of its very nature. The swing of the Pilgrim axe, year by year grew wider. The genius of the Puritan was constructive and self-reliant. Puritan colonies from the first were substantially self governed. Very early they declared to the world that "Governments are instituted among men deriving their just powers from the consent of the governed." But long, long years before this, the Puritan had disowned all ecclesiastical subjection to Priest or Hierarch, and insisted on the right of the people to organize and govern a church for themselves. They declared for "a church without a Bishop," long before they declared for "a State without a King." Substantially they defined a church as "A company of believers in Christ associated together for the Public worship of God, for the observance of Christian ordinances, and for mutual aid and encouragement in all Christian duties." They believed the powers of church government inhered in the people as afterwards that the powers of Civil government so inhered. Both in Church and State, developed last in the latter, was the Puritan ideal that power to organize and govern churches and communities rightfully sprang from the people. In the shining light of this Ideal, colonies were settled, churches and schools founded, governments instituted, and the ideal made practical on this Continent wherever the Puritan planted his feet. This ideal wrought in the frame of the Nation made it what it is. By such Puritans with such views, partly from East, but chiefly from Southampton, this church was formed.

Thompson in his *History of Long Island,* vol. I., p. 343, writes: "By the act of May 16th, 1669, the precinct of Bridge-Hampton and Mecox was declared a separate parish for the building, and erecting a Meeting House and to have and enjoy all the privileges and benefits of a distinct Parish." The same historian says, "Bridge-Hampton was at first called Feversham by the English." "The first Meeting House was built in 1670." I do not find the record of the act of May 16th, 1669, but think it hardly possible Thompson would state positively that such act passed unless he had good evidence thereof, and I assume that as an established fact. Prime says, (p. 199,) Bridge Hampton was made a distinct congregation nearly 30 years after the formation of the first settlement," and recognizes 1640 as the time of such settlement. Thus confirming the statement of Thompson. The question whether the first church was built in 1670 or later, is even more difficult to decide. Tradition fixes the date as 1670. Copying that tradition our church historians give that date. Prime fixes the date as "about the time of Mr. White's settlement," p. 109. Howell's Hist. of Southampton, p. 130, fixes the date as probably 1695. The vote of Town Meeting of July 20, 1686, gave to Isaac Willman 12 acres of land, &c. He "to make over to the Town 4 pole wide of his land, butting to Sagaponack pond, all the whole length thereof," &c., "for a highway," and "also so much land more as will contain a Meeting House, lying to the said highway, to be about 4 pole square about 14 pole from ye pond," &c., to which Willman agreed. Town Records vol. II., p. 110.

A vote for the whole Town to pay fifty pounds towards the building of a Bridge "over Sagaponack pond," passed the same day, and was confirmed by a Town Meeting held Aug. 24, 1686, *Ib.* At this last meeting it was "voted that ye inhabitants of Mecox and Sagaponack, that is *eastward of the Wading place* be released from paying their proportion of the yearly maintenance of Mr. Whiting *from October next,* upon condition that if they shall be without a minister there at Sagaponack for the space of a year, then they are to pay again to Mr. Whiting as formerly; to Mr. Whiting or the minister then officiating in the Town." Vol. 2, Southampton Town Records, p. 112.

At the same meeting, "It is also concluded by major voat of the said Town that there shall be by *November next,* laid out forty acres of land somewhere about Sagaponack or Mecox, at the discretion of the layers out to lye for the townes use to dispose of hereafter as they shall see cause."—*Ib.* There can be little doubt that this vote to lay out forty acres looked towards the assignment of land for a parsonage, which was followed by the vote to lay out sixty acres for that purpose in June 23d, 1691—*Ib.* p. 125, and by the actual laying out as reported April 24th, 1694, *Ib.* page 129.

The vote of July, 1686, acquiring land for the site of a Meeting House is in words looking to a building to be, rather than one already built, but not conclusively so. The vote to tax the whole town 50£ to build the Bridge, and the vote to release the people "East of the Wading Place" from paying rates to Mr. Whiting, all imply a church building already erected, or such progress toward it as assured its speedy completion. In the vote as to paying rates it is significant that the release was conditioned to take effect "from October next," and the vote to lay out forty acres "by November next" is likewise significant and imply that then, if not before, the Meeting House would be ready for the minister to be called, and which calling, as the votes show, was then expected. With all these concurring circumstances, we may conclude a Meeting House was built by or before that time. It was located about "14 rods" from Sagg pond, near the old and present Bridge, and on its western side, in the lot now owned by Silas Tuttle, of West Hampton. The roof of this house was thatched at first. Therein was a fire place. It might have been, and probably was about 25 by 35 feet in size. Therein the people of Bridge-Hampton worshipped until 1737, and therein Minister White preached over forty years.

The godly men who settled in Bridge-Hampton were probably organized there as a Christian Church, at least as soon as they built their meeting house, and as soon as by vote of the town they were to be released from paying rates to Mr. Whiting provided they settled a minister. They were clearly in a condition to settle a minister, implying the existence of an organized church, which church in the Puritan ideal might exist even without a Minister or officers. Tradition tells that in earliest times the people of Bridge-Hampton went to the Southampton church by the Ocean shore when the Bay was not running and by the Wading place when it was. Tradition further tells that the minister at Southampton sometimes preached in Bridge-Hampton, and the minister in East-Hampton sometimes preached in Sag Harbor. This was done before the two later colonies supported ministers of themselves. While in Southampton and East-Hampton churches, the Sacrament of the Lord's Supper was administered in the morning service down to within about a quarter of a century; it was administered in Sag Harbor and Bridge-Hampton invariably in the afternoon. It is a tradition that this difference of time arose from the necessity of the case, requiring the service of the same minister in one place in the forenoon of the Sabbath day, and in the other place in the afternoon.

All these circumstances, including the traditions of the past so corroborated, warrant the conclusion that a church was organized in Bridge-Hampton at least as early, if not anterior to 1686. A church to whom the minister in Southampton sometimes preached and to whom he administered the Sacrament of the Lord's Supper. This state of things may have continued many years before the coming of Minister White. Meetings for conference and prayer in private houses and churches by the devout minded were often holden without a minister, in early times, when the Sabbath was more sacredly observed than now.

THE MEETING HOUSE OF 1737
IN BRIDGE-HAMPTON.

"Southampton, April 5th, 1737. At an Election Meeting," &c., "Voted by ye town yt the people of Bridge-Hampton shall have liberty to build a Meeting House upon ye knowle on ye south side of Henry Wicks Land between Abram Howells House & Joshua Hildreth & it was a clear vote." Town records, vol. 3, p. 63.

This Meeting House was located about one-half in the street and the remainder in the enclosed lot about 30 rods east of the Esterbrook corner. The front door opened from the street opposite the pulpit, and at the east and west ends near the south corners were other doors. All these three doors opened directly into the audience room, there being no hall or vestibule. The church was a strong, heavily timbered building 38x54 feet not walled but ceiled with boards on the uprights and above. The posts projected within the ceiling some inches and were uncased but planed smooth. Large curved braces from the posts to the girts above held the building firmly together, and these also were smoothly planed. Six turned pillars resting on stones beneath the floor supported the galleries. Above the ceiling was painted white with a blue cornice around the outside underneath and above the galleries. The uprights were painted yellow, except that the window casings were white and the inner doors black.

The pulpit was panelled, painted green and retained that color until 1817, when it was stained in imitation of mahogany. In the centre was a semi-circular enlargement to accommodate the officiating minister. On its top in front was a dark colored cushion with tassels hanging from the corners. On the cushion was a large Bible, and on each side attached to the pulpit was a brass candlestick. The ascent to the pulpit was by a steep stairs—five steps—leading to a broader platform step, whereon the minister turning to the right, half around, opened the pulpit door and ascending two more steps entered the pulpit, the seat whereof was a naked board. Back of the pulpit was a window with two pilasters on each side. From the ceiling above the window secured by an iron rod fastened to the plate and its outer edge, hung the far-famed and indispensable sounding board. It was somewhat semi-circular with four angles projecting quite over the pulpit, and the most curious and singular piece of work in the house.

In front of the pulpit was a small pew, the floor of which was raised to the level of the lowest pulpit stair. The front of this pew was panelled, and the only seats were for one person on each side of the semi-circular enlargement of the pulpit. This was the Deacon's seat or pew, and was from age to age occupied by them who therein faced and overlooked the congregation. A Deacon in any other seat in time of public worship would have been deemed out of place.

A board attached to the front of this pew by hinges and turned up to a level with its top was the Communion table which was secured in its place by two braces from the outside to the panels underneath.

The passage from the front door to the pulpit, called the broad aisle, divided the lower part of the house equally, and one side was occupied exclusively by males and the other by females.

The seats were framed work of oak timber, very strong. On either side of the pulpit were the "short seats." On the side of the Broad Aisle the seats were called the "square bodies." In the different aisles were small seats for children. The gallery stairs were in the front corners of the house commencing near the end doors going toward the front about two thirds up and then turning abruptly toward the centre. There was a passage from the front door to the stairs leaving three seats next the ceiling which were occupied by colored people.

There were no aisles in the galleries. The seats there were partitioned in front across the middle as the dividing line between the sexes. They were six in number, extending without a break along the sides and front of the House. Over the gallery stairs were pews square and with seats all around except at the door. Both above and below the seats were open and free. The assessors who fixed the rates to be paid the minister at the yearly meetings directed the place where heads of families should sit. The old and honored in front, and younger in the rear. Thus the young passed from the seats for children in the aisles below to those back in the galleries, then to the front seats there, then in advancing years to the seats in the rear below; and if living to old age, moved perhaps to the very front. Thus it often happened that by successive changes from childhood to age persons had passed through the whole routine of seats from the smallest to the most honorable. When no rule of seating prevailed the elder often occupied the middle of the meeting-house, the younger deferring to them, took rear seats, and thus the rear became crowded and the front unoccupied. The order of seating while remedying this evil created another. Some thinking themselves as old, honorable, rich and deserving as others who were preferred in seats, left the meeting-house entirely. So that in 1816 all the seats on the lower floor were removed, pews put in their place which were yearly hired at auction wherewith the minister was paid. Even this change so offended a few that they forsook attendance on the church. The separate seating of the sexes thus ceased. Without material change the interior of this meeting-house remained from 1816 until 1842 when it was taken down. It had stood through the latter years of Minister White, all the ministry of Pastorals Brown and Woolworth for 105 years. The first sermon by the first Pastor preached therein, was from the text: 2 Chron. vi:18. The last by the Rev. Mr. Francis, June 12th, 1842, from Lev. xvi. 13.

The last meeting held therein was June 12th, 1842, when many converts at the Sacrament of the Lord's Supper united with the Church. Elder James H. Topping of those so united survives.

In January, 1843,* the present church edifice wherein we worship, was dedicated. It is 50x68 feet, "and for simple beauty, chaste neatness, just proportions and absolute convenience, it is not exceeded by any church in the County."

MINISTER WHITE.

Ebenezer White, the first minister settled in Bridge-Hampton, was born in 1672, and was the son of Ebenezer, born 1648, died Aug. 24th, 1703. The father is said to have married Hannah White, believed to be the daughter of Peregrine White, who was son of William White, the emigrant in the Mayflower, which Hannah was believed to be the mother of Ebenezer, the son. Minister White graduated at Harvard in 1692, and died Feb. 4th, 1756, in the 84th year of his age. He was ordained over the church here October 9th, 1695, but was actually here sometime

---

*Prime has this date December, 1842, which is an error.

previously. April 17th, 1695, he purchased of Jonas Wood and wife, of Elizabethtown, in New Jersey, ten acres of land at Sagabonac, "bounded North by land of Col. Henry Pierson, East and South by Highways, and West by the street." This was the original homestead whereon now one of his descendants resides. Minister White was unquestionably ordained over the church by a council after the congregational order. He officiated as minister until his resignation, June 15th, 1748, some 53 years. He is said to have been an able and useful minister.

MINISTER BROWN.

The Rev. James Brown, the second minister settled in Bridge-Hampton, was born about 1720, and died April 22d, 1788, aged about 68 years. He is reported to have been by one writer a native of Mendham, N.J., and by Thompson, in Hist. of Long Island, to have been a descendant of the Rev. Chad. Brown, of Rhode Island, and connected with the family made famous by Brown University. He graduated at Yale in 1747, was ordained over the church here June 15th, 1748, when Minister White resigned. Ebenezer Prime was moderator of the Presbytery at the ordination of Mr. Brown, and the exercises commenced with prayer by Mr. Horton. A sermon was preached by Rev. Sylvanus White, of Southampton, from Titus ii. 7 and 8 vs. The Rev. Ebenezer White then resigned his pastorate. The Rev. Ebenezer Prime then propounded suitable questions to the Candidate and the people in their representative body, the Committee taking their mutual engagements on both sides, and then made the ordination prayer during the imposition of hands, and gave the charge. Mr. S. Buell gave the right hand of fellowship, Mr. Prime addressed an exhortation to the people, Mr. D. Youngs made the concluding prayer; and after singing a Psalm, Mr. J. Brown, the Candidate ordained, pronounced the blessing. Minister Brown, in consequence of great bodily infirmities, resigned his charge March 27th, 1775, but resided here on his farm now owned by George Strong, until his death. He is said to have been "distinguished for great soundness in his theological views, and ably defended the great doctrines of the Reformation." I gather from tradition that he was of massive frame, melancholic temperament, diffident and distrustful of himself, of robust common sense, and very creditable scholarly attainments. October 23, 1754, at Brookhaven, on occasion of the ordination of the Rev. Benjamin Talmage, Brown delivered the charge to the people. This charge in print is the only like memorial known to the writer. It is pregnant with good sense, has marks of scholarship, good condensed logic, sound piety, ac-

curate study of and appeal to the Scriptures, much modesty and diffi-
dence. It is a production very creditable to the head and heart of the
author. Dr. Buell records the preaching of Brown in the great revival
March 22d, 1764, at East-Hampton, from Isaiah lxv. 24: "And it shall
come to pass that before they call I will answer; and while they are yet
speaking I will hear."

MINISTER WOOLWORTH.

The third pastor, Aaron Woolworth, D.D., was born at Long Meadow,
Mass., October 25, 1763, and died April 4th, 1821. He graduated at Yale
in 1784, and received the degree of D.D. from Princeton in 1809. Our
church records and the monument to his memory record his ordination as occurring Aug. 30th, 1787. Prime's Hist. p. 201, gives the same
date. On the following page in Prime the inscription on the monument
was erroneously printed April 30th, 1787, and Sprague in his Annals of
the American Pulpit repeated the error. He was ordained by an ecclesiastical Council which were present as delegates Rev. Samuel Buell and
Mr. David Talmage from East-Hampton, Rev. Henry Channing of New
London, Ct., Rev. Joshua Williams and Mr. Elias Pelletreau of Southampton, Rev. Zechariah Greene of Cutchogue, Rev. Richard S. Storrs and Mr.
Azariah Woolworth of Long Meadow, Mass., Rev. Samuel Austin of New
Haven, Ct. Mr. Channing was moderator and Austin scribe, Rev. Samuel
Buel preached the sermon, Mr. Greene offered the first prayer, Mr.
Austin the ordaining prayer, Mr. Channing gave the charge, Mr. Storrs
the right hand of fellowship, and Mr. Williams made the concluding
prayer. Dr. Woolworth was small in stature, not prepossessing in appearance; yet all authorities concur in declaring that "He was one of
the most able, discriminating and pious divines that Long Island was
ever blessed with." Prime speaks of his epitaph as written by the hand
of friendship, and adds: "He was all that therein is claimed on his behalf." It is said that Prime was its author.

Dr. Woolworth was a man of very great intellectual activity and untiring industry. He assisted students in preparing for the ministry. He
taught many students the classical languages. He wrote with apparent
ease, grace and power. In 1800 he communicated a long and interesting account of the Revival here of 1799 and 1800, which was published in the Connecticut *Evangelical Magazine* of the latter year, and
a somewhat similar account of the same Revival published in connection with the life and writings of Samuel Buel, D.D., about the same
time. His hold on the affection and esteem of his people was very

strong. When after a pastorate of about 34 years, he was borne to his tomb by them, their regret and reverence were heartfelt. Their gratitude and love as a tribute to his memory and worth are indelibly inscribed by them upon his monument. In the fervency of his prayers he was happy—in his strong faith singularly pre-eminent. An aged person many years since related to the writer an account of the Doctor's prayer for the recovery of an only son of a friend at Sag Harbor, then apparently in impending death. He prayed as Jacob did, "I will not let Thee go except Thou bless me," and added that the young man recovered.—(Note 2, see appendix.)

MINISTER FRANCIS.

The Rev. Amzi Francis was born at West Hartford, Conn., July 31st, 1793, commenced preaching here in September, 1822, was ordained pastor April 17th, 1823, and died here October 18th, 1845. The day previous to his ordination his examination by the Presbytery, met at Southampton, was sustained. At the ordination the Rev. Zechariah Greene presided. The Rev. Abraham Luce made the introductory prayer, the Rev. Ezra King preached the sermon. The Rev. Athrop Thompson made the succeeding prayer, Rev. Nathaniel Prime gave the charge to the Candidate, and Rev. Samuel Robinson gave the charge to the people. The Rev. Ebenezer Phillips made the closing prayer. Mr. Francis was of small stature, nervous temperament, his large speaking black eyes denoted intellectual and sympathetic action. He was scholarly in habit and appearance, studious, industrious, devout, intensely in earnest, spiritual, meditative, logical, small, one of God's own uncomplaining, patient, self-denying saints. The writer herein speaks from living heartfelt experience and knowledge.

REV. CORNELIUS H. EDGAR, D.D.

The Rev. Cornlius H. Edgar, D.D., was born at Rahway, N.J., in 1811, and died in Easton, Penn., December 23d, 1884. His first sermon in Bridge-Hampton was delivered November 23d, 1845. He was installed and ordained here June 10th, 1846. Mr. Harlow, of Philadelphia, introduced the ordination exercises; Mr. Edwards, of Smithtown, preached the sermon from the text: Acts x., 43. The Moderator, Rev. Mr. Evans, of Middletown, L.I., put the constitutional questions; the ordaining prayer was made by the Rev. Samuel R. Ely, of East-Hampton; the charge to the Pastor was given by the Rev. Mr. McDougall, of Huntington; the charge to the people was given by the Rev. H.N. Wilson, of Southampton, the Moderator made the concluding prayer, and the Pastor pronounced the benediction. Mr. Edgar remained pastor here until his resignation October 2d, 1853. He was tall, of commanding presence, in form symmetric, in gesture graceful, constitutionally positive, no trimmer, no idler. As a sermonizer he excelled. He was in manner impressive, in thought rich, logical, suggestive. A sound, strong, earnest, honest preacher of Jesus Christ. He did good work for the Master here.

REV. DAVID M. MILLER.

The Rev. David M. Miller was born in Elizabeth, N.J., June 12th, 1827, and died here June 29th, 1855. He was ordained here April 27th, 1854. The order of exercises were: Invocation by the moderator, Rev. Mr. Morgan, of Southampton; reading of the Scriptures and prayer by the Rev. Mr. Mott, of Rahway, N.J.; sermon by the Rev. Dr. Murray; charge to the pastor by the Rev. Mr. Reeve, of West Hampton, and charge to the people by the Rev. Mr. Hopper, of Sag Harbor; concluding prayer by the Rev. Mr. Mershon, of East-Hampton, and Benediction by the Pastor. Shortly before his death he was married to the only daughter of Hon. Hugh Halsey. His ministry gave promise of great usefulness, and attracted the strong affection and love of his people. His early death cut off the budding promise of his ministry. His funeral sermon was preached here by Dr. Murray, July 1st, 1855, and published.

REV. THOMAS M. GRAY.

The Rev. Thomas M. Gray, son of Rev. John Gray, D.D., of Easton, Penn., was a graduate of Lafayette College in 1851, and afterwards of Princeton Theological Seminary. He died at Salem Centre, N.J., December 24th, 1883, in the 54th year of his age. He preached here first Jan. 20th, 1856, from the text Luke x., 36 and 37 vs.: "Which now of these three thinkest thou was neighbor unto him that fell among the thieves," &c. He was installed here April 23d, 1856. The invocation was asked by the Rev. Mr. Drake, of Middle Island, the moderator; reading of the Scriptures and prayer by Rev. Gaylord S. More, of Babylon; sermon by Rev. Dr. Gray, of Easton, Penn.; constitutional questions and ordaining prayer by the Moderator; charges to the Pastor by the Rev. Mr. More; charge to the people by the Rev. Mr. Mershon, of East-Hampton; Benediction by the Rev. Dr. Gray, of Easton. The pastoral relation of Thomas M. Gray with this church was dissolved April 10th, 1866. As a companion few men were more amiable, more genial, more social or of more pleasing manners than Mr. Gray. After leaving Bridge-Hampton he preached in Derby, Conn., in Salem, Westchester County, N.Y. and its vicinity where he died.

WM. P. STRICKLAND, D.D.

William P. Strickland, D.D., was born August 17th, 1809, at Pittsburgh, Penn., and died July 15th, 1884, at Ocean Grove, N.J. He was a graduate of the College at Athens, Ohio, and in his 44th year received therefrom the degree of D.D. He was an industrious, accurate, profound scholar, and the author of many published volumes, including "A History of the American Bible Society," "Christianity Demonstrated," "Genius and Mission of Methodism," "Pioneers of the West," "Manual of Biblical Literature," "Life of Peter Cartwright," and other works. He was trained in the Presbyterian Church where his father was an elder and his mother a member. He said he was theologically Presbyterian, but entered the Methodist Church because he regarded its spirit as more intensely revival. He supplied this pulpit from May 13th, 1866, until October 5th, 1875 when he was duly installed by the Presbytery. The Rev. Thomas Harries was moderator, Rev. Andrew Shiland preached the sermon, Rev. Mr. Stokes gave the charge to the pastor, and Mr. Sproule to the people. Except a vacation of some six months in 1876 and 1877, when the pulpit was supplied by Rev. Wm. F. Whitaker, he preached until October 22d, 1878, when at his request on account of failing health he was released. He was spiritual, pure minded, of a lofty type, eloquent, impressive. Thus for twelve years he lifted and taught his people. Now we must ask:

> *"What to shut eyes has God revealed?*
> *What hear the ears that death has sealed?*
> *What undreamed beauty passing show*
> *Requites the loss of all we know?*
> *O, silent land to which we move,*
> *Enough, if there alone be love*
> *And Mortal hand can ne'er outgrow*
> *What is waiting to bestow!*
> *O, white soul! from that far off shore*
> *Float some sweet song the waters o'er.*
> *Our faith confirm our fears dispel,*
> *With the old voice we loved so well!"*

The Rev. Samuel Dodd supplied this pulpit for the three years preceding May 1st, 1882. Thereafter for a time the pulpit was supplied successively by the Rev. Mr.___Schaff, the Rev. Mr.___Frissell and the Rev. Giles P. Hawley now deceased, until just previous to March 1st, 1883, when the present pastor, Rev. Arthur Newman, was by Presbytery ordained and installed. The Rev. Wm. B. Reeve, D.D., was moderator. The opening prayer was offered by Rev. J.B. Finch, the ordaining prayer by the moderator, and the closing prayer by the Rev. Mr. Bowdish of the M.E. Church here. The Rev. J.D. Stokes preached the sermon, and gave the charge to the people. Rev. A. Shiland, D.D., delivered the charge to the pastor, who closed the services with the Benediction.

Minister White dying in midwinter was buried by his people in the old Sagg burying ground.

> *"When they laid his cold corpse low*
> *In its dark narrow cell*
> *Heavy the mingled earth and snow*
> *Upon his coffin fell."*

When in the last days of autumn 1775, Minister Paine, shepherd of the separate flock expired, his loving people reverently laid his mortal remains in the Hay Ground place of burying near their meeting-house.

When in 1688, Minister Brown, the long time victim of disease, finally gave up his life; his people tenderly laid his body at rest in the now much neglected burying ground at Scuttle Hole.

All that was mortal of Woolworth and Francis and Miller, was deposited by their sorrowing people in the cemetery near this church.

> *"They who die in Christ are blessed,*
> *Ours be then no thought of grieving!*
> *Sweetly with their Bod they rest,*
> *All their toils and troubles leaving;*
> *So be ours the faith that saveth,*
> *Hope that every trial braveth*
> *Love that to the end endureth*
> *And through Christ the Crown secureth."*

This church was probably Congregational until 1747. The condition of the gift of the 20 acre parsonage on the corner owned by Wm. H.H. Rogers, made March 20th, 1712-13 "to Bridge-Hampton for ye use of a Prisbiterian Minister & Noe other," seems to have been disregarded. Records vol. 2, p. 174. Although Minister Brown was ordained by the Presbytery, Woolworth was ordained by a council; the people then believing the connection with Presbytery dissolved, but were thereafter otherwise informed. From 1775 until 1794, no known vote of the church decided positively for such connection. The union was voted in the summer of that year and has continued. The circumstances were peculiar. The Separate Congregational Church was in being and many people preferred that form of Government. No Elders were elected until 1801, when four were chosen. Three more were elected in 1803. Not one of these seven was ever ordained, but acted without it. In 1811 six others were chosen who were the first ordained as such. The four elders of 1801 were Ebenezer White, who died the next year; David Hedges mentioned in the centennial Historical Address of 1876. These two had been many years deacons; Jonathan Rogers and Ezekiel Sandford were the other two elders. Rogers was a man of unusual powers of mind, long time a professor of religion outside the church, devout, wise in council, at one time a Judge of the Suffolk County Common Pleas. Sandford had been a member of the Separate Church. He was eminent in the gifts of singing, exhortation and prayer. It is said the meetings he attended were always interesting. These four first elders all men of mark and might, working with Woolworth wonderfully strengthened this church. The three elders of 1803 were Lemuel Pierson, Sylvanus Halsey and Lewis Sandford. The want of time prohibits more than mention of their names. It is believed that the session of this church have chiefly been good, prudent, sensible, devout men, not inferior to that of other churches. It is feared that one of their number, some sixty years since, fell through intemperance. Yet another elder stands out as a warning. Jesse Woodruff, elected as such in 1820, dying in 1857 at the great age of 92 years, fell into despondency and darkness and gloom, absenting himself from the public worship of God for thirteen years. Thereafter, on the 4th of September, 1851, over his own signature he publicly records the deeply affecting confession of his walking in sin and darkness. The wail of woe he utters is the echo of a past despair. His confession to his brethren expresses the deepest humility and penitence. His petition for permission once more to sit with them at the Sacramental Table seems tremulous with anxiety. This cry of a soul long in darkness, tempest tossed in doubt and fear, for a rest and peace unfelt is most pitiful. Luminous in this deep felt confession are the honesty, the intelligence, the agony of the man evidently in the words his soul prompted. In the like dark case may the like inspiration and desire to seek the Lord as "our refuge and strength" be ours.—(Note 5, see appendix.) He seemed gradually coming out of darkness thereafter, and very often attended public worship with more apparent hope and light until his death.

ITINERANT PREACHING.

Itinerant preaching was far more frequent in olden times than now. Itinerant ministers preached in churches and then often in private houses. Whitfield returned from his journey in New England, proposed to the Rev. Gilbert Tennent, of the Log College, to journey East, preaching to water the seed he had sown. The proposition was submitted to some ministers then attending the Synod in session at Trenton, New Jersey, who approved of it. About 1741 Tennent came to Bridge-Hampton, holding as is said, the first evening meeting ever held there. His first sermon preached was from the text Matt. v:20. "Except your righteousness shall exceed the righteousness of the Scribes and Pharisees ye shall in no case enter into the Kingdom of Heaven." One who heard this sermon, related to Deacon Stephen Rose an account of its astonishing impression, which account Deacon Rose reduced to writing. Tennent sketched the righteousness of the Pharisees as consisting in prayers and observance of rites and ceremonies. He presented with great power and effect the doctrine of Regeneration as exceeding the righteousness of the Scribes and Pharisees. While delivering this sermon he discovered some girls in the front seat of the gallery whispering and trifling and spoke severely: "You, young women! you sit there whispering and laughing when Damnation is sounding in your ears." It is said these words went to their ears with such power that they had no peace of mind until they were converted. The truth spoken by Tennent aroused many to great heart searchings. They said, "What preaching is this? what does it mean? we will enquire of our aged minister about it." Mr. White seemed reluctant to express any opinion concerning it, but finally said: "He sows good seed but harrows it in very roughly."

Tennent was followed by many others, and after him itinerant preaching became quite common.

NEW LIGHT MOVEMENT.

What was called the New Light Movement in Bridge-Hampton arose under the agency of the Rev. James Davenport, fourth minister of the church in Southold. He was the great-grandson of the Rev. John Davenport, of New Haven, was born in 1710, graduated at Yale in 1732, was ordained in Southold, Oct. 26, 1738, and dismissed from there in 1746. Davenport was an intimate friend of Ferris, a wild enthusiast who "claimed to know the Will of God in all things; that he had not committed a sin in six years; that he should have a higher seat in Heaven than Moses, and that no one in ten of the communicants of the church in New Haven could be saved." Ferris obtained an ascendency over several students and especially over Davenport. Some two years after his settlement in Southold, Davenport became "satisfied that God had revealed to him that His Kingdom was coming with great power, and that he had an extraordinary call to labor for its advancement." On one occasion he addressed his people continuously for nearly 24 hours until he became quite wild. In public services he raised his voice to the highest pitch, and that was accompanied with the most vehement agitations of body. His hearers were encouraged to express their distress or joy by violent outcries in public assemblies. And these things he pronounced tokens of the presence of God. He encouraged ignorant persons to address large assemblies. He claimed a right to sit in judgment on the character of ministers, and after examining them in private, often in his public prayers pronounced them unconverted, and so pronounced on those who refused to be examined. He informed the people that their ministers were unconverted and sometimes exhorted them to eject them. He encouraged dissatisfied minorities to form new churches. To this ardent, energetic, impulsive, deluded man, more than to all others, the New Light Movement in Bridge-Hampton must be ascribed. Under his influence a church known as the Separate or "New Light Church" was organized, and a church building erected about 1748. It had four roofs coming to a point in the middle, and hence was sometimes called "the peaked" or "picked church." It stood a few rods south of the Hay Ground burying ground on the west side of the road leading south by the dwelling of Elbert Rose to Mecox. Elisha Paine was settled over this church in 1752, and died here in 1775 at the age of 83 years. The church was disbanded, the building taken down and removed soon after the year 1800. It is now used as a dwelling and stands next south of the schoolhouse in the middle district, and is owned by Mrs. Mary C. Worthington. At this distance of time, in the absence of records, with a history written only by its foes, we may not clearly estimate the merits of the "New Light Movement." To some extent it seemed to be a protest of the activities of the church against its inaction. But its wild, unregulated, disorderly action prevented its progress and promoted its decay. Its bitter divisions weakened the power of the church. The darkness of a belligerent spirit extinguished the lights of Peace. Most disastrous for the good of the Parish was this new movement.

Deacon Stephen Rose was more fully versed in local and church history than any other individual known to the writer. He said: "Many spiritual minded godly persons, and especially many very excellent women belonged to the Separate Church." He spoke of their intense zeal, fervent devotion, purity of life, earnestness of purpose and spirituality of soul in terms so strong as to leave no doubt that he believed the "Separate Branch" in Bridge-Hampton was a branch of the true "vine."

CUSTOMS DISUSED.

Many customs of our Puritan Fathers in the church are now disused. Historic truth requires their mention.

FASTS AND THANKSGIVING.

The set days for Fasts and Feasts directed to be observed by the Church of Rome or the Church of England were not observed by our Fathers, who appointed such days for themselves. In the early settlements of this country dependence on an Almighty Power was deeply felt. When danger from the savage natives threatened, when epidemic disease raged, when long drought betokened famine, then and often days were set apart for fasting humiliation and prayer. As their Thanksgiving has become a National appointment, so for many years and until recently their fast days gave place to one annual observance in the month of March continued down to the middle of this century. These days were not appointed here as in New England by the Government, but by the several churches. They were very generally sacredly kept by the Inhabitants. Although "servile labor" on those days was not prohibited by law, it was almost universally by the custom of the people.

STOPPING THE CHURCH.

The minister, in olden times, at the close of services gave Notice like this: "The male members of this church are requested to tarry after the blessing is pronounced."

Such meetings called "staid meetings," were often held. Therein were appointed days of Fasting and Thanksgiving; therein delegates were chosen to attend the Presbytery. The acts and records of the session were read to the people at these meetings for their approval. At these occasions measures were taken to promote singing in the church. The hour of public worship and the intervening intermission were then and there arranged. Many other like matters pertaining to the church and public worship were there decided.

PRAYER FOR THE AFFLICTED.

From time immemorial until quite recently it had been a custom for the near relatives of a deceased person to request the prayers of the church that the death might be sanctified to them for their spiritual and everlasting good. On a Sabbath one or more after the funeral, according to an understanding, the family and near relatives sitting together clad in mourning rose when the minister read the request for prayers. The occasion was impressive in solemnity. The minister praying before the sermon implored the blessing of God on His people, on His cause, His church, His worship. When tenderly, devoutly, reverently he implored God to pour the balm of Divine consolation into the wounded hearts of fathers, mothers, brothers, and sisters, relatives and friends in words appropriate to the conditions of the case; when if any relative were far off on land or sea, he asked God to give them grace to bear the sad tidings; when with devout composure he asked that this dispensation of God's Providence might be sanctified to the more remote relatives, and finally to the whole church and congregation; then it was felt that the sorrows of one household were those of all. Then the help of the Divine Father the only reliance of all. Then the minister became the audible intercessor for all. The sympathy of a Puritan people with their brethren in distress and affliction was strangely tender and heartfelt. They made their God a witness to this. Does the disuse of this custom prove more sympathy now flowing in the hearts of their souls?

PRAYERS FOR THE SICK AND RETURNING THANKS FOR RESTORATION TO HEALTH.

In severe illness it was an old time practice to request the prayers of the church and congregation, that the sick might if consistent with the Divine Will be restored to health or be prepared to die. The family and friends of the sick united in this request which was read from the pulpit before the prayer preceding the sermon. The minister wrestled in great earnestness with God as the Great Physician of soul and body, praying for the restoration of the sick to health, and in protracted sickness prayers were so offered for several consecutive Sabbaths. These requests for prayer would be remembered at the prayer-meetings and generally at the family altar so that the illness was known all over the Parish, and the sympathy of the whole community extended to the sick.

When restored to health after severe illness a like request that the minister and church and congregation offer thanks to God for the preservation of life and restoration to health was made. The request was usually read, and thanks to God in prayer offered in Divine worship. With few exceptions this was a very general ancient practice.

PRAYERS FOR SEAMEN BEFORE AND AFTER A VOYAGE, AND THANKS FOR DANGERS ESCAPED.

In the early annals of the church it was a practice for the seamen and officers on the Sabbath before sailing to attend in the house of God and desire the prayers of the church and congregation to the God of the seas for their safety. On their return from the voyage they again presented themselves in the sanctuary when public thanks to God were offered for their preservation.

When one or a number of persons in pursuing their avocations were endangered in life or limb their preservation in danger was noticed on the next Sabbath. Thanks that in the providence of God they were delivered from impending jeopardy were publicly rendered.

PUBLICATION OF THE BANNS OF MATRIMONY.

The Duke's Laws required publication of the banns of matrimony by the minister, previously, or in place thereof the Governor's license authorizing the marriage to be solemnized. This publication of intended marriage between the parties named was termed "calling off." And after Sabbath meetings inquiry was often made, "Who were *called* off." The sentiment of the community, the practice of other Puritan colonies, and the requirements of law all constrained to this practice.

PROPOUNDING.

When after examination approved by the session, candidates were admitted to the church, notice of such proposed union was publicly given by the minister. This notice was given some one or more Sabbaths previous to their pubic profession of faith and covenant. It was given upon the theory that objection, if any, might be made to the candidate and the examination reconsidered. It was a custom of the Congregational churches, perpetuated in this and adjoining churches, and until late years deemed indispensable; so much so that when the writer was proposed as a member objection was made that he had not been "propounded" as the notice was called.

"The religious female Cent Society of Bridge-Hampton" was instituted July 6th, 1815, at the house of Dr. Woolworth, who efficiently aided the society in its commencement and continuance.

The records of this society for some thirty years are extant. The society often met at Dr. Woolworth's house, sometimes at the church, when once he preached a sermon, Oct. 22d, 1817, from the text Phillippians iv:3. At first the society numbered 33, and soon increased to 54 members, and thereafter to nearly one hundred. It received great encouragement from the Rev. Mr. Francis. It corresponded with other like societies on Shelter Island and elsewhere. It kept the missionary fire burning on God's Altar. It was the mother of succeeding benevolent societies that have been so great blessings to this church and to the world. There the mothers in our Israel prayed and toiled for the reign of righteousness. They wrought in cheerfulness, intelligence and hope. An absent member in 1818 sent her contribution in a paper whereon was written the following sprightly and graceful lines:

> *"Go, fifty cents, would you were more*
> *And thousands were your name,*
> *Then you might reach some distant shore*
> *And Spread a Saviour's name.*
> *But yonder Ocean's made of drops*
> *And particles of sand, or snow*
> *Can swell the lofty mountain tops*
> *Of Andes towering brow.*
> *The Lord can multiply your power*
> *More than the intrinsic worth,*
> *Go! do some good each passing hour;*
> *Go; help to bless the earth.*
> *Go; join your sister currents round*
> *And mingle as you flow.*
> *Go; help to heal the bleeding wound,*
> *And soothe the breast of woe."*

In Bridge-Hampton, as generally all over christendom, the women far outnumbered the men in church. In obedience, in zeal, in spirituality, in devotion they excelled. When on a fast day, Aug. 23, 1787, the members present renewed their covenant, Woolworth records the names of eleven male members only, and adds "there were a few other male members of church who were not present at this time." When on the 15th of June, 1800, the covenant was renewed, 14 other men appear to have covenanted, and 26 females the like.

REVIVALS OF RELIGION.

As no church records prior to 1787 are extant, all accounts of prior revivals of religion rest on other sources. Such revivals were, it is believed, almost unknown previous to the years 1741 and 1742, when occurred a general and powerful revival of religion, believed to be the first in this place. There was at this time a general and great awakening all over New England extending to Long Island. From the active agency of Mr. Davenport in this work, it has sometimes been called Davenport's Revival. Multitudes were converted. In the early days of some of the oldest persons living, the subjects of that work of Divine Grace described with the fervor of unforgetting love the scenes of this rare season. Tradition long preserved the story of the converts of that day. The venerable White was in his 70th year and within some six or seven years of the close of his ministry. There were exhibitions of excitement, of enthusiasm, of a zeal misguided and mistaken which called down his disapproval, marred his enjoyment and peace and a separation which probably led to his resignation and the appointment of his successor in the ministry.

REVIVALS.

In 1764 occurred the next general revival of religion. It was a work of great power. There were many converts, and with few exceptions they remained steadfast in the faith. The enduring test of time has set the seal of truth to this as a genuine work of God. On one occasion sixty were added to the church. The young converts of this precious season kept alive the coals on God's Altars during the long twelve years from 1775 to 1787, when this church was without a settled pastor. In this radiant light of Heaven, Minister Brown overcoming the natural despondency of temper and soul, felt the shining of the sun of righteousness. For more than ten years it encouraged him in the work which finally in despondency he relinquished.

In 1785 occurred another season of spiritual refreshing when many were converted. This has been sometimes called Mr. Fordham's revival for the reason that he officiated as a temporary supply for the pulpit at that time. It is believed that a few persons were then added to the church for the reason that at this time there was no settled pastor, and so runs the traditions of that time.

Another and well-known cause was the singular and prevailing aversion to union with the church. Over one hundred years ago and lasting down to within less than twenty-five years, there were in this and adjoining parishes very many heads of families exemplary in life, sound in doctrine, devout in demeanor, searchers of the Scriptures, constant in attendance on the public worship, prayerful in their household, hoping always for God's mercy in Jesus Christ, zealous and even jealous for the faith of the Gospel, and with all this never uniting with Christ's visible church. Sometimes it is believed the number of non-church male professing christians nearly equalled the number of the like who were members. It is now simply amazing to think of this most discouraging and disastrous state of things as then generally existing, and locally here more largely than elsewhere. Possibly, nay probably, the unhappy separation of the new lights perplexed and confounded young converts. It could not be other than a stumbling block. It will thus seem more clear why the number of converts often doubled the number of accessions to the church.—(Note 7, see appendix.)

In the fifteen years from 1785 to 1800 forty were added to the church. The next season of reviving occurred in the latter part of the year 1799, extending into the year 1800, usually called the Great Revival of 1800. New Year's day of that year "was signalized by the powerful operations of the Holy Spirit." Some were liberated from their bondage of sin; others were more deeply impressed than before. "Many were newly awakened." Dr. Woolworth wrote (in a sermon preached near the close of his life,) "The cloud of Divine influence completely overshadowed the congregation, and the rain of righteousness copiously distilled in every part. The arm of the Lord was revealed, and who did not recognize and acknowledge the power? The events of that memoriable [sic] season are distinctly within the recollection of many yet living; when under the influence of the Holy Ghost this house for three successive weeks was every evening crowded with hearers solemn as the grave, and listening as for their lives to the message of Salvation. In the course of a few months, more than one hundred and thirty indulged hope of having passed from death unto life." In the year 1807 some were hopefully converted. In 1808 several young ladies were seriously impressed. In 1809 the revival became general and every part of the Parish shared in the blessings of Salvation. Many youthful persons and some of middle age made profession of their faith and were gathered into the church.

In the winter of 1816 some mercy drops fell on this Parish and nearly thirty rejoiced in hope of reconciliation with God. This revival was not as extensive or general as the two previous seasons. The work was chiefly wrought in the north and west districts; it was the last occurring during the ministry of the lamented Woolworth.

In the year 1822 another outpouring of the spirit occurred and many, chiefly young people were converted. It was a sweet, interesting and pleasing work of Grace. At this time Mr. St. John was preaching as a stated supply, and as a consequence this has sometimes been denominated as Mr. St. John's revival. The writer cannot withhold his condemnation of such forms of reference to God's Reviving Grace as attributes the Divine work to any mere man.

In 1831 the ministers in this and adjoining Parishes resolved to hold meetings in August, for four successive days, in their respective churches. The meetings were holden and called "Four days meetings." The results were astonishing. The long prevailing paralysis of the church was ended. The slumbers of inactive christians were broken. The mighty cry of the church to God was heard. His people were revived. The impenitent were in alarm and terror. The agony of unforgiven souls went up in strong crying and tears to Heaven. The work extended as a whirlwind all over these Northern States. In that and the following years some sixty persons united with this church. The converts of that season, with few exceptions, gave evidence of a genuine, abiding, thorough work of Grace, remaining faithful unto death. The writer well remembers those impressive and even awful meetings— awful as exhibiting God's condemnation of sin. There Nettleton appalled the sinner with such flaming views of God. There father Jonathan Huntting besought the sinner to have mercy on himself. There Beers and Pillsbury warned the sinner of coming doom. There Francis held up the flaming letters of God's righteous Law. There the seraphic Joseph D. Condit showed to the sinner a Christ too lovely and pure to allow the presence of a sinner unrepentant, too gracious to reject the returning repenting wanderer. This is the unforgotten year of God, enduring on earth, in the Records of the church, unfading in the annals of Heaven.

Another season of reviving occurred in 1842. A much larger number of middle aged people were converted than in 1831, many of whom had passed unmoved through former periods of awakening. Nearly seventy persons, subjects of this work, united thereafter with the church. The last two revivals occurred during the ministry of the sainted Francis. He writes, March 20th, 1842: "The individuals previously examined were this day admitted to the communion of the church, no objection having been made to them. The number thus admitted was 30, among them were six husbands with their wives; twenty-four heads of families and one entire family."

From 1742, when under the preaching of Davenport, occurred the first named great revival, to 1842, the time of occurrence of the last, a century had fled. Nine seasons of God's special reviving grace have been noticed. They were occasions when peace, power and numbers augmented the church. Within the memory of many living the revival seasons of 1850, 1858, 1859, 1863, 1866, 1869, 1874, 1877 and 1883 are too recent to be forgotten or to be in danger of the wave of oblivion.— (See Note.) There have occurred special seasons in remote and later ages, when the Holy Spirit has been graciously shed abroad; when men seemed called to stand still and see the salvation of God.

> *"So sometimes comes to soul and sense*
> *The feeling which is evidence*
> *That very near about us lies*
> *The realm of Spiritual mysteries.*
> *The sphere of the supernal powers*
> *Impinges on this world of ours.*
> *The Low and dark horizon lifts;*
> *To light the scenic terror shifts;*
> *The breath of a diviner air*
> *Blows down the answer of a prayer;*
> *That all our sorrow, pain and doubt,*
> *A great compassion clasps about;*
> *And law and goodness, love and force,*
> *Are wedded fast beyond divorce.*
> *Then Duty leaves to Love its task,*
> *The beggar, self forgets to ask;*
> *With smile of trust and folded hands*
> *The passive soul in waiting stands*
> *To feel, as flowers the sun and dew,*
> *The one true life its own renew."*

Alexander Wilmot, born 1709, died 1744, graduate of Yale 1734, ordained pastor at Jamaica, L.I., April 12, 1738, is said to have been a native of Bridge-Hampton—vid. Howell's Hist. p. 305. The Rev. Herman

Halsey of East Wilson, in Niagara Co., N.Y., born July, 1793, oldest living graduate of Williams College, the Rev. Samuel Howell, son of Walter; the Rev. Wm. H. Lester, pastor of Presbyterian Church in West Alexandria, Penn., are claimed as native of Bridge-Hampton. Rev. Wm. Hedges, pastor of the Congregational Church in Jamesport, L.I., resided here some years before entering the ministry. Whether others have gone from here as ministers of the gospel of Jesus Christ is not known.

TEMPERANCE.

At a meeting of the session, Nov. 28, 1811, the recommendation of the Presbytery to the churches under their care, "Not to treat their Christian brethren or others with ardent spirits as a part of hospitality in friendly visits," was considered and "expressed their approbation of the same as a suitable means of discouraging that excessive use of such liquors which they are convinced is doing incalculable mischief for society, whilst they declare their readiness and resolution for themselves to conform to said recommendation; they also recommend it to all the members of the Church to do the same, and by their example and exertions in all other suitable ways endeavor to prevent the progress, and, if possible, destroy the existence of this species of intemperance. On the Lord's Day following, the above recommendation of the Presbytery, and what the session had done upon the subject, were laid before the whole church, who voted as follows: "That we approve of the measure recommended, and will for ourselves conform to it, and use our influence to induce others to do the same." This Letter of the Presbytery to the churches, Woolworth drafted. His voice was earliest and decided against intemperance. All his successors, and with few exceptions, the church have held resolutely advanced ground against intemperance and its unhallowed allies.

The second church built in 1737, standing 105 years, remembered reverently by the oldest worshippers, has therewith associated great historic interest. It had no tower, no spire, no bell. It was a barn in outline, without worn by the elements, unpainted, ungraceful; yet consecrated by the most thrilling scenes and the grandest events. Therein, in 1741, Gilbert Tennent had blown the trump of the Gospel in power. Therein, in 1764, George Whitfield preaching from Jude 21st verse: "Keep yourselves in the love of God," had made the spirit world seem real. There, in the later, riper ten years of concluding life, Minister White lifted his aged hands to bless this people. Therein Minister Brown during all the years of his active ministry, faithfully expounded the truth.

There for a generation Woolworth, animated, learned, logical, reasoned of "Righteousness, Temperance and Judgment to come." There, for a score of years Francis, serene, studious, fervent, devout with a fidelity equalled only by his great love, impressed the truths or Revelation on this people. The walls of this unadorned church of God witnessed the ordination vows of the last named three. The funeral sermons of the venerable White, the desponding, but faithful Brown, the animated and logical Woolworth, all were spoken under that o'er hanging sounding board in that high pulpit in this old church. Wonderful revivals of God's presence and power had here been displayed. Nine times had the Almighty "bowed the Heavens and came down." The feet of three generations and more had moved to its doors. The songs of three generations therein had praised God. The penitential cry of three generations "God be merciful to me a sinner" therein had risen. In the presence of God and men and angels three generations had solemnly there avouched and covenanted the Lord to be their Saviour. Hallowed by the memories of one hundred years; by the public worship of the long loved and lost, by the prayerful echo of voices unforgotten, although long silent; this church was the embodiment of all that memory holds dear, that hope holds bright, and faith holds precious. At Woolworth's settlement the church numbered only 33, members increased in 1818 to 179. During his ministry, including the year after his decease, 252 had been added, and 166 had died. During the ministry of Francis 147 were added, 93 had died, and at his decease 177 were in communion. When the ark of the Lord was removed from the old to the new edifice, the elder mourned while thinking of the spiritual grandeur of the ancient yet lacking in the modern structure. When Minister Francis was ordained the last sublime notes of the choir were:

> *"Arise, O, King of grace arise,*
> *And enter to thy rest;*
> *Lo thy church waits with longing eyes,*
> *Thus to be owned and blest."*

In the sentiment of that song, with all the younger people he longed for a temple condusive for the worship of Jehovah. Graciously he was permitted to assist in dedicating this church to God. For a few months he blew the bugle notes of the gospel's alarm, and then his voice was heard no more. The trumpet that fell from his hand was caught by his gifted successor, who saw throngs responding to the gospel's call. When Edgar removed with the heartfelt regret of many friends, the more youthful Thomas M. Gray reiterated not without response the message of Jesus Christ. The twelve years ministry of the eloquent, the gifted, the learned Dr. Strickland were years of a higher spiritual instruction in righteousness. In the answers from Heaven, in the numbers of converts and members, in the frequency and power of God's reviving grace, the ancient light of the older edifice pales before the grander effulgence of the new. The two hundred years of time marking the origin and being of this church, are long as measured by earthly affairs, are short in the eternal years of God. One more voice and witness for the world and the Kingdom that endureth forever.

> *"Oh, where are Kings and Empires now*
> *Of old, that went and came;*
> *But still thy church is praying yet,*
> *A thousand years the same*
> *We mark her goodly battlements,*
> *And her foundations strong;*
> *We hear within the solemn voice*
> *Of her unending song."*

CHAPTER VI

INTRODUCTION TO VOL. 1 OF THE EAST HAMPTON TOWN RECORDS (1649-1680)

Written in 1887 at the age of 70

THE TOWN OF East Hampton settled in 1649, in 1653 built and thatched a church. Tradition (probably correct) locates that church on the east side of the present burying-ground, opposite to and west of the house-lot of Lyon Gardiner. South of Lyon Gardiner and also on the east side of the street lived William Hedges. On the west side of the street then lived Thomas Baker and Thomas Osborn, and all within one-fourth of a mile of that church as a centre. Jonathan T. Gardiner, descendant of that Lyon; Jonathan Baker, descendant of that Thomas; Joseph S. Osborne, descendant of that same Thomas Osborn, are a committee chosen by their fellow townsmen to procure the publication of the ancient records of their town. They have invited the writer, a native of their town and descendant of the same William Hedges, to prepare an introduction to such publication. More than two and a fourth centuries have passed since the ancestors of these descendants with others, the first settlers, laid the foundations of the good old town of East-Hampton. Our forefathers wrought in harmony the great work of planting a colony which should endure for coming centuries. Side by side their bones are mouldering in the old "South-end" burying ground. Succeeding generations took up their work in turn to cease, and again beside each other there, to rest in the last long sleep. The animating sentiment, the impelling motive, the moving impulse, the sustaining fortitude, the elevating aims, the upholding faith, the cheering friendships, the darkening perils were similar for all. They were in life united and in death not divided. This invitation to the writer from the descendants of such sires, is enforced by the memories of eight generations of the dead. Their might shades make the call to him sacred.

The free Government and institutions of the United States of America were born in its early settlements. Of necessity first colonial communities were self governed. They were in a wilderness which must be subdued to sustain them. Wild beasts and wild Indians encircled them. They were visited by roaming tramps and vagabonds. Discordant elements divided them. Gaunt famine threatened. On every side without and within the dark cloud of danger hung over them. Untiring industry alone could keep away starvation. Fearless strength alone subdue the wild beast. Sleepless vigilance only secure from the savage foe. Organized power only could settle and put down individual grievances and quarrels. Combination only could build churches and schoolhouses, roads and bridges. Martial law only could gather power to repel the enemy. Self-preservation required self-government. Discord and disorder was ruin.

The government must embody the people's will or be a shadow. It must be strong to act or be defied. It must be swift to strike or fail of opportunity. It must drown all discord or be overwhelmed by it.

In such conditions were all the early colonial settlements. Therefrom sprang a hardy race who by unshrinking toil felled the forest, built villages and towns, made laws suitable to their requirements, instituted churches, organized armies and in self-reliant hope and courage founded a nation on the Western shore of the Atlantic. As truly as the river's source is found in remote springs and fountains those union forms the rolling stream, so truly the springs and fountains of these great States are found in the early settlements of this fair, free land.

The Records of the Town of East Hampton are more full, more clear, more continuous, more intelligent than are usually found in like early colonies. They contribute clear historic light wherein from the source in the past we may trace the causes which produced the present. Every native of the old town, every careful student of our National History will rejoice that these records by publication have become an enduring memorial to the world, and thank the sons of her early settlers for this generous contribution to the history of our nation.

From the settlement of the Town in 1649 until the conquest of the Colony of New-York in 1664, East-Hampton was practically self-governed. Left mainly to itself these fifteen years the colony gained an experience of self-control and self-reliance that education it for free institutions which in succeeding ages arose out of like experiences in all the old settlements of the country.

The Town Meeting was the originating, organizing, electing, legislating and deciding power. As early as October 3, 1650, at a Town Meeting then holden, called a "Court of Election," Thos. Talmage, Jr., is chosen recorder. Also "four men with the constable for the ordering of ye 'affairs' of ye Towne." The ordinances then and thereafter enacted were such as were called for by their peculiar condition. The oaths prescribed for the offices of Recorder, the three men, sometimes 4 and sometimes more, holding magisterial authority; the pound-master and constable are on pages 6* and 7. The four men or any two of them could try cases involving any sum under forth shillings. See page 7.

The Montauks were the most powerful and probably numerous tribe of Indians on Long Island, claiming tribute and service from all the other tribes at the time of this settlement. Even after the universal massacre of their warriors by the Narraghansetts, (see pages 174, 175-6) and the terrific ravages of the small-pox (see page 201), their number was large and stated in 1761 to be 180.

An alliance with the nearest settlement for purposes of security of defence and improvement of adjoining lands, was vital. The entry succeeding the earliest record of the Town Meeting shows the care taken to make this secure, (see pages 8, 9, 10.)

The order that all that are fit to bear arms be sufficiently "provided of such armes" and the prohibition to sell "power, lead, shot, sword, flint, gun or pistol to any Indian," (page 8,) show the sense of impending peril.

In all that required care for the general safety against outside foes, internal dissension, individual neglect, violence, fraud or injustice against oppression, avarice, theft, crime, disorder and vice, the Town Meeting fitted the Law for the emergency, and with heavy hand represssed all disorder.

Although the Town Meeting met often, sometimes monthly and sometimes "in 3 weeks," "or els the first wet day and all to appere at the beat of the drum" (p. 12); although the magistrates, generally "3 men" were directed to hold court "every month," (see page 17), yet it might be too long for an impatient litigant to wait until the sitting of either. In ease the real or supposed necessity so required a court could be demanded sooner provided the litigant paid the fees therefor (see pages 7, 74 and 424). The term "purchased court," or purchasing a court, occurring in these records simply means that the court was held at an extra occasion and the fees of the court were paid by a litigant and

---

*NOTE: All page numbers in this chapter refer to Vol. I of *East Hampton Town Records.*

were simply a compensation for the time of the court. In the sense that the judgment of the court was "purchased" or purchasable, a comparison of the ancient with modern tribunals or legislatures would do no discredit to the former.

The Town Meeting, the acorn out of which grew the stately oak of local and national government in these United States acted under so many occasions and emergencies that entire classification is hardly possible. The following may assist the reader in the study of the subject:

THE TOWN MEETING

Elected all officers—pages, 7, 45, 88, 99, 103, 113, 148, 180, 185, 187, 197, 200, 225, 242, 255, 274, 364, 366, 414.

Constituted Courts—pages, 7, 45, 154, 177, 227.

Tried important cases—pages, 22, 38, 87, 389.

Heard Appeals—pages, 27, 28.

Ordered Lands Allotted—pages, 15, 25, 151, 180, 181, 186, 188, 204, 267, 392.

Chose the Minister, &c.—pages 216.

School Master, &c.—page, 380.

Fixed their Salaries—pages, 16, 155, 183, 393, 404, 432.

Ordered the Church built—pages, 19, 20, 66.

Admitted or excluded Settlers.—pages, 7, 13, 18, 20, 91, 176, 182, 327, 371, 387, 395, 400, 421.

Ratified or annulled Sales of Land—pages, 13, 18, 20, 109, 154, 231, 327.

Assigned to Committees their duties—pages, 13, 18, 291.

Made police regulations—pages, 8, 11, 17, 18, 20, 21, 29, 71, 81, 101, 104, 192, 201, 367, 380, 422.

Imposed fines for absence from Town Meeting—pages, 7, 13, 14, 16, 17, 145, 251, 856.

Neglect to vote or accept office—pages, 28, 100, 145.

Ordered a prison—page, 57.

Licensed Taverns—pages, 61, 154, 370.

Appointed or provided for the Whale Watch—pages, 18, 29, 60, 87, 114.

Regulated the fencing and improvement of the public lands—pages 10, 144, 146, 148, 155, 185, 186, 190, 192, 197, 218, 220, 224, 257, 270, 327, 361, 367, 386, 388, 392, 401, 404, 423.

Chose military officers—page, 225.
Fixed times for burning the woods—pages, 17, 21, 220.
Expelled vagabonds—pages, 18, 20, 93, 371, 421.
Provided for highways, &c.—pages, 27, 60, 68, 22, 32, 46, 59.
Labor thereon, and footpaths—pages, 27, 71, 187, 224, 269.
Enacted Laws for strays—page, 272.
For settling Mechanics—pages, 307, 331, 338, 339, 349, 360,
   415, 416.

The entry of June 24, 1672, page 346, is significant. In the March of 1672, France and England had declared war against the Netherlands. Governor Lovelace had summoned the eastern towns of Suffolk County to assist in defending the Colony and contribute to repairing the fortification at New-York city. The Justices and deputies from these towns meeting at Southold, had determined that they would so contribute "If they might have the privileges that other of his Majesties subjects in these parts do have and enjoy." The determination "is well approved of by this town and they are willing to answer their part in the charge according to their act if the privileges may be obtained but not otherwise." The novice in history will understand that representative Assemblies were granted to Rhode Island and other colonies by charter, and had just been granted to New Jersey. This privilege so dear to free born Englishmen, inherited from Magna Charta, the safeguard against arbitrary taxation, is the privilege so earnestly desired by them, and the granting whereof is made the condition for their contributing. Thus early the sons of this old town evinced their undying attachment to the liberties of the citizen. The experiment of self-government conducted by them in their forest home for a generation had borne good fruit. In their own experience of nearly one-fourth of a century secluded from the hand of power, too obscure for the notice of rulers, they administered among themselves such laws, civil and martial, as suited their simple habits. Well they knew no laws made in Parliament wherein they were unheard, could fit their condition so exactly as their own taught them by their circumstances. In after years, through the voice of their representative, Samuel Mulford, they spoke for freedom. Its undying spirit burned in all their succeeding history. The resolve of this liberty-loving town was no more doubtful than the resounding echoes of Bunker Hill. If the heavy hand of despotic power found servility elsewhere in these old towns the unequivocal tones of freedom rang out as warning bells for the coming centuries.

This volume of the Records extends about thirty years from the first settlement. The colony was fairly launched on the political ocean where were sailing many like towns on the borders of the Atlantic. The members of the colony had increased. Dangers from the savage had lessened. Adventurous hearts panted for more acres and more room. John Osborn selling land at the east and acquiring much more at the west at Wainscott, was located there in 1670, and being so "remote from the town," in June of that year a grant of preference "to grind at the mill" is given him. The tradition that he was the first settler of Wainscott is confirmed by this and other entries in the records. His home lot taken by the settlers given to Thos. Smith, a blacksmith, who soon leaves, then dedicated by vote for a parsonage, is finally sold to Josiah Hobart, who settles on it and afterwards becomes High Sheriff of his county.

WITCHCRAFT

The wife of Joshua Garlicke, accused of witchcraft, by an order of the town meeting made March 19,1657, was directed to be taken for trial to Hartford. The testimony against her is scattered over the records anterior to and about the time of this entry. The result of this trial appears to have been unknown until lately. In the printed colonial records of Connecticut, pages 572 and 3, appears the following letter, and on the same page in a Note the letter is said to be in the handwriting of Gov. Winthrop, not dated, but must have been written some time in the spring of 1678:

LETTER TO EAST-HAMPTON.

"Gen & Loving Friends:
We having received your letter & findinge recorded a Court Order of 1649 wherein ye Court declared their acceptance of your Towne under this Government by your Agents Lift. Gardiner, etc., we shall present the same to our next Gen. Court for a further & full confirmation thereof: And ye meantime did take yt case which was presented from you into serious cosideration and there hath passed a legall tryall thereupon: Whereupon though there did not appeare sufficient evidence to prove her guilty yet we cannot but well approve and commend the Christian care & prudence of those in authority with you in searching into ye case accordinge to such just suspicion as appeared.

Also we think good to certify yt is desired & expected by this Court yt you should cary neighbourly & peaceably without just offence to Jos. Garlick & his wife & yet ye should doe ye like to you. And ye charge wee conceive & advise may be justly borne as followeth : yt Jos. Garlick should bear ye charge of her transportation hither & return home. 2ndly, yt your towne should beare all their own charges at home & the charge of their messengers & witnesses in bringing the case to tryall here & their return home—the Court being content to put ye charge of the Tryall here upon ye County's account."

Thus the only known case of accusation for witchcraft in East Hampton, for the trial of which the town authorities preferred to seek a higher tribunal, resulted in an acquittal, to the lasting honor of the town and the colony of Connecticut.

WHALING

The first settlement of the Town was located near the ocean, as if for convenience of whaling, which probably was even then a consideration moving to the enterprise. References to this adventurous business occur among the earliest records, and seem to indicate that the whole colony were interested and engaged and sharing therein. (See pages 8, 18, 29, 53, 60), even suspending school therefor, (p. 380). As early as 1668, Jas. Loper was here suing Renek Garrison for "non-performance of his agreement about going a fishing," p. 284. In 1672 he was attaching blubber of Nathanial Williams, p. 344. In May, 1673, he is acquiring a house lot in the Calf Pasture (south of Wm. Hedges' lot), p. 360. In December, 1675, he had married Elizabeth, daughter of Arthur Howell, and was making a marriage settlement on his wife, p. 372. The Records of Nantucket, under date of June 5, 1672, contain the draft of a proposed agreement with James Loper, of East-Hampton, to engage there "on a design of whale catching." It does not appear that Loper went to Nantucket on the "design." Possibly the bright eyes of Elizabeth Howell were a strong attraction and may account for the marriage and settlement and prosecution of whaling thereafter at East Hampton. The very successful prosecution of off shore whaling in late years at Amagansett, is but the continuation of adventure perilous but prosperous, conducted by the hardy sons of East-Hampton from the earliest times.

THE TITLE TO THE LANDS UNDIVIDED.

It has been a question often mooted whether the title to the lands vested in the town as a corporation or in certain proprietors, their heirs and assigns. Some expressions in the records appear as if the town as a town owned and controlled until allotted all the lands therein; but the proprietors who undertook the enterprise of settling the colony, purchasing of the Indians, instituting and building the church and schoolhouse, and subduing the wilderness, called themselves "the town." To all practical purposes for over an hundred years they were "the town." Their expenditures of time, labor, money, hardship and danger made the place habitable for themselves and others, and the enhanced value they deemed as justly an inheritance belonging to them and their heirs.

On page 66 is found "the charge for the Meeting House." Against the name of each land owner is set the amount he contributed, then the number of acres he was entitled to share in the undivided lands of the town; then his proportion due according to his share, then the balance due to or from him.

Thomas Baker contributed £3, 08s, 06d; he was the owner of 21 acres in all the yet undivided lands, he was bound to contribute £0, 13s, 1-1/2d; there was due him £0, 15s, 3-1/2d. Now, turning to page 342, where is recorded the land of Thos. Baker, we find he had "a one and twenty acre lot, vix: Home lot and plains with all privileges and appurtenances belonging to such an allotment." In other words, he had a right in the division of unallotted lands to that proportion, if he had received more than would be deducted, and if less, that would be made up to him in a future division of land.

All this agrees with the purchase of How by Baker, "what he now possesseth & what is or may belong to him with relation to his Lott as his right to his settling there,"   page   5

The 13 acre lot of William Barnes,	"	437
The 20 " " " Robert Bond,	"	445
The 13 " " " Richard Brooks,	"	447
The 21 " " " Thos. Chatfield,	"	451
The 20 " " " William Edwards,	"	474

These and others are simply illustrations of the principle admitted on the records, of individual ownership in all the undivided lands covered by the deeds, in proportions well understood and recognized in the allotments or divisions of lands whenever made.

The word "commonage" is often applied to these undivided rights in the unallotted territory, as on page 374, in the gift of John Mulford, senior.

CHURCH

There is no doubt that the early settlers of this town were strict Calvinists. Characteristic of their Puritan principles they called their church building "the meeting house." Neither in this or neighboring churches was any name sectarian or denominational given to the church as such. "The church in Southampton," in "Bridge-Hampton," in "East-Hampton," were so called from the village or town of their location, and only so called. When the venerable James, after a long service rested from his labors his loving people engraved on his tombstone no narrow epithet, but this: "He was Minister of the Gospel And Pastyre of the Church of Christ." The colony was happy in the choice of their Pastor. Minister James understood the Indian language, sometimes instructed the Indians and preached to them, and acted as an interpreter (Southampton Records, Vol. I, p. 160, Vol. III, p. 110.) He was learned, resolute, just, sincere, fearless, active, a powerful personality.

The colony were not less happy in the watchful regard of Lion Gardiner, who soon became one of their number and occupied the lot next that of Minister James with whom he took "sweet counsel." He was venerable for years, of large experience, both warrior and statesman. With the councils at Hartford or of the Sachem at Montaukaa, his influence was potent. The right of centuries revealing the weakness, the errors, the mistakes of the past, has left undimmed the radiant name of this magnanimous Puritan.

This volume covers the formation period of the town. The infant had grown to manhood. Under the tuition of Connecticut for the first fifteen years, East Hampton was cast in the Puritan mould. After the conquest of the New Netherlands in 1664, by the English, the entreaty of East-Hampton to abide with the colony of Connecticut was denied, p. 223, 241. In March, 1666, for their own safety they were constrained to purchase and hold under the authority of the Duke of York, by patent from Governor Nicoll—pages 353, 354, &c.

In June, 1674, after the reconquest from the Dutch, a renewed petition to be joined with Connecticut, is made in vain, p. 370. Yet for two centuries East-Hampton in untiring industry, in adventurous enterprise, in intellectual culture, in free aspirations, in modes of thought, in devotional fervor, was essentially Puritan. Disunited in government, it remained essentially in spirit a fragment of New England. The early history of the settlers reveals nothing of which their descendants need be ashamed. The transforming hand of the Puritan swept away its wilderness and planted the harvest. The free soul of the Puritan burst the bands of oppression and instituted freedom. The burning devotion of the Puritan revealed to the world a light that growing in radiance shall yet lead the millions into "the new heavens and new earth wherein dwelleth righteousness."

Bridge-Hamptons,
February 26th, 1887.
H. P. HEDGES.

CHAPTER VII

INTRODUCTION TO VOL. II OF THE EAST HAMPTON TOWN RECORDS (1680-1720)

Written in 1887 at the age of 70

THE ATTENTIVE READER closing the first volume of printed records of the Town of East Hampton, is assured that the elements of perpetuity have been so developed that by the natural law of growth, a larger life and progress was coming to the Colony. The settlers had overcome the first and the worst foes that imperilled their being. The close of King Phillips's war had removed all danger from the Indians. The most formidable wild beasts had been destroyed; the most venomous reptiles exterminated; unwelcome intruders had been warned and left for other homes. The patent of March 13th, 1666, from Gov. Nicolls, was thought to have assured their title to the purchased territory, beyond cavil. More than all, they had proved able to govern themselves. Rules, laws, customs, habits—had crystallized into a fixed system. In 1687, the population was:

Males	223	No. capable of bearing arms	98
Females	218	No. of merchants	2
Male servants	26	No. of marriages in 7 years	28
Female servants	9	No. of births	116
Male slaves	11	No. of christened	198
Female slaves	14	No. of burials	57
Total	502		

DOCUMENTARY HISTORY OF NEW YORK, P. 360, VOL. III.

The state of the Church, Oct. 5, 1704, as laid before the clergy at New York, then conveyed by appointment of Lord Cornbury and Col. Francis Nicholson, Governor and Lieutenant-Governor of the Colony, is thus given:

ACCOUNT OF SUFFOLK COUNTY.

In Suffolk County, in east end of Long Island, there is neither a church of England, minister, nor any provision made for one by law; the people generally being independents, and upheld in their separation by New England emissaries,"—See Documentary Hist. of New York, pp. 111 and 115, Vol. III.

The increase in population and adherence to their worship, "independent" of the established Church of England, now made them fit subjects for the rapacity of Governors commissioned for the very purpose of subverting representative government, and repairing their ruined fortunes by extortion from the Colonists. More insidious than the wily savage, more dangerous than wild beast, more relentless than the venomous serpent, these robber Governors were the mightiest foes of the Colony. In the communications of the Duke of York (afterwards James the 2d) to Gov. Andros, the danger of public assemblies was declared, and the Duke's opinion stated in the words: "Neither do I see any use for them." (See Bancroft's History U.S., Vol. II, p. 406.) In swift succession Governor succeeded Governor, each in the main baffled by the sturdy resistance of the people, no where more persistent than in East-Hampton.

The Governors were:

1664—Richard Nicolls.	1689—Jacob Leisler.
1667—Francis Lovelace.	1691—Henry Sloughter.
1674—Edmund Andros.	" —Richard Ingoldsby.
1677—Anthony Brockholst.	1692—Benjamin Fletcher.
1678—Edmund Andros.	1698—Richard Foote, Earl
1681—Anthony Brockholst.	Bellemont.
1682—Col. Thos. Dongan.	1699—John Nanfan, Lieut.-
1688—Edmund Andros.	Governor.
" —Francis Nicholson, Lieut.-	1700—Earl of Bellemont.
Governor.	1701—William Smith.

1701—John Nanfan, Lieut.-
 Governor.
1702—Edward Hyde, Lord
 Cornbury.
1708—John Ford, Gov. Lovelace.

1709—Peter Schuyler,
 Pres. of the Council.
 " —Richard Ingoldsby,
 Lieut.-Governor.
1710—Robert Hunter.

The three eastern towns of this County—Southampton, Southold and East-Hampton—were the back bone of the county, if not of the whole Colony of New York, in advocating representative government and resisting encroachments upon their liberties. As between the Colonists and the King, the governors were uniformly servile to him, and hostile to them. In this, Andros and Dongan, "the Catholic," were alike. Fletcher was "covetous and passionate." Cornbury "had every vice of character necessary to discipline a colony into self-reliance and re-sistance." (See Bancroft History of U.S., pp. 56 and 60, Vol. III.) The con-flict between our Puritan forefathers and these governors was long, unequal, and often resulted adversely to the people.

The conflict waged in 1681 for chartered rights, and representa-tive government never ceased until freedom won at Yorktown.

There was an attempt in 1682 to levy customs without a colonial assembly, which had been defeated by the Grand Jury, and trade became free just as Andros was returning to England. In 1683, the newly ap-pointed Gov. Dongan was instructed to call a general assembly of all the freeholders, by the persons whom they should choose to represent them. In October, 1684, the assembly met and claimed in a bill of rights as Englishmen, that "Every freeholder and Freeman should vote. Trial to be by Jury." "No tax to be levied but by consent of the assembly," etc. In 1685, in less than a month after James the Second ascended the throne, he prepared to overturn the institutions he had conceded. By ordinance a direct tax was decreed. The titles to real estate were questioned that larger fees and quit rents might be extorted, and of the farmers of East-Hampton who protested against the tyranny, six were arraigned before the Council. (See Bancroft's Hist. U.S., Vol. III, pp. 413-14-15.)

In May, 1686, Gov. Dongan was endeavoring to compel the people of East-Hampton to purchase a new patent at an exorbitant price, and they were resisting the attempt at extortion. The proprietor vote of that date regarding the four men on whom a warrant had been served, p. 186*; the vote of "the purchasers and proprietors of this town," June

---

*NOTE: All page numbers in this chapter refer to Vol. II *East Hampton Town Records* unless otherwise indicated.

11, 1686, choosing a committee for the defence of their rights; the committee vote of June 14, 1686, appointing "Leiftenant John Wheeler and Ensine Samuel Mulford" to defend the town's interest, p. 187—all relate to this controversy with the Governor.

July 29, 1686, ten persons complained to the Governor that the town will lay out no land to them, and he by order in council then directed Josiah Hobart, High Sheriff of the County, to lay out to each thirty acres. The written protest against this laying out, dated October 6, 1686, was deemed a libel, and an information to that effect filed by the Attorney General. Warrants issued for the arrest of Stephen Hedges, William Perkins, Jeremy Conkling, Daniel and Nathaniel Bishop, Robert Dayton, Samuel Parsons, Benjamin Conklin, Thomas Osborne and John Osborne. October 17th, 1686, Thomas James preached from the text Job XXIV, 2: "Some remove the land mark." Nov. 18th, 1686, Sheriff Hobart attested under oath to the text and, teaching of the sermon. The same day an order in council was entered that a warrant issue against Minister James on the ground that the sermon was seditious. A like information against him was filed. A warrant for his arrest issued Nov. 18th, 1686. He was arrested, and some three weeks thereafter petitioned the Governor for his release, reciting this as "the first tyme (for almost forty years of my being a minister of the Gospel) that I have been called to account by any authority I have lived under." (See *Documentary History of New-York*, pp. 351 to 360, Vol. III.)

The arbitrary power of Dongan prevailed; a patent was procured, dated December 9th, 1686, which secured individually to the holder all lands "then taken up and appropriated," to the purchasers all lands "unappropriated," "in proporcion to their severall & respective purchases thereoff," and gave to the Trustees of the corporation the pre-emption or first purchase right as to the *then* unpurchased part of Montauk. (See pages 194 to 204.) The patent is a mass of redundant verbage perplexing to the ordinary reader. The pith of the whole regarding title, is on page 198, which determines the sense and meaning of the instrument. Thus the proprietors obtained from the Governor a patent which confirmed their title to all the unallotted lands in the town as purchasers thereof, in proportion to their several contributions of purchase money. This was just what they had claimed from the beginning, and neither less or more. The consistency of the Governor in arbitrarily ordering a division of thirty acres each to those not entitled, and thereafter ignoring their claim, and by patent confirming title to the purchasers, is not apparent. It seems plain that the whole proceedings were designed to force the people to pay as they did pay the extortionate charge of two hundred pounds for the patent. Eighty pounds thereof was charged to Montauk. An extra amount was assessed to pay the costs arising "about mens protests," (p. 204.)

The people of the Town of East-Hampton claimed the right to be represented in a colonial assembly, and that taxes could rightfully be levied only by assent of their representatives. This was the burden of their grievance; this the reason why again and again they petitioned to be placed under the authority and jurisdiction of Connecticut where representative government was established. Only in the light of such claims of right can the records be properly read. The address voted at a general training, June 21st, 1682, (page 112). The appointment of a committee to obtain redress from the Duke of York, (pp. 112 and 113) in this view, are significant.

Samuel Parsons and Thomas Chatfield signed the letter dated March 10th, 1689-90, written to Leisler, reciting that "we have agreed to send over to his Majesty both a true narration of ye grievances we have suffered this many years under an arbitrary power, and a petition to their majesties yt we might be rejoined with Connecticut government as formerly, agreeably to the act of Parliament, yt all places (NE being particularly mentioned) shall have the same *privileges* they enjoyed in ye year 1660, restored unto them." (See Documentary History of New-York, Vol. II, page 187.) This recital is unequivocal, and makes the more clear many entries in the Town Records. The address to the Governor, dated Oct. 1st, 1685, (pages 169 and on) is not only a recital of the fact that formerly by "deputies" at Hempstead, "the whole Island being assembled in our representatives," but a claim to such representation "as a fundamental privilege of our English Nation," and the expression of a fear that by the denial of such privilege, "our freedom should be turned into bondage and our ancient privileges so infringed yt they will never arrive at our posterity." The address is said to have been written by minister James. It bears marks of his strong devotion to freedom. It is worthy of enduring remembrance as one of the luminous monuments of the ardent love of this people for liberty. The wise architect knows where and how to imbed in the deep foundations of the rising structure, strong bars of iron, to hold fast the springing arches, the massive walls, the spacious dome, the lofty spires. Like such a bar this "address" seems imbedded in the foundations of the fair temple of American Freedom. The expression of 1685 would develop by the laws of growth into the "Declaration" of 1776.

It does not appear that the town recognized Leisler as Governor. The Trustees' vote, September 2d, 1689, (page 240) authorized the committee to order and empower Capt. Leisler "to secure for this town's use, what monies is to be found in New York unjustly by tax or taxes levied on this town." In singular contrast the entry on page 260, Feb. 13, 1680, expressly names Sloughter Governor. Although the town had been constrained to pay an extortionate price for a Patent from Dongan, the stern spirits that panted for freedom still hoped and still fought on with unabated ardor for an assembly of representatives of the people. Neither Thomas James or Samuel Mulford (mighty names!) would tamely surrender the rights of a free born people to arbitrary power. The angel of American Liberty was unfolding his wings preparatory to a flight above the power of servile Governors, base-minded Lords or irresponsible Kings.

The student of history will scrutinize with intense interest the experience of this community in the improvement of lands in common. The compact village settlement, with small, narrow home lots, was convenient for the purposes of mutual protection, social enjoyment, education of the youth, religious worship, pursuit of the whale fishery and common improvement of outlying lands. On the one Main street the Colony was planted. It grew chiefly northward, and in two score years extended a mile in length. Outside of these home lots, the lands were tilled and pastured before and after allotment, in fields enclosed by fence made by the owners in proportion to their ownership. Each owner tilled his just number of acres to which he was entitled in the field devoted to cultivation, as he would have done had he fenced it separately. Each one turned in the number of cattle to which he was entitled according to the stint fixed for each, on the basis of his ownership in the lands pastured. The popular idea that a common of pasturage is an unlimited, unregulated right, is a popular mistake. "A right of common without stint cannot exist in law," vid. note *Blackstone's Commentary* vol. 2, p. 34, etc. Just as to a recent date the lands of Montauk were stinted for pasturage; so in early days the lands referred to were stinted for pasturage. Jonathan T. Gardiner kindly loaned me the April number of the "Magazine of American History" for the year 1883. The article therein entitled "Montauk and the Common Lands of East-Hampton," was contributed by Prof. John Franklin Jameson, of John Hopkins University. With much learning the improvement of lands in common here is sought to be traced back to New and Old England and the Germanic races who "Migrated to Britain."

The circumstances were favorable for such improvement; the location of the village settlement, the common interest and convenience of the people, and their general honesty all tended to make this experiment successful and lasting. But the infirmities of human nature come to the front in every age—in every race. The boys in meeting were sometimes unruly and required "looking after," by James Bird. (See page 113.) The owners of these lands seem to have required "looking after" in matters of fencing and common improvement. Very stringent rules were enacted—(pp. 102, 148, 165, 185, 217, 225, 265, 346, 401.)

Severe penalties were ordained—(pp. 125, 130, 148, 166, 209, 226, 266, 400.)

Fences were subject to the stern censorship of inspectors—(p. 191.) Delinquents in fencing were exposed by the initial letters cut on the fence—(p. 234.)

Yet all these failed to enforce the performance of the common duty, trespass occurred, fences were sometimes poorly made and sometimes not made at all. As time rolled on—except Montauk and certain meadows—the lands came to be improved in severalty and not in common. The Village system of settlement, the saving of fence, the saving of many drivers of cattle, the scattered lots of land, the habits of the people, seemed to call for the perpetuation of common improvement. The failure of the experiment here under most favorable circumstances, is in itself a strong testimony again at communism or any like system, that seeks to substitute the common in place of the several improvement of lands by their owners.

The Records abound in evidence that whaling continued to be an increasing and prosperous enterprise. Several companies were engaged in this perilous pursuit; young men came from Connecticut, New Jersey and other localities to share in the hazard and excitement of the whale chase, and often married wives at East Hampton. Farming and shoemaking soon attracted much attention, yet whaling was second only to agriculture. (See pages 77, 79, 86, 94, 95, 96, 97, 98, 99, 100, 101, 119, 120, 152, 153.

Incidentally through the accounts, we learn of events transpiring of which there is no other record. In 1682 we find a charge of £26 13s. 00d "to ye Carptr yt makes the gallery for the church," showing with other items that the people had been rebuilding and enlarging their church and constructing a gallery therein. (See pages 108-9-10-11.) Boards were carted from Northwest, and barrels carted down there; (see page 111) showing that their harbor or landing place at that time was Northwest. That there was a Fort, we know by the charge on page 107: "Stephen Hand for ye Gate of ye fort $0-5-00."

That they had a cannon termed "Great gonn," loaded at Montauk by Joseph Osborn; carted thence to Northwest by "John Cerles team" and

"John Millers Sen," we find from charges therefor, entered on page 247.

I find no positive recorded evidence locating the fort. I think probable it was near the church, if it did not enclose it. There the men carried their arms on the Sabbath at their meeting. That was the central rallying point when the New England settlements were assailed by the Indians, and a central point in East-Hampton. (See pages 32 and 54, Vol. II.) Just south were the graves of the dead, now extended over the site of church and fort, (if fort there was), as age after age enlarged the city "where the rude forefathers of the hamlet sleep." It is stated in the chronicles of East-Hampton that the burying ground had never been fenced. (See page 28.) June 16th, 1685, there was a vote to fence it "with a good peeke pale." (See page 167.) It seems probable it was then fenced. Forts were constructed by setting firmly in the ground half-tree sticks, some 8 to 12 feet long. Being split they were flat on the one side like a "pale," being sharpened on the top they were "peeke" or peeked. Dwelling houses here were so fortified and enclosed. (See pages 71, 301, Vol. I.) The burying ground was ordered to be so enclosed. It is not improbable that the enclosure of fort and burying place was then made by continuous lines of "pales." The early burial grounds were near the residence of the settlers. They were chosen for the purpose of being accessible; often on a hill as a conspicuous reminder of mortality, and an incentive to the living to defend to the death the graves of their dead from the savage foe. Nor is it certain, as has been charged, that the Puritans deliberately selected desolate, unsightly or unsuitable locations for this purpose, and with intent to exhibit disregard to the memory or sacredness of the dead. The vote referred to is as truly significant of the reign of the finer feelings as the vote of the town in April, 1685, when Thos. Squire was sick, that his taxes "were remitted," (see page 164) is evidence of; practical benevolence. Beneath the austere self-controlled demeanor of the Puritan, there breathed a gentle tenderness for the child of misfortune, a sacred reverence to the memory and the ashes of the dead.

June 16th, 1696, Minister James died. He had been partially disabled so as to require an assistant in the ministry for some years. For nearly half a century he had been an able and devout minister to his people, intelligent in the understanding of their rights as free-born Englishmen, fearless in their defence. Only with his last breath went out his watchful regard as their minister. In attestation of his conscious discharge of duty, his intrepid soul prompted the desire to be so buried as to rise facing his people on the resurrection morn.

In September, 1696, Rev. Nathaniel Huntting came to East-Hampton and commenced his ministry of fifty years there. He was wise in counsel, diligent in study, faithful in doing his work, devout in spirit and an untiring chronicler of the church and settlement. All accessions to the church, marriages, baptisms and deaths for half a century he minutely recorded. In this, he was faithful unto death. To the historian and genealogist his record is invaluable, and his work solid and enduring.

To these Puritans the voice of the minister was grave, his teaching serious; but the voice of the ocean, on whose shore they lived, was not less solemn. Within its depths countless human lives had perished. Their sad fate seemed to invite the desponding to join them there. The fascination was strangely attractive to the disordered mind, and often impelled to self-destruction. Its stormy roar hushed and awed the thoughtless. To the great souls who panted for freedom, it spoke encouragement. Its illimitable expanse symbolized the vastness of their thoughts. Its resistless wave was an emblem of the people's might. To the devout it spoke of the Almighty Maker. Its seeming quiet was beguiling as that of the serpent. The storm of its wrath who could withstand? Its soft evening murmur lulled the weary to rest. The unceasing beat of its billows echoed in the ears of the living. In its ebbing tides the souls of their dying had gone out. Over the graves of their dead rose the moan of its anthem. The fearful mysteries of ocean, mutable, majestic, measureless, are unutterable.

From the days of ministers James and Huntting to the present, the thoughts of the prayerful might read:

> *"And musing here I dream*
> *Of voyagers on a stream*
> *From whence is no returning,*
> *Under sealed orders going,*
> *Looking forward little knowing.*
> *Looking back with idle yearning,*
> *And I pray that every venture,*
> *The port of peace may enter,*
> *That safe from snag and fall,*
> *And syren haunted Islet,*
> *And rock, the unseen Pilot*
> *May guide us one and all."*

Bridge-Hampton, Sept. 30th, 1887.
H. P. HEDGES

CHAPTER VIII

THE CONTROVERSY CONCERNING THE SETTLEMENT OF SOUTHAMP-TON AND SOUTHOLD

≈⊘⊘⊘⊱

Delivered on October 1, 1889, at the age of 71

THE SETTLEMENTS OF Plymouth, Salem, Boston and those adjacent thereto would naturally be fixed by the voyagers on or near the ocean they had crossed and a harbor where supplies could be brought from the country they had left. Thereafter, in the selection of sites at Hartford, Windsor, Wethersfield, Saybrook, New Haven, Gardiner's Island, Southold, Southampton, East-Hampton, other elements complicated the problem. The interior was a wilderness, the home of the savage and the wild beast. The progress of the traveler was slow, dangerous and the road uncertain and hard to keep. The ocean, bay and river were more easily crossed. Colonies located thereon were more easily supplied, visited, succored and defended. In the wilderness, man to man, the hostile Indian might equal the hostile Englishman. On the ocean, bay or river one small vessel of the latter could beat the canoes of a continent. Not by chance or accident, or without careful thought were the early settlements in this country so located that the settlers could be sustained, supplied, visited, succored, defended. Thus fixed, the forest, the stream, the harbor contributed game and fowl and fish to sustain the pioneer. Thus established, he could export surplus products derived from the waters, the air or the earth.

Lion Gardiner, from Saybrook Fort looking over the waters of the Sound, saw with the eye of a soldier, a financier and practical business man the advantageous position of the beautiful isle that to this day bears his name. The Puritans of New Haven, from the heights of East and West Rock, saw over the waters the pleasant shores of Long Island,

136

and very early, knowing its attractions, its beauty, its health, its abundance, purchased and colonized Southold.

The Puritans of Lynn, embarking with a vessel under the command of Daniel How, left behind the territory of the New England colonies, and, preferring this island as a field of enterprise, settled at Southampton.

The choice of the Puritans who settled in the Hamptons or at Southold is confirmed by the continuing verdict of the ages and of our own time. What attracted them has attracted succeeding generations until the places where they planted their colonies have become the summer resort of thousands.

In the warm controversy concerning priority of settlement of Southold and Southampton I find little attention drawn to the precise question at issue or to the terms of the granting instruments. For these reasons chiefly I submit in the briefest manner my views on this question in the sacred cause of historic truth and historic light. As a native of East-Hampton and non-partisan inquirer I hope to do so free from prejudice or bias. The question is not whether some one individual first located in either town. On that issue the settlement of Gardiner's Island, now in the bounds of East-Hampton, would give priority to that town and exclude both Southold and Southampton. The question is not where a church was first organized. Such organization might be long after the settlement. Neither is it material which town first purchased from the Indians. They might—and did—locate in the towns prior to such purchase. Much less are the Indian deeds material. They are not the purchase, but evidence of a past purchase. The real question is, when was a settlement made in the name of and for the colonizing company by themselves or representatives of their number? Such representatives commissioned to build houses, plant gardens, erect fortifications and accommodations for later arrival of its members, who did arrive, would thereby commence the settlement. Their occupation would be the actual occupation of the company. Later accessions would not commence, but simply augment the numbers of the colonists. Both Webster and Worcester substantially define the word "settlement" as meaning occupation by settlers on the soil, and I mean it. Under date of March 10, 1639-40, by an agreement for the sale of their vessel to Daniel How, the persons therein named contract of the vessel "for the use of the plantacon," etc.; that "said Daniel shall not sell this vessel without the consent of the majority of the company:" "that the vessel shall be reddy at the Town of Lynne to transport such goods as the undertakers shall appoint—that is to say, three tymes in the year," etc. The times were fixed at the first, fourth and eighth month. This agreement expressly recognizes the formation of a company to found and plant a colony looking to the establishment of a church, or churches and a town. The vessel owned by the company was dedicated to this purpose and the dedication was recognized and respected in the agreement for sale. In thought, in resolve, in numbers, in means of access and means of support at this date a colony existed. (See Southampton Records, vol. 1, p. 1, etc.) To the eleven undertakers signing this agreement were afterward added eight more signers accepted by them and two more in a final declaration, dated the fourth day of the fourth (probably) month. The patent of James Farrett, agent for the Earl of Sterling, dated April 17, 1640, to "Daniel How, Job Sayre, George Wilbe and William Harker and their associates" gives to them the right "to sit down upon Long Island aforesaid, there to possess, improve and enjoy eight miles square of land or so much as shall contain the "said quantity," etc. "And that they are to take their choice to sitt down upon as best suiteth them." The rent was to be fixed thereafter by John Winthrop and the inhabitants "at their leisure" were required to purchase of the Indians having "lawful right" to said land. (Col. Hist. of N.Y., vol. 3, p. 628, new series, vol. 13, old.) By this Farrett patent the grantees and their associates had the option to locate anywhere on Long Island the equivalent of eight miles square. Without deed of specific territory, they had what was better, an option like a modern land warrant to locate covering the whole Island and excluding location by others, until they had selected or been given a reasonable time to select their land. Their grip held all over the territory and excluded all others. As matter of law Farrett could not convey so as to defeat their priority of choice. If he was intelligent and honest he would not try to do it, and as agent for the earl he is presumed to be both honest and intelligent. The emigrants had been tossed on the ocean, unsettled since their arrival, looking for a residence and resting place, standing as if on the tiptoe of expectation. A grant to them of the desired spot "to sitt down" under the simile of a wayworn traveler was a verbal painting of their condition. When in 1660, the Montauk Indians, hunted by the Narragansetts, had been driven to East-Hampton, in the counter bond to their conveyance, they reserved the right "again to sett down" at Montauk as expressive of their desire. (See E.H. Records, vol. 1, p. 174.)

Remembering the dates of the disposal of the vessel and of the patent in March, 1639 and April, 1640 (both meaning 1640,) we find on record an account of the discovery by the Dutch, in the yacht Prince William, of a party of Englishmen attempting settlement at Cow

Harbor; an order and expedition of twenty-five soldiers for their arrest, the advice given to surround them "unawares" at break of day, the arrest and march to Fort Amsterdam on the 15th of May, 1640, and the examination of Job Sayre, George Wilbe, John Farrington, Phillip and Nathaniel Kirtland and William Harker, all named among the undertakers aforesaid. The examination of these six pioneers discloses important facts; exculpating themselves, they admitted or testified that How and Mr. Farrett cut down "the arms of the State;" that these two had gone to Red Hill, (New Haven) with the sloop that landed them, with their "commission," meaning, probably, their deed of conveyance; that they (the witnesses) left, on their arrest, "two men and one woman and a child there to take care of their goods;" that they "had built a small house and were building another," not finished; that they came "to plant and build dwellings;" that "it was intended that twenty families should come; and if the land was good they expected a great many people." These men were discharged on the 19th May, 1640, then signing a writing reciting their coming to settle on the territory of the States General "without knowing the same, being deceived by Mr. Farrett. Scotchman," and a promise to remove from the territory "Immediately," [Vid. Col. Hist., vol. 2, p. 146, etc.] It is undisputed that an attempt to settle was made and defeated. Expelled from Cow Bay the eight men must take care of their goods, find their vessel and report to Howe and Farret. Where? At New Haven. There was their little vessel and there had gone Howe, the captain, and Farret, the agent, who had "deceived them." Howe was as much interested in founding colonies as Farret. Thereby freights and profits multiplied. He was proprietor in many purchases to that end. He was acquainted in New Haven and at home there on his vessel as much as anywhere. Subsequently both Howe and his son Jeremy removed from Lynn there. [See "History of Lynn" by Lewis and Newhall pp. 124 and 175.] Farret without doubt, went wherever called by interest and, without any fixed residence or strong ties elsewhere, could at New Haven overlook the territory in his charge better than at either Lynn or Boston, where sometime he was. The circumstances look to the continuance of the vessel and these men with her for a time in the harbor of New Haven. Until the success or failure of the expedition was known, Lynn was too remote a waiting place and Cow Bay rather near for both Howe and Farret, who were liable to arrest knew it. After this expulsion the expelled settlers would naturally, with their goods, rejoin the vessel at New Haven and claim that Farret should repay them the cost of transportation or barge hire and in his next patent, locating the territory purchased, he did agree to pay it. By deed dated June 12, 1639 (meaning 1640) Farret conveyed to Edward Howell, Daniel How, Job Sayre and their associates all lands "lying and being bounded between Peaconeck and the easternmost point of Long Island, with the whole breadth of said island from sea to sea, with all land and premises contained in aid limits, excepting those lands already granted to any person by me." * * * "in consideration of barge hire, besides they being drove off by the Dutch from the place where they were by me planted, to their great damage, and with a competent sum of money in hand, paid before the ensealing and delivery of these presents, all amounting to four hundred pounds sterling." By instrument dated August 20, 1639 (meaning 1640,) Lord Stirling confirmed this conveyance of June to Howell and others and also sales by Farret to John, Thomas, and Edward Farrington and Matthew Sunderland [Colonial History," Volume III., pp. 21 and 22] Farret, by his power of attorney, had authority to make a first choice in the land covered thereby to the extent of 12,000 acres, and in pursuance thereof had chosen Robbins Island and Shelter Island, sometimes called Farrett's Island and hence the exception in his grant to Howell. [Vide Thompson's "History Long Island," Volume II, 118 page. Thus by the deed of June Farret becomes a witness of this attempt to settle, in his own language, "where they were by me planted"—a witness to the expulsion, the payment of "barge hire," the large consideration of £400, and by his deed is estopped from denying these facts. Dutch and English alike were extending their settlements to fortify by possession conflicting territorial claims. If Farret designed to plant this company at the West as an intended barrier preventing Dutch aggression and protecting contemplated settlements further East, as is probable, he knew and anticipated the danger of expulsion. He knew the necessity that his vessel should be near at hand if his experiment failed and Howe knew the like. We prove this sloop to be at New Haven, not Lynn, with urgent motives to remain there and await results. It is there that the pioneers expelled from Cow Harbor probably rejoined the captain, Howe, a co-owner and proprietor, and Farret, the agent, with their "provisions" and planting and carpenter's tools, and from thence they probably pursued their voyage. No evidence is known showing a return to Lynn or any necessity thereof before effecting a settlement. Farret's deed in June was probably a deed to a company then located on the ground between "Peconic"—an Indian settlement at the head of the Bay [Vide "Colonial History of New-York," Vol. 3, p. 600]—"and the easternmost point of the island." The indignant reproaches of the company would constrain Farret to quiet them forthwith by a satisfactory deed. All the circumstances look that way.

There is every presumption for the continuance of the voyage and location at this date, and the burden of proof to the contrary is on those denying it. Right here let me say that this deed of June not only covers Southampton, but in the main, with the exception of the pre-empted islands Farret chose, might cover Southold by the terms, "With the whole breadth of the island from sea to sea." Certainly if Southold had been purchased this deed should not have been bounded so as to include "the whole breadth of the island." In this view the deed of June is evidence of the Southampton purchase, and more, is evidence that this purchase was anterior to because inconsistent with a co-existent or anterior purchase of Southold territory as a town. In referring to the instrument of June as a deed I use rather popular freedom than legal strictness. The deed of April was the deed relied on as the deed or conveyance by the settlers, accepted as such by all parties and shown to be such by the indorsement of Winthrop thereon fixing the amount of rent to be paid yearly to the Earl of Sterling "Made and dated 20, 8, 1641."

It will be clearly understood that I do not mean to say all the settlers were then there or that a church was organized or civil government instituted, but do mean to say that these pioneers expelled from the West did establish themselves at Southampton in June and then and there built houses for their coming associates, just as they had built before at the place of expulsion. The delay made it more imperative to hasten the settlement in Southampton. The option in the first deed covered all the island, and strictly no new deed was required, but simply an agreement of the parties on the location of the optional tract. The location naturally would be fixed by view of the parties on the spot, and acquiescence in the location by evidence in writing would not be given until after this view. While the deed of June 12 did not absolutely limit the eight miles square, except to prevent locating west of Peconic, it seems to have been made in confirmation of that in March, which was really the deed of premises undefined until the June writing defined them, probably after view thereof. The option "to sitt down" in April would not call for the locating instrument in June until the grantees had "sitt down."

The journal of John Winthrop singularly confirms the view suggested. Under date of 1640, fourth month (that is June,) it recites the purchase of land at the west end of the island; the agreement for the Indian right there; the commencement of building by ten or twelve men "with provisions;" the arrest and discharge, and then those words;

"Upon this the same men, on finding themselves too weak and having no encouragement to expect aid from the English, desisted that place and took another at the east end of the same island, and being now about forty families they proceeded to their plantation and called one Mr. Pierson, a godly learned man and a member of the church of Boston, to go with them." Consider: this contemporary witness, knowing all the history of these events, in his journal of June, 1640, speaks of this settlement by the Lynn men at the end of the island as an accomplished fact. Confirmed by circumstances and by this competent witness, the evidence of settlement in June, 1640, would seem to be conclusive. By "settlement," I mean the actual occupation of the premises conveyed or part thereof by the company of grantees or a part thereof in their name for them. In that sense, in June, 1640, the Town of Southampton was settled.

The Southold claim for priority of settlement is based on four grounds:

    I. Southold is older by purchase of the Indians.

    II. Southold is older by renting, purchase and improvement of lands.

    III. Southold is older by its union in civil government.

    IV. Southold is older by its organized church.

I. It is conceded that the settlement of both towns preceded the Indian purchase. [See "Whitaker's History," page 39.] The deed of December 13, 1640 for Southampton recites a previous payment of part consideration. A deed is not a purchase, but is evidence of a previous purchase. Conceding a purchase of Southold in August, it is not evidence of settlement prior to June, 1640, and is no conclusive evidence of purchase there anterior to the Southampton purchase.

II. It is claimed that Matthew Sunderland was settled in Southold in 1639 and that Richard Jackson's deed from Farret, dated August 15, 1640, and building a house and sale of house and land to Thomas Weatherby, mariner (and, I think, judging from location, a pilot,) by deed dated October 25, 1640 both indicate a prior settlement in Southold anterior to that in Southampton. But this deed from Farret to Jackson in August is antedated by Farret's deed for Southampton in June, and proves the priority of Southampton if it proves anything. Sunderland's settlement in Southold is a claim based upon a supposed lease of land there and payment of rent. On pages 201-2-3-4, Vol. 1, Southold Town

Records, are recorded two leases, both dated June 18, 1639, from Farret to "Matthew Sunderland Seaman, at Boston, in New England." The land leased is in Oyster Bay and on the sides of Oyster Bay Harbor, and not in Southold. One receipt is for rent of land at "Oyster Bay," the other for rent of land at "Boston Bay," possibly an error for Oyster Bay. Neither receipt nor any known receipt of the dates named shows payment of rent for land leased in Southold. In the Colonial Records, Vol. 14, old series, Vol. 3, new series, p. 500, it appears that this rent paid was for land in Oyster Bay. The leases, therefore, are affirmative evidence that Sunderland was then not in Southold, but a "seaman at Boston" locating afterwards at Southold, precisely when is uncertain. The confirmation of Farrett's conveyances by Lord Stirling, including those to Howell and others and Sunderland, purporting to be dated August 20, 1639, confirms his Oyster Bay purchases, and so far as we know nothing in Southold. This date, 1639, evidently is a mistake for 1640, made, perhaps, in copying, and is corrected by the date of deed of Farret of the 17th April. The same error in the year occurs in the deed of June 12.

III. Since the authorities of New Haven took title to the original site and territory of Southold, and it became thereby an integral part of the mother colony, of necessity its union therewith followed. But neither union nor settlement prior to June 1640, appears.

IV. The formation of the Southold Church in October antedates that of Southampton in November, 1640, about one month—the former in New Haven, the latter in Lynn.

A settlement on the soil may or may not antedate a church organized elsewhere to locate there and is inconclusive on the question.

In respect to its union with the mother colony and the formation of its church. Southold sustains her priority; in respect to actual occupation of the soil by planters, with intent to found both church and town in the name of and for the company and building, clearing, planting and preparing therefor; in respect to the ownership of a vessel to further the settlement of the projected colony and augment its numbers; in respect to the written constitution of undertakers as early as March 1640—in all these essential elements which may fairly constitute the settlement not of one or two individuals as such, but of a community, the Town of Southampton, in truth, is entitled to priority.

WOOD'S HISTORY.

Silas Wood, dating the settlement of Southold prior to that of Southampton, expressly states that the settlements of the English towns are by him dated from "their respective purchase of the natives" (p. 13.) Dating from the Indian deeds he fixes the settlement of Southold in October, and Southampton in December, 1640 (p. 10 and 13).

PRIME'S HISTORY.

Prime, assigning the priority to Southold (p. 64,) states that he dates the origin of the towns, etc., "from the time of the actual association of their respective inhabitants into a community for the exercise of civil or ecclesiastical government," *Ib.* While the tests assumed by Wood and Prime are inconsistent with each other, they are inconsistent with the acts. The constitution written in the cabin of the Mayflower and the constitution of the undertakers of Southampton preceded actual settlement, and the settlement of both Southold and Southampton antedates the Indian deeds. Wood and Prime state no attested fact contradicting the occupation, as herein claimed. The third patent of Farret, limiting the eight miles square to "grounds layed out and agreed upon," is recited in Thompson vol. 1, p. 328, and the date there omitted is given in Prime as July 7, 1640 (vid. p. 192.) The minute specification of boundaries in this deed at the west of Shinnecock, "where the Indians draw over their canoes," and at the east, "including the east line of the neck or island over against Farrett's Island," argues an acquaintance with localities probably unknown, except to settlers on the spot, and this reference in Prime makes him an unconscious and therefore more weighty witness against the statement of his history.

THOMPSON'S HISTORY.

In the first edition of Thompson he admitted the priority of Southold.

In the second edition, after more deliberation, he recites the *Journal* of Winthrop, as authority and makes no such admission, Vol. I, p. 324, and on. Hence he is a weighty witness to my prior claim of Southampton.

BAYLES' HISTORY OF SUFFOLK COUNTY.

Bayles, speaking of the expulsion from Cow Bay of the adventurers, says: "Some time during the month of June" (they) "commenced the settlement of Southampton," p. 305. Of Southold he writes: "The first settlement of this town was made in September, 1640," p. 360.

MUNSELL'S HISTORY OF SUFFOLK COUNTY.

In the very careful examination of this question by William S. Pelletreau, as impartial as careful, the results reached are that "there can no longer be any doubt that Southampton was settled in June 1640." See article Southold, p. 9. The deeds of Farret to Jackson and Jackson to Weatherly, recorded in Southold records, vol. 1, pp. 112, 113, are dated 1640 and not 1639. Pelletreau fails to find any evidence of settlement of Southold as early as June, 1640.

MOORE'S INDEX.

No more thorough or careful antiquarian of Southold is known than Charles B. Moore. He writes of Minister Young: "1640, October, organized a church at New Haven to be located at Southold."

HOLMES' ANNALS.

Holmes, writing of the expulsion, says: "The adventurers now removed to the east end of the island, where, to the number of forty families, they settled the Town of Southampton." p. 314.

HUBBARD'S *HISTORY OF NEW ENGLAND*.

Hubbard's recital after the expulsion implies an immediate removal and settlement at the east end of the island and Note 1 thereto at the foot of the page dates the settlement thus: "I, in June, 1640."

OGILBY'S HISTORY OF AMERICA.

This book was printed in London in 1671, and while living men knew the facts. On page 161 we read: "About the year 1640 by a fresh supply of people that settled in Long Island was there erected the twenty-third town called Southampton, by the Indians Agawom," which gives priority as a town in number earlier than is given to Southold, and the same priority is given in Edward Johnson's "Wonder Working Providence." See chapter XVIII of "The Planting of Long Island," and in Lechford's "Plain Dealing or News from New England," p. 101.

BRODHEAD'S HISTORY OF NEW-YORK.

This historian, reciting the expulsion, writes of it as leading "to the immediate settlement of the town of Southampton," vol. 1, p. 300.

This examination, prompted by no narrow, no illiberal, no jealous spirit, concluding in finding priority of settlement at Southampton, finds priority of union and ecclesiastical government at Southold. At the expiration of nearly two and a half centuries the organizing supremacy of Southold, the radiant genius of her great lawyers, the profound learning of her accomplished historian, the varied attainments of her efficient journalists, are undimmed. From her ample domains were carved the towns of Shelter Island and Riverhead, organized as at this day. Within these two towns flourish the free and self-sustaining institutions of church and state. Within the remaining limits of the ancient Town of Southold her organizing genius has upheld these institutions and created within herself a company for insurance, a bank for savings and two for circulation, all ministering to the prosperity of her people; all conducted with consummate wisdom and sterling honesty, all enlarging their sphere of operation on no uncertain basis. To the learning, the wisdom, the patriotism, the courtesy, the unfading honor of the old town and her sons, we pay our willing tribute with our parting word:

> *"Let foplings sneer, let fools deride.*
> *Ye heed no idle scorner-*
> *Free hands and hearts are still your pride,*
> *And duty done your honor.*
> *Ye dare to trust, for honest fame,*
> *The jury time empanels,*
> *And leave to truth each noble name*
> *That glorifies your annals."*

CHAPTER IX

CELEBRATION OF THE 250TH ANNIVERSARY OF THE FORMATION OF SOUTHOLD, L.I.

Delivered on August 27, 1890, at the age of 72

THE CONCLUDING remarks of my friend Mr. Smith allude in a most flattering manner to me, and are introductory to mine. Thereby I am in a position painful and embarrassing, because the herald's proclamation exceeds the speaker's power to accomplish, and the performance will fail to satisfy the sounding phraseology of the manifesto. The audience will please accept my disclaimer, and my honest desire to contribute to the interest of this occasion, as an apology for what I may say and fail to say.

Mr. Chairman: Speaking for the Town of Southampton to this glorious old Town of Southold, I might speak of the men here who for so long and many years have walked with the men there. I might even in my own personal experience speak of the aged men with whom I walked, with whom I talked and conferred, so that it may be said we took sweet counsel together. They have gone and we are here. But there is not time to speak of those who have here filled the ranks of social, business, and professional life, and it is fitting that I read, in order that I may condense, a few remarks which I suppose applicable to this case and this occasion.

MR. CHAIRMAN AND FRIENDS OF SOUTHOLD:

The questioner who asks whence came the volume of waters that the Hudson pours on the shores of Manhattan Island will find his answer in the far-off mountain streams that conjointly fall into that river. The student, inquiring into the origin of our system of confederated republics, will find it flowing from the early self-governed Colonies that occupied the ocean's rim, and moving west sent their cohorts from station to station until they reached the Pacific ocean.

In this majestic movement the colossal treasure of the New England Colonies is conspicuous. But their march is no more real, no more elevating, no more philanthropic than that of the early Colonies occupying Eastern Long Island. Southampton, Southold, and East Hampton, instituting government for themselves, allied early with New Haven or Connecticut, thereby became component parts of "The United Colonies of New England," and joined in the Westward march bearing the banner of Freedom. Their sons moved with the pioneers to the interior over swamp and morass, and marsh and river, up the Atlantic and down the Pacific slope of the Rocky Mountains. Their names are called in the halls of legislation, in executive positions, in judicial stations from center to circumference of these States and Territories. On whatever other questions these three Towns may differ, in their love of freedom, their devotion to the cause of representative government, their capacity to institute and perpetuate the people's rule, they agree.

As early as July, 1682, at a general training, the people of East Hampton drew up and signed a petition to Anthony Brockholst, the then Governor of New York, claiming the right of representation in a General and "Free Assembly," and that the imposition of laws and orders unauthorized by such Assembly was a deprivation "of a fundamental privilege of our English Nation." Thus, ninety years before the Declaration of Independence that town voiced substantially the principle that representation was a right of the people under the British Constitution, and taxation without it was a violation of the fundamental law. In this petition East Hampton, speaking for herself, the pioneer herald of freedom in the State, if not on the Continent, expressed the cherished convictions of the freemen of Southold and Southampton.

What elements of liberty were contained in the atmosphere of the British Constitution were wafted with the emigrants from England across the ocean to this New World. No oriental forms of obsequious servility, no betrayal of the people's rights, no surrender of freedom, disgrace the annals of these three Eastern towns. The lights that steady shine or sudden flash from the headlands of Montauk and Ponquogue and Horton's Point are no truer guides to the benighted mariner than were the aspiring souls of these three earliest English towns of the Empire State to the sorely tried men of their day.

November 1, 1683, Suffolk County, one of the ten original counties of this State, was organized, including six Towns, Brookhaven, Smithtown, and Huntington, in addition to the three easternmost. In celebrating the two hundred and fiftieth anniversary of the settlement of the Town of Southold, this day, we commemorate historic remembrances of the grandest import. We reach the mountain springs of the River of Freedom. We follow its flowing stream, commencing in 1640, less than a score of years after the Pilgrims first planted their feet on Plymouth Rock, past the wars with the Narragansetts, when brave Capt. John Youngs traversed the eastern entrance of Long Island Sound in an armed vessel of war and defended these towns from the appalling horrors of fire and murder and massacre that Ninigret, chief of the Narragansetts, sought to bear in his bloody pathway—past French and Indian wars—past the conflict on the unforgotten Heights of Abraham, where France and England wrestled for the sceptre of a Continent—past the siege and capture of Louisburg—past the unheeded protests of America against the Stamp Act—past the resounding shock of Concord and Lexington and Bunker Hill—past the ringing echoes of the famous Declaration—past the woeful day when Long Island fell before the foe, whereof the 114th anniversary occurs to-morrow—past Saratoga and Yorktown—past the glad hour of Evacuation Day—past one and a quarter centuries of Colonial vassalage—past the proud day when the corsair powers of Barbary were forced to forbear oppression and pillage and piracy—past the war of 1812, radiant with naval achievement, of our streaming meteor flag—past the war with Mexico, and best of all and more than all, thanks to the power Supreme, past the war of the Great Rebellion, down to the present promise of a union providentially restored to a consolidated strength in measure so vast as to beget the serenity of fearlessness, the assurance of peace.

The history of these old towns and this original county begun amid the beginnings of Colonial times, moves like an unceasing river's flow through all the tide of the Nation's life. Felt in its earliest pulsations, may it endure to the last heart beat of the Nation. Organized as towns and as a county generations before the Colony became a State or the States became a Nation, there is nothing of glorious sacrifice, of sublime achievement, of magnificent progress in the history of the Nation, wherein their sons were inactive or wherein their part was inglorious. In successive eras of the Nation's growth and grandeur, these old towns have contributed their best, their choicest offerings, and the Town of Southold not the tardiest of least.

As a native of East Hampton exultant in her past history, I present her congratulations to her sister Town of Southold on this anniversary in her long and bright career. As a resident of the Town of Southampton, careful for her fame, intrusted with her honor, called as her messenger, I express her sincerest regard and her profoundest interest in this celebration, and the remembrance of events so venerable for antiquity, so enduring in effects, so elevating in tenor, so transforming in power. As a delegate of the Suffolk County Historical Society, and speaking for the time as the representative of that institution and for the County, let me assure the audience that the County joins heart and hand in the memories of the day, and the unsullied history it is designed to perpetuate. Finally, as a private individual, past the allotted threescore and ten of the Psalmist, soon to hear the inevitable call, long intensely interested in the early history of these Towns and the County, let my last message to the good old Town of Southold come in petition for her welfare, her prosperity, her perpetuity, in gratitude for her unfading lustre, and let her devout aspirations ascend to the Great Father "as incense, and the lifting up of her hands as the evening sacrifice."

"Through the harsh noises of our day,
A low sweet prelude finds its way;
Through clouds of doubt and creeds of fear,
A light is breaking calm and clear.
That song of love, now low and far,
Ere long shall swell from star to star!
That light, the breaking day, which tips
The golden-spired Apocalypse."

CHAPTER X

CELEBRATION OF THE 250TH ANNIVERSARY OF THE VILLAGE AND TOWN OF SOUTHAMPTON

Delivered on June 12, 1890, at the age of 72

FRIENDS OF SOUTHAMPTON:

A N EMINENT New England logician and divine defined Truth as "the reality of things." If Truth be such in its unlimited domain, then History might be defined as the record of the Reality of past things. Born in the beginnings of time, its recording pen has written the story of age after age with augmenting minuteness and light, until it seems as if "there is nothing covered that shall not be revealed." Errors long uncorrected, mistakes long unrectified, events long misstated, characters long covered with unjust disgrace or undeserved applause; all these the impartial undimmed eye of history has seen and her voice unsparingly declared for the truth. If the myths, the errors, the mistakes, once accepted, now rejected, had been followed by a sound proportioned to the falsehoods exploded, the earth would tremble with the shock. Let us remember that history delights in certainty. The universal patented tradition of pedigree, "there were three brothers came over, one settled in Massachusetts, one in New Jersey and one on Long Island," even that elicits but an incredulous smile over the obvious illusion and the heavy strain on Long Island.

THE COMPACT FOR SETTLEMENT.

In the records of the town of Southampton is an Agreement dated March 10th, 1639, signed by some twenty persons therein proposing a settlement on Long Island. There is no known document so ancient proposing the settlement of a town on this Island by Englishmen.

To the inquiries of the Antiquarian and Historian this Instrument gives many full clear answers. It blazes with light concerning the origin, the settlers and settlement of the good old town of Southampton. It is entitled "The disposal of the vessel," because it disposed of it to Daniel How, reserving such use thereof as the contemplated colony might require, to found which it had been purchased. Yet it does more, far more than that. Framed at Lynn, Massachusetts, before the voyage began, which resulted in the removal of the Colonists with their families and goods to Southampton, it bound the signers to submit to righteous, to a fair division and improvement of the property purchased until a church was founded. It was an organic Instrument or Constitution for the Government of the future colony, as truly as that signed in the cabin of the Mayflower. The moment the colonists landed, this compact bound the settlers and never released its hold until some other authority superceded this original organic law. The organizing genius of the Anglo Saxon mind, its capacity to institute and enforce self-government, shine in letters of light in the very origin of the town, and antedate the voyage of exploration for the search and site of the future colony. Since those owning the vessel, thereby might claim exemption from the burdens of taxation, until their advances had been repaid, and dispute might arise, this instrument anticipated and limited such claim. The entire paragraph reads thus: "Forasmuch as we Edward Howell, Edmond Farrington, Edmond Needham, Daniel How, Josias Stanborough, Thomas Saire, George Welbe and Henry Walton and Thomas Halsey, Allen Bread and William Harker have disbursed four score pounds for the setting forward a plantation, and in regard we have taken upon us to transport at our own proper costs and charges all such persons as shall goe at the first voyage when those of our company that are chosen thereunto shall goe upon discovery and search and to begin and settle a plantation and furthermore in regard all such persons soe goeinge upon our account have in our vessel the freedom of half a tunne of goods a person it is thought meete that we the forenamed undertakers should not at any tyme or tymes hereafter be yable to any rates, taxes or impositions, nor be put upon any fencing, building of meeting house, erecting fortifications, building of bridges, preparing highways, or otherwise charged for any cause er reason whatsoever, during the time of our discontinuance in our intended plantation except that, in the fencing in of plantinge lots every man shall with his neighbors, fence or cause to be fenced, by the first day of April 10th wch shall be 1641."

The extract cited regarding exemption from taxes of the undertakers who were so called because they undertook to found the colony proves more, far more. It shows that some of the company chosen thereunto were to go on a first voyage "upon discovery and search and to begin and settle a plantation." Those going on that first voyage, resulting in the landing at Cow Bay and expulsion therefrom by the Dutch, were on a voyage contemplating no ending with that or any future expulsion. They were on a voyage destined to continue, until their commission "to begin and settle a plantation" had been executed. You will remember that no uncertainty, no doubt, no error can find room here. The record is positive, clear, full, unequivocal, as to the intent, purposes and continuance of the voyage. In confirmation of this original declaration of purpose the colonial Records of New-York (Vol. 2, p.p. 144-6, 150, &c.) show that eight or ten pioneers on this voyage landed at Cow Bay, built a house and were building another when expelled therefrom by the Dutch, 19th May, 1640. James Farret, agent of the Earl of Sterling, the then grantee of Long Island, had by deed, dated April 17th, 1640, intended for this company, given them a right to "sitt down" or locate anywhere on Long Island and "enjoy Eight miles square of land." By a supplemental deed from Farrett, dated June 12th, 1639, (meaning 1640) the location was fixed between Peaconeck, an Indian village at the head of the Peconic Bay, and the easternmost point of the Island "with the whole breadth of the Island from sea to sea."

The deed of July 6th, 1640, from Farret, limits the eight miles square west of Shinnecock at the Place "where the Indians draw over their canoes" and at the "East," including the Neck or Island (now North Haven) over against Farret's Island (now Shelter Island.) The deed of April conveys a right to locate. The deed of June limits the right within the expressed bounds. The deed of July finally and forever fixes the location. The voyage begun under the deed of April was intended to locate the territory conveyed and "to begin and settle a plantation." The locating deed of June after the expulsion in May implies a search and continuance of the voyage, and a location fixed between certain points, and in July defined and measured by unalterable natural monuments and bounds. To all objectors and all doubters we say this voyage begun in May was for the declared purpose of beginning and settling "a plantation."

The purpose was a continuing purpose, the voyage a continuing voyage until the chosen pioneers accomplished their mission and "began and settled a plantation." The confirming proof of compact and deeds create a presumption of settlement in June as yet unrebutted and which we submit the objector must rebut or yield his objection.

We show a cannon ball rolling down hill and that at some time it reached the foot. If time has effaced its track, if vegetation hid its course, no known obstacle intervening, the presumption that its course was continuous is irresistible, and not overcome by the objection "No one saw it go there." The May voyagers intending settlement as truly after, as before the expulsion, reached Southampton presumably in continuance of the original voyage no known obstacle intervening. It is incumbent on the objector to prove that the rolling ball stopped short of their destination and not demand of us to demonstrate that a continuing purpose continues.

If the voyage continued the settlement was in June. To prove Southampton settled by some subsequent voyage and not by this, the objector must overthrow the record and overcome all the probabilities of the case. In that day and for fifty years after, a voyage to Boston was so perilous that before sailing, the prudent landsman made his will and the pious seaman asked the prayers of the church for deliverance from danger. In 1676 Ephraim, son of this same Daniel Howe, in command of a vessel bound from Boston to New Haven, was shipwrecked and all on board including his two sons and three others perished, leaving him the sole survivor. (See Atwater's His. New Haven p. 190, and His. of Lynn, 0. 124.) Our pioneers had cleared the jutting points of Nahant and Nantasket, crossed the extended shoals of Nantucket, rounded the long Sandy Hook of Cape Cod. The Gay Head Indian may have seen their vessel enter the Vineyard Sound, evade the fearful rocks and reefs that lie North and West and South from that bold headland, steering wide from the sunken shore of No Mans Land. The gleaming eye of the Narraghansett might see them off the stormy Point Judith "high on the broken wave" and his tongue mutter malediction. In spite of sunken rock and hidden reef and jutting point, of yawning billow and muttered curse, they hold their way into and along that magnificent Sound that since has born the commerce of a continent. Does the objector insist that these men, again false to duty, voluntarily returned and encountered the perils they had overcome, when the perils before them, great as they were, might be little in comparison with those they had passed. There must be no unfair arguing by the objector from the present. The Beacon Lights that in 1890 flash warning from every point on our coast and illuminate our harbors and bays and sounds, the tolling bells that planted on our shoals tell us to sheer away from death, the lowing horn that sends its sounding signal through miles of mist and fog, not all or any of these in 1640 guided our fathers to these shores. Thus the conditions of the times, the circumstances of the case, rebut the presumption of a return voyage. And the records of the town of Southampton, earliest and first born of the English settled towns on Long Island and in the State of New-York, dissipating myth and conjecture and doubt, commencing the earliest of any town on Long Island continuing an unbroken succession of the present day demonstrate her title to priority of Settlement.

Wider reflection, ampler research and crucial controversy, confirm this title. Hence this memorable fifth semi centennial date, and this glad commemoration day.

THE SETTLEMENT ORGANIZED.

At the first the colonists occupied the rudest dwellings, the poorest among them partly or wholly underneath the surface of the earth. (See Records vol. 1 p. 79 vol. 2 p. 232 and Atwater's History New Haven p. 523). Within a few years thereafter comfortable and substantial houses were built. Edward Howell first of all the company styled *gentleman*, seems to have been the most wealthy and the Father of the Colony, (Records vol. 1 p. 40). Before the erection of a church edifice, Sabbath worship may have been held at his house as the amplest for the purpose. As early as 1645 allusion is made in the town records to a church previously built, probably in 1641 (Vol. 1 p. 37 and 38). Abraham Pierson the first minister held to the exclusive right of the church to govern, in both church and state. Adhering to this theory of government adopted by the colonies of Massachusetts and New Haven, which admitted only church members to vote or hold office, we can see why he was an ardent advocate for the union of Southampton by confederation with New Haven. Dissenting from the more liberal constitution of the colonies of Plymouth and Connecticut, he would consent to no alliance or confederation with either. On this question the minister and his flock differed, and their majority decision for union with Connecticut led to his early removal from Southampton. The antiquarian consulting the Plymouth Colony Records of acts of the Commissioners of the United Colonies of New England, might be perplexed to find, that at their meeting in Boston in September, 1643, New Haven had liberty to receive into her jurisdiction the Town of Southampton, and at a meeting of the Commissioners at Hartford in September, 1644, the same liberty was granted to the jurisdiction of Connecticut. (See Vol. IX, pp. 10 and 21.) The adverse views of pastor and people is the key to the conflicting applications and actions of the Commissioners. Going back in fancy a little less than five half centuries to some bright Sabbath morning, we might see some forty rude dwellings sheltering as many families, compactly clustered on either side of the then Southampton street. Each dwelling is fortified by enclosures of palisades, and all are guarded by a like surrounding fortification. Near the centre are both watch house and church. The rolling drumbeat of Thomas Sayre calls the worshipers, (Records, Vol. I, p. 51). Parents preceding children and servants move to the church. The deacons sit fronting the audience, who are seated according to rank and station, the men and women divided by a centre line. The soldiers with their arms are placed conveniently for defence near the door. Minister Pierson, serious, spiritual, severe, just, learned, logical, positive, presides over the assembly; with solemn air they await his utterance; with accent stern he invokes that Jehovah who thundered from Sinai. Perhaps his prayers, his exhortation, his sermon, declare his unalterable conviction concerning the foundations of human government. "The seven pillars," "wisdom hath hewn out," he interprets to mean seven men by whom authority is to be instituted and organized within the church, within it to be perpetuated forever. We know historically that the founders of Southampton resisted this narrow theory. Perhaps Henry Pierson, sometimes as positive and unyielding as the minister, Edward Howell, devout and self controlled, Thos. Cooper "the elder," Thos. Halsey, self reliant, aggressive, and others unconvinced, repel the argument. He the hammer, they the anvil from which every hammer's blow rebounded. Thus the minister of masterly logic, father of the first president of Yale college, born here during the father's ministry. (See Dexter's graduates of Yale College, p. 59,) failed to convince and carry with him his people. So failing, after some years he removed. All honor to that first band of English patriots, who in this their earliest experience, called to choose between the great principles of civil liberty and partiality for their minister, preferred principle above friendship, freedom above tyranny, the rights and manhood suffrage of the many, above government of the few, the rule of the people before the rule of the church. This resolve, made nearly five half centuries gone by, has been affirmed by a like long experience. For once the people, this people, *our* fathers, were right, and their minister, transcendently great as he truly was, was wrong.

THE EXPERIMENT SUCCESSFUL.

The colony at Southampton, remote from any other English settlement, divided by Peconic Bay from Southold and yet farther removed from the island stronghold of staunch Lion Gardiner, surrounded by wild beasts and wild Indians, set in the wilderness, was like a ship adrift on the ocean, its company uncommanded, unofficered, undisciplined, its course undetermined, its voyage undecided, its destiny unknown. Will the company select and submit to the command of the best men? Will they enforce discipline? Will they project a practical and practicable voyage? Will they steer straight for the destined port? Will they with united will man the yards, and as the elements permit or compel, spread the canvas or furl the sail? Shall they anchor in the desired haven? Or shall disunion and division leave them victims of their own folly, to founder in mid ocean?

With such anxious forebodings the friends of the Southampton colony might have watched its fortunes, waited anxiously for tidings from the lone settlement and heard with fear lest the news bring the story of disaster and distress, instead of hope and cheer. Has famine, gaunt and ghastly, thinned or exterminated their ranks? Has internal strife blotted out its victims from the face of the earth? Has imprudence and improvidence lost to them the means of sustenance and defence? Has wasting disease cruelly called them to untimely graves? Has some sleeping sentinel let in the watchful, prowling foe? Has the savage blotted out the light of civilization, the English set in his native wilds? Has the victor whoop of the Shinnecock drowned the battle cry of the Anglo Saxon? These are not only the inquiries of friends, but of the great heart of humanity, enlightened and elevated, the world over. At this distance of time, with little remnant of their surroundings but the solid earth whereon we stand, the vital air we breathe, the heaving ocean whose roar they heard, with bated breath we fancy their exposure, their solitude, their danger, and ask tidings of their well being or their doom. This colony may lose the knowledge of Jehovah and worship the unknown God. It may frown on schools and foster ignorance and vice. It may become besotted in intemperance, darkened in superstition, blind to the rights of freemen, unfaithful to human liberty, incompetent for self-government, the plaything of the demagogue, the object of scorn to the good and wise. It may transmit to future times the priceless treasures of ancestral piety, free born citizenship, enlightened intelligence, enlarged education, beneficent government, equal laws, organized industry. Unfaithful to its high mission it may blight and blast all these, and transmit to coming generations, the curse of aims, duties, privileges, possibilities, postponed, perverted, perished.

As time progressed all these questions were favorably answered. The company of settlers were brave, vigilant, intelligent, self-controlled, self-reliant, self-governed. Southampton contained within itself the powers of self-government; and more, it was capable of sending forth colonies endowed with like capacity and thus indefinitely multi-plying government by the people. It was like the first tree created by the Lord "yielding fruit after his kind, whose seed is in itself."

THE CHURCH IN 1690.

If after the lapse of the first half century from the founding of the colony we in 1690 survey the situation, there appears more commodi-ous and comfortable dwellings. The houses in the site of the town are multiplied. The old palisades, momentos of impending peril, have de-cayed and disappeared. There are flourishing outlying settlements at North Sea, Wickapogue, Water Mill, Cobb, Mecox and Sagaponack. There are scattered wigwams sheltering the dwindling remnant of the once powerful Shinnecock tribe, "at Sebonac," in the "Neck and on the Hills"; but west of that the territory of the town is an unsettled wilder-ness.

Cromwell and the commonwealth have flourished and fallen. The axe has struck off the head of the 1st King Charles. The 2d Charles, tri-fling, deceptive, dissolute, has figured on the stage. The 2d James, arbi-trary, narrow, treacherous, has fled to France before the Revolutionary storm of 1688. Mary and the Prince of Orange hold the throne of Eng-land. On a June Sabbath morning we look and find a larger and better church has replaced the second and smaller church of 1651, (Records, Vol. I, p. 90.) The Rev. Robert Fordham, minister from 1648 to 1674, ami-able, serene, spiritual, has rested from his labors. The short terms of Harriman, Fletcher and Taylor are passed. Not by drum beat, but by the bell, sent in 1693 to be recast in London, are the people called to wor-ship. Not as in early days when but a handfull responded to the call, but now in thronging numbers, from village and hamlet, in all the four quarters of the heavens, the people gather for worship. I see the bowed form, the trembling limbs, the lingering feet of Job Sayre, sole survivor of the original band of planters, move with feeble tread to the house of God. The Rev. Joseph Whiting, called from Lynn, the port of their embarkation, is minister. Learned, devout, sympathetic, he leads the worship in deep felt invocation, in solemn exposition, in yearning entreaty, in song of praise, in divine benediction. The hardy sons of the pioneers reverently listen to the voice of prayer, attend the preaching of the word, join in the song of praise. The ardent zeal, the sublime hope, the fervent faith of the fathers animate the sons. Fifty years of toil in subduing the wilderness, of battle with the wild beasts, of culture of the soil, of adventure on the sea, have not subdued the spirit, dimmed the eyes, or quenched the courage of these descendants of the band of pioneers who first founded this town. Temptation has not overcome them, unbelief has not depressed them, the world has not corrupted them, infidelity has not poisoned them. Strong arms, clear heads, brave hearts, lofty spirits here live to do honor to the memory and the name of their fathers.

THE CHURCH IN 1740, 1790, 1840.

In another half century ending in 1740 the commodius church building of 1707 stood in fair proportions. The Rev. Sylvanus White was minister, son of that Ebenezer, who was the first settled minister in Bridge-Hampton in 1695. The father was pastor there over half a century, the son here 55 years, both "faithful unto death." After another half century, a vision of the church, in 1790, would exhibit little change. The unmelodious, inartistic hymnology of 1690, has partially passed away in 1740, and in 1790 the reconstructed harmonies of Watts had expelled the barbarous verses of the former age. Although in 1790 there was no settled minister, some supply often officiated. The lifted curtain of an hundred and fifty years would show an audience large, devout, intelligent, clad in homespun, starr'd with revolutionary soldiers. We hear the pitch pipe's sound floating clear the keynote over gallery and aisle. We hear the hymn loved of the fathers, then so often, now so seldom sung:

> *"Lord, in the morning Thou shalt hear*
> *My voice ascending high,*
> *To Thee will I direct my prayer,*
> *To Thee lift up mine eye.*

The church of 1840 is more the subject of memory than of history. Yet justice demands mention of the then minister, Hugh N. Wilson, D.D., who filled the pulpit, with emphasis on the word *filled*. His profound learning, powerful logic, mellow wit, strong faith, have made an impression, indelible upon his people.

THE TOWN HAS INTIMATE RELATIONS WITH NEW ENGLAND.

The relations of the settlers with the Indians were generally peaceful. Both Pequots and Narraghansetts had invaded the tribes residing on the East End of Long Island, and at times extorted the payment of a tribute.To them the coming of the whites gave promise of an alliance that might shield the Island tribes, from the galling yoke and tributary burden, of Pequot or Narraghansett oppression. Hence in the deed of 13th December, 1640, the provision that the grantees, "the above named English shall defend us, the said Indians (*grantors*) from the unjust violence of whatever Indians shall illegally assail us." (*Records,* Vol. I, p. 13.) But the Indian was a barbarian, fickle, proud, selfish, resentful, subtle, wily, scheming, of uncertain temper when left to himself. Both Pequot and Narraghansett intrigued and conspired with the Island tribes to provoke war with the English.Thus the Shinnecocks, from fear of the tribes on the continent to which they were tributary, and suspicion of the English, whose power they dreaded, were as a magazine which the smallest spark might kindle to explosion. Each party were carefully watching the other. Hence the order on the records of January 21st, 1642, for training, and of October 9th, 1642, for a nightly watch. (*Records,* Vol. I, pp. 26, 27.)

In May 1645, probably influenced by Poggatacut, Sachem of Shelter Island, then the royal sachem, he, the sachems of Montauk, of Shinnecock, and Corchaug, offered their services as against the English to the Dutch.

The order of October 29th, 1645, as to bearing arms to the meeting house on the Lord's Day, directs that "the one side of the town shall bear armes the next Lord's daye and the other side of the town shall bear armes the next Lord's daye," &c. (See *Records,* Vol. I, p. 38.) The order of November 18th, 1644, enjoins those that bear armes "shall have a sufficient coslet of clabboard or other wood in continual readiness." (Vol. I, p. 34.) The word "coslet" is evidently a misspelling of corselet, denoting a breastplate or like defence against arrows. By order of May 67th, 1647, *all* were summoned to bear arms on the Sabbath.

The order of October 8th, 1650, enjoining the frequent training of soldiers and choice of officers, shows the sense of impending peril. (*Ib.* p. 67.) The direction in 1653 for distribution of powder and shot, again indicates the presence of danger. (*Ib.* p. 94.) In 1657 the town had been assailed and the assault repelled.The houses of Thomas Goldsmith and Mrs. Howell were burned. (*Ib.* p. 118.) The contribution to Goldsmith on account of this loss and "the fire money" named in the deed of John Ogden, refer to the tax levied on the Shinnecock tribe, to compensate the inhabitants for their loss. (*Ib.* pp. 65, 167.)

In 1655, at the meeting of the Commissioners of the United Colonies of New England, at New Haven, Capt.Topping, of Southampton, and John Young, of Southold, appeared with letters, &c., and urgently asked for powder and shot and aid, against Ninigret and the Narraghansetts. (See Plymouth Colony Records, Vol. X, p. 149.) The murder, by Indians, at Southampton, was incited, if not perpetrated, rather by Narraghansett than Shinnecock malice. (*Ib.* p. 98.)

The commission to Major Mason to go to Southampton with 19 men, &c., is dated May 15, 1657. (See Conn. Colonial Records, Vol. I, p. 299.) The vote of this town of 10£ to Major Mason, March 16, 1857, "given him as a gratuity," evidently relates to the hostilities of this period and the desired aid of this old Indian fighter. (See Records, Vol. I, p. 119.) Southampton and the neighboring towns of Southold and East-Hampton were all within the Narraghansett scheme of universal extermination of the whites, and devoted to destruction. Lion Gardiner, hero of Saybrook Fort, first English planter resident of the state of New-York, and Wyandanch, great sachem of Montauk, and finally of the whole Island, were fast friends to each other and to the whites. It is not improbable that their aid alone saved these towns from destruction. The blood of the sachem has long been extinct. To the many descendants of the honored Island Pioneer, we express our tribute of grateful remembrance. Gardiner may have approved and controlled the choice of site for settlement. His prior residence, knowledge of the country and Indians, and friendship with Wyandanch, would impel the locating company to consult him. The eastern shore of North Haven runs southerly in a line almost straight to the foot of Division street in Sag-Harbor, and thence to the ocean, marking, substantially, the dividing line of the towns of East and Southampton, and of the Montauk and Shinnecock tribes. If the friendship of the Indians could be attained, their hostility appeased or repelled, Gardiner would probably know. He knew that the waters, rolling without and within Southampton swarmed with fish, that her forests abounded in game, that flocks of fowl hovered in the air, that her magnificent ocean plain was unsurpassed for the production of corn and its life-giving summer breeze, that the outlook from the cliffs and headlands of her northern shore over her majestic Peconic Bay, was inimitable, and knowing would command.

THE TOWN HAS INTIMATE RELATIONS WITH NEW ENGLAND.

In the enterprise of colonizing Long Island, the aspiring minds of New England men engaged with zeal. How the Captain of the vessel was a freeman in Lynn as early as 1636, and in 1638 Lieutenant of the artillery company. Edward Howell was a freeman in Boston, who removed to Lynn and owned five hundred acres of land there. In the order of the General Court of 22 October, 1644, there is reference to the ten acre lot of Mr. Winthrop, and eight acres which was appointed unto Mr. Cole, of Hartford. (Vol. I, p. 33.) Winthrop was the referee chosen in the first Farrett deed to fix the rent. James Hampton was from Salem. (*Ib.* p. 130.) Appeals to the General Court at Hartford, were frequent. (*Ib.* pp. 83, 84, 122, &c.) Delegates from this town went regularly to the General Court at Connecticut. (*Ib.* pp. 119, Vol. II, p. 22.) Soldiers as Major Mason defended this town—soldiers from this town went to the Main. (Vol. I, p. 103.) Ministers from New England preached here. The like conditions, the like faith, similar purposes, pursuits, perils, thoughts, aspirations, predominated here as there. First of all and over all, was the same religious creed. Second and only second to that, was the like desire of great souls for political freedom in larger degree.

PURITAN THEORY OF GOVERNMENT.

Persecution confirms, consolidates and strengthens the persecuted. All history shows that it defeats itself. The persecution of the Puritans in England is no exception. Organized for mutual help, they fled to Holland, to Plymouth and elsewhere. Disowning all priestly authority they chose their minister from their own numbers and at will they deposed him. The church was one of equals, holding all powers within itself; a pure democracy. The duty of bearing one another's burdens, of mutual aid, of universal love, was of universal obligation. This theory, as they believed, derived and derivable from the Decalogue and the precepts of the Gospel, constituted every church an organic body, vitalized, perpetuated, controlled within itself. The logic of this theory of church organism and church constitution led to the like theory of civil government. Who could not see, that if within the church itself, independent of Priest or Hierarch or Ecclesiastical denomination, by the equal suffrage of her members, ministers could be chosen, government instituted, order established, organic life born and perpetuated; so in the colony or town, the suffrage of the people could organize government, create order, elect magistrates, enact laws. If within the church and by its suffrages power ecclesiastical was derived, the like power in the state from the suffrage of the community was derivable. The eagle eye of Elizabeth, the learned instincts of the 1st James, the presentiments of the 2d James and both the Charles' had discerned danger to the throne in the prevalence of Puritanism. The antipathy was not unnatural and not unfounded. If language had not formulated the epigram, "a church without a Bishop, a state without a King," they understood the tendency of Puritanism, and arrayed their royal power to drive it from the earth as a foe to be destroyed. Puritanism was ever a foe to tyranny and despotism, a friend to the people and their rights.

TOWN MEETINGS.

The political, organizing, governing genius of the Pioneers shown conspicuously in their Town Meetings. This meeting was composed of that body of Freemen accepted as such by the voters themselves, and those only. It was required that a Freeman be 21 years of age, of "sober and peaceable conversation, orthodox in the fundamentals of religion," and have a rateable estate of the value of twenty pounds. (See Baylis' *History of New Plymouth,* Vol. I, p. 230.) The suffrage was limited but not so far as to prevent the government in the main from being the wisest expression of the popular will. Six Freemen and one Magistrate being present constituted a quorum for business. (See *Records,* Vol. I, p. 88.) This Town Meeting, called the "General Court," because in the first instance it tried important cases, above the Magistrate's jurisdiction and heard appeals from their decisions, elected all town officers, and when convened for such election, was called a "Court of Election." (See Records, Vol. I, pp. 76, 83, 86, 87, 105, 108.) Of necessity the meeting must exercise powers of the widest scope, comprising subjects domestic, foreign, civil, martial, military, commercial, religious, national, sovereign. At the commencement, in Jan. 1641, (p. 25) the powers of the General Court are defined, including power to ordain magistrates and ministers of justice, to punish offences, and execute the decrees of court; "to make and repeale laws," to levy taxes, to hear and determine all causes, whether civil or criminal, &c. (Vol. I, p. 26, &c.) But even this definition was imperfect and limited. Who could correct the errors of the Town Meeting except the free and solitary, as an orb in space, must control itself or fall. Practically it did so govern. If an unwelcome inhabitant sought to intrude himself into their community they would not accept him as such. Whom they would they accepted and whom they would they rejected. A power as sovereign as that of naturalization, they exercised without scruple or doubt, and often forbid the entrance of convicts and tramps into their community. No drone was allowed in their hive. No crime escaped its prescribed penalty. The Records abound in instances of exercise of the highest powers. By the terms of the Indian deed of 13th December, 1640, the grantees were bound to defend the grantors "from the unjust violence of whatever Indians shall illegally assail us." This league or alliance, agreed to in the purchase of the territory and made a condition, was binding or considered so on the town or Town Meeting, which made or authorized its Magistrates to make regulations, rules, treaties or ordinances as a Sovereign Power dealing with the Indians. (See *Records*, Vol. I, pp. 22, 30, 37, 89, 90, 114, &c.)

It is intensely interesting to study the workings of this town government, by Town Meeting. The meeting all the while assuming increasing power because the circumstances required it and because no power was near enough to be felt, to reverse its acts. If an inhabitant desired to sell his land to a stranger, unless allowed by the town, he could no more then invest an alien with title than he can now do so under our present law of escheat. The power of the Town Meeting over the town territory, to prevent transfer of title to a stranger or unaccepted unnaturalized inhabitant was exercised as absolutely then as now by the State. (See *Records*, Vol. I, pp. 25, 49, 78, 90, 111.) The Town Meeting, composed wholly of proprietors, regulated the improvement, fencing, pasturage and division of lands. (*Ib.* pp. 34, 38, 42, 76, 77, 78, 79, 84, 85, 91, 98, 115, 129), imposed taxes, (*Ib.* pp. 39, 44, 118), directed the laying out of highways and labor thereon, the building and repair of bridges and sidewalks, (*Ib.* pp. 24, 53, 103, 114, Vol. II, p. 110.) It elected delegates to the General Court of Connecticut, (*Ib.* p. 119), it provided for the settlement of estates of persons deceased, (*Ib.* pp. 64, 65, 95, 109), it provided property inducements for the settlement of mechanics and ministers, (*Ib.* pp. 81, 84, 102,) it ordered a prison built, (*Ib.* p. 37), it voted a bounty for the destruction of wolves and wild cats, (*Ib.* pp. 31, 85, 185), it commanded aid to be given to the miller to obtain a fall of water, (*Ib.* pp. 78, 94), it regulated trade with the Indians, (*Ib.* pp. 22, 30, 60, 89, 90, 114), it controlled the whaling enterprise, (*Ib.* pp. 23, 91), it prescribed a watch and ordered a watch house built, (*Ib.* pp. 89, 164.)

These are but a few cases of the exercise of power by Town Meeting, and could be almost indefinitely multiplied. At an early day our ancestors had acquired experience in the method of conducting this meeting. In the Record of July 7, 1645, we read this: "It is ordered for the prevention of disorder in the Court that no person whatsoever, except the magistrate or magistrates, shall speak in any business which concerns the General Court unless he be *uncovered* during the tyme of his speech. And not to move or speak to any other matter until the former matter be ended. And that there be noe private agitation by any particular person to prevent the proceedings or issueing of any matters. And whoso shall make default shall be lyable to paye sixe pence and the constable shall distress upon the goods of the offender and to present the said fines to the next General Court."

Absence from the Town Meeting, or neglect to vote when there or refusal to accept office were punishable by a fine. (*Ib.* pp. 23, 30, 76, 103, etc.) That government by the people might not fail, attendance at Town Meeting, voting there, and acceptance and service by an elected officer, were compulsory, neglect finable. The fathers permitted no shirking of duty. Their system was *thorough*. Let it not be thought that order cost no struggle. Sometimes the authority of magistrates and the town itself was ridiculed and defied. Even the most respected pioneers would be overcome by wrath to unjust expression. But if Thomas Halsey "obstinately hindered the time of the Court," if Henry Pierson, venerated name! threatened if any man should strike his dog "he would knock him down," if Arthur Bostic challenged Mr. Stanborough "to fight," and if Mr. Stanborough unlawfully "rescued a distress," the strong hand of the magistrates, and Town Meeting as a General Court, censured and fined the transgressor. The heavy arm of Justice, embodied in Town Meeting, fortified by public sentiment, irresistible by public approval, compelled the delinquent to submit to the sentence, and acknowledge his fault or pay the fine. All resistance to the will of the people was overcome. All individual defiance and disorder was crushed out. (*Ib.* pp. 39, 401.) The Town Meeting moved with the momentum of the many and put down private and personal opposition. Fist law and shot gun law and chaos failed. Town Meeting reigned. Some of the most strong-willed, pugnacious, combative souls that first trod this continent, tried their individual strength against the collected will of the town. The beating wave no more moves the unshaken rock, than the individual wave of wrath moved the Town Meeting from its fixed position. The authority of government by the people for their good stood like a pyramid on its base, unmoved by all individual assault. The fiery chieftain whose pugnacity was a proverb in 1656, "for his unreverent carriage toward the magistrates, contrary to the order, was adjuged to be banished out of the town, and he is to have a week's liberty to prepare himself to depart," &c. (*Ib.* p. 112.)

After this signal failure to resist or subvert the authority of the Town meeting, resulting in the inexorable sentence of banishment, who could hope to overthrow an authority so firm, so invulnerable. If the Bull Rider of Smithtown failed to batter down the citadel of town authority, no one giant hand could do more. The American boy who remembers the Town Meeting of three and four score years gone by, its material and appetizing attractions, its athletic sports, the collected might of the yeomanry, the exalted wisdom and dread majesty of the moderator, the imposing array of strength and numbers, the overcoming vote of the majority, the shrinking, dwindling vote of the minority; to him, the colossal proportions of Town Meeting as a vital political force in the public history of the town, is not fancied or unreal. The French writer DeToqueville, some half century since, philosophizing concerning this subject, saw Town Meeting from the undiscoverable standpoint of France. Bryce, the late English writer on the American commonwealth, looking from the standpoint of the British Isles, saw through the splendors of the British throne that original foundation political institution known as Town meeting, and declared it "has been the most perfect school of self government in any modern country." (Vol. II, p. 276.) To the born American, undazzled by the splendors of the throne, unaffected by the electric light of rank, living

> *"Where none kneel save when to Heaven they pray,*
> *Nor even then unless in their own way."*

To him, the Town Meeting is the bed rock of American freedom, on which her free institutions and the fair temple of her liberties were reared. Child of the people ! born in the wilderness, cradled in peril, trained in hardship, surviving the challenge of disorder, the seductions of wealth, the arts of the demagogue, the frown of royalty, the cynic's sneer; may it live forever ! the beneficent gift of America to the unborn millions of every age, of every clime.

SOUTHAMPTON CONFEDERATES
WITH CONNECTICUT.

May 29th, 1643 the colonies of Massachusetts, Plymouth, Connecticut and New Haven, with the plantations in combination with them, adopted Articles of Confederation for their mutual welfare and protection. (Palfrey's *History of New England,* Vol. I, p. 262, &c. Atwater's *History of New Haven,* pp. 181-2.)

"March 7th, 1643-4, it was voted and consented unto by the General Court that the town of Southampton shall enter into combination with the jurisdiction of Connecticut." (*Records,* Vol. I, p. 31.) The order of Town Meeting of June 29th, 1657, fixes the date when the town was received into the combination, as "May 30th, 1645," (*Ib.* p. 136.) The combination with Connecticut made Southampton not only a member of the colony of Connecticut but also a member of the general confederation of the four colonies. Thereby, while Southampton was bound to aid in defending Connecticut and the whole confederacy, they were pledged, with all their power, to aid in her defence. (Palfrey's *History of New England,* Vol. I, p. 263, &c. Atwater's *History of New Haven,* pp. 181-2. Howell's *History of Southampton,* p. 5.) The confederation was called "The United Colonies of New England." It was represented and spoke by two commissioners chosen from each colony. The internal affairs of each town and colony were left to their control. Question of "offence and defence, mutual advice and succor upon all just occasions, both for preserving and propagating the truth and welfare," were controlled by Commissioners representing the colonies so leagued and confederated. Except "the exigency constrained", one colony might not engage in war "without the consent of all." Except "by consent of all," no two members shall be united in one and no new members shall be received. (*Ib.*) The appointment of men, money and supplies for war, were to be assessed on the respective colonies in proportion to the male population, "between the ages of sixteen and sixty," and "the spoils of war were to be distributed to the several colonies on the same principle." The concurrence of six commissioners controlled, and failing this, the questions being referred to the general courts of the several colonies, the concurrence of them all was binding. The Commissioners were to meet yearly on the first Thursday in September, and oftener if occasion required, at places prescribed. The choice of a President, the general policy of proceedings toward Indians, the return of fugitives from justice or service, the remedy for breach of the alliance by an offending colony—all these subjects were included in and provided for in the Articles of Alliance and Confederation (*Ib.*) Thus early on American soil, was instituted this first of all confederacies of the colonies, so complete in its anticipation of contingencies, in its conception of surroundings, in its adaptation to circumstances, that it endured assaults, external and internal, for twenty years, until the invasion and subjection of New Netherlands by the English, and the enforced rule of Royal Governors under the then Duke of York, in 1664, afterwards King James the 2d. This league so complete in its extent, so just in its provisions, so wise in its principles, so practical in its policy, comprised in its scope the democracy of the Town Meeting, the representation of Towns in the Colonial Assembly, (called also the General Court,) the representation of the united colonies in the body of Commissioners. Seemingly complex, it was in reality simple. Its machinery was well fitted for the work it had to do.

In all local and town affairs the practical knowledge of the yeomanry of the town, assembled in Town Meeting, was superior to that of any non-resident, however wise. They knew their wants, their grievances, their interests, their ability and inability, their circumstances, and could best devise measures for relief or redress. The delegates of the towns composing the colony assembled as its legislature and highest court, representing the whole and every part of the colony, could wisely legislate and decide for all. The Commissioners of the united colonies representing their union and clothed with powers that covered and only covered subjects of general concern, affecting the welfare and safety of all the so united colonies, could best legislate for the union. It is needless that I stop here to show that this machinery of government by towns, by colonies, by confederated states foreshadowed what was to come. The thought of the hearer outstrips the words of the speaker. Before the recital ends comes the flashing conviction that in the early history of these colonies the free institutions of this wonderful nation of the United States was born. The self-constituted government of Southampton and other early settlements in their Town Meetings or general courts was an ancestral immunity transmitted to posterity out of which the modern Town Meeting was born.

The delegates from all the towns in a colony assembled as its Legislature, to ordain and enact laws for the general good, and called the General Court of the colony, foreshadowed the state governments which were born of the colonies. The confederation and union of the four colonies of New England, including in the colony of Connecticut the towns of Southampton, East-Hampton, and afterwards Huntington and Setauket, predicted the coming union of the colonies and of the Independent States. By the laws of growth, by organic development, in modern scientific terminology by *evolution*, this transfiguration must transpire. The Provincial Congress must grow out of the Colonial Assembly. The Continental Congress and Confederation must grow out of the root of the New England confederacy and union. By a logic and a law, in politics as universal as simple, as immutable, as eternal, as the law of attraction, the one must precede and produce the other. At the time of this confederacy in the New England colonies, of which our town was part and parcel, the civil war was raging in England. The Long Parliament was sitting. The first Charles was claiming as regal the same power which Parliament, under the British constitution, claimed as pre-eminently its own. The conflict between these two involved all the strength and energies of old England. New England unhelped, uncared for, unnoticed, must defend, protect, preserve herself, or perish. Thus in 1643, out of the necessities of the case, the impending peril so near, the far off absence and constrained neglect of old England, was born the union of the New England colonies.

REPRESENTATION.

Writers upon Representative and Confederated Government have sought by the analogies of the Achaean League, of the Grecian and Roman Republics, of the Swiss Cantons, of the Dutch Republic, of the Iroquois or six Indian allied nations, of Ecclesiastical and Church government, to derive therefrom the origin of the Government of these United States. Theories these, *all* far fetched. Our magnificent constellation of republics and their union were born upon our own soil, nurtured by successive generations of freemen, evolved from colonial childhood and *"The United Colonies of New England."*

CAUSATION.

At the time of the Union the colony of Plymouth contained eight towns; Massachusetts thirty; Connecticut, including Saybrook and Southampton, six; and New Haven, including Southold, five. (Palfrey's *History of New England,* p. 275.) Forty-nine organized democracies, represented in four colonial assemblies, and all in the Commissioners delegated to act for the union, the seed corn which planted grew from ocean to ocean. It is improbable that the early colonists had any thought of an independent republic in voyaging over the Atlantic, or in their exile on its western shore. To Winthrop, compeer of our fathers, came the vision of a renovated England in America, enlightened, purified, spiritualized, dominated by loftier principles, aiming at higher results, moving, towards a higher destiny. (*Ib.* p. 110.) Independence, as an object attainable, and to be attained, came as the hard alternative of degradation and servility, postponed until forced to command regard. Sudden as the lightning flash it broke out of the clouds and storm of war, and the whole electric air of the continent felt its flame of fire. Yet sudden, and startling, and surprising, as was the battle cry of Independence, who can doubt that the long school of hardship, the long experience of Freemen in the government of their towns, the early establishment and maintainance of churches and schools, the training of their militia, the constant watch and guard against the savage, the

conflict with the Pequot, and Narraghansett, and Mohawk, the wars
with France and Spain, the siege and capture of Quebec and Louis-
burgh, the temerity and defeat of Braddock, the masterly retreat of the
young Provincial Washington; the whole antecedent history of the settlements on the western shores of the Atlantic, from Plymouth Rock,
for over three half centuries, was but an augmenting stream of causa-
tion that burst all barriers of thrones or dynasties, cast away all obstacles of Kings or Nobles, called for the reign of the people and that only.
Even Franklin and other great souls, laboring earnestly for the redress
of wrongs, like the prophets of old, unknowing the meaning of the revelations made to them, awoke as from the profound sleep of submission to the battle call for Independence.

THE REVOLUTIONARY WAR.

The wave of the Revolution found the Town of Southampton comparatively populous. The census of 1776 showing 1,434 people residing
east of the Watermill, and 1,358 west thereof. All were animated by the
burning spirit of Patriotism. All who were liable to military duty were
enrolled, officered, organized, armed. The second regiment of Suffolk
County counted nine companies of 760 officers and men, commanded
by David Mulford, of East-Hampton, Colonel, and Jonathan Hedges, of
Bridge-Hampton, Lieutenant Colonel. East-Hampton furnished two
companies, Bridge-Hampton two, Sag-Harbor and Bridge-Hampton
jointly two, and Southampton three. In addition to this the regiment of
minute men commanded by Col. Josiah Smith, of Moriches, called from
Southampton one company commanded by Capt. Zephaniah Rogers,
numbering 61 officers and men, and another from Bridge-Hampton
numbering 59 officers and men. Of these selected minute men, Elias
Pierson, Corporal in Capt. Rogers' company, stood 6 feet 6 inches high,
tallest of the tall. The relative importance of the county of Suffolk and
the early history of its towns is shown by many facts, and briefly thus,
"581 quota of Suffolk, 200 of Queens, 175 of Kings, 58 men to reinforce
the Continental army at New-York, June 7th, '76." (See Onderdonk's
Revolutionary incidents of Suffolk and Kings counties, p. 27.) The latest
research shows that the whole force of Eastern Long Island was engaged in the disastrous battle named from the Island whereon it was
fought. Thereafter very many joined the Continental army, and the defence of the people and stock on Long Island required the presence
there of every available man. The subsequent military occupation of
the Island by the British, broke up the regiments organized or organiz-

ing by the Americans there. Time fails to tell the story of that armed occupation. Who can photograph the depression of defeat, the confusion of the fleeing, the consternation of the defenceless, the quartering of hostile troops, the extorting of supplies by the British, the destruction of supplies by Americans, each grasping to starve the other and thereby starving the people, plundering by the lawless of both, insults of the brutal, the provoking exultation of the foe, the sullen submission of the subjugated, their fears for the safety of absent friends fighting for freedom on land and sea, defeats of the American army magnified, their victories belittled, every aspiration for independence answered by the raven cry "Nevermore." If the amenities of Gen. Erskine sometimes let in a gleam of light, the barbarities of Major Cochrane soon transposed darkness for light. For seven years after the battle of Long Island her patriot people endured the blighting scourge of the conqueror, the gnawings of unsatisfied hunger, "the pinching hand of poverty," the shivering, wintry blast, the horrors of hope destroyed; seven vials of wrath poured out upon her inhabitants and her soil. Washington said that Long Island furnished him, of all places, the earliest and most correct intelligence of movements of the foe. Not until Evacuation day were the pent-up patriot passions of this people released from the hydraulic pressure of British power. No town in the old thirteen states welcomed Independence with a louder shout than Southampton.

CELEBRITIES.

Nor is this town undistinguished by men whose names have been illustrious. Is a councilor wanting in 1665? Capt. Thomas Topping of this town is chosen. Is a speaker required for the Assembly in 1694? Henry Pierson of this town is chosen. Does the great city of London in 1773 require a High Sheriff to repress disorder and execute decrees of courts? This town supplies the officer in the person of Stephen Sayre, a native born citizen, friend of Franklin, friend of freedom. Does the Empire State demand a chancellor to preside over its High Court of Equity? Nathan Sandford, a native of this town, is appointed thereto. Does the old county of Suffolk summon her selectest sons to preside over her courts? What town but Southampton can furnish in succession judges like Hugh Halsey, studious, upright, learned, or Abraham T. Rose, eloquent gifted, accomplished. For three successive Presidential campaigns the village of Bridgehampton supplied the successful candidate for election, in 1840 Gen. Abraham Rose, in 1844 Judge Hugh Halsey, in 1848 Judge Abraham T. Rose, each actually voting for the elected candidate. Does Japan seal her ports against all Christian intercourse and commerce? Mercator Cooper, master mariner, stem of the old Southampton stock, rescues from starvation and death twenty-two Japanese, and in 1845 boldly enters the prohibited port and returns them to their native land, bearing in his mission of humanity at the most head of the whaleship Manhattan, the stars and stripes, (excepting the limited Dutch traffic) the first Christian flag that floated in Japan air, the first Christian ship that entered a Japan port, the first Christian master who dare defy the nation's sentence of exclusion. What shore so desolate? what solitude so secluded? what island so remote, that the ships of Sag-Harbor have not visited? In all her long history the sons of Southampton have upheld her honor, in the sphere of adventure, of music, of painting, of the arts, of learning, of legislation, of the legal, the medical, the ministerial professions.

THE PURITANS' MERITS.

Let it not be said that the theme is hackneyed, that language has acquitted itself in proclaiming the sublime self-denial, the heroic fortitude, the Spartan courage, the devoted patriotism, the steadfast faith, the fervent piety of the Fathers, that art has paid its debt in monuments of magnificence to commemorate their virtues, that learning has meted its full measure to perpetuate their remembrance. Neither language nor learning nor art can adequately express the lofty ideal they attained; the self-consecration they made. Early in the dawn of historic light, the patriarchal characters stand out like giant profiles; masterly types of personified virtues, priest and prophet, sage and lawgiver, hero and bard, at long intervals succeed each other. It was not inappropriate that the pen of Jehovah should outline the perfected piety of Enoch, the persevering obedience of Noah, the unreserving faith of Abraham, the unfaltering trust of Job, the great loving heart of Joseph, the lofty patriotism of Moses, the resistless valor of Joshua, the superhuman strength of Sampson, the strategy and songs of David.

These great spirits gave for their posterity and for the race their utmost in word, in deed and life. The long self-denial, the unfailing patience, the undoubting faith, the stern justice, the high resolve, the pure patriotism of our fathers, seem allied to the greatest and first-born of the sons of earth. No mere human words, no monuments of art, no expression of human learning, however exalted and however graceful, will exhaust the subject or overpay the debt humanity owes to the founders of the infant colonies of this transcendently great, free and happy nation. Let music sing its highest harmonies, let eloquence attain its loftiest utterance, let painting portray its most exquisite lines, let statuary unfold its grandest conception, let monumental art lend its perfected ideal, let poetry breathe its selectest sentiment, let piety consecrate her purest offering, and then, ah, then, the light that shines from the Pilgrim's tomb, the song his soaring spirit sings, the sentiment his life made real, shall be more radiant, more elevated, more pure, then all expression of art, of music, of eloquence. Since the founders of this town first landed on its shores, eight generations have come and gone. The innocence of infancy, the joy of youth, the vigor of maturity, the decay of strength, the decrepitude of age, the inevitable end, have chased each other. On this fleeting hour, and on us now living, has devolved the sacred duty of celebrating this day, and commemorating the memory, the history, the solid worth of our ancestors. Standing over the crumbling consecrated dust of eight generations who have followed them, as wave follows wave, the solemnities of the occasion are severe. To the ears of their dying came the ocean's moan; with the ebbing of its tides their lives went out; over their burial place sounds its unceasing requiem roar. Inheriting their names, receiving the fruit of their toils, depositors of their fame, entrusted with their free institutions, children of their affection, guardians of their graves, let us cherish their achievements; let us treasure their traditions; let us preserve their principles; let us honor their memory; let us transmit, unsullied and unimpaired, our bright inheritance to succeeding generations.

One of our own untiring antiquarians has recorded the tradition, that at the first landing of the Pioneers one of the number, a woman, said: "For conscience sake, I'm on dry land once more!" This expression of a past disquiet, of a present gratification, is impressed upon the spot, which from that day to this has borne the name of "Conscience Point." Name not inappropriate and not unknown to the Argonauts of Southampton. For "conscience sake" their fatherland is forsaken. For "conscience sake" they crossed the stormy ocean. For "conscience sake" they suffered and they toiled. In all her long career, inscribed on the banner that floated over Southampton, that streamed in her pure air, that signified her ruling motive, that impelled her to action, was written her watchword, "Conscience." No insignia of rank, no emblazoning of heraldry, no bearings armorial, no symbol of command, so appropriate and so true. Till time shall end, till the earth shall be dissolved, till "the elements shall melt with fervent heat," let her watchword be unchanged. Aye! in that grand concurrence of the Nations called by the Archangel's trump to hear the eternal equities, inscribed on her banner, may there be nothing more unworthy than her own glorious countersign, "Conscience."

As if responding to the utterance of the mighty shades of the dead, let us live as they lived, let us look as they long looked for the coming triumphant march of their principles. Burdened with the weight of years, your speaker in this public utterance, (possibly his last), cannot forget the generations vanished, the mutability, the mortality of all humanity.

> *"A few more storms shall beat*
> *On this wild rocky shore,*
> *And we shall be where storms shall cease,*
> *And surges swell no more."*

Nor will we forget the cheering promise our history portends. Rescued from all perils, triumphant over all foes, undivided by all differences, you, with me, will look forward to advancement of the nations, to the progress of humanity, the elevation of mankind; you with me will say:—

> *"Hail! to the coming singers!*
> *Hail! to the brave light bringers!*
> *Forward I reach and share*
> *All that they sing and dare.*
> *The airs of heaven blow o'er me:*
> *A glory shines before me*
> *Of what mankind shall be,*
> *Pure, generous, brave and free.*
> *A dream of man, and woman*
> *Diviner, but still human,*
> *Solving the riddle old,*
> *Shaping the age of gold!*
> *The love of God and neighbor:*
> *An equal-handed labor;*
> *The richer life where beauty*
> *Walks hand in hand with duty.*
> *Ring, bells in unreared steeples,*
> *The joy of unborn peoples!*
> *Sound, trumpets far off blown;*
> *Your triumph is my own!*
> *I feel the earth move sunward,*
> *I join the great march onward,*
> *And take by faith while living,*
> *My freehold of thanksgiving."*

The natives of the east end of Long Island made frequent visits to New Amsterdam, Hartford, and sometimes as far north as Boston. On the 24th of May, 1645, the Sachem of Shinnecock, Wittaneymen, with forty armed Indians, appeared before the Director and Council of New Netherland, at Fort Amsterdam, Manhattan Island, and offered their services. Therefore he and his Indians were permitted to embark in one of the Company's vessels and were sent up the Hudson river to discover the Indians who were then at war with the Dutch. Having discovered their whereabouts, he was to attack them, and to return, when he would be rewarded as he deserved. This duty he performed, and five days later brought in the head and hands of one of the enemy. Wittanymen is the Sachem, called in the East-Hampton deed of 1648, Nowedinah—the "seeker." It is probable that he derived this latter title from the above fact, that he was to spy and to seek out the enemies of the Dutch, who were Indians living about Esopus Creek. The Indians frequently changed their names from similar happenings in their lives. On the same day, (May 29th, 1645) having shown what he could do, Wittanymen again appeared before the Council of New Netherland, declaring to be empowered by his three brothers, to wit: Rochbouw, the greatest Sachem of Ahaquatuwamuck (Shelter Island and parts adjacent), Momoweta, Sachem of Corchaug, and Wyandanch, Sachem of Montauk, and stated in his own name, as well as in that of his brothers that they had taken under their protection the villages named Unkechaug (on Mastic Neck, Brookhaven,) Setauket, Secatogue, (Neck at Islip,) Nissequogue (a locality on the river of the same name,) at which place the Mattinecocks then resided, and Rockaway, and requested to walk in friendship. The Council promised them peace and protection as long as they and the villages named, remained in their duty. These 47 armed Indians, were probably not all from the Shinnecock tribe, but were culled from the bands ruled by the four brothers. (*Col. His. N.Y.* Vol. XIV, p. 60.)

The year previous (1644) the brothers, with Yoco or Rockouw, at their head appeared before the Commissioners of the United Colonies of New England at Hartford, on the same errand, and asked for a certificate of protection, which was given them. (*Plymouth Col. Records,* Vol. IX, p. 18.)

That both the Dutch and English considered it policy to propitiate the Indians of Long Island in every way that lay in their power, is amply proven by many of the early records. In 1647 it came to the notice of the Council of New Netherland that the Sachem of Massapeag in what is now South Oyster Bay township, had excited, by gifts, some Indians to war against the Dutch and English, and that they were resolved to destroy the English at Hempstead, while they were in their fields harvesting, to which plot the chief of Corchaug (Southold town), Momoweta and his brothers at Montauk, Shinnecock and Shelter Island had agreed. Although the Dutch considered this an idle report of the English, they believed it to be of sufficient importance to send Sec'y Van Tienhoven, who understood the Indian language, in a sloop to the east end of Long Island to enquire of the chief Momoweta of Corchaug, whether the report be true or not, and to present the chief and his brothers with three cloth coats and some trifles. This record from the Dutch archives seems strange when we consider that at this period harmony did not prevail between the nations and the settlers. At this time the Shinnecock Sachem and probably most of the tribe were residing on the north shore at or near Sag Harbor. (*Col. His. N.Y.* Vol. XIV, p. 79.) Even as late as 1675 Gov. Andros would not permit the Indians of Rockaway, Unkechaug and parts adjacent to assemble at Secatogue (West Islip) for a Kintecoy, "to sing and to dance," and directed the constable of Huntington to take away their arms and to order the Sachems to proceed to New-York to meet the Governor. (Col. Hist. N.Y. Vol. XIV, p. 709.)

Complaints were frequently made against the Dutch, who at that period, as well as to-day, were born traders, eager and greedy, for the skins, wampum and other commodities that were produced by the red men and procured by easy barter. This greed often led them into waters not under their jurisdiction, thereby causing trouble and annoyance to the English settlers who found their red neighbors in possession of implements of war, obtained in some way unknown to them, thus becoming a constant source of worry and anxiety to the simple tillers of the soil. The following is the result of a complaint from the town of Southampton against Govert Loockmans, of the sloop Good Hope; he is often mentioned in the Dutch records. On Sept. 28th, 1648, two sailors appeared before Cornelis Van Tienhoven, the Secretary of New Netherland, and declared it to be true that they had been in the months of October, November, 1647, with Govert Loockmans in his bark along the coast from New Amsterdam, Pehehetock, (Peconic) Crommegouw, (Gardiner's Bay) and New Haven, during which voyage they did not see, nor even know that Loockmans himself, nor any of his crew, had directly or indirectly, traded or bartered with the Indians, there or elsewhere, any powder, lead or guns, except that he made a present of a pound of powder to the Chief Rochbouw in Gardiner's Bay, and bought two geese from him, and half a deer at Pahetoc,

(Peconic or Pehik-konuk, probably Indian Island, Riverhead town). It means a "small plantation or village"), with powder without having given or exchanged anything else.—(*Colonial His. N.Y.* Vol. XIV, p. 94.)

The complaint is referred to in a letter from Gov. Eaton, of New Haven, to Gov. Stuyvesant, at New Amsterdam, dated May 31st, 1648, as follows:

"Janua. the 3d, 1647, a complaint was brought from the English att Southampton, that Govert Lockoman had bynne latelie trading with the Indians of those ptes, who reported that after he had sould them some coates he declared that if they would buye more, with everie coate hee would give a pound of powder, which pcured him a quicke markett and soe furnishes the Indians with powder that they could sell to the English; and the same Indian further testified that Govert wisth them to cutt of the English and the Dutch (to such a worke) would furnish them with peeces, powder and shott enough, wch soe provokes the Engl. at Southampton, that had they order they would have staide Govert and his vessell."—New Haven, *Col. Records,* Vol. I, Appendix p. 524.

CHAPTER XI

EARLY SAG-HARBOR

—◦◦◦—

Delivered on February 4, 1896, at the age of 78

PRELUDE.

THE FORERUNNER spoke of him who should come after as one "whose fan is in his hand, and he will thoroughly purge his floor and gather the wheat into his garner, but he will burn the chaff with fire unquenchable." Reverently, and not unaptly, History might be so personified, as a being whose fan is in his hand to drive away the chaff of error, of misconception, of falsehood, and burn it with unquenchable fire and gathering the wheat into an unperishable garner. Without such exalted views of the office of History, the annals of the towns and villages of our free land cannot be properly told.

The Indian name of that part of Sag-Harbor lying in the part of East-Hampton was Wegwaganuck, or Wigwagonock.

Your fellow citizen, Wm. Wallace Tooker, is a lifelong student of the Indian tribes of this Continent and their language, and is an authority on the subject. He locates their village on the North Shore below Sleight's Hill, or Fort Hill, where ancient shell heaps denote an Indian Settlement. He derives the name from Wequae-adn-auke, which signifies "land or place at the end of the hill."

As descriptive of the location, we perceive the name to be peculiarly appropriate and accordant with Indian custom. The abundance of fish and clams in the vicinity would naturally attract Indian dwellers, and tradition says their wigwams stood in the neighborhood of Round

178

Pond at the west, long after the towns of East-Hampton and Southampton were settled, for over half a century. The Indians were migratory rovers, and this vicinity would be a convenient stopping station between the Montauk and Manhanset tribe at Shelter Island.

THE TOPOGRAPHY.

The surface of the earth in and around Sag-Harbor has undergone a change since its settlement, almost incredible. Originally the meadow swept nearly across Main Street at the junction of Main and Madison Streets, and encroached still more northerly, striking the cliff where now is the blacksmith shop of John Fordham. From that cliff Turkey Hill rose and gradually fell, until it was lost in the swamp between that and Meeting House Hill, on which now is Masonic Hall. That swamp closed Main and probably Madison Streets, in the vicinity of the residence lately of George Kiernan, formerly the Heman Bassett house. Turkey Hill was slid into the north and west side of Main Street to the depth of 4 to 6 feet, which made that passable. Meeting House Hill was moved into Main, Madison, Washington, Division and Hampton Streets, which before were all impassable.

The south side and east end of the Watch Case Factory building stand on the north edge of an old swamp. This swamp, or ravine, covered quite an extent of territory east of the Old Burying Ground, Meeting House Hill and Turkey Hill, and its waters flowed down Burke Street into the harbor.

There was a hill or ridge from the Burying Ground west, to and including the course of Main and Garden Streets. Turkey Hill, sometimes called Cliff Hill in early days, was said to be 50 or 60 feet high on the shore bluff. All the houses on the east side of Main Street were built into it. It extended just south of the corner of Main and Washington Streets.

The Cove west of Conkling's Point was deep. Vessels were there built and launched in the days of Captain William Johnson Rysam. Captain Prior, ship builder, had his shipyard there. Later on and some 50 years ago ships' ways were there.

Gull Island, reported anciently as much larger, cultivated, and used as a pasture field according to tradition, has dwindled into insignificance. The meadow, anciently much more extensive, has diminished and is disappearing.

An amusing tradition has survived the wrecks of time; in substance that Wentworth, residing on this meadow, was the last person who attempted to pasture on Gull Island. Taking them by boat, he left a couple of donkeys to pasture there. Whether the pasture was poor or the tide too high, the donkeys left and it is said reached home before their owner, familiarly known as "Pap Wentworth," did.

Anciently the tide ebbed and flowed over most of this meadow. In the early settlement of this County the meadows furnished almost the only winter feed for cattle and horses, and hence were very valuable, and allotted as soon after the settlement as possible. It seems to us singular that it was deemed the precious portion of Sag-Harbor, and all settled nearly a hundred years before the upland there.

This meadow was the place where the stocks were thrown, by some roguish person or persons, some time in the last century. Esquire Samuel L'Hommedieu, father of the late Esq. L'Hommedieu, to vindicate the outraged majesty of the Law, offered a reward for evidence to convict the offenders. But who they were remains to this day a secret undivulged.

Otter Pond was originally a sheet of fresh water, separated by a high ridge from the Cove. It derived its name from the fact that otters were anciently caught there in great numbers. Mrs. Betsy Sherman, mother of the late Luther L. Sherman, formerly lived in a house south of Otter Pond, and remembered that her father, Silas Edwards, often told her that when he was a young man, he frequently caught otters there in his seine.

In 1783 the present inlet was cut to the Cove. All the male inhabitants turned out to assist in digging it, and were rewarded, according to tradition, with a barrel of New England Rum. The object was to make this pond a fish pond. Striped Bass and other fish were formerly taken from it in abundance. In 1793, by consent of the proprietors of the Pond, the Trustees of the Town transferred their right therein to John Jermain, "with the privilege to set mills on the stream," and liberty to dig across the road that leads from Sagg to Sag-Harbor, in order to let the waters of Crooked Pond and Little Long Pond into said pond, &c. This was the grant for Major Jermain's mill.

Thick woods covered Sag-Harbor and its settlement. The boundary line between the towns of East-Hampton and Southampton is recorded in 1695, as a marked pine tree over against the eastern point of Hog Neck.

James Howell's infant son died June 4th, 1767, and was the first person whose remains were buried in the Old Burying Ground. Mrs. Abigail Price, daughter of James Howell, related this fact, and added that her mother used to cry because her babe had been buried all alone up in the woods.

At that time the woods, it is said, came down to the houses of Benjamin Price and Ephraim Fordham on Madison Street, where is the house late of William Buck, deceased. As late as 1800 woods came nearly to the Old School House on Madison Street. My early impressions recall no houses south of the Old Burying Ground, except Brister Miller's, Daniel J. Harris' and Mehetable Franklin's; say some seventy years ago.

North Haven Bridge, built some 65 years ago, in my day took the place of an old ferry, before that the usual route of travel. But practically, North Haven, and Brick Kilns, and Noyack, were suburbs of Sag-Harbor, after it ceased to be a suburb of North Haven, which was first settled.

THE ROADS.

The first road from East-Hampton to Sag-Harbor came through Pine Swamp to the North of Northwest Creek, following the landing opposite Turkey Hill, just east of where stood the shop of the late Jedediah Conkling. It ran so close to the bluff that at high tide one wagon wheel would be tilted upon on the bluff and the other depressed in the water. The road from Sagg ran from the point where Sagg and Wainscott road intersect, north of Long Pond, came out north of the house of Samuel T. Hildreth, deceased, and south of Otter Pond, passed the old Jesse Halsey house and between the Cove and Otter Pond, and skirting the Cove and west edge of the Meadow, to the landing near the old Toll Gate of the North Haven Bridge, following some part of Glover and West Water Streets.

The Bridge-Hampton Road came down along the present Brick Kilns road, and struck across just in front of the house of Samuel T. Hildreth, deceased, at Ligonee Brook. Nathan Fordham, Esq., grandfather of Nathan Y. Fordham, deceased, is reported to have given the present Brick Kiln Road from the Jesse Halsey corner and taken the old one in exchange.

The road from East-Hampton at an early day was changed so as leave North West Creek and come out at the east end of Eastville, and later was cut through the slough as at present. The Sagg Road, also later, and some 125 years ago, left the present route near Elisha King's residence, and ran west to the old landings.

Formerly Main Street, winding now, was much more circuitous. Probably at first a much more crooked path, sometimes running west to avoid the swamp just south of David Hand's corner, sometimes di-

verging easterly from the meadow, until fixed habitations and structures prevented the authorities from diminishing the magnitude or
number of its curves and angles. After the great fire of 1817 the course
of Main and West Water Streets is said to have been moved some 30
feet east. It is said Esq. Nathan Fordham gave West Water Street, or a
large portion of it. The descendants of Braddock Corey claimed that he
donated Union Street.

Benjamin Glover dedicated to the public the street that bears his
name. He built and resided in the house now occupied by Captain
David P. Vail, and owned and sold in house lots on that and other
streets, the large territory formerly known as "Peter's Green".

Suffolk Street was laid out and settled in my day. The streets south
of Joseph Crowells' corner, and east of Madison and west of Division
Streets, and all east of Division and west of Hampton Streets, and south
of the point of intersection in Hampton and Division Streets, were also
laid out and settled in my day.

THE SETTLEMENTS.

Southampton had its landing at North Sea. East-Hampton had its landing and warehouse at North West. The roads to Sag-Harbor were indi-
rect and circuitous. The slough near Rattle Snake Brook obstructed the
present straight route from East-Hampton. The swamp north and east
of Meeting House Hill, and that crossing Main and Madison Streets,
were all hinderances to a settlement, but Sagaponac and Mecox were
growing, and in 1686 Merchant Howell lived in Poxabogue and had
procured his goods from the landing and storehouse at North West,
and to facilitate their conveyance cut a road through the woods east of
Poxabogue, to this day called "Merchant's Path."

In the accounts of the Trustees of the Town of Southampton, in
1707, William S. Pelletreau funds this charge, "For going to Sag-Harbor
to evidence for ye town 3s. 6d.," which he states to be the first
recorded mention of the name. Some thirty years after occurs the first
mention of the name on the town records. It is sometimes called the
Harbor of Sagg, and unquestionably so called because the residents of
Sagg used the locality as their landing and harbor.

Uniform tradition dates the settlement of Sag-Harbor about the
year 1730. At first the places of refuge from a storm were mere holes
dug in the cliff on the north side of Turkey Hill. Then huts were constructed to shelter fisherman, and then small houses. all tradition
agrees that all these were located at the north declivity of Turkey Hill.

The first houses were set in the Hill, one story under and one above ground.The first of the houses were on poles or stanchions.The rear of the American Hotel still shows the remains of Turkey Hill and shows that they were perched on the brow of the Hill.

This settlement preceded wharf building some thirty years, and the allotment by twenty-five years.April 3d, 1739, the town meeting voted to sell to Samuel Russell for four poles of land at Sag-Harbor adjoining to his meadow, indicating that he was residing at Sag-Harbor, &c.In the drawing of the 12 acre division in 1761, Lot No. 12 is set to the heirs of Samuel Russell, showing him then deceased.This Russell is the first recorded settler of Sag-Harbor, and his lot was near the west side and north end of Main Street. Russell has been located near the corner of Main and West Water Street, and also on or near the Albert Hedges premises. I think it not improbable that Braddock Corey occupied this lot in the Revolution.

The Trustees of the Town, May 5th, 1742, appointed a Committee to choose a place for a wharf at Sag-Harbor, "but not to charge the town."April 7th, 1761, Nathan Fordham, Jr., and James Howell, obtained from the Town of Southampton the liberty and privilege of "building a wharf and setting up a try house at Sag-Harbor, &c., the town reserving the privilege of landing their whale upon said wharf at all times, and they shall receive it into their try house and try said whale on reasonable terms."

The first whaling vessels were sloops, cruising near the shore, which, after capturing a whale or whales, carried the blubber and bone into the harbor, where the bone was prepared for market and the oil tried out.This was the beginning of an enterprise that thereafter carried the whaling fleet into unknown oceans.

Tradition reports the first landing to have been at "Zachery's Point," near where was the cooperage of Charles T. Dering. Zachery Sanford was the father of Peter Hildreth's wife. Hence was derived the name of the Point and afterward from Hildreth the name of "Peter's Green."

As the channel formerly swept in shore from old North Haven Bridge to near Conkling's Point, probably different places were used for landings as circumstances varied. All tradition agrees that the first wharf was built just east of the old North Haven Bridge, probably about 1761, or just before. It may have been a mere bulkhead adjoining the channel. From the unwillingness of the town to incur "any charge" for wharf building, we infer that those interested in shipping in early days, were obliged to construct at their own expense, rude facilities for mooring and lading and unlading vessels.

We know that in 1760 three sloops owned by Joseph Conkling, John Foster and some others, called the "Goodluck," "Dolphin," and "Success," cruised for whales in Latitude 36 degrees North. (See Thompson's *History of Long Island*, Vol. 1, Page 349.)

Thus early maritime enterprise progressed in spite of discouragement and lack of proper facilities for commercial purposes.

THE ALLOTMENT.

In November, 1738, a large part of the Town of Southampton was allotted. A middle line, commencing at the East-Hampton boundary, was run to near North Sea, and lots laid out on either side; those north and south being respectively called the "Great North Division" and "Great South Division."

On the town record in connection with these divisions we find the name of Sag-Harbor. This North Division extended substantially to the old bound of Union Street, which ran west from the East-Hampton line to the northeast corner of the Old Burying Ground, and thence southwesterly to the house late of Jeffrey Fordham, before that, of Braddock Corey, father of John B. Corey, and thence toward Main Street, ending in the vicinity of the house of the late Miss Sarah Fordham.

November 18th, 1745, a survey of the lower part of Sag-Harbor was made, and followed by a division of seventeen lots and seventeen amendments. These lots commenced at "the clift," and ran south about as far as where Main and Madison Streets unite at or near David Hand's corner. They extended west from Division to Main Street. The lots varied from 24 to 40 feet wide.

The first lot at "the clift" was at or near the blacksmith shop of John Fordham. Washington Street lies between the 5th and 6th amendment. With the exception of the meadow this is the first allotment of land in the Southampton part of Sag-Harbor below Union Street, and demonstrates that at that time the settlement must have been a mere hamlet. This allotment was drawn November 19th, 1745.

November 30th, 1761, a survey was returned of what was called the twelve acre division, and the lots so surveyed were drawn, comprising substantially all the land unallotted between the old line of Union Street on the south and a line commencing at David Hand's corner, and running east to Division Street. It is said that a stone wall marked this north line of Division between these allottments, and it was between the lots formerly of Edw. C. Rogers, deceased, and the lot now of Dr. Wheeler, formerly of Captain Nathan Fordham, father of

Samuel and Oscar Fordham. Lot 1 was at David Hand's corner. Lot No. 15 was north of and on Union Street. All these 15 lots were bounded west by Union Street. Two lots, No. 16 and 17, and some amendments to lots 5 and 6, were laid out northwest of Union Street. The 51 lots in the Great North and South Division drawn together aggregated something over 14,000 acres.

The 51 lots and amendments drawn in Sag-Harbor were only some 39 or 40 feet wide. All village or city lots. They were therefore exceptional and dimunitive in size, demonstrating faith in the future coming of commerce and the importance of a Port of Entry, that would call for and sustain a large population. As these lots had two or more fronts, they could be and were subdivided into four or five times as many house lots. Prime's *History* states, "Between 1760 and 1770, while as yet the commerce of New York was carried on principally by schooners and sloops, this little untried Port had opened a small trade with the West Indies in larger craft."

Col. Gardiner at that time owned and employed two brigs in that business, while several smaller vessels were engaged in the fishing and coasting trade. At this early period two or three sloops cruised in the Atlantic a few degrees to the south, for whales, which were then so plenty, that more or less of them were taken every year by boats along the whole southern coast of the Island.

THE WHARVES.

Writers have not agreed on the date of the building of the first wharf, and have given a date a score of years too late for that of the Long Wharf. The volume of business and the population would largely depend on wharf accommodation, and hence the importance of the date. It is a fixed fact that in April, 1761, Nathan Fordham, Jr., and James Foster, obtained from the Town of Southampton the privilege of building a wharf and try house. No substantial wharf was then existent.

It is probable they erected a wharf that year, just east of the old North Haven Bridge, where the channel made near the landing. The wants of the coasting, West Indies and whaling enterprise, all imperatively called for such a wharf and would not be denied. It may be assumed that his old wharf was the place. February 12th, 1770, the Town of East-Hampton, by their Trustees, made a grant of liberty to build at Sag-Harbor a wharf. "Beginning at Southampton on East Patent line where Southampton grant for said wharf ends, and to run northerly thirty rods, said wharf to contain forty rights, reckoned at twenty pounds a right." This grant recited the name of William Nicoll, of this County, and the names of nine residents of the Town of Southampton as petitioners therefor, and also recited that "Trade and commerce are in general a benefit to mankind, and in particular to the inhabitants of this town."

We have proof that the Long Wharf was built about that year. Captain David P. Vail loaned me a bundle of ancient documents. One of them is a deed dated April 25th, 1771, by which Thomas Foster, cooper, conveys to Daniel Fordham, victualer, half a share in the new long wharf at Sag-Harbor. By another deed dated December 1st, 1773, Jeremiah Hedges, physician of East-Hampton, in consideration of £17, conveys to David Gelston, merchant of Southampton, one share of the great Wharf and Storehouses at Sag-Harbor, being 1-40 part. "September 15th, 1776, wharves at Sag-Harbor crowded with emigrants." This statement occurs in Onderdonk's Revolutionary Incidents in Suffolk County and refers to the flight of people to Connecticut. April 21st, 1798, the Commissioners of Highways of the Town of Southampton, in a description of a highway running west from the northeast corner of the house of Captain John N. Fordham, refer to the "Old Wharf" as included in the Highway.

September 5th, 1808, the Trustees of the Town of East-Hampton convey to the people of the State of New York, a parcel of land covered with water, from the end of the Sag-Harbor Wharf extending northerly three hundred feet. This was the grant for what was called the State Pier at Sag-Harbor, constructed by the authority and at the expense of the State.

Thus we find the Long Wharf constructed some years anterior to the Revolution. The Old Wharf disused and a part of a highway in 1778. The State Pier at the angle at the end of Long Wharf built about 1808.

By successful stages the commerce and shipping of Sag-Harbor outgrew the Old Wharf in 1770, outgrew the Long Wharf in 1808, and more than four score years ago had conducted an enterprise that extended in vastness to the farthest oceans, yet not without disaster and disappointment and hope deferred, that cried:

> *"O dread and cruel deep, reveal*
> *The secret which thy waves conceal,*
> *And, ye wild sea birds, hither wheel*
> *And tell your tale.*
> *Let winds that tossed his raven hair*
> *A message from my lost one bear,*

Some thought of me, a last fond prayer
Or dying wail."

THE OLD MAP OF SAG-HARBOR.

At the Centennial celebration of the Church here in 1868, William H. Gleason, the orator of the day, exhibited a map of Sag-Harbor as it was in the Revolution. A mere rough outline drawn from recollection, probably with the aid of John B. Corey, Eleazar Latham, Captain Jesse Halsey and others. This map shows the location of the old and new wharf. It marks two windmills on the shore between the wharves and one west of the old wharf or West Water Street. It locates Esq. Nathan Fordham in the old Jesse Halsey House, above Otter Pond, and the road south and west of his house, then bending east and north between Otter Pond and the Cove, skirting the shore of the Cove, and so north to those windmills on West Water Street.

This map, partly right and partly wrong, is correct in locating Duvall on the west corner of Main and West Water Street. It locates Daniel Fordham on the De Castro premises, where afterwards and in my early days, Robert Fordham kept tavern. It locates Peter Foster south of Fordham, then going south comes Truman, then Timothy Hedges, then James Howell, where stands the American Hotel. The Nassau House is marked on the bluff East. Joseph and Edward Conkling are marked on Hampton Street. Ephraim Fordham is marked near where is the residence of William Buck, and Benjamin Price opposite. Next south of Duval is marked Benjamin Coleman, who I think was grandfather of the wife of Ezekiel Mulford. Then came Uriah Miller near the south part of the Albert Hedges premises. Then Joseph Gildersleeve, probably an error. Then Braddock Corey and John Foster, who is located about at the south corner of Main and Howard Streets. On the east side of Main Street is located John Edwards, the father of John Edwards, who resided at the Old Farm. This house is located near where stands the Robert Douglass House on the north edge or in the swamp that then crossed the Main Street and perhaps Madison Street. South of Edwards came Thomas Ripley and South of him Daniel Havens. Five houses are located north of Scoy's corner on Main Street. Six houses are marked on the west side of Main Street below Nathan Fordham's. Three houses are marked on the east side of Main Street. Two houses are marked on Madison Street. Including the Norris and two Conkling houses with the Jesse Halsey house, we get in all 20 houses, and if a house marked as burned (probably by the British) in the Revolution is included, then 21. But Truman, Ripley, Daniel Havens and John Edwards are not included in the census of Sag-Harbor as I understand it. Yet there remain fifteen houses marked and practically identified as there in the Revolution.

In the census of Southampton, east of the water mill, sworn to July 4th, 1776 (Memorable Day), there are two groups that seem to include Sag-Harbor. One group beginning with Anthony Sherman includes, following his name, Nathan Fordham, Nathan Post, Obadiah Gildersleeve, John Woodruff, Eunice Quithall, Grover L'Hommedieu, Captain Samuel L'Hommedieu and Joseph Gibbs. The tradition that Anthony Sherman lived south of the Otter Pond and the occurrence of his name next to Nathan Fordham's, who was a known occupant of the Jesse Halsey house, proves him there. John Foster's known location near the corner of Howard and Main Street would indicate that the five names preceding his were residents. Nathan Post, I think, was a mariner, and afterwards master of a vessel sailing from this port to the West Indies.

The map may have mistaken the name and called it Joseph, when it should have been as in the census, Obadiah Gildersleeve.

Gibbs, I think was the schoolmaster, or of his family, and thus by the census and tradition we locate these ten families in Sag-Harbor.

The census taker appears to have gone down Main Street, and after enumerating Gildersleeve's family, left for another work. But tradition speaks of the early settlement of Main as more complete than any other street, and therewith this view of the census accords. When next the census taker visited Sag-Harbor he probably began with George Fordham and family, who removed to East Haddam, Connecticut, as a refugee in 1776, and continued to reside there after the Revolution all his life, and ended with William Duvall, Innkeeper, at the corner of Main and West Water Streets, whence he crossed the then Ferry to North Haven. I so judge because the third name after Duvall is Constant Havens, the eighth and ninth names he takes are Doctor Jonathan Havens and John Pain, all known residents of North Haven. The two latter large landholders. Doctor Havens was the grandfather of the late Jonathan Havens, and John Pain the great grandfather of Charles W. Payne and Mrs. Joseph Fahys.

The 32 names of families which he records, that seem to be residents of Sag-Harbor, are:

GEORGE FORDHAM.	JAMES HOWELL.
NATHAN FORDHAM.	JAMES WIGGINS.
SILAS NORRIS.	SILVANUS WICKS.

COL. JOHN HURLBUT.

TIMOTHY MATTHEWS.

JOSIAH COOPER.

SAMUEL HOWELL.

JOHN HUDSON.

URIAH MILLER.

JONATHAN CONKLING.

DANIEL FORDHAM.

JONATHAN HILL.

BENJAMIN COLEMAN.

JAMES STORE.

WID. TEMPERANCE FOSTER.

TIMOTHY HEDGES.

WILLIAM DUVALL.

WID. ELIZABETH HICKS.

WID. HANNAH LATHAM.

WID. SARAH BOWDICH.

WID. SARAH TARBELL.

HUBBARD LATHAM.

EDWARD CONKLING.

DAVID SAYRE.

JEREMIAH GARDINER.

WILLIAM BUTLER.

EPHRAIM FORDHAM.

BENJAMIN PRICE.

WILLIAM HALLOCK.

BRADDOCK COREY.

In this group eleven names occur which are on the Map. In the former group three names occur which are on the Map. In all fourteen names, which, for convenience, are starred, are on both Map and census.

The name of Braddock Corey occurs next to Duvall. The tradition is that he came here from North Haven and located on the lower part of Main Street, before building the house late of Jeffrey Fordham, and herein tradition and the census agree. But tradition and documentary evidence, indicate as residents of this place Hubbard Latham, David Sayre and Col. John Hurlburt.

In the Suffolk Gazette of June 8th, 1807, John Hurlbut advertises for sale his premises where "he now lives" in Sag-Harbor, from which I think his residence was thereafter and not before that in Bridge-Hampton. He resided on Main Street between Union and Jefferson Streets.

John Hudson, Jonathan Hill, Jeremiah Gardiner, Widows Tarbell, Latham, Hicks and Foster making ten to add to the fourteen names above starred and practically identifying twenty-four revolutionary heads of families resident in Sag Harbor. The census is correct. The difficulty is to locate the forty-two families named in the census here, and to reconcile map and census. Tradition, obviously incorrect, limited the number to twenty at the Revolution, and on that erroneous theory the Map was made. Six names occur on the Map that are not on the census. They are John Edwards, Thomas Ripley, Daniel Havens, Peter Foster, Truman and Joseph Conkling. Foster may have been in the Widow Foster's family, and Conkling in that of Edward Conkling's family. The other four names I think must have been those of late residents. Ripley, with his father, Capt. Joseph Ripley, came from Dartmouth, Mass. Documentary evidence in the possession of Charles W. Payne shows that from 1791 to 1802, Thomas P. Ripley, than a young merchant, was in partnership, under the firm name of Payne & Ripley, with his great grandfather, an old man and wealthy merchant and landholder on North Haven, who built the Point House in 1802, and after many years of merchant life died in 1807.

Coleman came from Nantucket, and was grandfather to Julia Prentice, the wife of Ezekiel Mulford. Edward and Daniel Havens named both on the map and census, seem to be grouped with residents of Noyack or Brickilns, which were more populous in the Revolution, or soon after it, than now. At this distance of time it was a work of arduous labor to locate even twenty-four of the probable forty-two Revolutionary residents of Sag-Harbor. Sifting loose tradition, scanning old documents, rubbing moss from old tombstones, allowing for failing memory, connecting hearsay by recorded testimony, all this is necessary. And the work accomplished shows the population and the commerce of Sag-Harbor, at the Revolutionary era, had developed to a relative degree of importance.

By the capture of Louisburg in 1758, and of Quebec in 1759, the predominance of the power of Great Britain on this Continent was established, and thenceforth the field of commerce became more extended and the profits of commercial enterprise more secure.

These conditions, anterior to the Revolution, were favorable to the growth of Sag-Harbor, and made it a centre of trade and commerce at that day beyond the diminutive estimate of dull tradition.

In 1810 the returns of the census according to Spofford's Gazeteer, showed in Sag-Harbor eighty dwelling houses and tonnage of shipping of about 5,000. Its whale fishery on the coast of Patagonia and cod fishery at New Foundland and elsewhere are there noticed.

SAG-HARBOR IN THE REVOLUTION

At the Revolution the clearing in Sag-Harbor, excepting Main Street, extended little if any above the old line of Union Street.

After the battle of Long Island, in August, 1776, Sag-Harbor, with all the Island, came in the possession of the British Army, which with strong hand, ruled the territory. The people were robbed and plundered by the British, to prevent possibility of supplies from here for the American army. They were robbed and plundered by their countrymen, to prevent the British army from living thereby. Language fails to picture the misery of the devoted patriots of Long Island.

A garrison of the British held Sag-Harbor. Its officers were quartered on James Howell, whose daughter, Mrs. Abigail Price, remembered their capture by Meigs' Expedition in May, 1777. They constructed a breast work, enlarged and strengthened by palisades on Meeting House Hill occupied by the garrison. Tradition tells that some of the soldiers died and were buried in the first burying ground west of the church, where formerly were grave stones, and where, in excavating, human remains have been found east of the houses once of Henry B. Havens and Oliver Fowler, and of Robert J. Power. That the Revolution temporarily paralyzed the growth and commerce of Sag-Harbor is unquestionable.

Anterior to the Revolution a church had been organized, about 1768, after the Presbyterian form of government and faith, with a small church building on this Meeting House Hill. It is probable this first burying ground, so near the church, may have been for a time deemed to be, or become, a part of the church lot. Cemeteries were often conjoined in the same location with churches. It is conjectured that the use of the first burial ground was designed to be temporary. Its occupation and desecration by the British in the Revolution, may have confirmed the people of the village in the resolution to abandon its use entirely, and accept instead the old one on Madison Street, devoted to that purpose some eight years previous.

The remains of a loaded gun barrel, iron bolts and chains, found many years ago in excavating in this vicinity, were thought to be Revolutionary relics.

When Meigs burned the supplies acquired by the British, and captured the garrison and officers, the British fleet in the harbor cannonaded the port with intent to aid their countrymen. Then James Howell put his daughter, afterwards Mrs. Abigail Price, in his cellar for safety. This circumstance she, with others, vividly remembered. Perhaps at this time the house was burned, which tradition imputed to the British soldiers.

These supplies destroyed in Meig's expedition were extorted from the farmers in the Hamptons. Stephen L. Hedges, of East-Hampton, had it from his grandfather, Captain David Hedges, that he was impressed to cart hay to the British forces in Sag-Harbor. My father told me that his father, who was a larger farmer, was compelled to furnish hay in like manner; that my grandfather drove one yoke of oxen ahead, with a load, and my father, then a little boy, followed with another load. This hay was unwillingly furnished, with the promise of compensation. After its destruction the promise was broken and pay refused by the British, to the loss, in some cases, of large sum by the sufferers.

Deacon John White, grandfather of the present John E. White, of Sagg, was in Meigs' expedition, and may have been in part its guide. He gave me an account of it. The company of American soldiers crossed from Guilford, or Sachems Head, in thirteen whale boats, under convoy of two armed sloops, carried the boats across a narrow neck of land west of Greenport, rowed to the foot of the beach and left their boats in the woods hid under guard, marched to Ligonee, forced two British soldiers in the house of Silas Edwards, then used as a hospital where patients were cared for by these soldiers, and who acted as guides, by whose aid the officers at James Howell's were captured, the fort was surprised, and the garrison taken. Under fire of a schooner of twelve guns and seventy men, Meigs' men burned twelve brigs and sloops, one a vessel of twelve guns; 120 tons of hay, 10 hogsheads of rum, and a large quantity of corn, oats and merchandise, and returned to Guilford in twenty-five hours from the time of embarking, without the loss of a man, and with ninety prisoners.

This exploit was a star of hope in the darkest night of the Revolution.

SAG-HARBOR IN THE WAR OF 1812.

The attack of the British on Sag Harbor, in June, 1813, was a failure as disastrous as the Revolutionary success was brilliant.

The British fleet lay in Gardiner's Bay, commanded by Commodore Hardy. A launch and two barges, with 100 men, attempted to surprise the place by night. They landed on the wharf, but an alarm had been given previously and the guns of the fort were used with such effect, that they set fire to one sloop only and retreated in such haste as to leave a large quantity of guns, swords and other arms behind them. The flames were speedily extinguished by the Americans, who suffered no other loss.

Captain David Hand, of Revolutionary memory, preserved as a relic, some portion of the arms, and his grandson, Captain David P. Vail, has treasured the mementos from his grandfather until now. Captain Henry Green and John Gann were sentinels on the wharf at this time. Green told me that he heard a boat and challenged it, and obtaining no answer, fired. Knowing that a return fire would follow, he jumped behind a large spile, that receiving the enemy's shot protected him. He then ran from the wharf, continuing the alarm. He said that Gann's gun missed fire, and as he ran past him, Gann was on his knees picking his flint and saying: "I want to get a crack at them." His Irish blood, in its enmity to England, was true as steel.

Does Great Britain know the burning resentment of the millions of Irish Americans who pant for war against her? Her arrogance in 1776 cost her half a continent; continued, it may cost her untold retribution.

In connection with the flight of the patriots from Sag-Harbor to Connecticut, to escape the consequences flowing from British rule here, after the disastrous battle of Long Island, the following notice published in the New London Gazette of January 17th, 1777, is interesting:

"Thomas Dering, John Foster and Thomas Wickham, or either two of them being appointed by the State of New York to receive, examine, and report on the several claims against said State for transporting families, stock and effects from Long Island to Connecticut, all persons who have any such accounts unsettled, are desired to bring them in for settlement to Ephraim Fenno's, inn holder, at Middletown, the third Wednesday, Thursday and Friday in January and February next, where attendance will be given to adjust the same. They are requested to give particular account of the names, and number of the families, and owners, of the effects, and the places from and to, which they were removed, and to be certified by the committee of the several towns where they live."(*Middletown,* Dec. 11th, 1776)

DISTRESS IN A FIRE.

A most calamitous event took place in this Port on Monday last. About 2 o'clock in the afternoon, a small barn in which there was some hay, was discovered to be on fire. The barn was contiguous to the thickest part of the settlement. The buildings were all wood, and very dry, and the wind blowing almost a gale. Such was the rapid progress of the flames that notwithstanding the utmost exertion of the citizens, in three hours about twenty of the best houses and most valuable stores in the place, together with fifteen barns, and other buildings were consumed. The scene was uncommonly distressing and destructive, as most of the buildings were stores full of various kinds of merchandise, and provisions, and such was the rapid advance of the fire, that the people had not time to remove them to places of safety.

A large quantity of the goods, furniture and clothing was removed from the storehouses into the streets, where their owners were obliged to abandon them to save themselves from the heat, the falling timbers and burning shingles. This awful visitation of Providence has left a number of families and poor widows houseless and dependent upon the charity of the public; has reduced others from a state of comfort and ease to poverty, and has greatly lessened the means of the rich, by consuming much of that capital they were employing for their own benefit and that of their fellow citizens.

THE FIRE OF NOVEMBER 14TH, 1845.

EXTRACT FROM THE *CORRECTOR* OF 22ND.

The fire in this village commenced about half-past 12 on Friday morning in a commission room for furniture and other articles, in the Suffolk buildings, and destroyed the hotel (Oakley's) and stores; Huntting's store, with the three dwellings at the west side of it, thence down the wharf as far as there were any buildings, on both sides, then the store of A.H. Gardiner, Phelps' Hotel, and everything up the street, on both sides, stopping after burning Tinker & Sons' on the east side, and A.G. Hedges' on the west, as likewise a number of dwelling houses and other buildings on the streets east of Main Street, and we are not much out of the way when we assert that there were somewhat in the neighborhood of ninety-five dwelling houses, stores, warehouses, tradesmen's shops, etc., destroyed; turning out over forty families to seek shelter in houses already fully stocked, or abide the peltings of the winter's storms; besides a good number being thrown entirely out of business, or their business much damaged.

What the total loss may be it is almost impossible to come to any correct conclusion, as the very sufferers themselves cannot speak with any degree of certainty. Fifty-seven stores, shops and warehouses were destroyed, besides stables and barns. If we were to state the loss at some $200,000 to $250,000, perhaps we should not be much wide of the mark; although some have calculated it much higher. The night was remarkably fine, and but little wind, until the air was so rarified by the excessive heat of the flames as to create a strong current. Some saved three-fourths of their goods, some half and some less, but few lost all. The sufferers are:

J. HILDRETH.	C. S. SLEIGHT.
H. G. BASSETT & CO.	S. HALLOCK.
C. S. HEDGES.	HOWELL & HAVENS.
OAKLEY.	A. H. GARDINER.
ROBINS & BROWN.	PHELPS HOTEL.
T. KIERNAN.	LAWRENCE & OVERTON.
DERING & FORDHAM.	RIPLEY & PARKER.

T. BROWN.

WM. WILCOX.

MOTT & STREET.

G. & H. HUNTTING.

H. CROWELL.

C. DOUGLASS.

N. & G. HOWELL.

H. COOPER.

DOUGLASS & WADE.

T. FOSTER.

SUFFOLK CO. BANK.

J. C. FOWLER.

WADE & RUSSELL.

J. SMITH.

S. & B. HUNTTING & CO.

S. L'HOMMEDIEU.

N. COMSTOCK.

MULFORD & SLEIGHT.

W. M. COOPER.

A. OVERTON.

A. G. HEDGES.

W.A. SIMONS.

J. CROLIUS.

E. C. ROGERS.

P. ROGERS.

WM. H. NELSON.

G. R. LOPER.

E. H. SMITH.

G.V. OAKLEY.

E. PHELPS.

A.A. EDDY.

P. P. KING.

D. CONGDON.

D.Y. BELLOWS.

OCEAN HOUSE.

COOK & GREEN.

S. S. SMITH & CO.

T. P. RIPLEY.

GARDINER & SEALEY.

S. PITCHER.

J. HAVENS

G. H. COOPER

W. F. HALSEY.

THOMPSON.

S. HAVENS.

TIFFANY & HALSEY.

G. D. CHESTER.

T. HOWARD.

D.A. JENNINGS.

Z. ELLIOT.

OFFICE OF *CORRECTOR*.

J. HOBERT.

FRENCH.

MRS. PEASE.

N. TINKER.

T. VAIL.

N. S. LESTER

E. MUFORD & CO.

BABCOCK,.

J. G. LEONARD.

E. L. SIMONS.

J. CONKLING.

O. SLATE.

J.A. COOK.

STEWART & CROWELL.

B. BABCOCK.

G. HOWELL.

H. STEWART.

MRS. WOOD.

WILLIAM TAYLOR.

MRS. REEVES.

STEAM MILLS & PUMP.

MATHEWS, AND A FEW OTHERS.

The fire of 1845 ran south on Main Street on the west side to the north walls of the three brick stores owned by Major John Hildreth, where for nearly fifty years I had my office, and on the east side to the dwelling and store of N.S. Lester (now torn down), north of the Union

School building. I remember that fateful night. Doctor Abel Huntington, Collector of the Port, declared that these brick stores saved Sag-Harbor.

The fire of 1817 was limited, I am informed, to nearly or quite the same lines.

NOTED LOCALITIES.

On Meeting House Hill, in old times, stood the stocks. Later they were moved to Madison Square. The Whipping Post, relic of a barbarous age, stood near where the old liberty pole was erected, in front of Hunting's store, near the north end of Main Street. The one an emblem of brutality, the other of American Freedom. In or near the front of the dwelling and store of Captain Oliver Fowler, stood the Hay Scales. They were literally scales of such ponderosity, as in my youthful imagination seemed to rival the seven wonders of the world.

The spider-legged windmill on Peter's Green, tended by Peter Hildreth, demands recognition. The rope walk of the elder Samuel L'Hommedieu, Esq., near by, a long covered shed, was a familiar object in the landscape. Beebee's mill, on Sherry's Hill, moved its might arms to the impelling breeze, fufilling its mission in fitting the grain for human sustenance.

The embanked fortification on old Fort Hill frowned defiance to our country's foes. The art studios of Hazard Parker and Hubbard L. Fordham invited the enthusiast in the fine art. The shop of Ephraim N. Byram was an attractive centre of mechanical genius; its unassuming proprietor the greatest attraction it contained. The Arsenal, depository of cannon and military stores, and used by Henry P. Dering, sometimes as a Post Office, more a Collector's office. Arms and ammunition below, records and law above, rightful juxta-position; it was an emblem of the Federal Power of the Nation over which its Flag floated, not unbecoming a Sea Port whose commerce extended to "earth's remotest bounds." The Salt Works, on North Haven, was a part of the landscape from Sag-Harbor in my early days.

The Light House on Cedar Island was unknown until about 1838. The early commerce of this Port was conducted with few of the safeguards and facilities of modern times.

THE WHARF THE CENTER OF ATTRACTION.

In the whaling days of Sag-Harbor the wharf was the great centre of attraction. It was its receiving and its impelling heart. Its avenues were arteries whose currents were impulses therefrom. Its streets were veins whose returning rills flowed therein. For it the coopers' adze swung swiftly. For it the mills hurried through their grist. For it the rope-walk groaned with tiresome toil. For it the boat builder plied his knife. For it the blockmaker's gouge moved. For it the sailmaker's needle flew. For it the carver's fine shavings fell. For it moved the carman's truck.

Go back with me fifty years and stand as I then stood on Sag-Harbor's dock. Look with me as then I looked on an industrial enterprise; that out of the depths of the sea, impoverishing no human being, brought millions to our shores. Who can measure the diversified labors it employed. This ship has just arrived, worn, grimy, soiled, her masts, and spars, and sails, and rigging, and hull, battered and weather beaten, all need to be renovated. Her supplies furnished, her casks stowed. Her defective masts and spars fitted. Her bottom coppered. Her rigging and sails renewed. Mighty hands heave her down to be corked and sheathed and coppered. Carpenters replace defective timber and plank. Painters smooth and decorate and gild. Masons set up and try works. Riggers, keen of eye and strong of nerve strip the ship, from the tip of her taper top gallant mast to her cut water, and replace, and renew, and wind, and knot, and tar, and tighten, till all is strong, and trim, and taut. All this for one ship. Multiply this by a score and a half, and you get some idea of the volume of majestic movement, of human industry, that flowed to the wharf in olden time.

When the clock struck 12, the army of mechanics and seamen that marched from thence, might fight a seventy-four gun ship. Returning from dinner before the bell struck one, they might take that ship of the line over which floated the Commodore's flag. Those were grand days. The hands of the laborers received their reward. The varied skill of the artizan obtained due recompense. The care and thought of the merchant secured ample remuneration. The venture of the enterprise was amply returned. Comfort, plenty, wealth came. The last to a few. The others to all. Then Sag-Harbor was cosmopolitan. Her citizens had visited all Continents, navigated all oceans, experienced all vicissitudes, sailed in all climes. Representatives of all nations walked her streets. The Sandwich Islander, gentle, docile, mild; the Feegean, loud, tattoed, barbarous, not unfrequently were seen. One of her ships, under command of Captain Mercator Cooper, had been the first to enter the prohibited ports of Japan. Another, the ship Cadmus, had brought Lafayette to our shores. One of her citizens, Zebulon Elliot, father of your Secretary, had been in the Miranda expedition.

Speak to her people of the farthest Isle, of the most desolate coast, and the answer would be, "Yes, I've been there."

Names of vessels absent in 1841. Months and days. Names of master. Barrels of sperm. Barrels of whale oil. Pounds of bone, and managing owners.

The foregoing table at one view exhibits the extent of the whaling commerce of the Port of Sag-Harbor in the year 1841. The ships Hamilton, Romulus, Phenix, Zenophon, America, Ontario, Huron, and Barque Concordia, did not return that year. Luther D. Cook contributed the foregoing statement for Thompson's *History of Long Island,* in which it was published.

VESSELS.	MOS. & DAYS.	MASTERS.
Washington	20—1	Wm._____
Fanny	20—27	S. W. Edwards
Thomas Dickeson	20—	Wickham S. Havens
Henry	10—20	John Green
Columbia	20—18	Lawrence B. Edwards
Thames	22— 2	Jeremiah W. Hedges
Neptune	20— 6	Shamgar H. Sleight
Panama	33—25	Tho. E. Crowell
Bark Franklin.	—21	David Youngs
Roanoke.	8—15	Ben. J. Glover
Dan. Webster	22—10	Ed. M. Baker
Triad	21— 4	Isaac M. Case
Ann	20—17	Ezekiel H. Curry
Portland	23—	Wm. M. Payne
Delta	22—10	Seth Griffing
Barque Noble	10—18	James Sayre
Brig Seraph	10—25	Geo. W. Corwin
Arabella	22—13	John Bishop, Jr.
Hannibal	10— 4	Lewis L. Bennettt
Gem	10—24	Theron B. Worth
Bark Nimrod	12—10	Albert Rogers
Ship Hudson	23—23	Sam. Denison
Ship Byard	12—	Francis Sayre
Ship Acasta	10— 2	Syl. C. Smith

Total number of arrivals, 20 Number of tons, 9,722—6,726—58,827—482,119.

Wickford	3—18	Davis Miller
Camillus	13—22	Ezekiel H. Howes
Bar. Marcus	15— 8	David Loper
Cadmus	29—	Henry Nickerson, Jr.
Washington	12—13	Rob. N. Wilson
France	37—17	Rob. L. Douglass

From the like authority, I copy from notes in the same history the following. From the statement furnished by him, it appears that in 1837 there were twenty-three arrivals and twenty-nine departures of whaling ships from this Port; the number of men and boys employed on board of which exceeded eight hundred. To appreciate the extraordinary progress made in this business, it is only necessary to remark that in 1815 there were but three ships owned here, yet that in 1838 the number had increased to twenty-nine, being an addition of twenty-six ships in twenty-three years. It shows also how much may be ac-

SPERM.	WHALE OIL.	IBS. BONE.	OWNERS.
82	2,436	22,214	Huntting Cooper.
120	2,060	25,500	N. & G. Howell.
247	3,780	38,000	Muford & Sleight.
154	1,900	14,358	S. L'Hommedieu.
63	2,955	25,207	Luther D. Cook.
139	3,077	26,884	Thomas Brown.
30	2,695	22,206	S. & B. Huntting.
440	3,376	29,000	N. & G. Howell.
227	2,636	20,246	Chas. T. Dering.
123	1,509	12,028	Wiggins & Parsons
340	2,810	26,271	Mulford & Sleight.
241	1,406	11,291	H. & N. Corwin.
428	1,764	14,640	Mulford & Howell.
320	2,051	16,201	S. & B. Huntting.
328	1,560	12,484	H. & N. Corwin.
245	1,132	6,945	Ira B. Tuthill.
180	315	3,000	Sam. H. Landon.
178	2,130	16,200	N. & G. Howell.
59	1,611	9,459	S. & B. Huntting
52	2,200	14,690	Huntting Cooper.
110	1,533	13,419	Chas. T. Dering.
298	1,682	15,858	Luther D. Cook.
104	1,244	7,432	H. & N. Corwin.
	1,920	14,900	Mulford & Sleight.
100			David P. Vail.
201	1,409	11,377	C. T. Dering.
832	904	4,070	N. & G. Howell.
553	1,473	12,000	Mulford & Sleight
130	1,123	9,500	Wiggins & Parsons.
402	3,636	26,730	N. & G. Howell.

complished by a spirit of enterprise, so characteristic of the American people, and which is nowhere more nobly portrayed than in this department of our navigation. It is calculated by Mr. Cook that from 1804 to 1837 there were 198 arrivals of whaling vessels at this Port, producing 338,690 barrels of whale oil, 40,509 barrels of sperm, and 1,596,765 pounds of bone. In 1834 and 1835 there were seventeen arrivals, amounting in the aggregate to 6,361 tons to each vessel. In 1837 there were twenty-three arrivals, producing 8,634 barrels of sperm, 31,784 of whale oil, and 236,757 pounds of bone.

During the same year the departures were twenty-nine, including one from Jamesport, one from Cutchogue, and two from Greenport, all bound to the South Atlantic. In 1838 the tonnage employed was 11,700, to which may be added 5,437 of enrolled and licensed tonnage, employed in the coasting trade, making 17,137 of tonnage from this Port. During the year ending January 1st, 1841, there arrived in this district nineteen whaling ships, the contents of which were 3,479 barrels of sperm, 29,436 of whale oil, and 232,182 pounds of bone; equal to 107,000 gallons of sperm and 912,600 of whale oil, of the value of $600,000. Between the 16th of June and 20th of December of the same year, there sailed fifteen ships, four barques, and one brig to the South Atlantic, Indian Ocean, New Zealand, New Holland, Crozett Islands, and the N.W. Coast. The average duration of voyages of the whalers that returned in 1840 was little short of 16 months.

The tonnage of 1841 was 13,945, besides two ships and two brigs added during the year, and the quantity of produce 6,726 barrels of sperm, 58,827 of whale oil, and 482,110 pounds of bone; the net proceeds of which was $863,000. The whole value of the fleet (43 vessels) with its outfit, amount to at least $900,000, and the number of officers and seamen is 1,025. There are now more than forty vessels in this business, which with those from other parts of the district, increase the number to fifty. Henry T. Dering, Esq., the present Collector, states the arrivals in 1842 at fifteen, bringing in 24,410 barrels of whale oil, 4,175 of sperm, and 192,000 pounds of bone.

The whole number of vessels now employed in the whaling business from this district is fifty-two, the registered tonnage of which is 17,317, and the number of hands employed 1,217.

EARLY RESIDENTS IN SAG-HARBOR.

Mrs. Miranda Beers, daughter of David Gibbs, the old schoolmaster, even in 1791 states that she was told by her grandmother that she remembered when there were but three houses in Sag-Harbor. The grandmother was Prudence Fordham, sister of Esq. Natham Fordham and daughter of Nathan Fordham, who lived at the Old Farm. She died in 1808, aged 82 years. Her sister married Bowditch, who lived in a house formerly of one Norris, on Turkey Hill. When she was fourteen years old she came down through the woods all the way to this house on the bluff, and then there were only two other houses there. This was in 1740. In very early days Joseph Conkling had a house on the spot where now stands the residence of Mrs. William R. Sleight. The grandson, Edward Conkling, lived south of the residence of Captain Wickham S. Havens, where Henry Conkling lived.

John Foster's father had a brick store before the Revolution, near where William R. Street's shop used to stand. At the close of the Revolution he returned and found his store entirely demolished. This Foster was a noted mathematician, and jokingly used to say he could tell how many solid feet there was in a load of brush.

NOTABLE CHARACTERS.

Hubbard Latham, a native of Noank, Connecticut, came here in 1760, and was for many years an active business man and prominent citizen. He was born January 4th, 1746, and died November 16th, 1813. His possessions were extensive and his enterprise large in mercantile and maritime directions. Not one of his twelve children survive. Eleazar Latham, deceased, son of Eden, deceased, was a grandson of this Hubbard.

Whatever concerned the traditions and early history of this place was garnered in the memory of Eleazer Latham. To the Historian and Antiquarian he freely gave invaluable aid as the writer gratefully attests.

Daniel Fordham, one of the first settlers of Sag-Harbor, was there as early as 1769, was brother of Esq. Nathan Fordham. He had a wife Phebe; daughters, Frances Wentworth and Charlotte Kirtland; sons, Samuel, Nathan, Jairus, Thaddeus, Joel, Frederick and Daniel. His son Samuel died young, before his father, leaving a daughter Elizabeth. The late Hubbard L. Fordham was a son of Jairus and grandson of this Daniel, who was a large landholder and active business man, engaged in the early enterprises of Sag-Harbor. In 1769 he is called in a deed, Mariner; in 1771 a Victualler, and in still another in 1780, Innkeeper. His tombstone records his death June 12th, 1816, in the 86th year of his age.

SOME NOTED RESIDENTS.

Captain Stephen Howell was born October 23rd, 1744, and died January 18th, 1828. He was an ardent patriot and engaged in the battle of Long Island. Pelletreau records him as notably one of the first who erected storehouses in this village, and the first to engage in manufacturing business, which was a sperm candle factory, located near the old gas works. As early as 1785 he was engaged in the whale fishery, which his sons Lewis and Silas successfully continued, and his grandsons Nathan P. and Gilbert H. Howell continued, until it proved a losing enterprise.

Col. Benjamin Huntting, of Southampton, born 1754, died August 17th, 1807, was early engaged in both the West India Trade and the whale fishery. His sons Samuel and Benjamin, and afterwards Gilbert and Henry H. Huntting, were largely interested in the whale fishery and mercantile business at the time of its brightest prospects and suffered in its disastrous downfall.

In quiet humor, sound judgment, clear perception, business insight, large views and a generous heart, few men excelled Col. Samuel Huntting. Friend and helper of my early days, to thy memory I cannot withhold the expression of my undying gratitude.

The Nathan Fordham, who with James Foster, in 1761, received from the town authority to build the first wharf, was grandfather of Pelatiah Fordham and the late Nathan Y. Fordham. He was commonly called Esq. Fordham. He resided in the old Jesse Halsey house. He owned immense landed estates, including some hundred of acres at Chatfield's Hill; a large territory south of Otter Pond Bridge; all the land south of the Hedges' house on the west side of Main Street, and other lands. He died May 18th, 1805, aged 84. Upon his tombstone in the old burying ground was inscribed this memorial: "He was one of the first who commenced the settlement of this place."

His son John Nathan Fordham married first Jane, daughter of John Foster, who was mother of Pelatiah Fordham, and second Charity, daughter of Jesse Halsey, at the head of the Pond, who was the mother of Nathan Y. Fordham.

This son, John N., kept the tavern on the corner of Main and West Water Street, and is said to have laid out Meadow Street, as his father, Esq. Nathan, laid out and gave West Water Street to the public. On this famous corner in my early days was the noted Inn of Pelatiah Fordham, while across the street was the Inn of Robert Fordham; rival taverns; both were conducted by men experienced and inheriting ancestrial gifts to excel in their calling.

The old Long Island Inns were marvels of house comfort, of delightful dinners and rare good cheer. The Sag-Harbor hotels were no less famous in their day than their contemporaries [sic]. Pelatiah Fordham, commonly known as "Duke Fordham," is reported to have entertained the novelist, J. Fenimore Cooper, at his hotel. This fact I know by the testimony of eye witnesses, but tradition, unreliable often, asserts that Cooper therein wrote his first romance entitled "Precaution." In this case tradition is probably founded on hearsay. Strangely, and lately, there came into my hands a copy of a letter written by his daughter, late Susan Fenimore Cooper, dated January 7th, 1891, to Rev. William Remsen Mulford, of New Haven, in which she states that the time the novel was written her father resided at Angevine, near Mamaroneck, and when a child she heard him read the manuscript to her mother, which was written there.

That Cooper owned in the Ship Union engaged in whaling from Sag Harbor, and at one time under the command of Captain Jonathan Osborn, of Wainscott, there is no doubt. In his "Sea Lions" Cooper immortalized the name of Ebenezer Sage, physician and philosopher.

The old house and inn of Daniel Fordham was sold to someone who tradition tells started to move it to Sagg. When it got as far as the lot south of E.C. Rogers, deceased, the wheels broke, and the mover declared he would go no father with it. He bought the next lot and set it there, from whence Dr. Wheeler removed it to the lot in the rear of the residence of Robert J. Power, where it now stands. It had been the Inn of Daniel Fordham, and when there on the lot afterwards of Robert Fordham. Aunt Dence Fordham, grandmother of George Bassett, deceased, remembered to have danced there when a girl.

It had been the residence of Captain Nathan Fordham, and there his sons Samuel and Oscar were born. Of origin long anterior to the Revolution, its history is coeval with the early days of Sag-Harbor.

What days of roistering merriment. What ministry of good cheer. What cures of sorrow. What exultant welcomes, has it witnessed. Small, of one story, it seems diminutive; but its history in duration, in variety of event, in eras of magnitude, overshadow that of the palatial residence of modern times. The beams of its rooms, gifted with the powers of utterance, could tell of the secret joy that gladdened the patriotheart when came the glad news of Burgoyne's surrender, of the exultant thought that welcomed the tidings of the capture of Cornwallis, of the triumphant cheer that went up to Heaven when the British evacuated New York, and their fleet, discomforted, sailed from our shores. They could tell of the hopes and fears expressed when the ship Argonaut, in September, 1817, sailed under command of Captain Eliphalet Halsey around Cape Horn into the Pacific, owned by Silas and Lewis Howell; the first ship to double Cape Horn. They could tell of the glad welcome that was given her captain and crew, when in June, 1819, she returned with 1,700 barrels of sperm oil. They could tell of the first billiard table set up in Sag Harbor on the meadow, to the scandal of the place, as some then thought. They could tell of the house on the lot of the late Captain Charles Smith, burned in the Revolution by the British. They could tell of the dark and desolating day of the embargo. They could tell of the consuming disastrous fires of 1817 and 1845. They could tell of Henry P. Dering made Collector of the Port under Washington, in 1790, and continued in the office until his death in 1822; a man of signal ability and executive capacity; sometimes postmaster of the village, and always active. A gentleman of the old school, cultivated, educated, honored.

He had a solitary deer which he sent to Gardiner's Island to be temporarily kept there by his friend John Lyon Gardiner. By letter dated October 8th, 1804, Gardiner wrote to him that the deer, in attempting to swim off the Island, was drowned, and enclosing some lines written by Isaac Conkling, then a student with Dr. Sage; as a sample, I quote:

"In mournful numbers Muses tell
Why starts the tender tear,
By cruel death my friend has fell,
My much lamented deer."

This old house, endowed with the power of utterance, could give the whole history of Sag-Harbor. It could tell of every sloop, and schooner, and brig, and ship, that ever sailed from this Port. It could tell of the whaling enterprise from first to last. Men may decry it, and belittle it, and vulgarize it, and yet before the Revolution, the whale fishery trained a band of seamen that in the long contest for Independence fought with honor on the ocean under the stars and stripes.

Paul Jones would not undervalue these seamen, his contemporaries and fellow victors of undying name. In the War of 1812, disastrous on land, with naval achievement by sea, the whalemen formed the solid foundation of our marine force, fellowmen and sharers in the work, and the glory, and the spirit, embodied in the names of Decatur, and Porter, and Hull, and Lawrence. To the unjust and not improbable sneer, "Sag-Harbor has done nothing."

The old house may truthfully respond all that I have uttered and more. Solitary and alone this Port pioneered the way to an enterprise so profitable, and so vast, that although other ports and places followed the same pursuit, this Port, in the magnitude of her marine, in the enterprise, exceeded that of all the other Ports of the Empire State.

In this day we hear much of athletics from the Universities and Colleges of our own and other lands, and, to the reader of the classics it seems as if the ancient Grecian games were reviving. As if on our own soil the contests Olympic and Isthmian were renewed. For such a training the world never saw a school superior to the whale fishery, or a place better fitted to develope the strength and endurance of the physical man, than the whale chase. There was excitement sufficient to arouse the most phlegmatic temperament, danger so far imminent as to demand the utmost vigilance. A chase that called for the utmost exertion of strength, and the last power of mortal endurance.

The eye must be quick to see, the judgment sound to estimate, the arm strong to heave, the nerve steady to direct, the mind self reliant to guide. In such a school the youth of this port and the adjacent villages were trained. In physique, in ambition, in manhood, in fertility of resource, in self reliance, unexcelled on this or any other continent. The onset of a thousand men so trained would be a shock no feeble force could withstand.

Mad Anthony Wayne might well ask for such men to storm Stony Point. Let others undervalue the whale fishery as a nursery of our merchant and our military marine. Let us do it exact and equal justice. We speak of that of which we know. We attest that wherein we have had experience. The whale fishery bore to the navy of the United States the man who upheld her flag in all her wars on the sea, as its fruits. And Sag-Harbor as her fairest flower gave to the Military Marine of the Nation, that unsullied name to maintain her honor, Admiral Oscar F. Stanton.

THE NATURAL ADVANTAGES OF SAG HARBOR.

In the early history of Sag Harbor the Indian bore exclusive sway. His wigwams were at intervals on its northern shore, and dim tradition speaks of them at Round Pond. The big meadow and marsh, the extended swamps, the sandy and roundabout roads retarded its development. But its harbor, a gem of beauty, was capacious, comparatively deep, well land locked, and with good roads, easy of access from the Hamptons, and of central location. The products of the soil accumulated, and the surplus called for export. Beef and Port, Butter and Hides, Staves and Casks, Shoes and Boots, Cattle and Horses, Wood and Hay,

Corn, Rye, Oats and Potatoes, Whale-oil and Bone, looked for a market in New York, or Boston, or the West Indies.

Out of this surplus product began the commerce of Sag-Harbor. It has survived the shock of the Revolution. It has outlived the paralysis of the Embargo. It has not perished in the disastrous fires of 1817 and 1845. It has not expired in the failure of the whaling enterprise. Her beautiful harbor, the beneficent gift of God, remains. Whatever future disaster may come, that except by the convulsion of nature will be our lasting inheritance and advantage.

FIRST BILL OF LADING.

Shipped by the Grace of God, in good order and well conditioned by Francis Pelletreau, in and upon the good sloop called the Portland Adventure, whereof is Master under God for this present voyage Richard Hartshorne, and now riding at anchor in the harbour of Sagg, and by God's Grace bound for New York, to say: Five barrells of Beef and nine barrells of Pork, two Furkings of Butter, two ditto Cranberry, and one ditto of Eggs, for the proper Accompt and Risque of Francis Pelletreau and goes consigned to himselfe. Being marked and numbered as in the Margent, and are to be delivered in the like good order and well conditioned at the aforesaid port of New York (the dangers of the seas only except), unto Francis Pelletreau or to his assigns. He or they paying Freight for the said goods sixteen pence per barrell, and four pence half penny per Furkin, with primage and average account added. In witness thereof the Master and Purser of the said sloop hath affirmed two bills of Lading all this of this Tenor and Date. One of which two Bills being accomplished the other is to stand Void. And so God send the good Sloop to her desired Port in safety, Amen.

Dated in Southampton ye 26th of November, 1731.
Rich'd Hartshorne.

Beef F. P. B.
Porke F. P. P.
Cranberry F. P. C.
Eggs F. P. E.
Butter F. P. 1 to 2

The above is, I believe, the oldest document relating to "Sagg-Harbour" as a port. W .S. Pelletreau.

THE NEWSPAPERS.

The following items contained chiefly in Thompson's *History of Long Island* are interesting:

"The first Newspaper ever printed on Long Island was issued in this Village by Frothingham,:David Frothingham, May 10th, 1791, entitled the 'Long Island Herald,' which he transferred to Selleck Osborn June 2nd, 1802, who changed the title to the 'Suffolk County Herald.' On the 20th February, 1804, he relinquished the establishment to Alden Spooner. The title was again changed to that of 'Suffolk Gazette,' which was continued by Spooner till Feb. 23, 1811, when the further publication of a newspaper here was abandoned. The 'Suffolk County Recorder' was commenced by Samuel A. Seabury, October 19th, 1816.

"October 18th, 1817, the same was altered to 'American Eagle,' which was discontinued in four years thereafter. August 3d, 1822, 'The *Corrector*' was established by Harry W. Hunt. September 16th, 1826, a paper called the 'Republican Watchman' was issued by Samuel Phillips, and about 1844 was removed to Greenport. July 14th, 1859, the 'Sag-Harbor Express' was first issued, edited by John H. Hunt. 'The *Corrector*,' now edited by Hon. Brinley D. Sleight, is the oldest newspaper published in Suffolk County. That and the 'Express,' still edited by J.H. Hunt, are issued weekly. Thus more than a century ago and earliest on this Island, the light of the press shone at the 'East End.'

CONCLUSION.

We speak of the history of Sag-Harbor as of a locality. In a proper and a large view of the subject it is an Epitome of the History of the Country. It antedates the Revolution by nearly half a century. It began in a wilderness. The strong arms of her early settlers cleared the forest. They levelled the hills and cast them into her swamps and marshes. They constructed her commodious roads and avenues. They built her dwellings and stores. They constructed her wharves and warehouses. They prepared the way for her commerce. They instituted her schools. Go back to 1796, one hundred years, and Jesse Hedges, grandfather of Charles S. Hedges, a graduate of Yale College, was teaching some sixty scholars, showing the regard of this people for education. Go back to 1797, and the Rev. Daniel Hall was preaching in the old church erected some twenty-nine years before that, the truths of Holy Writ, showing the regard of this people for the life that is everlasting. Go back seventy years and more and look in the rear of the store of Josiah Douglass, and find a well selected library of choice books (from which I remember to have read *Plutarch's Lives, The History of Greece,* and the *Battles of Alexander the Great,* and Cooper's *Romance of the Red Rover*), showing the literary culture of this people.

In industrial progress, in educational advancement, in literary culture, in spiritual development, the history of Sag Harbor is in miniature, the history of this vast Republic. In the contribution of early ship building and extended commerce, made by Sag-Harbor to the Country, her citizens may rightfully exult. The unexhausted deposits of subterranean oil were discovered just as the whaling enterprise was waning, and dealt it a deadly blow. It is no dishonor of ours that destiny deprived us of our source of support. That the sons of Sag-Harbor were driven to other fields of industry and enterprise, in other regions and beyond the mountains, even to the shores of the Pacific.

The lessons they here learned cannot have lessened their love for the Honor, the Glory, and the Flag of their native land. In the most extended enterprise of their day the Fathers of Sag-Harbor carried the Stars and Stripes to the Arctic and Antarctic circles. In the spirit of the Fathers, let the sons emulate and excel the untiring industry, the hardy toil, the independent resolve, the patriotic purpose, that animated the hearts of their sires. It is hard to submit to defeat and disaster, and disappointment. Yet these lessons, so bitter to endure, may purify, and ennoble, and enrich the nature. Even of the great Master we read that he was "made perfect through suffering."

The presence of manufacturing industry relieves the gloom that hung like a cloud so many years over this beautiful village. We hope it is the dawn of a larger enterprise and a brighter day. Other villages and states may have gained the good citizens Sag-Harbor has lost. Other coming days may give to Sag-Harbor some return for the great loan she has made for the benefit of others.

In closing this paper I am deeply impressed that what I have essayed to do is less, far less than what I cannot do. My limits prohibit adequate notice of the masters, mariners, officers and seamen, who sailed from this port a half century ago. They prohibit enlargement on the unsullied integrity of Josiah Douglass and Charles T. Dering, or the bluff honesty of John Budd and William Rysam Mulford, or the abounding energy of Thomas Brown and Gen. Henry H. Huntting, or the genial suavity of Cornelius Sleight and his son William Rysam Sleight, or the sound judgment of Major John Hildreth, whose three brick stores stopped the progress of the desolating fire of 1845, or the logical power of Thomas Foster, or the ardent nature of John Sherry, or the methodical movements of Luther D. Cook, or the intellectual refinement of Henry T. Dering, or the hardy seamanship of the Smiths—Charles, Thomas, Freeman and Daniel. These men, all useful in their day, have gone to the house appointed for all the living. And me. Ah me! Shall I say as has been said:

> *"I feel like one who treads alone*
> *Some banquet hall deserted,*
> *Whose lights are fled, whose garlands dead*
> *And all but he departed."*

Nay, rather let me with serene courage, with subdued passion, with grateful emotion, with rigid impartiality, with reviving memory, with thanksgiving to the Universal Father, live to record the virtues of the loved and lost.

One subject omitted thus far will survive the wrecks of time, will live in the eternal years. The Fathers in 1768 organized and built on Meeting House Hill a church, where at the beat of drum they assembled, and many years worshipped and heard a sermon read, all without a minister.

In 1817 they took down that church building and on the same lot erected another church edifice. In 1843 they commenced the construction of the present Presbyterian Church. Time wears out the dwellings of men. Time crumbles into dust their houses of worship. Time cuts short the life of mortal man, but the church, the living church of Jehovah, in endless succession moves on, in immortal vigor, and immortal youth. Men perish age after age. The organic church built on no material power, founded on no mere human hope, resting on no unstable faith, endures. Our forefathers, discerning the imperishable power of the Church of God, organized their community upon its beneficent, its elevating, its enduring bed rock. In the early days when they could ill afford to sustain a minister, the elder Esq. L'Hommedieu (as his name imports the Man of God) conducted public worship, and heard from the young answers from the Catechism, always concluding his prayer with that memorable ascription "Now unto the King eternal, immortal, invisible, the Only Wise God, be honor, and glory, forever and forever, Amen." Deacon Job Hedges was a living power in the same church, a light for years. This generation knows nothing of Thomas Ripley, whose clapsed [sic] hands denoted perpetual prayer, whose devout demeanor spoke of indwelling peace, whose placid eye told of the triumph of the spiritual. He was eminently the Father of the Methodist Church here.

The memory of Marcus Starr may yet linger in the minds of some in this audience. I see him now as for the last time in life I saw him a generation gone by. His name was a synonym of unquestioned honor and honesty wherever known. If his devotion found most appropriate expression in the liturgy and ritual of the church of England, who can deny that its utterances rise to the loftiest ascriptions of Praise; sink to the depths of profoundest Penitence; breathe out the most urgent desires for spiritual aid from Him from whom "all blessings flow." To his untiring zeal more than to any other may be attributed the institution here of that grand old church we call "The Episcopal."

Some few of my audience may have seen David Hempstead. Large of frame, of Afric type. Uneducated, with little of this world's goods, there reigned an indwelling spirit in the soul of that man born not of earth, nor of man, nor of the power of man, an invisible presence that transformed him from the image of the earthly to the resplendent image of the Heavenly. He was a living epistle known and read of all men. Who can deny that God made this man his witness in the African Church.

During my ten years' residence in Sag Harbor the Baptist Church was built. If I were called on to name the men whose active zeal largely contributed to found and perpetuate this church, whose devotion kept alive and burning its fire of worship, to what should I attribute it but to the spiritual ardor of Uriah Gordon, and the unfailing faith of Nathan Comstock.

There is another name connected with another church which in my early years was not often alluded to with favoring notice. But time and the nearness to eternity magnify the unity and lessen the differences of Sectarian thought. A few old men will join with me in naming Michael Burke as the founder and the sincere devotee, the earthly angel of the church we call the Roman Catholic. Divering creeds have divided churches, and in other places sometimes so far antagonized, as to blast their influence. To the credit of the churches of Sag-Harbor her history knows no such dark blot. For three-score years and more I knew her record of voluntary toleration, of charitable allowance, of fraternal recognition, of tranquil amity.

Here practically I learned of a faith that rests upon the Universal Love of the great Father. The littleness of man made creeds that distort the symmetry of Divine Revelation. For this grand lesson of a boundless, undying, God like Love, to the church of this place of any and of every name, I return my poor meed of sincere thanks. In sentiment and in spirit with you I say and sing:

"One sole baptismal sign,
One Lord below, above,
One faith, one hope divine,
One only watch word, love.
From many temples though it rise,
One song ascendeth to the skies."

Standing before you on this occasion which from the nature of the subject calls for our regard, having attained that age which renders it possible and probable this may be my last public utterance to you, what transcendent interest comes to me when I think that it is my Farewell. That soon the Angel whose summons all must obey will call my name. I hope in His Mercy serenely to answer the call.

In the dawn of Divine Revelation the Patriarch said: "Few and evil have the days of the years of my life been." In its meridian splendor I doubt the propriety of the expression and personally declare the reverse.

"And so beside the silent sea
I wait the muffled oar;
No harm from Him can come to me
On ocean or on shore;
I know not where His islands lift
Their fronded palms in air,
I only know I cannot drift
Beyond His love and care.
O brothers! if my faith is vain,
If hopes like these betray,
Pray for me that my feet may gain
The sure and safer way,
And Thou, O Lord; by whom are seen
Thy creatures as they be,
Forgive me if too close I lean
My human heart on Thee!"

CHAPTER XII

THE 250TH ANNIVERSARY OF THE SETTLEMENT OF THE TOWN OF EAST HAMPTON

Delivered on August 24, 1899, at the age of 81

HISTORY HAS RECORDED, eloquence has described, poetry has exalted, art has emblazoned the sterling virtues of the Puritan. Their landing in the desolation of winter is a story oft told and ever remembered, when

> *"The breaking waves dashed high*
> *On a stern and rock-bound coast,*
> *And the woods against a stormy sky*
> *Their giant branches tossed."*

It is a field in which it is thought the last sheaf has been bound and the fullest harvest gathered, where even the gleaners have searched for the ears which eluded the reaper's sickle, where your speaker, amid the toils of an arduous profession, wrought in the bi-centennial celebration in 1849 and at intervals since then, and by your invitation on this memorable occasion. For this invitation, for your lifelong friendship, I return sincere thanks.

The history of East Hampton is a subject worthy of the grandest effort and full of the loftiest inspiration. Who that has drank deep at that fountain has not found his theme expanding as time progressed, dilating as study opened up new and more charming views, larger and more moving thought. The theme exhausted? No! While literature endures, while liberty survives, while morality lasts, while piety bears its immortal fruits, while gratitude is fragrant with sweet and sacred memories, the name, the fame of other Puritan shall be radiant with light and enduring renown; undimmed by age, its star shall brightly shine.

> *"Watchman, will its beams alone*
> *Gild the spot that gave them birth?*
> *Traveler, ages are its own,*
> *See, it bursts o'er all the earth."*

Let the sons of East Hampton recall the history of their forefathers, their manly courage, their unyielding independence, their obedience to law, their enforcement of order, their devotion to education, their regard for humanity, and they will breathe an air too pure to nourish vice, too lofty to submit to degradation, and be fired with an ambition greater than human glory and a covetousness grander than of gain.

When was the town of East Hampton settled? This question, historically not insignificant, has received little consideration. If the settlement of one individual or family is regarded as the settlement of the town, then East Hampton is the oldest English settled on Long Island. The first practicing lawyer in New England, Thos. Lechford, kept a note book of his work from June, 1638 to July 29, 1641. In that book is a record of the deed of Pommanoc Sachem and his wife, of the island called Manchonat to Lion Gardiner, commander of the fort called Saybrook fort, dated May 3d, 1639. This deed of Gardiner's Island antedates all Indian deeds relating to Eastern Long Island. By deed, dated old style, March 10th, 1639, new style, 1640. James Farrett, agent for the Earl of Sterling, conveyed the same island to Gardiner "which he hath now in possession, which island hath been purchased before my coming, from the ancient inhabitants, the Indians."

Thus, in March, 1640, Farrett records the fact that Gardiner is "in possession." This antedates all other known English possessions in or near Eastern Long Island, and accords with the undisputed tradition that Gardiner's Island was the first English settlement in the State of New York. Since the island lies within the bounds of East Hampton it follows that with more than the shadow of argument that town may claim precedence as the first town settled by Englishmen in this State. The learned historian of Southold arguing priority for that town on the ground of prior individual occupation thereby argues from a fact that would give priority to East Hampton as a town first settled, and defeat the very claim he makes that Southold was the first settled town in the county.

If the question of the settlement of Gardiner's Island be decided it may be claimed that of the town is still undecided and still recurs: When was East Hampton settled?

The copper vane surmounting the old church showed conspicuously two dates, 1649, 1717. By uniform tradition the first was that of the settlement of the town, the second that of the building of the church. It may seem a crime akin to sacrilege to question the accuracy of the former date. If, with veneration, for a century and a half, five generations have looked up and accepted this date as a verity, who dare doubt, or deny, or challenge its accuracy? But history admits nothing but truth. Tradition, hearsay, conjecture, subjected to her severe scrutiny are often found erroneous. The student of history owes unswerving allegiance to truth: as a sworn witness he must "tell the truth, the whole truth, and nothing but the truth."

This audience will remember the deed from the Indians covering East Hampton to Montauk Highlands given to Theophilus Eaton, governor of the colony of New Haven, and Edward Hopkins, governor of the colony of Connecticut and their associates, was dated April 29, 1648, although Hopkins' assignment thereof to the people of East Hampton was dated April 16, 1651. It is shown by the town records that the people had long waited and long urged as their right the delivery of this assignment which recites that 30 pounds, 4 shillings, and 8 pence was advanced by him to Thomas Stanton and others who made the purchase and was repaid by the inhabitants of East Hampton. As a matter of fact settlement generally preceded purchase of the Indians and did so in the towns of Southampton and Southold and probably in this town. In the deed to the governors "their associates" are parties. It is a fair inference that these associates who advanced money for the purchase of the town intended settlement and did soon remove there, probably in 1648, if not before. They would not leave their money long invested without using the land it had purchased.

Preparatory to the settlement of the main body of emigrants, a pioneer party would prepare log cabins as temporary shelter and secure a stock of provisions for sustenance. This was the case both in Southampton and Southold. The wives and children of the emigrants required shelter from the pitiless storms. Common humanity demanded that an advance company of pioneers should construct shelter, plant corn and prepare for the reception of the main body of emigrants. All parties admit a settlement of this main body in 1649. But if that was preceded by a preparing party in 1648, that year is the correct date. If we can find corroborative traditionary or other evidence therefor, although slight, it would go far to establish the fact. Such confirming tradition exists and strangely enough has been overlooked. In 1806 Lyman Beecher, then minister in East Hampton, had, as contemporaries and associates, many remarkably shining lights, not the least of whom, as a congenial companion, was John Lyon Gardiner, noted as an antiquarian and literary man, studious, cultured, correct. He gave to Beecher from his treasured historic stores the fruits of research, of tradition and legend, which were transferred to his historical sermon, delivered January 1st, 1806. On page seven of that sermon the writer says:"One of the natives of Montauk who died about fifty years ago, aged it was supposed an hundred years, and who if she did not herself recollect the first settlement of the town, must have lived so near that period as to have received correct information, used to relate to persons now living the following anecdote, viz.: "That six families first planted themselves at the south end of the town; that they were discovered by some Indians that were on a hunting party; that the chief warrior applied to the Sachem living then at Three Mile Harbor for leave to cut them off; that the Indians who made the discovery were called in and interrogated. Did they invite you into their houses? They did. Did they give you to eat? They did. Did you experience any harm from what you ate, did it poison you? It did not. The reply of the Sachem, turning to his warriors, was: 'You shall not cut them off.'" Indian history was perpetuated by tradition and their aged women were their select repositories. Their traditions were remarkably reliable and this accords with known facts and is inconsistent with none. It accords with the list of first purchasers, given in the same sermon, viz:"John Hand, Sr., John Stratton, Sr., Thomas Talmage, Jr., Robert Bond, Daniel Howe, Robert Rose, Thomas Thompson, Joshua Barnes, John Mulford." (Capt. Daniel Howe probably did not reside here then and perhaps two other purchasers may not have been there then, leaving but six families as above.) Unless new negative testimony appears it would seem as if we must fix the settlement in 1648, and antiquarians have for many years so thought. Recompence Sherrill, deacon, died in 1836, aged 98 years; Eleazor Miller died in 1788, aged 91 years; Stephen Hedges died in 1737, lacking not quite six months of one hundred years. The last named must have remembered the facts of the settlement. The second must have known them from him. The first was nearly threescore years old at the time of Beecher's sermon and in frequent and friendly conversation with him. If the tradition of the whites as to the settlement contradicted that of the Indians it must have been known and declared. So far as is known the white men do not contradict the red men. The Colonial records of Connecticut show that East Hampton was accepted under their combination, November 1649. It must have then been an organized town with a settlement anterior. Historians differ in dates. Wood dates the settlement of towns from "purchase of the natives;" Prime dates from "their organization in civil or ecclesiastical government." The date on the old church vane may be according to Prime's standard and yet later than that of the pioneer settlement.

THE CONSIDERATION FOR INDIAN LAND.

The fair name of the Puritans has been bitterly assailed by their foes, because the price paid for the Indian's land seemed so inadequately small. They assert that the piety of the Puritan, his assumed regard for the conversion of the Indians, his philanthropic professions, did not prevent his taking advantage in buying his land. With the sneer of contempt, with the finger of scorn, with exultant triumph, their foes point to the consideration paid for the town purchase. Twenty coats, twenty-four looking glasses, twenty-four hoes, twenty-four hatchets, twenty-four knives, one hundred muxes, a kind of awl for making wampum, as a bargain bearing on its face a base fraud, and in itself a transparent cheat; substantially the same charge is made against all like transactions and purchases, whether made by individuals as Lion Gardiner or by associations as founders of towns. Remember war, pestilence, disease, intemperance had so decimated the Indian tribes that they occupied from four to ten times the land required for their sustenance even in their wild state. The consideration then paid was equivalent to forty times its value now. If the Indians had given to the whites three-fourths of their land for occupancy and culture, the remaining fourth thereby would rise in value exceeding that of the whole. In our day Government has given alternate sections for railway construction, It has donated homestead to actual settlers. It has fixed a nominal price on the public lands, and its policy is a vindication of the conduct and character of our forefathers on this question. In after years in the acquisition of Montauk the whites paid to the Indians hundreds of pounds, which rise of value due to their settlement thrice repaid the Indians for any lack of consideration in the original purchase. A wilderness, wild, neglected, forlorn, must not be measured by its value redeemed, cultivated, developed. The shallow thought that with no reflection condemns our fathers, with it must exonerate them from over-reaching. "Seek other cause 'gainst Roderick Dhu." On the records of the town some evidence confirming this conclusion appears. Daniel How, master of the vessel that brought the emigrants to Southampton in

1640, was a purchaser of the town of East Hampton, and owned a house there which, with all his rights in the purchased territory he conveyed to Thomas Baker by deed dated May 10, 1650, for twenty pounds. It is probable that this was the most commodious and valuable house in town. In November, 1651, the town meeting voted to pay Mr. Baker "eighteen pence for every Lord's day that the meeting shall be at his house." If after the settlement and erection of houses and organization of government in church and State the best house in town and a share in its unallotted lands sold for so little the whole unimproved territory must have had a small market value. In the assignment of the Indian deed from Edward Hopkins dated April 16, 1651, the consideration was named at £30, 4s., 3d. In view of the fact that Manhattan Island was purchased for baubles estimated at $24 in value, not one-third the amount paid for East Hampton, excluding Montauk, it ill becomes the citizens of the metropolis of this continent to condemn our forefathers in their purchase.

MIANTONIMOH.

In Scribner's *History of the United States,* Vol. II., p. 92, is recorded a speech of Miantonimoh, the great sachem of the Narragansetts, reputed to have been made to Indian tribes from Massachusetts to Long Island, designed to unite them in a league for the destruction of the whites, wherein he said: "We are all Indians, as they are all English, so must we be one as they are one, otherwise we shall be all gone shortly. For you know our fathers had plenty of deer and skins, our plains were full of deer, as also our woods, and of turkeys, and our coves full of fish and fowl. But these English have gotten our land. They with scythes cut down the grass and with axes fell the trees. Their cows and horses eat the grass, and their hogs spoil our clam banks and we shall all be starved. Therefore it is best for you to do as we, for we are all the sachems from East to West, both Moguakues and Mohawks, joining with us, and we are all resolved to fall upon them at an appointed day. And when you see the three fires that will be made forty days hence in a clear night, then do as we and the next day fall on and kill men, women and children, but no cows, for they will save to eat till our deer be increased again." This bit of Indian eloquence, which seems to have been the prototype of many Indian speeches since, was probably never made by Miantonimoh, but put into his mouth by some clever savage to work him harm. Capt. Gardiner, nevertheless, believed it to be his, and reported an intended massacre of the English to Mr. Haynes at

Hartford and Mr. Eaton at New Haven. Massachusetts was appealed to for aid, and the sachem was summoned to Boston to answer the accusation. The only evidence against him was the hearsay testimony of his enemies. This evidence, though accepted at Hartford, New Haven and Plymouth, was not believed by the Massachusetts magistrates. It may be thought presumptuous in the writer to question the authority of a history vouched for by the great name of William Cullen Bryant, yet I more than question, I deny, the correctness of the history and the conclusion of the authorities of the colony of Massachusetts, and for these reasons: This speech of Miantonimoh was reported by Wyandanch direct to Gardiner as stated in the chronicles of East Hampton, published by the New York Historical Society. In addition, as there stated, the Narragansett sachem said: "I have come secretly to you because you can persuade the Indians and sachems of Long Island what you will. Brothers, I will send over fifty Indians to Block Island and thirty from there to you, and take an hundred of Southampton Indians with one hundred of your own here," etc. Thus we see Miantonimoh as reported by Wyandanch had arranged the minutest details of a plan for a union of all the Indians on Long Island to destroy the English, and had promised aid and fixed the number of men to be furnished from his own tribe. These minutiae omitted in the history as if designed to discredit the charge against Miantonimoh, and destroy the credibility of his reputed speech, seems like a device unworthy of a historian. The Manhansett and Shinnecock tribes in 1642, the precise time, although not positively committed to this policy by hostile acts were so far unfriendly as to be easily persuaded into a confederacy to destroy the whites. (The four sachems of Shinnecock, Shelter Island, Montauk and Corchaug in May, 1645, were ready for war in the interest of the Dutch and in 1647, against the Dutch.) (See Col. Hist. of N.Y., vol. xiv., p. 60, and vol. ix, p. 18, etc. See address of H.P. Hedges at 5th semi centennial of the town of Southampton, noted at the end by Wm. H. Tooker.) Gardiner was a witness on the spot, and knew the Indian language and tactics. Wyandanch was his friend and the friend of the whites, as true as steel. Both were well known in New Haven, Hartford and Plymouth, and there believed. If Massachusetts, more remote from the place, knowing less of the men concerned and less of the facts, disbelieved, yet the proof satisfactory to the three nearer colonies, should be accepted by history, although she dissented. It is too late to question the intelligence, the veracity, the character of Wyandanch or Gardiner. Their fair name and fame will go down together to the remotest time. They have stood the test of centuries. They will wear the unfading garlands of immortality.

TRAITS OF PIONEERS.

The first settlers of East Hampton were men of enterprise, courage, self-reliance, industry, perseverance, self-denial. Founders of colonies require these strong traits of character. From their earliest records we read that they established a school, thereby proving that they cherished education. That they were pious men is shown by their instituting a church, erecting a meeting-house and settling and supporting a minister. Their whole history attests their courage and self-denial. Their works attest their industry and perseverance. Indolence is always a sin condemned by the judgment of mankind, by the test of experience, by the word of Revelation, by the example of our ancestors. Hard work was their lot generation after generation. Health, strength, prosperity were results. Their intense hatred of idleness may be aptly condensed in the Spanish proverb, "While the devil tempts other men the idle man tempts the devil." As an inheritance to their descendants they transmitted the safeguards of industry. More wonderful, still, they organized and perpetuated popular government. I say more wonderful because other races have established colonies, have extended territorial greatness, enlarged their conquests and failed to exercise the cohesive organizing power that welds individuals into harmonious and enduring communities and nations. When East Hampton was born it was born a town, having within itself all the elements of an organized community. The colonies of the Latin or French and Spanish race were consolidated and kept in being by power and prestige from without, by the despotism of the sword. Witness South American from the Isthmus to Cape Horn. Witness the colonies of France from Quebec to New Orleans. The Anglo-Saxon colonies inspired with memories of Magna Charta, contained within themselves the living, binding, organizing power out of which union, consolidation, government was evolved as by a law of their being. From its earliest day to the present in East Hampton the town meeting was a power before which dissent, discord, disorganization disappeared. The resistance of the individual was overcome by the united momentum of the mass. The town meeting was the acorn from which grew the compactness of the State and the magnitude of the nation. The phalanx of the Greeks overcame the loose martial array of the Asiatic races. The consolidated power of compact, Anglo-Saxon organization prevailed over lack of cohesion in the Latin races.

ARCHITECTURE.

Pioneer life admits small space for ornamental arts. The useful demands too much for culture of the beautiful. In the chronicles of East Hampton allusion is made to the dwellings which succeeded the first rude huts of the settlers. It is there stated: "They were built after the same fashion as those in New England. Their outward form and architecture much resembled the salt box which hung in the kitchen of every house, and which was humorously said to have formed the model of the builders throughout New England," etc., and to be borrowed from the style of those in the Netherlands. These dwellings, two-story in front on the south and one story in the rear, were often by addition made, in after years, a double house. After the Revolution the double, two-story dwelling was the prevailing style. After 1835 the single house, end and front to the street, with two stories, was the fashion. Thus the age of a dwelling may be very nearly decided by its form, its finish, its windows, which all the while grew larger in number and size.

THE PURITAN LIFE.

Sometimes in pleasantry, oftener in animosity, the precision, the sternness, the intolerance, the devotion of the Puritan life have been criticised adversely. It has been said by their descendants thoughtlessly, by their adversaries deliberately, that admitting their merits "I would not like to live with them." Much less would those critics of the Puritan desire to live with his contemporary adversaries, with their laxity of morals, their intolerance of legitimate restraint, their devotion to the divine right of kings, their exclusion of popular rights, their limited sphere of conscience in worship, their oppressive system of tithes and low standard of ministerial duty and life. Association with them would not elevate or emancipate. Non-conformity in England to-day bears the yoke of ecclesiastic and governmental oppression. Puritanism to-day in this fair land has borne the beneficent fruit of universal disenthrallment. "I would not like to live with the Puritan" may be true. But it is true not because they were more intolerant, more indolent, more ignorant, more immoral than their contemporaries. It is true because human progress has made this age the grandest for human life of all the ages; because the advancement in science, in arts, in literature, in morals, in ministration to human comfort and happiness have made this age transcendent in all the elements of enjoyment, far, far beyond all past eras of the historic world. I go back in memory to the scythe and sickle, to the fire on the hearth, and "the old oaken bucket," to the whizz of the wheel and the thump of the loom, to the tallow dip and the tinder box, to the flail and the riddle, to the crackle and swingle and hatchel, to the flint-lock King's arm, to the smooth-bore cannon, to the slow-sailing packet, to the lumbering mail stage, to the days when no fires warmed the church, no coal warmed dwellings, no gas lighted houses, no steamships traversed oceans, no telegraphs encircled the earth, no anesthetic allayed pain, no inoculation warded off death. To those days neither the friends nor foes of the Puritans would go back. Heirs of the past, enlightened by its experience, enlarged by its contributions, emancipated from its burdens, unconfined by its limitations— no one would willingly sink the joyous life of this for the dimness of the past age.

THE STANDPOINT FOR A VIEW.

The judgment of any age should be from the standpoint, not of this, but of that age. It is most incorrect and unjust to view and declare from the elevation of this age the depression, the intolerance, the grossness of the times of the Puritans. In Presbyterian Scotland cockfighting was practiced as late as 1790, (vid. *Chambers Book of Days,* vol. i, page 238). In Episcopal England bear-baiting and bull-fighting were practiced as late as 1802, and were not abolished until 1835. Within a century an appointed paid official waked the church sleepers. Attendance on church was compulsory. Neglect to attend was by law finable so late as the ninth and tenth years of the reign of Queen Victoria, when compulsion was abolished. Serfdom survived in England until 1660, and in Scotland until the reign of George Third. It is with ill grace that the voice of England or Scotland or their adherents utters condemnation of the narrowness of the Puritan. "Why beholdest thou the mote that is in thy brother's eye, but considerest not the beam that is in thine own eye?"

THE MINISTER.

In the colonial life the minister was the religious and political instructor of the people; often the referee to settle their differences, and a medical practitioner and adviser, held by them in reverence and affection now almost unknown. Their life was hard, narrow, uneventful, secluded. He became a friend, a traveler, a newspaper, an inspirer of thought. His prayers, like Jacob's ladder, began on earth, ended in heaven. His sermons, like links of logic, formed a chain in a demonstration followed by his hearers with an intelligent delight wherein time was not wasted but wanted by the hour. If he dwelt with emphasis, now unknown, on the sovereignty of God, and gave small place for His love and mercy, it was a phase of teaching as effectual then, as now it would be vain. That was an age when willfulness required unconditional submission; this when the sunlight of Divine benignity charms and wins the soul as never before.

THE HALF-WAY COVENANT.

The civil government of New Haven and Massachusetts derived power from the Church. From the Church the State was born. Church members only could vote and they only were qualified for official position. Hence the pressure to enter the church as an avenue to the right of suffrage and of official station. Strange that the door of the church was the door for ambition to worldly preferment, and alliance with the church was the way for alliance with the world. Hence a pressure to enter the church and hence a lowering of the standard of membership to let in the office seeker. Out of this state of affairs grew a limited church membership which required the candidate to profess belief in God, in the divinity of Jesus, in the sacred Scriptures and a promise "to train his children in the nurture and admonition of the Lord." Then without profession or claim of a divine renewing the candidate was entitled to the sacraments of the church for his children, including baptism, and thereby became a qualified elector entitled to vote and hold office. The church records of Minister Huntting show that this modified form of church membership had traveled from other colonies to this town, and was practiced here and known as "The Half-way Covenant." While it is true that this town did not require church membership as a prerequisite to vote or hold office, it is equally true that this modified church membership here prevailed and trouble grew out of it. In the "great awakening" that wrought a spiritual revolution in New England, the "New Lights" denounced, and their conservative adversaries upheld, the half-way covenant. Over this question the fire of theologic wrath flamed and burned. Whitfield, Davenport, Edwards, Brainard thundered against this, to them, corrupt practice. For this the people of Northampton drove Jonathan Edwards from the pulpit. Mankind has been from earliest ages divided into advocates of experiment or experience, conservatism or progress, new ways or old ways. "New Lights" or "old lights." These men were the men of progress, the "new lights" of their day.

In the latter days of Minister Huntting, so gentle, so scholarly, so devout, so faithful, so beloved of his church, there gathered a cloud which biographers have not dispelled. Of the years when he laid down his ministry, and after that his life, the record is silent. Why? Why was the sainted Brainard importuned to fill the pulpit and thrice invited to become the pastor? He sympathized with Jonathan Edwards, was affianced to his youngest daughter, who watched over him in failing health for months in her father's house, was at his deathbed, and within four months thereafter departed this life. (See Life of David T. Stoddard by Joseph P. Thompson, page 9. Note: Brainard died Oct. 9, 1747. His tombstone is in Northampton and will speak forever). Why was the eloquent, the learned, the brilliant Samuel Buell called to minister here? Why was Jonathan Edwards of world-wide fame invited to preach his ordination sermon? You may ask these questions. History will ask them and find the answer. These men and this church repudiated the "half-way covenant," which Minister Huntting, an "old light," sustained. A monition to the old that sometimes we may err and that it is not always the young who are in the wrong. May the sweet grace of humility last in the garland of graces, and forever be ours to exhibit and enjoy.

LANDS READILY TRANSFERRED.

In England burdensome restrictions hindered the transfer of lands. The policy there favored perpetuity of possession and the upbuilding of a landed aristocracy. The forms of conveyance were technical, verbose and cumbrous. With marvelous celerity all this mass of lumbering formality brought here by the fathers was consigned to the oblivion where it belonged. With strong common sense they stripped conveyance of its useless jargon, and retaining the wisest rules, disposed of their lands in the simplest way. By vote in the town meeting they disposed of lands and the vote with them had the force of a deed duly signed, sealed and delivered, and was deemed to convey title unquestioned and unquestionable. In Connecticut by law and vote of town meeting conveying lands was legalized, and confirmed to pass title. Anciently it probably would be so interpreted and construed here. Whether it is so now with all the five half centuries of free institutions, is more than doubtful.

LANDS DEDICATED.

If a land owner maps out a street or public park, and exhibits such a map to the proper authorities of an organized community, with the declaration that he dedicates forever such street or public park, designated by monuments and bounds, and such authorities accept the same for the use and purpose stated, then, without deed, without other writing or act, instanter, with the rapidity of lightning title vests in the public, and the dedication is complete and binding on all the parties as an act irrevocable. By such a method of conveyance, so simple, so open, so truly American, the town meeting voted and dedicated to the public, highways, streets, burial grounds, church sites, squares and school-house lots. Thus, by like vote thousands of acres of land were allotted in severalty to the proprietors thereof. Thus by like title this beautiful Main street, unsurpassed among the Hamptons, spacious, neat, graceful, picturesque, the crown and glory of the town, was dedicated by the fathers to the public, an enduring monument of their perception of the beautiful.

CHARLES I.

Charles I., of England, was a tyrant, deceitful, perfidious, aggrandizing all power in the prerogatives of the Crown, and crushing the liberties of the people guaranteed by the British Constitution. France paid him money wherewith to betray and enslave the people he governed. His son, Charles II., added to the vices of his father a shameless licentiousness that made his court the most dissolute and immoral England had known. Charles Barnes, an early settler in East Hampton, was its first schoolmaster. Let us see when we find another Charles. The tax list of East Hampton in 1675 has 42 names and in 1683, 70. The deed for Montauk in 1687, has 35. The equalization of three Montauk purchases in 1748 has 127. The general association to stand by the Continental Congress was signed by every man in East Hampton capable of bearing arms in 1775 and it numbers 260. In all there are names summed up 534, covering over a century and the name of Charles never appears. If evidence was wanted to show how our ancestors prized freedom and detested tyranny what could be more conclusive than this avoidance of even the tyrant's name on their records age after age.

IN THE REVOLUTION.

East Hampton, in the patriotism of her townsmen, in the unity of her people, in the devotion of her sons, is surpassed by no town in the county or State. Her seven years' subjection to hostile arms after the Battle of Long Island, the banishment of her bravest sons, the pillage of her harvest by friend and foe, derided by the British conqueror in his exultation, despised by Americans for being conquered, her condition was sad and forlorn. The bitter cup of poverty, of subjection, of oppression, of bondage was hers to drain to the dregs. With rare fidelity, with the intuition of literary genius, with imagination true to reality, with romance based on fact, Miss Mary B. Sleight, in the book entitled "*An Island Heroine,*" has delineated the unyielding, unsubdued, incorruptible devotion of the sons of East Hampton to the cause of Independence and the freedom of the thirteen colonies of British North America. The descendants of Revolutionary sires elsewhere organized are nowhere more universal than in East Hampton.

HUNTTING MILLER.

I remember an evening sixty-eight years ago in the east room of the dwelling then owned by my father, now the home of John H. Mulford, son of Samuel G. Huntting Miller was visiting my father, and both were born subjects of King George III. Miller was over seventy-five years of age, of a ruddy countenance, with long hair white as snow, a ready talker, a genial companion, repository of a vast fund of legend and tradition. Dressed in his blue surtout, marching up the north aisle of the old church he seemed a venerable relic of a generation long gone by. I see him now as I saw him then, intensely alive, practical, just, in patriotism ardent, in righteousness a Gibraltar. He spoke of the sufferings of this old town in the war of the Revolution, of the British soldiers quartered on our citizens, of their lawless depredations, their unprovoked abuse, their wanton insults, their vulgar insolence, their assault on Captain John Dayton, the historic incident on Pudding Hill, the inhumanity of the ruffian Major Cochran, the great care taken by the British to suppress news of the battles of Bennington and Saratoga. Animated with the theme the old man acted his part to the life. The stage may simulate nature, but no feigned character can equal the living reality of his narration of memorable events, and when he told of the vain attempt of the British to conceal the triumph of American arms his exultation knew no bounds. The glad news could not be suppressed. In that night of deepest darkness the day-star of victory illuminated the gloom of despondency and despair. To hear Huntting Miller describe the effect of the news from Saratoga and tell how in low, suppressed, accents the citizens of East Hampton spoke one to another, "Burgoyne is taken! Burgoyne is taken!" was to hear that which in thrilling interest, in magnitude of extent, in enduring results to the nation and to humanity, no narration of Homer, of Euripides, of Shakespeare can exceed. The genius of American patriotism, the memory of undying self-denial, the magnanimity of immeasurable love of freedom dilated and filled and fired the soul of this old resident and typical citizen of East Hampton and eye witness of the Revolution, with power beyond expression. May his devotion to his country be unforgotten.

"Be thy virtues with the living
And thy spirit ours."

On this same memorable evening my father asked, "How old is this house?" Huntting Miller said, "My father told me this house was at least seventy-five years old when he first knew it and that must have been seventy-five years ago," to which add the sixty-eight last years and we find its age over two centuries.

THE OLD HOUSE

was probably the home of Josiah Hobart, high sheriff of Suffolk county, and soon after passed into the Mulford family, and was, in the Revolution, the home of Col. David Mulford, a near neighbor of Dr. Buel and often named by the author of the *Island Heroine* in that romance. The Rev. Ebenezer Phillips owned and occupied it during his ministry. It was for twelve years my father's home. And now in the course of human events it is again inhabited by John H. Mulford, a house-holder of the same family name as in ante-revolutionary days. Over its threshold haughty sachems have marched, within its rooms the officials of King George have feasted. It has witnessed festal joys and echoed with bitter laments. Within it high hopes have been nurtured. Blighted and blasted they have gone out in darkness. Aspirations have been cherished sometimes to become realities, sometimes to vanish. Within its walls seven generations have been born, seven generations of the dead have thence been borne. There pallid lips and faltering tongues have whispered, as in our extremity we may do:

> *"O Thou that for our sins did take*
> *A human form and humbly make*
> *Thy home on earth.*
> *Thou that to Thy Divinity*
> *A human nature didst ally*
> *By mortal birth;*
> *And in that form didst suffer here*
> *Torment and agony and fear,*

So patiently;
By Thy redeeming grace alone
And not for merits of my own
O, pardon me!"

How boundless is history. In its study, "Hills o'er hills and Alps o'er Alps arise." In miniature that house has a history of the centuries it has lasted, the occupants it has sheltered, the visitors it has entertained, the events it has witnessed. If the history of one house, one family name, is of such transcendent interest, how much more that of an old town colonized within less than a generation after the Pilgrims struck Plymouth Rock? Colonized by those, some of whom must have been familiar with the emigrants in the Mayflower. Thus the legends, the traditions, the history, the spirit of the first Pilgrims at Plymouth flowed on in continuous stream to our day and time. Venerable, delightful, dear East Hampton, identified with the early and later history of the nation, with its colonial life, with its Indian wars, with its aspirations for freedom, with its sufferings in the good cause, with its revolutionary agony, with its organic constitution, with its restored Union; her history is in part the career, the life, the history of this great nation. Let us aim to do nothing to sully the fair fame, the good name, the rich inheritance of our native town and native land.

I read of the majestic march of the Roman armies, of the returning movement of that vast horde that stormed and sacked imperial Rome, of the momentum of the Tartar host, of the swelling tide of Turks that surged over eastern Europe and threatened to overwhelm the continent. Vast as were these movements, terrific as was the shock of armies, perilous as was their influence on the destiny of nations, in magnitude of result, in sublimity of movement in its effect on the destiny of mankind, the march from the early settlements on the Atlantic shore to the shore of the Pacific is indescribably more beneficent and grand. The movers cut down the forests of a continent in their march, built vast cities, navigated rivers whose currents flow over thousands of miles, and lakes that are inland seas. They carry commerce and learning and the arts and Christianity with them. Colleges rise on the sites of a wilderness, church spires point heavenward. Humanity owes its debt of gratitude to these pioneers of industry, of education, of morals. A continent is redeemed, a confederation of the states is consolidated, a nation is born. In this march across the continent, in this beneficent mission to mankind, in this emancipation of a continent let us exult that our dear old East Hampton bore no ignoble part.

COMMERCIAL INFLUENCE.

Commercial influence somewhat affected East Hampton from its earliest days. Its era of meridian brightness may be dated from 1815 to 1850. The splendor of the achievements of Commodore Porter and Stephen Decatur, the undying courage of the heroic Lawrence gave to their great names a lustre that prompted parents to perpetuate their memory by like christening their sons. When J. Fenimore Cooper wrote the *Water Witch*, with appropriate fitness he located her mysterious and wonderful commander as a native born and bred in East Hampton. When he set forth the *Sea Lions*, he made Harry Gardiner her adventurous and hardy commander and she sailed out of Gardiner's bay. In my early days the language of common life largely borrowed its metaphors and expressions from the sea. We did not walk, we "drifted along;" we did not rise, we "turned out;" we did not retire, we "turned in;" we did not interview a person, we "hailed him," or "spoke him;" we did not converse, we "had a gam;" we did not relate an anecdote, we "spun a yarn;" we made no memorandum, we "made a log;" we did not run, we "scud;" we were not sick but "under the weather;" we did not ride towards a place, we "steered" for it; we called Northeasters "Levanters" and one's vehicle his "rig."

DEATH!

To the young the lessons of decay and death speak with a sound faint and afar off. To the old the roar of that ocean we shall sail so soon, grows more audible and nearer. The doom of two hundred generations gone casts its dark shade before our advancing steps. The few living contemporaries of our youth and early manhood admonish us of the brevity of human life. The majestic voice of the fathers of East Hampton calls from on high, "Come!" The sweet spirits of our mothers in the far-off Land say "Come!" The living, enduring Word enlightens the doubt and darkness that hangs over our pathway and says, "Come!" The Grand Architect of the Universe, who sent the circling worlds from his Almighty hand, whose law suns and stars obey, before whose power nothing is too vast, in whose notice nothing too minute, "who knoweth our frame and remembereth that we are dust," ever his resistless call rings from the o'er arching Heavens, "Come!" Admonished of our frailty, our weakness, our mortality, reminded of our intimate relation to the generations gone and those yet to come, not forgetting our obligations to the one, or our duties to the other, let us so live that the summons to us to look our last on earth, our first on the new, enduring life, shall find us so doing without remorse, without regret, without despair, in the sweet hope of the Father's outstretched hand and welcoming smile.

THE ATTRACTIONS OF EAST HAMPTON

to the early settlers were not few. The bounding deer ranged in her forest; myriads of wild fowl hovered in her air; her waters and shores abounded in clams and oysters; fish swarmed in her lakes and bays. Much of her land was meadow ready for the scythe. A large portion was fertile and responsive to culture. In the calm the scenery ministered to the sentiment of the beautiful, in the storm to the sublime. The mighty leviathan of the ocean was a prize alluring and remunerative. In other localities subsisted the straggling tribes of Indians, but in numbers none equalled the Montauks. If the savage with his bow and arrow could subsist much more the civilized man with superior arms could live. The convenience of harbors and waterways as facilities for travel invited commerce. The landscape was lovely, the air pure as ocean and bracing as ever blew, the climate genial. These attractions drew them to this fair inheritance as their lasting earthly abode. And the same continue and increasingly continue to attract the brain workers of the continent to East Hampton. The wearing cares of business, the mental strain of competition, the disasters and disappointments of human life, the monotony of arduous effort impel the soul to cry out

> *"Oh for a heart of calm repose*
> *Amid the world's loud road,*
> *A life that like a river flows*
> *Along a peaceful shore."*
> and the answer is found here.

The map of the county of Kent whence came our fathers shows the sea on three sides: the map of East Hampton does the like. The similitude of residence in the old and new world was striking and was another attraction to this location. The points of interest now were so then. Travel now from the centre to any direction and you attain some locality of historic interest, some landscape of rural loveliness, some valley of serene peace, some outlook of charming beauty, some expanse that reaches far, far off into the sublime unknown. Go west and the ancient hamlet "Jericho" speaks of an age that makes it historic, and

"Georgica, its little sister" utters a like voice; and Appaquogue, more ancient still, an Indian name, carries the thought far back to the thousands of years past and the barbarian ages that antedate all history and
end in dim oblivion. Go father and between the creeks find the
dwelling and the grave of Capt. John Dayton, the mighty hunter and
hero of the Revolution, whose life is an integral part of the history of
this town and the Empire State; go farther still to "Wainscott" opens to
the eye its plain and pond of diversified beauty. Go northwest and the
significant names of "Toilsome" and "Hardscrabble" tell us of the arduous labors of the fathers in the "Northwest Plains," and farther on
within thirty feet of the third milestone now obliterated, "Sachem's
Hole" marked the place where the bearers of the body of Poggatacut,
royal sachem of Long Island, rested and laid his head on their weary
way from Manhanset, now Shelter Island, to the burial ground of
sachem kings at Montauk. Farther on and unmistakable, now much
filled up, is the "Whooping Boy's Hollow," of dread and mysterious
memory, from whose depths the ghost of the murdered boy uttered
unearthly cries, as if in the agony of dissolution and death. Farther on at
the foot of the hill on the shore where now is Sag Harbor once stood
an Indian village whose name I call Wequagannock, but which no living man except my antiquarian friend, Wm. Wallace Tooker, can rightly
pronounce. The buffs and shores of "Northwest" big and little, present
rare and romantic views. "Three Mile Harbor" has its hills and vales, its
"Indian Highway" where once Indians lived and died. It abounded in
fish and clams on which they feasted. The piles of buried shells tell of
their presence in the long time ago, and there the sachems ofttimes
lived. The salt meadows of "Acabonac Neck" furnished food for the
stock of the early settlers and were highly valued. "The Springs" suggest
an oasis and "The Fire Place," when the fire was kindled, conveyed its
message to Gardiner's Island that a visitor was coming and awaiting
the boat from there. What scenes of varied charm, what legends of dim
romance, what diversified life all these could tell. Traveling east we
glance at the "Hook;" on the left leave "Freetown," significant name of a
bondage past; we ask is "Pantigo" a word of Indian or English deriva-
tion? Did some one of the aborigines long time ago, we know not
when, say something we know now what, construed to sound Pantigo,
we know not why? Or did some tired English traveler whose reluctant
feet trod their weary way over these plains, mindful of exhausting effort and exhausting breath, give name to the place where in long-
drawn syllables he walked and said, "Pant I go?" "Egypt," symbolic of
plenty in time long gone by is so now. "Amagansett," first fair daughter

to East Hampton, needs no bird plumage on her hat to heighten her charm as she turns her beauteous head eastward to look on her "Promised Land." "Napeag" waste and wild, has its meadows and its mosquitos as in the long time ago. Ages on ages past, old Ocean, by some caprice in its slow current, deposited the sand which formed the beach and joined Montauk, then an island, to that other island which ended in Amagansett. And yet the very wildness of Napeag attracts the artist's eye. "Montauk," the favored home of the Indian, the abode of the Royal Sachems and the royal tribe, unique, secluded, solitary Montauk. The aborigines by thousands have here lived, by thousands have here died. This vast graveyard of many people, of a strange tongue, of many generations in the past unknown, imparts to the spectator its melancholy and its meditative charms, and its hollow voice utters in impressive tone, "No trifling here." March south and the old burial ground holds the consecrated dust of the fathers and eight generations of their descendants. What eye can look unmoved upon its graves? Go father and "Mill lane" and Plain tell of the old horse mill of earliest times, and "Pudding Hill" of Revolutionary days. Go father still and

THE OCEAN!

the element of most attractive interest, of most elastic mood, of most illimitable expanse, of most varied expression; ocean from plain and dune and hillock appears to gladden the eye, dilate the lungs, purify the body and inspire the soil. Mountains may speak to fancy, rivers may whisper of beauty, lakes may express the thought of space; but ocean in vastness of expanse, variety of voice, murmur of music, moan of lament, dirge of woe, roar of wrath is inimitable, incomparable, unconfined, fearful, sublime.

THE UNDERTOW.

Old ocean bounds East Hampton south from the tip of Montauk to the Southampton line. It attracts visitors, it promotes health, it dispels malaria. Its products sustain human life; its mighty surge tells of power; its moan sings the dirge of the thousands sunk in its depths. Woe to him that falls in its undertow. Shall I give an experience with it in the long time ago? It is dangerous for a speaker to make himself his subject, yet you may fairly say that a life of more than four-score should be fraught with a message of hope, of instruction or warning, and demand its deliverance, and I comply. Go with me to the ocean shore early in

October, 1842, where with Mr. Sanford, a former principal of Clinton Academy, and Mr. Livingston, the then teacher, our mutual friend Samuel B. Gardiner had taken us for a ride to Appaquogue. Sanford went in bathing and by urgent request of all I did also. The surf was high, the water cold. I swam out some thirty rods and returning, when near the shore, after long, exhausting, unavailing effort found I could get no nearer. There was a bend in the shore; at each outer end the high waves broke and their momentum carried the incoming waves toward the centre. The waters gathered there must recede, and returning underneath the incoming wave flowed seaward, and rose to the surface at a point where its volume overcame it. That was the undertow. Woe to the swimmer who unwittingly strives to overcome it. If he soon finds out his danger and turns at right angles out of it, well! If he persists in the contest with the current he is doomed. Unconsciously I had persisted near to the point of exhaustion. The chilled waters almost froze the life blood. The shore recedes. The horrors of death got hold of me. Even at this distance of time I remember the minutest circumstance attending this fearful event. My companions alarmed for my safety, ran down from the bank where they had been watching the wave, with that interest wherewith ocean beguiles the onlooker. I remember revolving the question, Can I float until help is brought from Appaquogue and Georgica or Jericho to launch a boat and pick me up? Just as I was about to speak of this, appeared a mighty rolling incoming wave and with the rapidity of light it flashed upon me, That vast body of water will overcome the undertow. On its swift crest I put forth all my power and gained. Another like mighty wave and another desperate struggle for life and yet another still flung me on the beach and hurled me back as the wind whirls the feather, and still another wave threw me further up, and with desperation, hands and feet buried in the sand, I crawled on the shore. Panting, gasping, freezing, unable to stand, a victim rescued and barely rescued from the undertow. Great God! What a deliverance! An experience of impending death, of unexpected safety. An experience of the power of memory and the power of conscience all but supernatural. The reverberating thunder is not more audible, the lightning flash is not more visible than, in the danger of impending death, the voice of conscience and the flash of memory. As in a panorama all the past life unrolled instanter. As in the day of Judgment, over all other voice swells the voice of an accusing or acquitting conscience. O God! With what an awful power I saw the buried past revive in that dark hour and all its ghastly memories live again! Agnostics may ignore, skeptics may doubt, infidels may deny the reality of a coming judgment. For all that it is true and is coming. How do I know? I have been there. I have known the unrollment of life in an instant of time; the condemnation of conscience reechoing the judgment of the eternal equities; have been in the valley and shadow of death, from thence I bring tidings of a coming Judgment that will ring in the transgressor's ear in the Resurrection morn, as clear, as loud, as real as the trump of the Archangel. O man! overcome in the undertow of unhallowed indulgence, of beguiling intemperance, of consuming covetousness, of engrossing worldliness, of dismal and disappointing crime, think not to avoid the sentence of Jehovah. You are gone, forever gone, unless you sheer out of the undertow and stand on the abiding rock. In the undertow of vice, of sensuality, of selfishness there is nothing but danger and delusion and death. There is an Almighty hand outstretched for your deliverance. Take hold of it and you are rescued. Fail to do it and you perish.

REVISITING SPIRITS.

Do the spirits of the dead revisit the scenes of their earthly life? Are there memorable occasions when the genius of the place returns to its former abode? Lion Gardiner, Puritan, pioneer of commanding genius, of iron nerve, of winning ways, of pious spirit, of far-seeing intellect, who wrote to Winthrop for a young minister for this town, believed to be none other than Thomas James. Lion Gardiner, unsullied name! Does his undying soul revisit the scenes of his mortal abode and his earthly life? Divested of the tenement of clay does it view the ground whereon his feet have trod, the places where centered the interests, the hopes, the toils, the aspirations of his life, here?

Thomas James, preacher of the everlasting gospel of righteousness, in the first old thatched church, to the Indians at Montaukett whom he sought to win from their wild pagan ways to the faith that is "the substance of things hoped for and the evidence of things not seen," does he come back to his unique tomb, haunt the spot where stood that old church, journey to Montauk where he had catechised the Indians in Bible truths?

Does the meditative soul of Minister Huntting from some hilltop in Heaven cleave its way to the spot of his earthly ministry, where sleep the bodies of those who heard his earnest words, and followed his clear logical thought? Does it hover over the ground whereon stood the sanctuary of 1717, wherein so long he preached the fearful truths of a Revelation mysterious and divine?

Does the ardent, patriotic, undying soul of Buell from its high abode, return to the place where he so long lived and so grandly wrought, and look for and lament the ruin of that church edifice sanctified by his ministry of half a century? But for him, no Clinton Academy would have graced the village and town of East Hampton with the glory of its light.

If Samuel Mulford lives in the spirit land, does his thought go to me locality where as a patriot and hero he suffered and wrought that future generations might be free? Does he there see a spirit nobler, loftier, grander than his own?

Or those mighty souls of the Revolution, the Mulfords, David and Ezekiel; the Gardiners, Abraham the Colonel, and his son Nathaniel or the Millers, Eleazar and his son Burnet, or Captain Thomas Wickham, or Captain John Dayton, and many others? These! Do they in presence review the past and descend to the fields of their mortal career? Is their high purpose transmitted to this present generation and these money-making times? Our creed enjoins no prayers to saints; it forbids no following after their bright example, no marching in their footsteps, no imitation of their virtues. It forbids not the belief in their invisible presence, in their profound interest, in their devout approval of this celebration. If the veil of mortal flesh that hides their presence from our sight, that stops our ears to the music of their song, that dulls our perception to the message they speak were rent in twain then we might see and hear and know their spiritual form, their celestial song, their high-souled words. However lofty our ideal it would fall far beneath the reality. Spirits of the immortals! Of the founders and the fathers of this honored town, live! Live forever in the hearts of your children!

CHAPTER XIII

THE SEA
—~~~—

Delivered in January 1900 at the age of 82

MR. HENRY P. HEDGES. MR. CHAIRMAN, LADIES AND GENTLEMEN OF
THE BOARD OF AGRICULTURE OF THE STATE OF CONNECTICUT:

IN YOUR NAME your indefatigable secretary invited me to speak of "the
sea" as distinguished from the land. With pleasure and thanks for the
high privilege I accepted.

Your secretary knew that I was born and had [been] raised on Eastern Long Island over four score years, that there in our earliest and latest days and over our graves is the ocean's roar, our unceasing harmony
in life, our dirge in death.

He knew that by location we with you were attracting commerce,
trade, manufactures, and development of our waters, away from the
culture of the soil. By steam power the world competes with the
farmer, so that in our old routine of staple crops, corn, oats, wheat, our
labor is measured by that of the serf and not of the freeman. The shores
of Long Island and of New England have become the summer resort of
increasing thousands of visitors, thereby modifying the culture of products of the soil, and seemingly destined to work an entire and a paying
revolution in agriculture operations. The day is not quite here, but is
coming. Meantime the farmers on opposite shores of Long Island
Sound are asking each other across the waters, "What shall we do to
live as freeman ought to live, training our children so that they will
know their rights, and knowing, dare maintain?" Underneath all indus-
tries, all arts, lies the bed rock of agriculture. It may be depressed, and
is so now, but out of the deep comes the voice of hope. Adjust the cul-

ture of the soil to the changed conditions. Develop all that the waters will produce. All that dews and rains will not fail to nourish here as elsewhere they often fail to do. Utilize labor-saving means. Prepare for more and more summer visitors, more and more fresh products of land and sea. This adjusting era is the time to try our faith and courage. Farming fail! Never, until man can survive without sustenance! This is the time for farmers to say as seamen say when chasing whale, "Now for a long pull, and a strong pull, and a pull all together."

By the logic of location New England and Long Island are the sanitarium of the nation. The mountains of the former and the shores of both have made them so. The historian of New London writes, "Here lies Connecticut and Long Island forever looking at each other from their white shores with loving eyes, linked as they are by the ties of a common origin, congenial character, and similar institutions, and guarding with watchful care that inland sea which, won from the ocean, lies like a noble captive between them, subdued to their service and enclosed by their protecting arms."

Our food contains a large quantity of water. The amount would be nearly as follows:

Of these twenty articles of food two contain fifty per cent. water, six less than that, and fourteen more. In this list, fluids like tea, coffee, cocoa, and soups varying eighty-five to ninety-six per cent. of water do not enter. Enough appears to show that more than two-thirds of our food is water.

Of these 20 items, Long Island produces all except the oranges, and Connecticut almost the same, and both largely by proximity to the sea, its waters forming so much of their substance. In two of our towns, cauliflower estimated at 162,500 barrels, at $2.00 per barrel, and amounting to $225,000 were shipped this fall. Our county is reported to produce more cauliflower than all the other territory of the United States. Cabbage, cucumbers, onions, beets, turnips, strawberries, and asparagus are cultivated at a profit in our county. Potatoes are our largest crop with a paying average yield and so fine that the price in the New York market ranges from ten to twenty-five centers higher per barrel than those raised elsewhere. The more water a crop contains the less it draws from the soil, *a problem* we are now studying. Our blue fish, striped bass, and Blue Point oysters cannot be unheard of. The product of our great South Bay alone is estimated at nearly $2,000,000 in shell and other fish. Ninety-six steamers of the American Fisheries Company report a catch of menhaden this season at 262,500,600, valued at $1,000,000; taken chiefly in waters adjacent to Long Island.

We speak of the "waste of waters" because they cover nearly three-fourths of the earth's surface, as if in the Divine harmony of creation, God had mistaken the just proportion of land and water. We forget that the food we eat contains no less proportion, that man in his living organism solid and fluid, is in miniature and symbolism not unlike the globe we inhabit. Think of a temporary drought, and the famine that follows. Think of its continuance and of augmenting misery. Think of a world where no water is, and you think of a climax of torment chosen by inspiration to portray the agony of Dives, because torment can go no farther. If, as a subject of thought, land is pregnant with profit to the farmers, water in its necessity to give profitable results for his toil, in its grateful ministry to satisfy thirst, in its cleansing power to purify the body, in its beneficent service to bear the products of land to remotest shores, in its facility to furnish food—as a field for the finest skill, the most adventurous enterprise, the most significant genius, the most daring valor, ocean yields nothing to land. Its study may satisfy us more fully of His wisdom in the creation of the world, who "hath founded it upon the seas and established it upon the floods."

Does the configuration of the continents tell their possibilities? Asia, with her 30,800 miles of coast line, has one mile only of coast to 459 of surface; Africa, with 14,000 miles, has 623 miles or surface to one of coast; South America, with 14,500 miles, has 420 of surface to one of coast; North America, with 24,500 miles, has 350 of surface to one of coast; Europe, with 17,000, has 156 of surface to one of coast; Japan, in location, seems to Asia like the British Isles to Europe, and is the only Asiatic power aroused from the lethargy of ages to the benefits of commerce. The map shows Africa and South America with smooth coasts like two vast Russian territories, wide at the topics, tapering towards the poles, and unfitted for marine supremacy. Europe puts out cape and promontory, peninsula and headland on all her three water bounds, and smallest of continents has hands and arms, feet and legs, lacking in other continents, that successively have made Greece and Rome, Venice and Portugal, Spain and Holland, victors in ocean war. Is not her greatest proportion of coast mileage the preponderating cause? The United States, with climate genial, two oceans almost encircling three sides, her border lakes, her abounding arterial rivers, her mineral wealth, her ship-building material, her varied, immense, and yet undeveloped production, bears on its surface capacity for a commerce in volume yet unknown in the world's records, and a naval supremacy unrivaled by any single power on other continents. In the War of the Revolution, and of 1812, the British fleet rode triumphant in Gardiner's

Bay; our patriotism should prevent the like presence of that or any other fleet in coming ages. And England, our mother-land, with her 2,000 miles of coast line, her magnificient harbors, and unbounded enterprise, England, from the days of the great Armada, has maintained a commerce world wide, a colonial empire encircling the globe, a naval supremacy that successively wrested the sceptre from Spain, Portugal, Holland, and France, and made Waterloo possible. Her larger coast line, three times longer than that of France, enables her to raise more seamen, and hence her supremacy. The map of the British Isles speaks this to the eye.

Write the history of the Mediterranean Sea, and you write the history of the ancient world. On its shores rose Tyre and Sidon, Egypt and Troy, Greece and Rome, Carthage and Venice, Spain and France, at different times predominant on the sea, and thereby over other nations. It has borne the navies of victor and vanquished. The story of the Argonautic expedition in quest of the golden fleece, the fate of the 1,183 ships sailing from Greece to the siege of Troy, the ignominious overthrow of Xerxes, the battles of Thermopylae, Marathon, and Salamis, the mighty names of Scipio and Hannibal, of Pompey, and Caesar, of gods and demi-gods, live with the records of this inland sea. If the historic end of the word extends back forty-five centuries, the history of this sea covers eight-ninths of that era. What the Mediterranean Sea was to the ancients, the Atlantic is to the moderns. Transportation now from London to New York is as expeditious as formerly from Athens to Egypt, or Rome to Carthage. The power that is supreme on the Atlantic is invincible against the world. Great Britain accepts and acts on this principle as an axiom. The United States may wisely do the same.

The examination of the sea coast is a wonderful study, showing some compensation for every disadvantage. The rocky shores of Maine and Massachusetts, down to the vicinity of Plymouth, abounds in harbors of safety from the perils of fog, wind, and wave. The sandy shores of Cape Cod and its vicinity, failing to open harbors, are not so perilous to life and ship as a rock-bound coast. The more rocky and dangerous part of the Connecticut shore opens to the mariner more frequent havens of refuge. The shores of Long Island present like features. It is as if the creative power in tenderness for the navigator with increasing perils had provided increasing avenues for escape. As if on the rock and on shore he had written in lines of lasting endurance and monuments of His mercy and His goodness.

Surrounding waters laving shore, and stopping there leave the land an uninhabitable, unproductive, parched waste. He who made them enveloped them with an encircling atmosphere miles on miles in height, with a benign power when heated by the sun to lift into its embrace from sea and ocean, lake and river, pervading volumes of water, and carrying it over isle and continent, drop it from the clouds to enrich and rejoice the earth. The parched hills of Connecticut in dearth and drought, telephone to the sea, and clouds, the great water-bearers in the heavens, move over the sphere of desolation and drop their precious freight in gladness on the soil.

The current from the North Pole flowing south freezes this continent nearly through Labrador, bringing with it icebergs, and making adjacent land a cheerless desert. Across the Atlantic, in nearly the same latitude, lie the British Isles in marked contrast, with genial climate. Why? The Gulf of Mexico, almost encircled by this continent, receives from the coast of Africa a vast stream following the southeast trades, heated under the Equator, which, coursing around the gulf, is projected from its northeastern rim with a velocity powerful enough to run near our coast, and temper our climate somewhat north of Montauk Point, where it is seaward about 110 miles. Thence it moves in a curve, bathing the shores of the British Isles, bearing warmth, fertility, comfort. Writers have termed the Gulf of Mexico the great teakettle of Great Britain. Blot out that gulf and England loses her genial climate, her abounding prosperity, her favored lot, and, perhaps, her naval supremacy.

Understanding something of the magnitude of this subject and of the qualities evoked by ocean life, we can better estimate whether national pre-eminence is promoted by maritime location, whether the seacoast concerns the character, welfare, comfort, attainments, momentum of its residents. If it were practicable by vote to do so, would the borderers on Long Island Sound, on the Connecticut River, on the magnificent harbor of New London, vote to fill them up, exchanging land for water? This case is put no because of a doubt what the vote would be, but, if God has *so* made one part of this country, which we know, that we see in it the working of a hand, as wise, as beneficent as it is mighty, may we not infer if the little we see speaks thus, what we do not well see and know, may speak the same language and evince the same benignant design, thus enlarging our contentment and confirming our faith.

What traits of character does life on the sea develop? The sight of a sailor three sheets in the wind may satisfy the surface thinker of the imprudence and improvidence of seamen, and seemingly stamp his character, yet, a drunken sailor is no more an index of seamen, than a

drunken farmer would be of farmers. In a long life of intimacy with seamen I have observed some qualities of mind and heart, brought out by
conflict with wind and wave. What elements are more baffling and uncertain? To-day a calm, to-morrow a storm; now all sun, and now all
darkness; now in mid-ocean, and now on a lee shore; tides now rising,
and again receding; streams, and currents, and eddies, and whirlpools,
coming we know not when, going we know not where. What occupation can demand or educate to more careful forethought than that of
the navigator? The popular notion that ascribes to the sailor the trait of
thoughtlessness is a popular mistake. He is, and necessarily must be, a
man of intense forethought.

The oar and sail were joint ship-moving powers until past the days
of the roving Vikings. Topmasts superseded the heavy single mast after
the day of Columbus; high castles aft for officers, forward for seamen,
were not disused until after the time of the great Armada, and our word
"forecastle" has survived its literal meaning. If the curve, the least impediment to water, was undiscovered until our day, the like in the plow
to the furrow so remained. It is something to know how to put your
hand on any rope in a full-rigged ship the darkest night, which a landsman knowing not, knows himself "a land lubber." I risk nothing in calling the seamen inventive; I need not say the sailor is enterprising, his
calling stamps him that; I need not say he is broad minded, his voyages
to remote regions make him so; conflict with elemental forces com-
pels him to be resolute. His life is eminently a continued combat to
overcome obstacles, and a man's measure is his power to overcome opposing forces. The more he can overcome, the stronger he is, and the
more he weighs in the scales that measure power—so weighed the
sailor will not fail to attain the full standard of manhood. Responsibility
he cannot avoid, and, hence, is self-reliant; in the calm he must be patient. Squalls are quick, emergencies sudden, and must be met by
thought as quick, decision as sudden. In the long night watches the
stars in the heavens speak to him, "Day unto day uttereth speech, and
night unto night showeth knowledge." He becomes not only a quick
and a precautionary, but a deep thinker. Among the most profound
thinkers I have known may be numbered the master mariners from
our own seaports. We of the land tread the marked and beaten road,
the voyager on the ocean finds no guideboards and no milestones.
With the most watchful vigilance the heavens may be darkened so
long, or the elements rage so furiously, as to make his location uncertain and his shipwreck unavoidable. He often meets those who have so
suffered, and knows not when their hard lot may be his own, hence his

gentleness to the unfortunate and his known generosity; virtues found nowhere else more conspicuously.

If athletics, now so prominent in college life, mean anything in enlargement of strength, health, and life, the conflicts of the sailor with opposing elements mean more, because one is temporary, the other enduring contest. Admit all that the victor in the boat race can claim, victory is bought at the expense of the vanquished. In the whale chase the trophy gained by the victor is so much rescued to add to the world's wealth, and costs no humiliation of defeat. In all naval victories our athletic whalemen, made more so by training, have been a conspicuous element in achievement.

If mountains are the stronghold of freedom, its cradle in infancy, its grave in death, the ocean is not less its nursery and abode, swung from all obstructions of shore, all unmeaning restrictions of society, rocked on the surges of its vast expanse.

> *"Our thoughts as boundless and our souls as free,*
> *Far as the breeze can bear the billow's foam;*
> *Survey our empire and behold our home."*

This transport of being, this ecstasy of disenthralment, this largeness of thought, is the impulse of which freedom is born and ever lives.

LAW.

On the land man is subject to law as enacted or adjudged by influences, temporary, local, sectarian, municipal, narrow. On the mighty deep no village ordinance, no restricted legislation, no purchased legislature rules. What the universal judgment of mankind dictates, freed from all that is local or transient, that is law. Extend through to the widest bound of man's discernment, go down to the bed rock of everlasting equity and justice, go up to eternal harmony, and find the law of nations and of the stupendous ocean. From the day of Noah, God Almighty's master mariner, intellectual enlargement was born of the mighty deep. I need not name the great navigators of ancient or modern times. The great naval commanders of our own land are a living and a lasting testimony thereto. What enlarged wisdom, what profound sagacity, what discreet decision, what heroic valor, what intuitive genius, what faultless statesmanship glorifies the name of the victor at Manila?

Did not he who had power over wind and waive, power to magnify the loaves and fishes—to discern the miraculous draught—to know the heart of man, know the profound thought, the high-souled courage, the unshrinking fortitude, the adaptability for unmeasured devotion born of a life of conflict with the sea, and knowing this, not in ignorance, not by chance, but in infinite wisdom choose, as witnesses of His teaching, heralds of His divinity, apostles of His kingdom, ministers of His gospel, fishermen of Galilee, who would with abiding constancy, with every power of body and soul attest that gospel to man while living, nor shun to seal its truth with their last heart-beat and last expiring breath.

LIGHTHOUSES AND LIFE-SAVING STATIONS.

The slow progress of humane relief in war, of aid to indigence, of universal philanthropy, has been equaled regarding the safety of life and ship in commerce.

Over Long Island Sound is borne the products of continents, yet, until 1795, no lighthouses shone from our dangerous Montauk Point. Eight lighthouses erected by the states in 1789 were ceded to the general government. In 1820 the whole number in the United States was 55, and in 1852, 325. We now see from the hills of Eastern Long Island eleven lighthouses.

Life-saving stations in this country originated in Massachusetts in 1789, in huts built on her coast. Congress first gave aid to this object in 1847, efficient service began in 1869.

From November 1, 871, to June 30, 1890,

Reports show property			lost	$23,474,747
"	"	"	saved,	65,503,935
"	"	"	involved,	89,275,682
"	"	persons	"	46,061
"	"	"	saved,	45,516
"	"	"	lost,	543
"	"	"	succored,	8,691

THE BENEFITS OF COMMERCE.

Commerce enlarges thought, comfort, convenience, power, happiness. Gathering the experience and knowledge of many nations it makes them the treasure of all. Under its benign reign barbarism is local or impossible. What coal has done to warm this shivering world, what petroleum has done to illuminate its darkness, what India rubber has done to shield the human form from the tempest's wrath, what quinine accomplishes to dispel disease and death, are all the achievements of commerce. Through its ministry the men of Java and Brazil raise the coffee that adds delight to our breakfast. The Chinaman produces the tea that gives its charm to our evening repast. Toilers in Cuba and the Sandwich Islands are manufacturing our sugar, and in the East Indies producing our fragrant spices. The whole world pours its rich contributions into our storehouses.

FISHERIES.

You ask me what I know about fisheries? I know that in early manhood I have seen on our ocean, miles on miles, far as the eye could reach, fish in one solid mass, and have often known, 1,000,000 of menhaden taken at one haul (say 50 wagon loads). Now our shore fishing is nearly abandoned to steamers. In my boyhood wild pigeons in flocks of uncounted thousands came just after wheat harvest. I have seen not one in a score of years. The fate of the wild pigeon is coming to our menhaden, blue fish, and striped bass, is coming to the seal as it came to the buffalo. I remember when a few whale ships cruised out of Sag Harbor on the coast of Brazil, returning in six to eight months with full cargoes. Then the search extended to the Falkland Islands, around the Horn, and Cape of Good Hope, and into the Arctic Ocean, where the whales have been driven as a last refuge. The industry that numbered in our Sag Harbor nearly seventy ships, and in this country nearly 700 that always could man a navy with men as strong and brave as the world ever saw, was overdone, and now has dwindled from colossal to infant size. Our shore fishing for menhaden, striped bass, and porgies, almost destroyed by steamers, leave us yet a paying chance in catching cod and sturgeon, and on an average three or four whales each winter. Thousands of men devote their time to catching eels, clams, and oysters, and to cultivating oysters as a crop, which is an immense and a growing industry in Long Island and Connecticut waters.

In our quiet homes, secure from wave and storm, unexposed to the hazards of maritime enterprise that often loses all, enjoying the comforts of a life removed from poverty or riches, let the husbandman think of his tranquil life, his undisturbed repose, his sweet peace of mind. He has not his fortune where the wave or the rock may wreck it, he incurs no danger of breaking rope and swaying mast. Many perils lie in the seaman's way. Let the farmers' exemption fill his soul with sweet content.

The shores of continent and island first attract inhabitants, both savage and civilized. To this Long Island and all the archipelagoes witness. The emigrants to this country, with wise foresight, first located on river banks. In peace they brought to these shores the wealth of the deep and of far-off lands. In the Colonial Wars, in the Revolution, in the War of 1812, in all the history of this free land, seamen have borne with honor the nation's flag on ocean's wave. New England cannot afford to blot out her naval history, or close her seaports to the commerce of the world. Shut up these and her power, her prosperity, and her controlling mission are gone.

The disappointments, the casualties, the disasters that occur on land are frequent and sad. Those that come on the sea are still more frequent, more unavoidable, more calamitous. A shipwreck, attended with loss of life, is a view of desolation and wretchedness that seen is stamped forever in the memory of the beholder. The swaying, pounding, rocking, groaning ship, the unfurled flapping sails, the stranded and breaking cordage, the straining spars and masts, the symmetric structure that seemed instinct with life, marred and shivering in the death agony, the remorseless, surging billows that are rolling over the wreck and submerging and drowning men, this is a sight to freeze the soul with horror. What fearful amplitude of meaning belongs to the word *wreck*, the wreck of ship, the wreck of souls. The barque ship, *Edward Quesnell*, wrecked on our coast some sixty years bygone, bound to a New England port, was one of the saddest scenes my eyes have ever witnessed.

On the bank of the shore near the shipwreck were twelve drowned men, laid in a row as they were drawn from the wild, cold waves. To this day that vision of death stares me in the face, as perfect, as fearful, as pitiful, as heartrending as then.

Some twenty years ago, within less than two miles of my dwelling, the ship Circassian came ashore. A large force of workmen went on board to lighten and work her off. In the night when the tide made full and the prospect was fair to sledge her over the bar, the wind suddenly changed from blowing off to blowing on shore. The ship was on the bar, rising on the incoming wave, falling and pounding as it receded. That she must soon break in the middle, and sink the crew and workmen with herself, was inevitable. Some twelve or fifteen Indians of the Shinnecock tribe were on board, tall, athletic, powerful young men, the flower of the tribe, when they saw that death was coming did they sing the pagan deathsong of the Indian of two hundred and fifty years ago? Thanks to a Christian church and training; no! The listeners on the shore, helpless to save the imperiled seamen, heard a hymn, in our last living hour we may long to repeat. Over the noise of the groaning, breaking ship, over the shriek and howl of the tempest's wrath, over the ocean's roar, they hear in the melodious and melancholy strain those Indians sing:

"Jesus, lover of my soul,
Let me to thy bosom fly,
While the billows near me roll,
While the tempest still is high;
Hide me, O my Saviour, hide,
Till the storm of life is past,
Safe into the Heaven guide,
Oh receive my soul at last."

When the surf breaks in a bend of the shore the surges roll to the center of the crescent. Gathered there, they recede underneath the incoming wave, and rise to the surface seaward at a point where the momentum of the outward current overcomes the incoming wave, that is, the undertow. Woe to the man that remains in it. If he shears out of it he is safe, resisting it he is gone. Every bathing season finds victims to the undertow. I was once in it, and near to impending death; memory flashed as lightning all the past, conscience spoke in thunder tones. Do I believe in the last judgment? I know it; I have been there.

THE MYSTERIES OF OCEAN.

What mind has comprehended them? Man may ascend the loftiest mountain, tunnel and explore the deepest cave, mine the ore miles deep in the pits of the earth, but who has descended to the unfathomable depths of ocean or explored her hidden caverns and her deep dens? On the land we close the eyes of our dead and tenderly convey their bodies to the grave; on the engulphing sea no tender hand of kindred blood with sympathetic touch closes the eye, no grave of mother earth marks the place where the seamen sank. From the days of infant commerce, from historic times, the ocean has swallowed up treasure inconceivable, lives innumerable, navies uncountable, and in her depths we know not when, we know not where, lie strewn the navies submerged, the treasures hidden, the ghastly bones of the drowned, and over all this mystery roll the waves that guard their story until "the sea gives up its dead."

You look from a height, and feel an impulse to plunge below. A being the embodiment of all evil tempted one, the incarnation of all good, to cast himself down from a pinnacle of the temple, assailing this weakness in our nature. A look on ocean so fascinates and attracts; its vast expanse, its measureless power, its surging billows say, come to the disordered mind; the attraction to suicide in its wave is fearful. It seems a monster, hideous, yet alluring against which resistance is vain, from which flight is impossible. Fascination overcomes horror, the soul surrenders, and surrender is doom.

The sweat that bedews the brow of manly labor, dampens the forehead in death, in all the ages from the equator to the poles, is born of the world of waters, and is borne from we know not what spring or fountain, rill or rivulet, lake or river, or through what devious way of the heavens above or the earth beneath. The tear that drops from the eye of humanity in transports of joy or depths of woe, from the first inhabitant of the world over its wide expanse in all the centuries of recorded or unrecorded time, is born of that might ocean, whose billows break on the shores of all the continents, whose winds convey its waters over every cape and island, every hill and headland, every valley and plain, above the highest mountain, to fall in reviving dew or refreshing rain in the remotest land; the gift of a power as beneficent, as mighty, who is never limited, never partial, never narrow, but in universal benevolence maketh "the rain to fall on the just and unjust."

The centrifugal force of the revolving earth at the equator so far exceeds that at the poles as to raise the dimensions there and diminish them at the poles. Of the two diameters of the globe, that at the poles is about twenty-six miles the shorter. The centrifugal force at the equator just balances its additional diameter; stop the revolution of the earth and the ocean rolls to the poles, leaving the equator bare and uninhabitable; set in motion again, and the equator is submerged. An Almighty hand has moved, and infinite wisdom balanced antagonizing forces.

In all the migrations of water, in all its unnumbered changes in the ocean, in the wave on shore, in the upper air, in its descent from above, in the running rill or rivulet, not a drop is lost; the full measure is maintained, the minutest particle is undestroyed. We may believe that like it in its purity, its mobility, its endurance, virtue, honesty, righteousness, regardless of creed or sect, will abide all change, all ages, all adversity; undiminished, undimmed, indestructible, imperishable, guarded, preserved, secured, by the omnipotent Jehovah.

How wonderful is the circulation of the blood in the human body, impelled from the heart by the arterial channels to every part of the system, and returned there by the veins; to keep up its perpetual round while life endures. So the rising and receding tides of the living, mighty ocean pulsate through its vast expanse, preserving it from stagnation and death.

The water we drink is conveyed from center to circumference, and in response to manly labor, runs from every pore in purifying perspiration, ministering health and happiness; so the warm air lifts up out of the ocean into its sublime heights its waters, and moving clouds on every breeze traveling to far-off regions, drop their burdens and baptize anew grass and flower, fruit and tree, and performing its mission, by rivers that "to the ocean run," returns again, forever to keep on its beneficent, everlasting round. God's mighty mechanism in His material universe in ocean has its counterpart in the miniature mechanism of His creature, man.

FARMERS OF CONNECTICUT. Adverse forces have wrought against the farmers of Long Island and against you. We helped build the Erie Canal, and thereby built up a competition of the boundless west against ourselves. Water that had been our gain became our loss. We shared in the taxes levied to purchase and procure territory additional to the limits of the thirteen colonies, and did so adversely to our financial interest. When the national government laid on us our share of the burden of constructing railways to the Pacific, it compelled us to contribute to find a market for a vast area to our disadvantage. For four score years the tide has been against us. Think not that I came to mourn, I come to rejoice with you that the march westward from the Atlantic shore has been the majestic, the benevolent march of civilization and freedom. Our temporary loss has been the nation's glory and its gain. "It is a long lane that never turns." What was our transient detriment will prove our abiding advantage. If we have contributed to build up and enrich the mighty west, it is that for health and strength their people must come east to recuperate. The multiplying thousands that have moved towards the Rocky Mountains in thronging and increasing thousands return their summer delegation to our shores, and the days of our prosperity draw nigh. If we have been tributary to the prairies and valleys of the abounding west, in return they are becoming tributary to us. If for a hundred years we have sent there out best and bravest with our treasures, our prayers, our tears, the investment will repay us all it cost, and more.

Finally, the ocean world is replete with moral lessons. It is forever salt. Where in the deep caverns of the earth is that vast, inexhaustible deposit that keeps it so? Whose Almighty hand has measured to the ocean this enduring element? The air takes up the water *fresh*, leaving the salt; whose infinite, adjusting wisdom gave it the power to thus discriminate for man's good? The ridge at the equator and depression at the poles exactly balance the revolution of the earth on its axis. Whose divine mechanism contrived this harmonious adjustment?

The Gulf Stream poured in, and whirling around hundreds of miles, so comes out as to warm North America up to Newfoundland, and dividing, runs south, to do the same for France, Spain, and Portugal, and north, tempering the British Isles, Norway, and Sweden. By those impelling hand was this beneficent stream poured on coasts, otherwise bound in perpetual ice? The equatorial heat causes a vast volume of evaporation, replaced by polar streams, cooling there the air and water, that otherwise would be intolerable. By whose wise, creative power was this arranged? Our little pools of artificial make stagnate and die. God's mighty ocean, with tides and currents ever moving, is ever pure. Who can view the ocean in its vastness, unity, adjustments, mechanism, power, its benign office and mission, without emotion, without thanksgiving, without praise to Him "from whom all blessings flow"? If he who undevoutly contemplates the stars is mad, is not he who undevoutly sees "the works of the Lord and his wonders in the deep" also mad? To the seaman and the farmer, both living near to nature, by it the Creator speaks. A bard of your own New England has sublimely said:

> *"The harp at nature's advent strung,*
>   *Has never ceased to play;*
> *The song the stars of morning sung*
>   *Has never died away;*
> *And prayer is made and praise is given*
>   *By all things near and far;*
> *The ocean looketh up to Heaven*
> *And mirrors every star.*
>   *Its waves are kneeling on the strand*
> *As kneels the human knee,*
>   *Their white locks bowing to the sand,*
> *The priesthood of the sea.*
>   *The winds with hymns of praise are loud,*
> *Or low with sobs of pain;*
>   *The thunder organ of the cloud,*

The dropping tears of rain.
The blue sky is the temple's arch,
Its transept earth and air,
The music of its starry march
The chorus of a prayer.
So Nature keeps her reverent frame
With which her years began,
And all her signs and voices shame
The prayerless heart of man."

CHAPTER XIV

SAG-HARBOR IN THE REVOLUTION

Delivered in 1907 at the age of 90

THE HISTORICAL SOCIETY of Sag-Harbor invited me to write a paper with the title aforesaid, and gave me six months' time wherein to do it. I consented because although over 90 years old, the subject was interesting, congenial, instructive. My father was born a subject of King George, Third, and knew much of the olden time, and had transmitted its traditions to me. I had known and conversed with Revolutionary soldiers, and the duty seemed imperative to rescue from oblivion the memorials of our conflict for Independence which might otherwise perish. If I died in the work it was so exalted God would not frown.

Sag-Harbor in the Revolution was a port and point of magnitude. It was the strategic centre and key to all Eastern Long Island. Its history is connected with the progress of that war from beginning to end, read as if isolated narrows and degrades it. Every man capable of bearing arms, in the Towns of East-Hampton and Southampton, wherein Sag-Harbor was included, as early as the summer of 1775 had signed agreements to sustain the measures of Congress and the union of the colonies, to maintain their opposition to the tyranny of Great Britain, and pledging sympathy and aid to their brethren then besieged in Boston. This was their spirit through the battles of Lexington and Concord, fought April 19th, 1775, and Bunker Hill fought June 17th, 1775. The guns planted on Dorchester Heights, compelled the British Army to evacuate Boston, March 16th, 1776, when New England was free. Thence the British fleet and army sailed into Long Island Sound and their consolidated force overcame the American at the battle of Long

Island on the 27th of August, 1776. Thereafter all Long Island, and soon New-York City, was possessed by the British and held until Evacuation day, November 25, 1783. Burgoyne's Army, moving from Canada, was designed to connect with the British army moving from New-York, and thus bisect the colonies and divide their forces. His surrender at Saratoga, October 17th, 1777, with 5,752 prisoners, defeated the design and weakened the hostile army. The surrender of Cornwallis at Yorktown, with 7,073 prisoners, October 29th, 1781, was fatal to Britain's design and confirmation to American hope. At Boston the British army must evacuate or starve. At Saratoga Burgoyne must surrender or starve. At Yorktown Cornwallis had no other alternative. With merely the experience of a backwoods soldier Washington had burst open an admiring world as a strategist and leader unexcelled in his own, if not in every age. Be it remembered that, while New England was free by the flight of army and navy from Boston and Northern New-York by the capture of Burgoyne and the sunny southland by the victory at Yorktown, the city of New-York and all Long Island was still under subjection to British rule. The severity of their sufferings, the weight of their burdens, the bitterness of their lot, instead of alleviation, was intensified. Despair drove their foes to greater barbarity, more galling insults, more sullen and savage executions. Robbery, rapine, theft, outrage abounded. Tradition has transmitted many, oblivion has covered more of this history of depravity and crime overshadowing Sag-Harbor, Suffolk County and all our Island.

The 32 dwelling houses reported to be in Sag-Harbor, at the taking of the census of the Town of Southampton, July 4th, 1776, did not include East-Hampton, wherein probably Joseph Conkling, father of Edward, Doctor Jeremiah Hedges, a surgeon in the Revolutionary army and perhaps a Russell and others may have resided as well as Timothy Hedges, grandfather of the late Capt. Jeremiah Hedges. Its magnitude must be measured more by its trade and commerce and shipping than by its number of houses. It was in this state as a seaport second only to New-York city. All North Haven and Little North West and Brick Kilns, and most of Noyack were precincts of this centre. The products of farms and forests, hides, tallow, beef, pork, hoops, slaves, cattle, horses, shoes, grain, salt fish, &c, from all Eastern Long Island were shipped at Sag-Harbor for the West Indies and for trade in other markets.

NOTE—By the record of deeds in Suffolk County it appears that Jonathan Paine, Jr., of Southampton, sold lands to Joseph Jacobs and also 1/3 of a sloop called "Charming Betsey" now lying at Sag-Harbor June 13th, 1764. By deed dated April 6th, 1784, Thomas and Philetus

Howell sold to Stephen Howell land and meadow at Sag-Harbor 75 acres bounded N.E. by Cook Seaman and Nathan Fordham, East by the highway, South and West by John Woodruff, North and West by the beach.

In the State Library is a list of officers reading thus: "Eighth company. Capt. Samuel L'Hommedieu, 1st Lieut. Silas Jessup, 2nd Lieut. Edward Conkling, Ensign Daniel Fordham," vide Geo. R. Howell's Hist. p. 72. All Sag-Harbor names and showing an organized company probably chiefly residing there, and in its vicinity and near the date of the Battle of Long Island.

The Revolutionary career of Capt. David Hand has been recorded, and I need not enlarge on the acts of the old hero, a resident of Sag Harbor whom I well knew.

In 1846, Henry Onderdonk, Jr. published a book entitled "Revolutionary Incidents of Long Island. Prison Ships." In the quotations from that storehouse I shall in this paper often omit the title, but for reference mark the page.

"While the British were in Boston their vessels occasionally carried off stock from Suffolk County." The journals of the Provincial Congress contain the following:

"Juy 5th, 75. The people of E. and S. Hampton pray Congress that Captn. Hulbut's company now raising for Schuyler's Army, may remain to guard the stock on the common lands of Montauk, (2,000 cattle and 3 or 4,000 sheep) from the ravages of the enemy." Journ. 75, Onderdonk p. 19.

"July 31st, 75. Congress allow Griffin and Hulbert's companies to remain to guard stock." Jour. 75. Onderdonk, p. 19.

"April 3d, 76. In consideration of the defenceless state of east part of Suffolk Co. the 3 companies raised for Continental service were continued there." Onderdonk p. 26.

Some sixty years ago I had the correspondences and journal of Capt. Hulbert from Samuel L'Hommedieu and read and returned it to him. He lent it to his nephew Samuel L. Gardiner, and in New-York city it was taken from Gardiner's hat and disappeared perhaps forever. From this journal and letters I learned that his company on Montauk was stationed at Shagwonnack, that they were supplied with arms, ammunition and provisions by the people of the town through Burnett Miller and Stephen Hedges their committee, and that on the 7th September, 75, the companies having marched off to Montauk, Hulbert and his men were supplied with guns and ammunition; and were afterwards stationed at Fort Constitution.

Not stopping for comment we continue the narrative by citations chiefly from "Onderdonk's Incidents."

"Dec. 3d, Hugh Geston allowed to go to L.I. for 300 bushels of salt." p. 7.

NOTE—I think Gelston was going to get this salt from the old salt works on Hog Neck, located on or near the Old Mitchell farm, lately owned by Samuel L. Gardiner, deceased, and probably operated by the Revolution time or before. The salt was produced by evaporation of salt water.

"New London, Feb. 5th, 79. Last Saturday the Ringer, a British Privateer Brig, of 12 guns, that had been cruising in the Sound, was taken from a wharf at Sag-Harbor, after a short resistance, by the brig Middleton, Capt. Sage, sloop Beaver, Capt. Havens, sloop Eagle, Capt Conkling. On Sunday these 3 again sailed for Sag-Harbor, where they discovered 7 British vessels just arrived, one a brig of 8 or 10 guns, when a fair prospect appeared of making capture of the whole, but the wind ahead, the Middleton struck on the Middle ground, in beating up the Harbor, 1/4 of a mile from the shore, where she was bravely defended for 4 or 5 hours by her crew, against an incessant fire from the brig, and several field pieces on shore; after being hulled by 30 shots under water, and the vessel careening by the tides falling, the guns could not be worked, all except 4 left the ship, and were taken on board the other 2 vessels. Those on their return took 2 brigs from Cork, via N.Y., with rum, wine and 12,000 bushels of oats, for the troops on Long Island." p. 80.

This is the report by the Americans. I now give the same by the British.

"Hog Neck, 11 o'clock at night, Feb. 1st, 79. Sir. At daybreak the brig "Middleton" and 2 sloops of 14 and 10 guns each, were seen standing in for Sag Harbor. Betwixt 8 and 9, they came within cannon short of the King's armed vessel, which fired 3 shots ahead of them, neither of which being answered, the "Neptune" fired at them, which was returned on their side, hoisting rebel colors, and still standing on until they came within each of the guns on shore, which having thrown a few 12 pound shot at them they stood out from the Harbor towards the end of Hog Neck; long shot was then exchanged for some time, till the rebel brig having the appearance of being aground, or having met with some accident, a 12 pounder was moved down to the end of long wharf, which being nearly on a level with the water, had the effect of deterring the sloop from giving her much assistance: while I crossed over to Hog Neck with the infantry of the British Legion and the 3 pounder attracted to it, from whence we bore with such advantage on her, that she struck to us, but unfortunately, having 5 whale boats on board all the crew except 3 got off, and the sloops immediately left the Bay. We met with but one accident, a corporal being wounded:

Chas Cochran, Maj. B.,
Legion commanding troops at S.H." p.80.

To Sir W. Erskine,

This Major Cochran was noted for barbarity, and tradition has transmitted his name as infamous. He was killed at York-town. His account is specific, and probably correct, but does not speak of the captain of the 2 brigs from Cork laden with rum, wine and 12,000 bushels of oats, of which he had not then heard.

"Feb. 16th, 14 companies light infantry. 25 March, 700 at Southampton; Gen. Clinton at Southampton with about 2500 troops, 25 sails in and near Sag-Harbor, 12 or 14 drive on Gardiner's Island by a gale, N. London." p. 82.

"April 15th, N. London, 5 French prisoners escaped here from L.I. who say there are only 500 foot and 50 horse at Southold, and 700 men at Sag Harbor, with 2 field pieces, which force is kept there, to facilitate the taking of wood and hay from Sag-Harbor. A fleet of 16 sail of wood vessels, and a 12 gun brig lie there and a ship with provisions lately from N. Port. Before her arrival provisions were so scarce that the inhabitants were obliged to kill poor milch cows for food, and the troops sickly. Gen. Clinton was returning to N.Y. after throwing up some breastworks &c, in conse-quence of a report that Gen. Parsons was preparing for an attack on Sag-Harbor, with 40000 troops." p. 82.

"Riv. Oct. 2, '79. N. Lon. Sept. 22. A requisition having been made, to Gen. DeLancey of L.I. Militia, to furnish 500 men, to parade with their blankets on Aug. 23, to march for Brook-lyn, to be employed in repairing and constructing new works there; 210 of which were to be from Suffolk County, who were also to furnish and send to the magazine at Brooklyn, 50000 fascines, 9 ft long, and stripped of leaves, 25,000 pickets, from 3 to 40 ft long, 5,000 faisings or stock-ades from 9 to 10 feet long, and 6 to 8 in. thick, 5,000 railing of 6 or 7 ft. The inhabitants having refused to comply, the following letter was sent to Gen. Delancey.

N.Y.Aug. 26th, 79. Sir, you will signify to the People of Suffolk Co., that if the requisition is not immediately complied with, a detachment of troops will be sent into the district, and every person who shall refuse, shall be turned out of L.I. and their farms will be all for the support of those who have suffered from reach attachment to Government."

Rawdon, Ad. General." p. 86.

"Sept. 22, '79. N. London Gar. Last Friday 35 young men came from L.I. to Saybrook, who left their homes on account of being ordered to work on the fortifications on the west end of L.I., apprehending they should be ordered thence to the West Indies." p. 87.

"Wm. Fowler and John Strong, in the armed boat Wm. the Conqueror, took a small skiff in Acabonic Bay, Aug. 23d, 81, with 300 lbs. coffee, and 120 lbs. tea." p. 80.

"N. London, Nov. 30. Last week Major Davis and Capt. Grinnell being ashore at Sag-Harbor with several men, were betrayed and taken prisoners by a Hessian major and 20 light horse. They had 2 armed boats with them which the enemy were about setting on fire, but Capt. Wickham in an 8 gun sloop from Stonington about the same time coming to near the boats brought them off." p. 106.

Refugees from Long Island and Sag-Harbor. After the Battle of Long Island and the hostile occupation by the British, those active in the American forces thought it unsafe to remain, and fled in great numbers to Connecticut. I quote this, "170 voters refugees from Suffolk now in E. Haddam, Lyme, Saybrook, Killingworth, and Guilford, petition the N.Y. Legislature April 10th, 77. They want to be represented in convention." 70.

"Saybrook, June 12th, 77. Petition of 45 Suffolk County Refugees for relief and permission to pass over to L.I. for forage for their families, and bread corn growing on their land, which otherwise will fall into the enemies' hands." p. 70.

The first quotation shows 170 voters residing in 5 localities desired to vote for representatives in the provincial congress convention, or Assembly of New York.

NOTE—Governmental authority at the commencement of hostilities was vested in committees. After that in the Provincial Congress, sometimes called "the convention." The 4th Provincial Congress met July 9th, 1776, and assumed the name of "The Convention of Representatives of the State of New York." The first constitution of this State was adopted April 20th, 1777, in the stress and storm of war. Legislative authority was then vested in the Senate and Assembly.

In fact those representatives were then residing on Connecticut, and could not reside in this county. They were Thomas Wickham and Burnett Miller, of East-Hampton. The second quotation shows 35 refugees in Saybrook alone, heads of families, refugees begging for relief, and among the signers are Daniel and Ephraim Fordham, Oba. Jones, Lewis Stanborough, the first three residents of Sag-Harbor, and the last in its vicinity. If we could ascertain the number of refugees from Sag Harbor it would aid to estimate from other places, and I now examine that question.

"1777. Feb. Petition to Governor Trumbull to remove flax, wood, stock, etc. from L.I. to Conn." p. 70. Signed by Samuel L'Hommedieu, David Sayre, Silas Norris and Nathan Fordham.

"1776. John Hudson of Sag-Harbor at Stonington. Oba. Gildersleeve (1778) of Sag Harbor at Saybrook." p. 79.

"1777. July 3d, Obs. Jones, John Hurlbut, (both of Sag-Harbor) and Thomas Dering gave permits to refugees going to L.I." p. 70.

"1780. Nov. Daniel Fordham and George Fordham want permits to cross to L.I." (both were of Sag-Harbor) p. 90.

"1782. Nov. Nathan Fordham of E. Haddam wants to go to L.I. with his family." p. 108.

Dr. Jeremiah Hedges probably resided in Sag-Harbor by the Revolutionary time and Joseph Conklin and he were in Conn.

We then list the Refugees and locate them as follows:

1. John Hulbert, Col, at East Haddam, Conn.
2. Samuel L'Hommedieu.
3. Nathan Fordham, at East Haddam, Conn.
4. George Fordham, at East Haddam, Conn.
5. Ephraim Fordham, at Saybrook, Conn.
6. Daniel Fordham, at Saybrook, Conn.
7. Edward Conkling, at Stonington, Conn.
8. John Hudson, at Stonington, Conn.
9. Obadiah Gildersleeve, at New Haven, Conn.
10. Silas Norris.
11. David Sayre.
12. Obadiah Jones.
13. Doctor Jeremiah Hedges*
14. Joseph Conkling.

*NOTE—Doctor Jeremiah Hedges was a graduate of Yale. He died in Sag-Harbor in 1797. His grave and tombstone are near the northeast corner of the old burying ground there.

Out of the 32 dwelling houses reputed to be in Sag-Harbor at the Revolution, 14 men most active for independence, and fearing for their lives, fled from happy homes and became exiles and refugees for their country's cause in Connecticut alone, in many cases with their families. Nearly one-third of its fighting force in number, full that in weight, transferred from Sag-Harbor, so weakened to strengthen Connecticut. I think it probable that one-fourth of the war force of Suffolk County and perhaps all Long Island, were refugees and remember these were the marked men of their towns. High souled, haters of despotism, ardent lovers of liberty, burning for the conflict: call to them the war song

> *"Lay the proud oppressors low,*
> *Tyrants fall in every foe,*
> *Liberty's in every blow."*

and their brave hearts and master passion responded as lions for the charge.

The 170 refugee voters understood that Long Island in possession of the British army, could not choose representatives to a patriot convention, Congress or Assembly, and to obtain representation there, their votes alone could avail, and their representatives must come from the refugees, another evidence this of weakness here and strength transferred there.

The Petition of 35 Refugees at Saybrook, to bring from Long Island supplies to their families in Connecticut, is significant to the same condition and reveals the destitution present and impending.

Many years gone by my Aunt Sally Hedges, then over 90 years of age, told me on the night on which she was born, in March, 1777, that her father had down cellar, a sow and pigs, and in his bedroom, sheep and lambs, and was compelled to that to keep them from British robbers and save his family from starving—think of this as a picture of the wretchedness in the Hamptons, in Sag-Harbor and all over our Island. The American armed forces said if they did not get our provisions they would feed the British, and the British said if they did not get them the Americans would. Both sides robbed and plundered, and both justified it. The residents here were ground between the upper and nether millstone. Roving outlaws, with eagle eye, looked for prey, spies left no secluded nook unsearched. The thousands of sheep and cattle, pasturing on Montauk in summer and driven home in winter, would feed an army, and all sides coveted and plundered this drove until, as we have seen, the inhabitants were compelled to kill their milch cows or starve.

The marches and counter marches of hostile forces on eastern Long Island, the movements of vessels and fleets in bays, streams, ocean and sound, the many plundering raids and robberies recorded and unrecorded, related here would be confusing and enlarge this paper beyond proper bounds. What bears directly on the history of Sag-Harbor we must not omit.

EXPEDITIONS TO SAG HARBOR.

Writers have not failed to notice the Meigs expedition. Its magnificent achievement was so striking, its success so illuminating in the darkness of the times as to demand rehearsal. It was not the solitary expedition to Sag-Harbor. In 1779, in the last of January or 1st of February, Captain Sage in the brig Middleton, sloop Beaver, Captain Havens, sloop Eagle, Captain Conkling took from Sag-Harbor wharf, the ranger, a British Privateer brig of 12 guns. Again on Sunday sailing from New London, the brig Middleton grounded, and her crew was rescued by the other two vessels which, returning took 2 brigs with rum, wine and 12000 bushels of oats. Here are two more expeditions to Sag-Harbor, noticed by Onderdonk, and quoted formerly in this paper. Quoting from the same authority I have noticed the expedition of Major Davis and Captain Grinnell in 2 armed boats who were betrayed and taken prisoners and the boats rescued from the enemy by Capt in his 8 gun sloop from Stonington. This counts fourth in expeditions, and was made in November, 1781.

NOTE—The Hessian and Light horse men who captured Davis and Grinnell probably were on North Haven and these may have been betrayed by some one then engaged in the salt works there.

THE WHALE BOAT

was easily propelled by oars or sail, of little draft, built for living in all winds and weathers, and had much carrying capacity, was easily handled, and almost all "East Enders" in it, were at home. John White, of Sagg, piloted Meigs in his whaleboat expedition. Major Davis and Grinnell were in whaleboats, with crews, more or less, Grinnell and Wickham were refugees, and the first two were from Sag-Harbor. Wickham was from East-Hampton and was father of Sarah wife of Judge John P. Osborn of Noyack. The weight at his front gate was 2 welded grape shots fired by the British in their attack on Stonington.

THE OATH OF ALLEGIANCE.

When the British army got possession of Long Island commissioners were appointed to compel the inhabitants to take the oath of allegiance to King George, and those refusing were liable to be treated as rebels and prisoners of war, subjected to the law of their captors with all the indignities of insults, chains, prisons, disease, starvation, and often death. What should they do? Take the oath and live? Refuse, and die? They took the oath but in heart were as devoted to their country and as hostile to their oppressors as before. This is a subject avoided by writers, but fidelity to historic truth demands expression. When residents of Sag-Harbor and the Hampton's took this oath, as they in fact did, they reasoned thus: Refusing, I die with no benefit or help to my family, friends or country's cause; living, I may be a help to all ministering to aged parents, to sick and dying of family and friends, protector of wives, sisters and children from brutal assaults on their purity and honor. In law and orals, fraud or force annuls a deed or contract, and undue influence voids a will, and why not an oath? To hold an oath procured by force, valid, is to hold force the law and above the right. When Col. Gardiner as commissioner, with a company, surrounded the house of Col. Jonathan Hedges, of Sagg, and at the point of the bayonet compelled the old hero to take the oath, what else could he do? What else could Col. Hedges do? It was this or death. They were both known as patriots then and after.

If Col. Gardiner did not compel Col. Hedges and others to take the oath he was liable to all the penalties of Martial Law just as Col. Hedges was if he did not take it. At this very time Nathaniel Gardiner, son of Col. Gardiner, was a surgeon in the American Army and served as such until the end of the war. Who can doubt the patriotism of the father? This question was settled by the patriots of Suffolk County themselves by agreement to take the oath and send a committee to the British authorities. Onderdonk p. 46, states that "E. and S. Hampton will meet Sept. 14, '76, at Sag Meeting House to appoint." It could not but be fully argued and agreed then and there to take the oath. The name and repute of Long Island has suffered and sunk lower in the estimation of people not so subjected more from taking this oath than it deserves and I think unjustly. When they have been tried in the furnace of fire and come out of it, they would better know how to pity the distressed.

Howell's *History of Southampton* p. 78, states that "This town also furnished four surgeons for the War of the Revolution, Henry White, Shadrack Hildreth, William Burnett and Silas Halsey." He should have added Samuel H. Rose, of Bridgehampton. East-Hampton sent Nathaniel Gardiner, and Sag-Harbor Jeremiah Hedges. These seven absent must have stripped these towns almost, if not entirely, of medical relief and is another addition to the agonies endured.

At what a cost of privation Sag-Harbor obtained independence. The victors' hostile flag floated before the eyes of her native born freemen. The victors' shout of triumph saluted their ears. Her wharves, stores and houses held by her adversaries. Her shipping gone. Her trade ruined. The products of her field seized by her foes and often robbed by professed friends. The aged and infirm and sick, dying and dead without medical relief. Her sons fugitives in the armies of Liberty and privateers, that heroically assailed their enemy, or in prison ships or dungeons. Her daughters subjected to the approach of soldiers of a garrison whose desire was their dishonor, whose every victory brought them nearer to the gate of despair. All threatened with pestilence, with gaunt famine, and all last to look on the retreating ships of their country's foes and last to re-echo the glad hurrah for Freedom and Independence gained. When the British ships sailed from New York they took thousands of royalists, born Americans with them—not one from Sag-Harbor. Her sons and daughters were true to the harmonies of Union and Independence.

In the War of the Revolution and that of 1812, the British fleet anchored and held supremacy in Gardiner's Bay. No son of Long Island should wish a hostile flag again to float therein, secure in triumph. At any and all cost our navy should be such as to forbid that recurrence. As a child I remember the intense, universal boiling wrath of the American people against England. No sign of the times is more cheering than the harmony now between them.

PRISON SHIPS.

There was a tradition that Major Davis, of East-Hampton, taken prisoner, died in New-York by poison in his chocolate. I have not heard that any citizen of Sag-Harbor perished among the thousands who were imprisoned in the Sugar House and prison ships there. The memory of those martyrs should never be forgot.

> "Oh, if there be on his earthly sphere,
> A boon, an offering Heaven holds dear,
> Tis the last libation Liberty draws
> From the heart that bleeds and breaks in her cause."

HOUSE TAX.

By act of Congress passed July 14th, 1798, a tax was imposed on all houses and December 11th, 1800, Jonathan Rogers of Bridge-Hampton, as surveyor, made a list of all houses, including therein the territory of the towns of East-Hampton, Shelter Island and nearly or quite all of Southampton. In the great fire of 1837 that swept over Sag-Harbor, most of the houses were burned as well as the church. The loss was so great that the port was reduced almost to beggary. I give a few cases of houses taxed with valuation, amount of tax and name of owner:

OWNER.	VALUE.	TAX RATE.	AMT. PAY
Duvall,: William	$675 00	2 10	$2 03
Fordham,: Daniel	1,687 50	4 10	6 75
Fordham,: John	472 50	2 10	0 95
Fordham,: Nathan	421 37	2 10	0 85
Howell,: Stephen	843 75	3 10	2 50
Howell,: James	675 00	3 10	2 03
Hedges,: Jesse	703 18	3 10	2 11
Howell,: Silas	1,265 62	4 10	5 06
Latham,: Hubbard	1,012 50	4 10	4 53
Hommedieu,: Samuel	810 00	3 10	2 43

The following named houses then taxed now stand in names of present owners as correctly as I can give it:

OLD OWNER.	PRESENT OWNER.	VALUE	TAX.
Joseph Conkling,	Thomas Lister,	$675 00	$2 03
Thomas Beebee,	Mrs. C. G. Vail, once Satterly,	517 50	1 55
Ephraim Fordham,	George Bassett, lately,	191 25	0 38
Thaddeus Fordham,	Mrs. H. T. Hedges,	196 87	0 39
Luther Hildreth,	late John Budd,	450 00	0 90
Hurlburt, John,	Mrs. Sage, once John Osborne,	562 50	1 69
Daniel Hall,	now Douglas,	450 00	0 90
John Jermain,	Mrs. Russell Sage,	849 75	2 53
Peleg Latham,	late Geo. B. Brown,	1,125 00	4 53

By act of Congress of the same date owners of slaves were taxed each 50 cts. for each slave and Nathan Fordham, Hubbard Latham and Henry P. Dering were each taxed for 1 slave in Sag-Harbor.

CONCLUDING THOUGHTS.

The historian gathers materials from the conflicting accounts of opposing parties, and traditions, sometimes and not seldom, antagonizing each other. He must weigh, sift, discriminate and if afraid of labor is unworthy the name. When I began this paper (now far outgrown expectation) my interest became intense. Within my soul there seemed a voice crying, "Unless you possess the subject, the subject will ever more possess you." The Historical Society of Sag-Harbor, and my many friends there, are entitled to my most arduous effort. Poor as the work is, it is the best the infirmities of age allow. The patriotic devotion of our Revolutionary fathers, their toils, their hardships, their self-denial, their heroism, living in the remembrance of their sons, may they inspire them to attain the exalted idea of their ancestors.

CHAPTER XV

MEMORIES OF A LONG LIFE

Delivered in 1909 at the age of 92

DEDICATION

EDWARD DAYTON, of Hardscrabble, in the Northwest Plains, was a schoolmate of mine in Clinton Academy and so far as I know is the only surviving me. He is venerable for age. He and I are the only survivors of the two boats crews that killed the whale in 1838. We are both descendants of the founders of East Hampton. He has resided all his life at an outpost of the town. He has forwarded, fed and lodged many a strayed, broken down, hungry and belated traveler. I never heard that he ever refused aid to such or turned the hungry away. His life of honest industry and helpfulness to the needy and unfortunate is worthy of any tribute I can give. To him now living I dedicate the "Memories of a Long Life." That I think he has not lived in vain and that I have so remembered him in his declining years may be, I hope will be, a sweet memorial to him.

Bridgehampton, February 4th, 1909.
H. P. HEDGES.

∞∞∞∞∞∞

MY ENVIRONMENT.

I was born in the house late of James H. Topping, Wainscott, on Monday, October 13, 1817. Commencing life on the first working day of the week, I have been a hard worker all my days.

The memory of early sorrows soon vanishes. That of early joys abides. The never failing attractions of Wainscott Pond deeply impressed my mind in infancy and childhood. What boy ever saw a puddle of water without wishing to wade in? What youth ever looked on a pond without anxiety to explore its mysteries? Before I was eight years old I knew Wainscott Pond from shore to shore, from shoal to deep. There I gathered the fragrant and beautiful lilies. There caught minnows on a pin book. There paddled the old canoe. Borne on its bosom time flew unheeded, disappointments were forgot. Hope gilded its expanse; truth dwelt in its depths; joy centered in its bounds. At the distance of more than four score years, I remember how the rays of the morning sun glinted and swept over its placid bosom—how its setting beamed and glorified water and shore. This one feature of sweet nature wrought healthy hope and cheer in my young life. Out of it was born perception of the varied beauties impressed on this material world, by the hand of its mighty Maker.

This pond was the eastern bound of my father's farm. It was bounded south by the *ocean*.

OCEAN!

The varied *phases* of ocean stamp varying impressions on the mind. Ages long gone by Homer, looking on the Mediterranean sea, moved by gentle winds, sung of "the countless smiles of Father Ocean." The poet Pollock, viewing its measureless power, called it "strongest of Creation's sons." Burns, in the farewell to his native country, with forebodings of evil, wrote:

> "'Tis not the surging billows' roar,
> 'Tis not the fatal, deadly shore.
> Tho' death in every shape appear,
> The wretched have no more to fear."

Byron, with view of its vastness, wrote in the Corsair:

> "On the glad waters of the dark blue sea,
> Our thoughts as boundless and our souls as free.
> Far as the breeze can bear the billows' foam,
> Survey our empire and behold our home."

The changeful moods of ocean are always alluring, impressive, mysterious. Its repose is that of power, its wrath the wrath of a world.

Sometimes its music is as low as the moan of the dying soul—at times loud as the thunder of elemental war. In every form of its face, in every tone of its harmony, in every war of its wrath, there is the unfailing impression of immensity. The waves of the same ocean that beat on our shores eat on those of other continents. The billows that break on our Island are of the same ocean whose surges strike the icy barriers of either pole. We may not analyze, we may not define, we may not be conscious of the impressions ocean writes on the heart, yet they are suggestions of the vast, the boundless, the mysterious, the sublime. The child, the man, the philosopher, alike, are attracted, allured, beguiled, entranced, by the view of ocean. What it was to them that from my early days it was to me.

From the hill whereon stood my father's house, looking west a fourth of a mile, was the two-rod road or highway, between the towns of East Hampton and Southampton, in the old records called Wainscott Plain. What littleness constrained those two towns to limit this highway, with all their wealth of land, to the narrowness of two rods? Looking north some fifty rods was the *old School House*. The Burying ground near by was just east and north of it. The main, north and south road ran through "Wainscott Hollow" west of the school house. Formerly the sources of Wainscott Pond ran from the north far up, into the pond. The road east and west was made passable by filling the stream with sand from the near bank west, and hence the same "Sandy Bridge," given to the road and the little pond north of it. The marks of the excavation were clear in my childhood, and now may not be wholly destroyed. On this little pond we skated in winter, and slid and played "bendigo" and got lots of fun and wet feet.

The Burying Ground, as I remember it, not now in its neat and decent well-kept state, but in its neglected, forlorn condition four score years ago, unfenced, overgrown with briars, brambles and bushes, nest of vermin, was an object of dread and abhorrence. To me it was the Home of Horror, the haunt of ghosts. In the light of day I saw nothing there to please the eye. In the shades of night fancy conjured strange and shapeless forms and ghostly sights. I gave it a wide berth and moved on the run. As years passed superstition fled. Reverence expelled abhorrence. There I saw laid to rest the remains of John Strong, a *Revolutionary* soldier. There are entombed the companions of my childhood and youth. There rests the mortal form of saints who testified to truth living and dying. There were buried the bodies of my only two sisters, dying in childhood. When, at short intervals, my mother lost her daughters, Maria and Phebe, her heart almost broke. There lies buried the body of my oldest brother, Thomas Sanford, and that of his wife. The precious dust of generations dead, whose lives cheered the houses of the village, and whose death darkened and saddened the families they left lonely and desolate, consecrate the old burying ground as a monument dedicated to all that memory holds sacred and affection most dear. God's Acre! The return to earth of all that were earth-born.

The Wainscott Burying Ground stands to-day a demonstration of the advancement of the finer feelings of mankind over those of eighty years ago.

The old School House near, if not on, the exact site of the present one, was shingled all over, and time worn. The frame was of hewn oak timber, grown probably near by. It was hoary with age when I first knew it. Rats, for convenient travel, had gnawed holes here and there; mice scampered on its floor and sides and hid in its crevices and cracks; birds had pecked holes in its gable ends. In the winter its loft had been storage room for the seine. In its northeast corner was a cupboard, for what purpose nobody knew; in its dark recess naughty boys were shut up until the terrors of confinement were supposed to have wrought reformation. No stairs ran aloft and climbing was the only way to get there. Twilight by day and cimmerian darkness by night reigned in the loft. Hideous spirits and imps of evil were believed to dwell under the roof of that old attic. To keep me quiet in my childhood, the school mistress told me I might be sentenced to climb up and stay in that dread abode, where were "scorpions, and sarpents, and where Hidingijo lived." Who Hidingijo was and how he looked? What was the shape of scorpions! How big the "sarpents" were? I knew not. That all were bad I believed, and fancy dilated visionary forms into images of horror. The impressions of early dread and fear wrought in the soul, remain, indelibly imprinted in remembrance, and they remain with me—A lesson that we should beware how we misslead [sic] and terrify and torture the infant mind. Perhaps I went to school to Aunt Ailsie Osborn, great aunt to Oliver, and got these gostly [sic] legends there. I seem to remember being in the old school house, and hearing her say such words, and that she set me to picking seeds out of cotton, before the cotton gin came in general use. In this dim era of dawning memory, distinctly as I recall the sayings and legends, the personality of the speaker is in a haze so thick that whether that is fancy or fact, I dare not affirm. All babies grow in and grow out of this haze, and I must have soon outgrown it. In this old school house Jane Edwards taught me to spell and read. She was young, patient, conscientious, intelligent, considerate. I was bubbling over with irrepressible activities and perpetual motion, a living torment and trial. I remember her instruction with gratitude. She did the best she could. Long since she has entered on the enduring life. I render to her my sincere thanks, and hope that even in the unknown spirit land she knows my repentant heart, reads it, as living in the mortal body she could not. Disbelieving all the mummery of spirit rappings, I profoundly believe in the preeminent intelligence of the soul unclogged with the impediment of material mortal habitation.

John Cooper taught in this old school house some two or three winters in my early boyhood. Profound in scholarship, stern in discipline, exacting in requirement, he rued the school as rigorously as an army controlled by martial law. No trifling was allowed, no idleness overlooked, no offense unpunished. His commendation was rare, his rule that of an age long past, his policy that now not tolerated.

Robert L. Hedges, commonly known as "Bob," presided over this school two or three winters, I think, succeeding Cooper, and not far from 1825 and 26. I was then reading in the English reader, writing after the copies he made and figuring on the three foundation rules of arithmetic. As a teacher he was zealous to enlighten and unfold the scholars' powers. He was elastic in tact, sharp in shrewdness, quick in perception, humorous in mood, unrivalled in wit. Those who knew him well had for his talents admiration, for his unfailing wit a welcome, for his failings pity.

John Cooper and "Bob Hedges," life long school masters, were noted characters in their day, with rare ability, with high aspiration, with large acquirement, with keen penetration, with all the faculties required to attain eminence in the learned professions, they failed to obtain the rank they might have achieved and failed because they lacked not genius, not opportunity, not circumstance, but that self control which makes man the wise master of all his acquirements and all his powers.

In the night, about 1826 or '7, the old Wainscott school house was in a blaze. The flame shone on the windows of the room, where, in a trundle-bed, I was sleeping. My brothers ran to the fire. This was the first building I ever saw burned. Chauncey Osborn, then courting his wife, Miranda Hand, at her father, James Hand's house, first saw the fire and gave the alarm. The first witnesses coming saw in the bushes of the old graveyard in the chair used by the school master, the only chair kept in the school house, a man sitting whom they did not clearly recognize. The house burned to the ground. Tom Hopping, poor, crazy

"Tom," was charged with the crime, arrested, imprisoned and tried, but not convicted. On his examination he professed ignorance of the cause of the fire, suggested that on account of the wickedness of the people fire might have come down from Heaven, as it did on Sodom and Gomorrah, and that for the same cause, it might come down on more houses. Tom's apparent stolidity and concealed shrewdness, and the indistinct recognition of witnesses, saved him from conviction. In long after years it was reported that he confessed to carrying the fire-brand from home, a mile through the street, and setting the torch to the building.

Poor Tom! Gone! Long since gone!

Thus perished the old school house! It must have been nearly a hundred years old, perhaps more. Full three generations of youth there learned their letters. Three generations, at 5 o'clock meetings, had worshipped therein. It was hallowed by the prayers of sincere and humble worshippers. Its walls had echoed and re-echoed with sacred hymn and psalm sung by devout and honest tongues. Centre of primary instruction, centre of seine meetings, centre of religious worship, it had been an institution of enduring benefit and blessing.

Cut in the boards were initials of many students. Cut on its south side was the outline of a full rigged whale ship, "Andes," or "Union," I think the former. Cut in its rude seats and desks were notches and outlines of figures and faces and animals and birds, rude, unsymetric work of jacknives, by inexpert boys—raw specimens of struggling art. All these marks of past generations of boys passed beyond recovery with the destruction of the old school house. Its loss would have been irreparable except for the better one that took its place, and the better one that replaced that.

In the second school house Thomas Rose, brother of Col. Edwin, and Josiah White, both of Bridgehampton, were school masters, previous to 1832. The men who taught and scholars they had in my day are all gone. Albert Hand, David Edwards, James H. Topping, Chauncey Osborn, Isaac O. Hopping, Silv Pharaoh, afterwards King of the Montauk Indians, and others—*all gone*. I can recall no living soul who was with me, a fellow student, in either the old school house, or in the one following.

Knowing both, in the present graceful structure the third in my day. I see such an advance as might confirm the faith of all who believe in the progress of our countrymen in education, intelligence and moral elevation.

THE NEIGHBORS.

Looking west, across the northern end of Wainscott pond, from our dwelling was seen the old double, two-storied house, probably built by John Osborn, first settler in Wainscott, about 1670, from whom the present Oliver S. descended in the eighth generation from the original Thomas, first settler in East Hampton. The beams in the walls over its rooms, the strange paneling of wainscoting, the vast fireplace and chimney, all tell of remote antiquity. The house is its own witness of an origin not far removed from the time when Wainscott was first settled.

Tradition credits this John with great physical strength, courage and hardihood, much shrewdness and commanding personality. It says he got a cannon well charged, tied a rope around the muzzle, told the Indians to pull on it and when they were in a string in front fired and killed the whole lot. Wainscott and Georgica ponds abounded in fish and eels, the ocean was there, the forest was wide, water fowl and game were plenty. The location could sustain a considerable fraction of the Montauks, and Wainscott in time of the settlement, was not improbably the seat of a large section of that tribe. It is probable the Indians were numerous, thieving and troublesome, perhaps threatening. He might have found it necessary to frighten but not to kill, nor do I believe he did kill one. The tradition I heard eighty years ago. Traditions sometimes grow like gossip. Both badly need sifting.

Every village and town is subject to change. Its inhabitants desire to know what changes time has wrought.

Before my time there had been a house on the south side of the road, west of Jeremys Creek, about a half mile or more northeast of Mrs. Lucia Conklin's corner, where was an excavation, the remains of a cellar. In passing that, my mother told me Taylor Osborn's house was there.

Just South of Capt. Jonathan Osborn's house, was a very old house where, I was told, Deacon Jacob Osborn resided in his lifetime and that he tended the spider-legged mill, which stood just southwest of it and, as I remember, in the street. I remember that Jacob Hopping tended that. The house was burned sometime before 1831.

Between the houses of Morgan Topping and John Hand once stood a house in which lived Elias Hand, a soldier in the French and Indian War. That house was burned before my time.

In Wainscott Hollow, north of the burying ground were ditches, marks of enclosure, where, as I was told, long ago lived a George Strong. In an angle of the road some quarter of a mile northeast of Lucia Conkling's corner, formerly lived a William Miller on what Elisha Osborne (not Continental) called his "Bill lot." North of Lucia's corner, on another road lived a Zebedee Osborne, rearing there (as told me) a large family. The house which Carl Hopping built on or near the site of the Deacon Jacob Osborne house, was moved to Madison St., Sag Harbor.

The dwellings standing in Wainscott in my early days and before 1831, beginning east were as follows:

1. *Polly Talmage*, widow of Jeremiah, lived in a house in the northwest corner of Capt. John Dayton's Neck and east of Jeremys creek, and her children were Jeremiah, Jason, Ezra, Timothy and Harvey, *the whaleman*; Betsey and Mary.

2. *Daniel Hopping* lived in a hollow a few rods north of Capt. Jonathan Osborn's house, and had son, "Tom Hopping," and daughter, wife of Charles Payne.

3. *Capt. Jonathan Osborn* lived in the house now standing, and had wife, sister of Sam Schellinger, and daughter, wife of Gurden Halsey, and sons Jonathan, Abram, Isaac, Conkling and David.

4. *Elisha Conkling* lived in an old house on the site where Lucia now resides, and had sons Abraham, Elisha H. and Nathaniel, and daughters Amy, Jerusha, Mary and Nancy.

5. *Elisha H. Conkling* lived in the house where now resides D. Edgar Talmage, and left two daughters and sons Geo. W. and Cornelius.

6. *Jacob Hopping* lived where now his grandson Jacob O. resides, and had daughters Mary, Nancy and Caroline, and sons Osborne, Carl and Isaac. This house stood end to the street, and Sam Schellenger on a cannon ball in the centre turned it round front to the street when I was a boy.

7. *Elisha Osborn* lived in a house on the site where his son Chauncey afterward resided, and left daughter Charlotte, and sons Malines and Chauncey. This Elisha, in the Revolutionary War, was in Connecticut, and to distinguish him from the Elisha next named, was called *"Continental."*

8. *Elisha Osborn* lived in the old John Osborn house now standing, and had wife Mary, and sons Thomas and David, and daughters Lucretia, Fanny and Betsey.

9. *James Edwards* lived in the house where now resides Oliver S. Osborn, and had wife and daughters Jane, Harriet and Phebe.

10. *My Father* lived in the house where now resides Morgan Topping.

11. *James Hand* lived in the house where now his grandson John H. resides, and had wife Chloe, and sons James, Sylvester, John, Reuel, and Albert, and daughters Polly, Matilda, Fanny, Julia, Miranda, and Elizabeth.

12. *John Strong* Revolutionary soldier, lived where now his great grandson Charles W. resides, and had sons John, Sylvanus, Saul and Abner, and daughters Hannah, Martha, Mary, and Emeline, and perhaps another.

13. *Jesse Strong* lived where now resides the widow of Edmund T. Strong, his deceased nephew.

14. *Bethuel Edwards*, elder in the East Hampton church, lived where afterwards his son David A. did, and had sons Josiah and David, and daughters Esther, Mary and Sophia.

15. *John Edwards*, lived where afterwards Jared D. Hedges did to whom he sold.

One or two families in the town of Southampton near the town line once belonged to the Wainscott District School. These fifteen houses all in the East Hampton town, comprised Wainscott as I remember it previous to, and about 1831.

From this data thus given, the decline or progress of Wainscott can be reckoned for the past seventy years and more. Families can be located and their history followed, genealogies traced, and some facts secured from oblivion.

On Wainscott Plain, secluded from the commercial, the mechanical and traveling world, in these fifteen dwellings, lived the farming community, who were descendants of the Pioneer settlers. Without exception all were tillers of the soil. James Hand was a weaver, Bethuel Edwards a shoemaker, James Edwards, his brother, a carpenter, and Jacob Hopping the cooper in this settlement, and when the wind blew, its miller.

A Pioneer requires within himself resources unknown to residents of a large community. He must construct his own domicile, provide his own food, clear his own land, till his own soil, defend his own fireside; sometimes fighter, sometimes cook, sometimes farmer, then trapper, then hunter, then mechanic, tailor, carpenter, smith, cooper, architect. Occasions the most sudden, emergencies the most pressing, dangers the most appalling, call for invention, hardihood, courage, resolution, decision, perseverance. His watchfulness must be unsleeping. His labor must know no respite. He must be his own priest, his own physician and lawyer. If there is in the man hidden power pioneer life will disclose and develop it. The self-reliant, inventive, resourceful powers of the American people were born in pioneer settlements.

How much was sold out of Wainscott, compared with the little bought or brought in, would be a marvel to this age. The clothing, almost wholly, was made from the flax and wool raised there. The shoes were made from hides of cattle grown there. From head to foot the apparel was raised, kit, woven, carded, spun, cut, sewed, fitted at home. Straw hats made at home covered the head in summer, caps, woolen and fur of wild animals, were worn in winter. John Strong, the Revolutionary hero, had killed a fox and had the skin made into a queer looking old cap, with tail hung behind and nose pointing before. Funny, hardy, jocose, old Uncle John with his unique cap, his jolly ways, his abounding humor, his beguiling stories of the Revolution Times, welcome guest always, most welcome in long winter evenings, most welcome in huskings, where he made the hours seem short, and the ears flew fast. His picture would be a bonanza, and now is vivid in my eye.

James Hand's dwelling was a few rods north of one nearest to our house. His son Sylvester, married the sister of Alden Spooner, Editor of the *Suffolk Gazette*, in Sag Harbor, and afterwards of the *Star*, in Brooklyn, N.Y. He took the paper and was a great reader. The family were intelligent, friendly, social, musical experts on the flute or fiddle, nimble and graceful in the dance, full of life and spirits, and there from a toddling infant to a big, awkward boy, I enjoyed many happy hours, and there found congenial conversation on reading and books, attractive, sympathetic, inspiring. They lent me their books, told me of the Sag Harbor library, had books from there, and led me to petition my father to buy a share in the library. When he went to Sag Harbor he took me to the library kept in Josiah Douglass' store, where I selected and brought home the treasures of Literature. To the patience, the consideration, the intelligence of this family I am indebted for a propelling force, that led to literary culture. Such a thoughtless boy as I was must have been a trial—None are now living to whom I can say, Thanks!

When I first remember, the soil had been tilled on the rule of skimming off all that could be got and returning as little as possible. It is said the Indians taught the first settlers to fertilize corn with fish. Bunker fishing with shore nets was in practice and then almost the only element of fertilizing the soil, except the little barn-yard manure the farmers made. A few acres would be kept in better condition near home, for mowing grass, wheat, barley, rye, etc. Very largely, other lands were cropped with corn and oats and left unseeded to grow briars, daisies, five fingers and a little grass, where the cows and horses pastured. Hardly less than five and often ten acres were required to pasture a horse or cow. The crops of grass and grain were *meagre*. All the grain was stored in bins in the attic except corn, which was mainly put on poles over the barn floorway, and some ears of corn went up garret. Elisha Osborn had a basket rigged for hoisting by a rope and single block and thus got his corn over the floorway. A little wheat was raised. Rye and corn bread were mostly eaten. Samp, hominy, johny-cake and hasty pudding were usually the stand by for winter. Salt pork, seldom beef, often fish both fresh and salt, supplied food in summer. There was plenty always, frugality always, waste never. The process of renovating lands, of painting houses, of wheat bread as a staple article of food dates after my early days. Captain John Dayton raised "a bloody great hog, he weighed twelve score" that was when I first remember the weight of swine.

CHIPS.

A writer has said "Critics have been perplexed to know the design and connection of the Ninth Eclogue of Virgil. Some of the lines are exquisite, but, like a heap of flowers, they seem to be thrown together without order or sequence." The same writer believes the case to be this: "He had in his note book a collection of splendid fragments, too good to be thrown away, and was driven to the awkward expedient of telling the story of a poet, turned from his home, who sang these lines, and thus found a string to tie his discordant flowers together."

I have no basket of flowers, but propose to write some disconnected matters in this number and therefore entitle it "Chips."

DRAWING THE SEINE!

Fishing for bunkers was an enterprise that enlisted all the activities of the people of Wainscott. When it was "fishing weather" and a school of fish seen, "the watch" on the beach banks swung his jacket as a signal, and a basket on a pole set up out of "the scuttle" on top of a house made "a weft." Then horns blew, boys yelled, men halloed, and all hands ran to the beach. Either for fishing or whaling a like "weft" was made and a like race to the beach. Whaling and fishing were both convenient, congenial and animating activities in Wainscott.

One day when all the militiamen were gone to "a company," not "a General Training," someone "made a weft," and all the boys and old men gathered on the beach, screeching, foolish boys, halt, lame, rheumatic, old men, everyone in every other one's way; a sight to behold! Uncle John Strong told Elisha Osborn, *"Continental,"* to let him take the rope, and untie the hard knot his brother-in-law, "Continental," was in vain wrestling with. "Continental" answers:

"John you can't untie it.

John says to "Continental," "There aint no such word in the book as *can't.*"

"Continental" says, "Some folks are *dreadful full of grammar."*

That old, queer, abortive hauling down the boat, loading up the seine, tying on the ropes with a "bowline," coiling ropes, shoving off, casting the net, hauling it ashore and getting *Nothing,* was a comedy enacted to the life, that beat any theatrical exploit I have seen in all the varied experience of the seventy-five years since it occurred on the sea and shore of Wainscott plain.

The Inspectors of Election eighty years ago sat, in East Hampton one day, more or less, and afterwards in Amagansett, Northwest, Wainscott, etc., moving from place to place and holding the polls open, with the same boxes, and in Wainscott remaining a half day. There in the old school house, among others John Strong and Elisha Osborn, "Continental," voted, and had, as often they did, a friendly tilt. Abraham Parsons Esq., one of the Inspectors, had lost a steer which he described by age, color and earmark, inquiring of those present for knowledge of it.

Strong says, "'Continental' has such a steer."

Parsons says, "who *is 'Continental?'"*

Strong says, "Elisha Osborn"

Parsons says, "why do you call him 'Continental?'"

Strong says, "we call him 'Continental because he is just like continental money, he is *good for nothing."*

Let no one think of this anecdote as otherwise than a pleasant contention of wits. Elisha Osborn, the "Continental," was a worthy, substantial, honest, intelligent, good hearted man, with a streak of droll humor that in most cases gave him the advantage in the conflict of wits.

Tom Hopping, working for my grandfather, at the dinner table said:

"Deacon Hedges what will you take for all you are worth?"

The Deacon says, "I will take forty thousand dollars, but Tom, where will you get the money?"

Tom said, "I will go to Gardiner's Island, mortgage all the property I buy of you and bring you the money."

Then Tom hesitated and finally said:

"Mind you, Deacon, Betsey is in the bargain."

Betsey was the Deacon's youngest daughter and Tom's proposition about Betsey became a by-word.

The tone of public opinion in Wainscott was intensely American and Patriotic. Through all the minor differences of opinion, there ran an overpowering stream of sentiment, anti-aristocratic, anti-British, anti-monopolistic. The memory of the wars of the Revolution and of 1812, were unforgotten and unforgiven. Wrongs suffered were thought to be unatoned, unrighted, unavenged. The American people were as sensitive to foreign criticism as a raw school boy, and as resentful when it was adverse. In their serene majesty and conscious power they are now unmoved and unruffled by like utterance.

In my day, in public sentiment, I know no variation so vast as that from the former extreme sensibility to foreign opinion to the present calm indifference. I record with regret, a condition in the body Politic now so corrupt, compared with former days. I do not believe, in my youth there was a *purchasable vote in Wainscott*. Now, in cities, Judas has such a following that he seems to have attained a popularity that threatens to nullify the example of *all the other Apostles*. When the government of this Republic is for sale to the highest bidder, the Nation will have fallen into that deep abyss in which have perished the dead nations of past ages—Will the sun of our National prosperity be eclipsed?

How wonderful is the power of association! The thought of eclipse reminds me that as a young boy, reading Cooper's *Romance of the "Red Rover"* between the school hours at mid-day, I witnessed the most complete eclipse of all my life. The stars came out in the darkness, the fowl went to roost at dark,—Night reigned. I was compelled, for lack of light, to give up reading. *"The Red Rover"* was first published in November, 1827. The eclipse, I think, must have occurred February 12, 1831, as foretold in the Almanac of Thomas Spofford, wherein he says, "In New York, beginning at 11:15 a.m." Much condensed knowledge may be gathered from almanacs, which are signs of the age, its manners, its progress, its failures, its follies, its thoughts, its superstitions, its wit, its wisdom. From a child up to date I have read almanacs with pleasure and profits.

SABBATH THOUGHTS.

Is the Sabbath of rest an ordainment of God? Has He written in the constitution of man the law of six days labor and the seventh of rest? In a long life of arduous work, my individual opinion may count for something. Just as a clock must be wound up to keep it going, so the human system must be wound up by supplies of food, fluid, sleep, repose. The machine runs a few hours only without these, and without, soon runs down, into disorder, derangement, disease, death. I believe the fourth commandment is written in the frame work of a man as truly as it was in the tables of stone by the finger of Jehovah, that the Creator has so made man that to do the most, achieve the most, reach the highest he must refresh, recuperate, wind up, by rest one day in seven, from manual or mental labor, that this is a law inherent in man, made for his well-being, conducive to the health, the comfort, the long life, the higher and purer life, the enjoyment and the devotion of man.

You ask me to prove it. [Answer: the proof is not remote, not old, not hard to find. It exists in our own history, at our own doors.]

When our forefathers came to this continent the wilderness stretched from ocean to ocean, a habitation of wild beasts and wild Indians. The work they had to do was the most stupendous demanded of any people in all the annals of recorded time. Their march from ocean to ocean, their transformation of a continent, their work, the most onerous and beneficent in all history, was a labor of six days, with rest on the seventh. They did more manually, mentally, morally than in like case the same number of men ever did and did it better. Show us more work, swifter work, better work anywhere, by any people, without the Sabbath rest! Show half as much before you disallow or disavow the Sabbath! In the body and soul of man his Maker has indelibly written the Law of the Sabbath. That law is a condition of success, a benign and perpetual blessing to the human race. Victorious achievement attends its observance. Misfortune, failure, calamity, follow in the footsteps of the Sabbath breaking man, or nation. I have known in families of my acquaintance, often three generations, sometimes five and sometimes six, and know whereof I affirm. Regard for the feelings of surviving kindred prevents personal mention of Sabbath breakers and their disastrous career. Such considerations, not lack of proof, constrains me *not* to say what I might say. Man may sometimes successfully cheat his fellow man, never his Maker.

If conscience is the rightful, regnant, supreme voice of the soil; if the lower, animal, selfish, degrading attributes of man ought to be subordinate to the mental and moral; if the spirit is superior to the flesh; if the earthy is earthly and returns "earth to earth, ashes to ashes, dust to dust:" if the soul survives in enduring, immortal, indestructible life; if God, uncaused, self-existent, lives, not as fancied in the classic mythology of Greece and Rome, a mere superhuman being, with like appetites, propensities and frailties, like selfishness and passions, but in the inconceivable loftiness of the God of the Bible, whose care, whose providence, whose tenderness, whose love are expressed in the life and mission of Jesus, His representative on earth; if all this be true is one day in seven too much for him to claim and can man, in view of his welfare, give him less?

THE BIBLE!

Men who read and know much of the Bible almost always are devout believers. Men who read and know of it little are generally the objectors and disbelievers. It is simply ignorance against knowledge, misunderstanding objecting for cause originating in itself. Tom Paine's assault on the Bible, all unfair, all partisan, all predjudiced [sic], was well known to me before I attained manhood, but not before I knew enough of the Bible to see how shallow, unfounded and false his logic was. Tacitus says, what men wish to believe they easily believe. Tom Paine wished to disbelieve and easily did so. From him through all like him, down to Bob Ingersoll, the same rule applies.

The Bible, begun ages before Homer sung, ended nearly fifteen hundred years before the art of printing, the mariner's compass, or gunpowder were discovered, was a Revelation to the world when practically in a dark, benighted, barbarous state. From first to last it was ages in advance of all heathen, all barbarian, all contemporaneous thought. It was more humane, more merciful, more just, and taught a system of life and laws more beneficent and regardful of the wrongs of the innocent and oppressed, more denunciatory of the oppressor, more exalted in the light it shone on the spirit land, more worthy in the power, the wisdom, the purity, the perfection, attributed to its Jehovah, than Homer, or Plato, or Virgil, or Horace, or any Heathen genius had attained. Read of the Gods of Homer, the realm of Pluto's gloomy reign and follow down the Mythology of Greece and Rome, to the day of its downfall. Then read the Bible, always higher than human thought, wiser than human wisdom, purer than human virtue, grander than human conception, a light to the mind in childhood's simplicity, in manhood's strength, a light to every soul, in every age, in every land. *Read!* And say, if it does not bear the stamp of a Divine original.

GOOD BYE TO WAINSCOTT!

In the early spring of 1831 my father moved into the house in East Hampton lately the home of Samuel G. Mulford, deceased, and in July after it I bid good bye to Wainscott and began life in the village of East Hampton. As early as 1823 I had attended school in Clinton Academy, and at later dates a few weeks only. I remember being there when David Gardiner, M.D., was its scholarly principal, and when James M. Huntting was instructor and once instructed me by pulling my hair.

East Hampton Centre was then, as now, the capital of the town. At Town Meetings, General Trainings, celebrations of the Fourth of July, and Sabbath day worship I had been there. Yet Wainscott was home. With many a long lingering look behind, with many a pang at leaving the house where I was born, Wainscott Pond, where I had fished, and swam, and rowed; the mighty ocean, inspiring thought of boundless expanse and power; the neighbors, whose friendship and tenderness was so dear; the playmates whose company was so congenial; all these strong ties bound me to my old home, and all were broken in going to East Hampton.

EAST HAMPTON!

Out of the harvest field, tanned almost to the color of an Indian, with hands hardened by toil, with ankles scratched by briars, feet stockingless, pants too short to cover ankles, a growing, awkward boy of nearly fourteen, I entered the classic shades of Clinton Academy, the most conspicuous mark for criticism, and raillery, and ridicule and jest in the whole school, and perhaps the most sensitive. Jeered at, hooted at, ridiculed, scorned, despised, the butt of the whole school, what could I do? What could I say? How could I defend myself? Backward in studies looking to a farmer's life, unsophisticated in the ways of the fashionable and social life, struggling with the geography of the earth and problems of Arithmetic, and rules of grammar, I might suffer in silence, and be the tail end of the kite. Was there any other way? When not long after, it was announced that my father intended to send me to college the outburst of astonishment and ridicule rose to appalling magnitude. A few years ago Nathan Dimon told me, his father was told my father proposed to send his son Henry to college, and in surprise his father said, "What! Is he bright?"

Other students were more advanced. Stern Randolph Campbell was principal. Himself a hard worker, he drove the school with a discipline and momentum that made it a race in study, and thus he drove me. His aim was to find the maximum of capacity and put the pressure up to that. I was in this dilemma: If all my powers of thought went in study of books nothing was left for self-defense, then I must suffer in silence. Passive virtue may be the most exalted of all the virtues. But boys seldom rise to that, and I had not got there. I must and could and would defend myself. I must meet ridicule with ridicule, taunt with taunt, scorn with scorn, gibe with gibe, and so meet as to down it. If I studied school books less and the art of ridicule more, self defence compelled. If Randolph Campbell frowned he had less cause than he thought. If in the conflict of vituperation I achieved readiness of retort that compelled my tormentors to retreat in every charge, retreat in every assault, flee in every battle, fear more than date, self defence was the cause, and the assailants taught and provoked and trained the assailed.

I studied the art of (I hate the word, but none occurs to express what I mean so fittingly as this) *blackguarding* so effectually that my adversaries tacitly agreed to an armistice and then and not till then, I went for scholastic acquirements with a will.

Of all the teachers and scholars there then I can recall only one now living. If I am not mistaken Edward Dayton was in the class in geography when I was under Randolph Campbell and I heard him answer the question, "What is the highest peak in the mountain chain of the Andes?" by saying, "Chimborazo is the highest peak." Strange that after the lapse of more than three score and ten years this incident is uneffaced. Honest, old, substantial "Ed Dayton," of "Hardscrabble," on the "Nor'west Plains," and owner of a good many of its acres, life-long tiller of the soil, life-long friend of the writer, only living witness of the times and scenes I have been describing, say if the story I have told is not a frank and fair relation of facts! Mr. Boughton, editor, and you, gentle reader, if in making this narrative true and full I had to *blow my own horn*, it was because there was left none beside.

In my dilemma, a schoolboy of this generation in the same case might or might not do as I did. Just now I cannot stop to preach. Readers may consider and meditate on the facts. My preaching may follow but not just here and now.

How new students are looked over and scrutinized and criticised and measured, boys know, and girls know, and society women and men know. From the common school to the university, from the social circle in the village to the like in the largest city this measuring and scanning of a new comer is universal, and unceasing. Elihu Hedges came to Clinton Academy soon after my entry there. He came from up the Hudson, and, probably with consciousness of this overlooking, when we were gathered just before school began, jumped on top of a desk, clapped his hands, crowed, and began, "Beloved friends and fellow mortals, rattle snakes and snapping Tortles."

CLINTON ACADEMY.

Clinton Academy had been a Pioneer light in education almost a half century when I entered it, in the midsummer of 1831. In youth the residents of East Hampton had been instructed there. In maturer life its results were conspicuous in intelligent thought, higher aims, wider influence, enlarged capacity, superior knowledge of public affairs. The darkened streets of a village, by the touch of electric torch, in an instant are illuminated and glow with light. Clinton Academy was the educational torch that illuminated the intellect of our town. Mind on mind, like star on star, shone resplendent in its air, radiated in its sphere, charmed in its social life, swiftened thought and animated expression. From far and near students gathered there. From New London came John Brandagee, brother of Augustus, Jo Lawrence and one or two brothers, Elias and Shaw Perkins; from Brooklyn, Ben Hoogland, John L. Gardiner M.D. and Charles H., minister of the everlasting Gospel; from N.Y. City, James Norton, Pearsall Norton and another brother; from Smithtown, the Smiths, John Lawrence and Joel; from Huntington, Abel K. Conkling; from Moriches, Jesse W. Pelletreau; from Southold, Wm. Huntting, Ben Goldsmith, Joseph C. Albertson, Elias Luce and D. Fanning Brown; from Sag Harbor, Howells, Gilbert H. and Augustus, Wm. and Gilbert H. Cooper, and Stephen D. Topping; from Sandy Hill, N.Y., John Hempstead, Luther Sleight and two brothers, Ogden Edwards, Judge of the Supreme Court of New York and grandson of Jonathan, the greatest metaphysician of the age, had there a son, Jonathan and two other sons.

This catalogue (not full) of my fellow students shows that the fame of Clinton Academy was wide spread and well established. As an institution preparatory to a college course it was a necessity, an educational force found nowhere except in the like few existing academies. Its star shone bright in the constellation of like stars. Now union schools supply the place of and have supplanted this and many other academies throughout the land. Let not this detract from their fair fame and their former usefulness and merit.

Clinton Academy achieved for the girls as much as for the boys. To the charms of female beauty were added the animated light of intelligence; to the grace of form, the soul of understanding. The young ladies there were conspicuous for acquirement in scholarship and shone in elevating, purifying light in the domestic, social and literary circle. As years rolled on they won the garlands of substantial worth.

A.D. Candy and Joseph D. Condit were teachers in the academy before 1831, and were followed by Randolph Campbell, a Mr. Sandford, Z. Rogers, Ely, Robert D. Gardiner and James Harlow, under whom I studied. They were able, scholarly men and faithful instructors. Candy, Condit, Gardiner and Harlow married East Hampton ladies. President Tyler married Juliana, daughter of David Gardiner, confirming proofs of my former statement.

EXHIBITION.

The spring term closed with dramatic performances termed the *exhibition*, in which the young ladies and gentlemen represented the characters. Tragedy and comedy both were under contribution in this grand display. It was the crowning event of the year to which all eyes looked, for which all hearts beat. In my history of East Hampton, the programme for the exhibition given April 10th, 1821, is printed, conveying some idea of its magnitude. Tickets were sold, actors were exercised, parents and friends interested. The Academy would be crowded. The amateur stage was the central object on which all eyes were turned. There I first saw representations of the dramatic art. In time I too became an actor, studying the power of personification, in tone and emphasis of voice, expression of countenance and feature, variety and vehemence of action. I had the actor's fever in some dialogue taking the part of "Dr. Pangloss" in a comic piece. The fever raged furiously. I thought no aim more enticing than that of the actor, no ambition more gratifying than that of the theatre. Oh! if I could only belong to a traveling company of actors, and going from town to town, rehearse and represent, in comic character to the delight and astonishment of listening audiences, the parts I thought I could well act, then my ambition would be atained. I was almost ready to run away, in hope of finding and joining such a band. How often boys are saved from their own folly. When I recall how as a boy I wanted to find danger only to risk it, sport only to engage in it, adventure only to trifle with it, it is a wonder I have two good eyes, two sound legs and an unbroken head. If to the sailor "There's a cherub aloft that takes care of poor Jack," a like "cherub" seems to care for boys.

TRAVELS!

In the spring of 1834 or 5, Augustus Howell, Henry Gardiner and myself, schoolmates, broke the monotony of study, by a journey to the cities of New York, New Haven, Hartford, and home by way of New London. A horseback ride to Montauk Point probably had been our longest trip from home. The tide of travel was by packet from Sag Harbor to New York. We sailed thence with Capt. Charles Smith, in the sloop Gen. Warren and got in Peck's Slip in a little more than two days. There were some dozen passengers, among them Cyrus Hitchcock, Lawrence Edwards, and Capt. Harry Green.

Capt. Nathan Fordham in the sloop James Lawrence, sailed at the same time. The voyage was a race from start to finish. Captain crew and passengers all were determined to beat and left nothing undone to achieve it. In hoisting or lowering sail, reefing or hauling in the sheet, gybing or wetting sails, all worked with a will. Capt. Charles was a thorough seaman, hardy, athletic, ambitious, honest, resolute, watchful, active and in his chosen element, a type of the best navigators of Sag Harbor in its maritime splendor. He was a man of sterling worth, an individual interesting to mark, watch, and study, no ordinary, common man, but capable of high thought and heroic act. He was vigilant, in every minutia, prompt in every command. I can see him now, in compact, muscular build, looking out forward, and hear him in ringing tones say to Ishmael Ward, his Indian sailor, "Luff a leetle Ishmael, when it blows hard." Poor Ishmael! One night he was on deck, and soon missed, and appeared no more, how or why no one knew, the sad and mysterious end of many a seaman. By a close shave Capt. Charles got the Gen. Warren into Peck Slip just ahead of the James Lawrence.

The Clinton Hotel in Beekman street, nearly opposite the old brick church of Dr. Spring, was the then great hotel of New York, and there we stopped. We saw the sights. By stage we rode out to Harlaem; Canal street was up town; Above Broome street New York was suburban. Capt. Harry Green took us under his protecting wing and escorted us to the theatre, where Fanny Essler danced, and the drama was glorified. To me the first night's display was a real transfiguration, the gilt real gold, the spangles genuine, thunder and lightning all a reality, actors and acting all natural, and all to the life. Not so the second night. Then the illusion vanished. Tinsel was tinsel, gilt nothing else. Acting was acting, thunder and lightning a hollow sound, the whole exhibition a mockery. The repulsion was complete. The theatre lost all charm. I was cured, disenthralled for all after life from theatrical fascination. With some interest I have witnessed the play of the "Old Homestead," yet the illusion of that first night never returned. The magic of the stage has been an empty bubble, expelled by the sober realities of life.

By steamboat we went from New York to New Haven, stopping at the Tontine Hotel, visiting the college buildings, viewing the neat, white, country-like cottages, the grand and graceful elms, the simple, solemn, decent cemetery, and admired the beauty of a city that still retained so many delightful features of the country.

By stage through Middletown, and Wethersfield with its prolific plots of onions, we went to Hartford, another capital of the Nutmeg State, and there saw the famous Charter Oak, visited the Asylum for the insane, and that for the deaf and dumb. Hartford had more costly structures, apparently more conveniences for trade, and more city like appearance. From outward look I got the impression that it was better for business and New Haven better for learning. By steamboat we came down the river from Hartford to Lyme, stopping at many landings, and all manner of Haddams, East, Middle, etc. At Lyme we put up at Bacon's Hotel. It was reported that he believed in the general remedial efficacy of steam, and had apparatus for taking a steam bath and was a steam doctor. Some one told us he took a steam bath, and the attendant kept him shut up in it a long time, until the old fellow was almost boiled. It may have been all a story yet we boys laughed long and loud over it, and had lots of fun about it. It was the time for river shad. In their season they are delicious fish, and none of their kind beat those of Connecticut river. How we three hungry boys loaded up on shad was both amusing and astonishing.

We went by stage from Lyme to New London, over a rough, rocky country, abounding in stone walls, and boulders. In one place stone and rock almost covered the ground, and the driver told us there was where Noah hove out his ballast. New London was then a notable whaling port. Its harbor was deep, capacious, sheltered. Its commerce was considerable and growing. The Groton monument stood with only a few farm houses visible near it. Its population and enlargement now must be eight or ten times more than then.

In the little packet sloop *Bee*, commanded by Capt. Rogers, we came to Sag Harbor and home. The journey was time and money well spent. We got more correct and enlarged views of life, of the geography and extent of our country, of its inhabitants, its manners and customs, and in our boyish lingo, half comic, half serious, we were "acquainted in large cities."

YALE COLLEGE.

In August, 1835, I was examined, and by a hard rub, admitted to the Sophomore class in Yale College. In mid-autumn I started by steamboat from Sag Harbor, running up Connecticut River to join my class. I left a good home, congenial companions and conditions for a strange, untried, uncertain career. When the steamer parted from the dock, in an instant all this burst upon me. As the distance increased the thoughts grew more alarming. I was going to live with strangers, in an unknown land, where no guardian, guiding hand, no sympathetic, congenial friend, no one to love or care for me might be found. The outlook was appalling. All that John Howard Payne (whom I had well known) wrote of the delights of "Home, Sweet Home," that I was leaving, flashed over me. *I was Homesick.* Looking back nearly seventy years, I thank God that my home was such that its ties were hard to break. The boy that leaves it with gladness, or without regret, fails in the finer feelings, or his home fails there. If he scorns his home, except it be the abode of scorners, Woe! Dire Woe, awaits him!

I was not well fitted to enter the sophomore, which is the hardest year in college, and like members of my family, matured late in life. It was hard work to keep up with the class, studying so much by lamp-light, with poor, smoky, whale oil, strained and so inflamed my eyes that they were permanently weakened for all after life. There was no impairment of vision but loss of power of long endurance. Eyes that had never tired before now tired soon. After fighting through sophomore year progress was easier to the end.

The catalogue of Yale for 1835 and '6 shows students thus: Freshmen, 135; Sophomores 87, Juniors 111, Seniors 81, in all 414; theological students 63, law students 31, medical students 60, total 568.

Multiply that number by 5 and you get a result very near to the present army of students in Yale. A growth and patronage deserved by the virtue, the purity, the fidelity, the learning of a band of instructors whose fame is coextensive with civilization.

The class of 1837 was one of the most illustrious in the college annals. Among its graduates were Morrison R. Waite, Chief Justice of the Supreme Court of the United States, William M. Evarts and M. Edwards Pierrepont. The class of 1838, of which I was one, graduated 70 members. In numbers less than the average, it made a record useful rather than brilliant. There were few shipwrecks. There are now living John K. Bartlett M.D., probably *of California*; Richard E. Butler, of Louisiana; Hon. William F. Cooper, of Nashville, Tennessee, a most distinguished jurist; Chester Dutton, of Kansas, eminent and successful farmer, nearly 90 years of age; Rev. William T. Doubleday, of Bridgehampton, N.Y.; Theodore S. Gold, of West Cornwall, Connecticut, an eminent scientist and instructor, long time secretary of the Board of Agriculture of that state, and the writer.

I soon found that exercise was essential to health, and took long walks, generally in the early dawn of winter mornings and at other times. In these walks I met the venerable Jeremiah Day, President of the college, the professors, tutors and others, some of whom were widely known. Counted with these morning walkers, seeking health, and with few exceptions attaining longevity, were Judge David Daggett, sometimes a lawyer of eminence, a distinguished judge, a senator of the United States, in person large, tall, strongly built, of majestic presence, clad in short pants, top boots, his hair powdered, he was the personification of a gentleman of the old school, so old, that he with his grand, courtly manners, was almost the sole, solitary survivor. Noah Webster, the author of my old spelling book, the great Lexicographer, I often thus met, a tall, slender, nervous man, with a pale scholarly look, light eyes, massive forhead [sic], quick step, just a thinking machine. When his big dictionary first came out the word "everlasting" was not in it, and Prof. Kingsley, the wit of faculty, said he "could not see how the word 'everlasting' could not be got in such an everlasting dictionary." Webster had the large, overhanging eyebrows that, it is said, marked the Webster family, the great Daniel and others. At this time he was living with Prof. Chauncey A. Goodrich, who married his daughter, and after his death edited and enlarged his dictionary.

Prof. Goodrich was a man with great learning, and a great heart. He cared for me, counseled me, encouraged me, inspired me to literary achievement more than I expected or deserved. Thanks and honor to his memory!

Sophomore year generally decides whether the student will remain through the college course or leave. If his eyes, brain and body can stand the hard strain of that year, he probably will pull through and graduate. I got time to eat, sleep, exercise and passably learn the tasks assigned, with no surplus power to do much more. When this hard fight was over, Junior and Senior years gave more leisure to look beyond lesson books, and open my eyes on the larger, outer, living world. By mastery of elementary knowledge in the classics and mathematics, we advanced to higher flights therein. We pondered on the great truths of Natural Philosophy and Astronomy, studied History, got a smattering of the French language. When seniors we received instruction largely from the President and Professors.

President Jeremiah Day, a man of sweet, serene temper, purity of purpose and life, endowed with eminent, mathematical and logical powers, lectured on our studies in intellectual and oral philosophy and natural theology, himself a practical illustration of the precepts he expounded. The elder Silli, man, enthusiastic, brilliant, inventive, eloquent, lectured on chemistry, mineralogy, geology, and by magnetic power drove the great truths into our dull comprehension. Prof. Kingsley, a man of keenest perception, sharpest wit, largest literary achievement, purest style of expression and profoundest thought, lectured on language, history and its varied sources, and sketched a system of chronology. Prof. Olmstead, an intense, practical, studious, thoughtful genius, lectured on the principles of natural philosophy, mechanical powers, meteorology, etc. Prof. Goodrich, great hearted Goodrich, profoundly versed in lexicography, lectured on language, rhetoric, style of expression, oratory, pronunciation, verbiage, obsolete, inacurate [sic], improper, redundant, etc.

Nathaniel W. Taylor D.D., President of the Theological Department, was a man of great intellect, strong in argument, pure and benevolent in life, resolute in purpose, independent in thought. In the pulpit, his lofty forehead, pale, scholarly face, dark, luminous eye, animated countenance, marked him a power not to be overborne or silenced. I have seen no man who filled the Pulpit, with emphasis on the word "*filled*," with more dignity, more majesty, more power of presence. Lyman Beecher, perhaps more eloquent, more magnetic, more popular, certainly more fortunate, was so strongly attached to Taylor that by his request his body was buried by the side of Taylor's grave in the New Haven cemetery. These two great chieftains of the Church Militant, emancipated from the tenets of an impracticable, obsolete, unscriptural creed, fought for and won a battle for principles that made theology more consistent, more practical, more defensible, in advancing "the Faith once delivered to the Saints." Dr. Taylor lectured to us on the Evidences of Christianity.

I now have notes of lectures in college, as follows:

> Olmstead on Natural Philosophy, 16 lectures; on Astronomy, 21 lectures; on Meteorology, 3 lectures.
> Daggett on the History and Constitution of Connecticut, 4 lectures; on the Constitution of the United States, 9 lectures; on the Law of Nations, 4 lectures.
> Goodrich on eloquence, 9 lectures; on style, 7 lectures; on the use of words, 13 lectures.
> Kingsley on History, Chronology, etc., 10 lectures; on Language, 12 lectures.
> Dr. Taylor on Evidence of Christianity, 14 lectures.
> Total number of lectures 122.

This large, varied, valuable mass of lectures, by men in their day eminent in their several spheres of acquirement, convey no little amount of instruction to the thoughtful student. In one of Olmstead's lectures he stated that the highest buildings in New York City were the New York University, 108 feet; The City Hall, 107 feet; the Astor House, 96 feet. The modern sky scrapers now look down on these structures as of pigmy proportions.

Whatever may be said in disparagement of the Yankees, it cannot be denied that they were and are eminently able and successful instructors. In my day New Haven blazed with intellectual light. There I heard lectures from James Silk Buckingham, an English gentleman, distinguished as a traveler and explorer. There I heard lectures from George Combe, the great Phrenologist, on his system of Phrenology. There I heard John Bell, afterwards candidate for President of the United States, and Congressman Graves, of Kentucky, who shot and killed Congressman Cilley, of Maine, address the people on the politics of the day.

The clergy of Connecticut were an intellectual and moral force not often excelled.

On the Sabbath in the chapel, Prof. Eleazar T. Fitch stately ministered, a man of fine literary taste, profound thought, logical mind, earnest, impressive manner, pure and simple life. His sermons were systematic, symmetric, cohesive, converging to a prearranged conclusion, enforced and emphasized by eloquent, practical, pathetic appeal. He was a workman worthy of the high position he nobly filled. Grant his premises and his argument demonstrated his conclusion, as inevitably as the well sped arrow flies to its mark. Sometimes Dr. Taylor filled the pulpit with his grand personality and there once preached his most eloquent sermon, on the text, "What is Truth?" Sometimes Joel Hawes D.D., of Hartford, tall, commanding, long armed, of fair countenance, clear, blue eye, kindly, winning manner, great intellectual and emotional force, preached. Sometimes Noah Porter D.D., of Farmington, (father of the Noah afterwards President of Yale), preached. He was a man of remarkable intellectual and spiritual presence, pale, calm, restrained in manner. His air of devotion seemed seraphic, his hold on the spiritual an embodied reality, his converse with Heaven a habit, his prayer a patriarchal invocation to a very present God with whom he walked. Once Lyman Beecher preached there in the morning and in the Centre Church in the afternoon. He carried the audience with him by main electric force. He was reported to have advised his theological students to write sermons thus: "Make a point and set a candle on it." He formulated a striking thought and by similie [sic] and figure illustrated it, thus exemplifying his teaching. Once Adoniram Judson D.D., life-long missionary to Burmah [sic], translator of the Bible into the Burmese language, preached. His saintly sacrifice of himself to this great work was known throughout Christendom. Nothing in his appearance attracted attention. In form he was of good size with light eyes, light complexion, light hair of the Anglo Saxon stamp, and an air of repose more than animation. In his calm way he began to speak of his mission to Burmah. Warming in interest every fibre [sic] of his body moved with emotion, every feature of his face shone with animation, every movement of his hand was an expression of his soul, every utterance of his lips a trumpet call for sympathy and aid to the poor, benighted, suffering, stricken, millions of his beloved Burmah. His appeal was a revelation on the meaning of the word *Transfiguration*.

Daniel Webster came to New Haven about 1837, and had a rousing reception in the Center Church. Charles B. Hosmer, my roommate in No. 76, North Middle College, was a more partisan Democrat than myself as a Whig. I asked him if he was going to hear Webster. He said: "Yes! I am going to hear the old aristocrat, old federalist, Hartford conventionist and bluelight." We got a good seat, well forward in the gallery, where was a good view of the platform and personages thereon and of the audience. The large church was closely packed with the most prominent and intellectual representatives of the intelligent city of learning.

Webster was then about 55 years old, about 5 feet, 10 inches in height, broad-shouldered, large-chested, compactly, heavily and strongly built, with ponderous head, majestic, towering forehead, dark, deep set eyes, large and noble looking features, in presence the most imposing man I ever saw in all my life. To the casual observer, from the first glance, there flashed back the impression of power of body and mind, the power of a champion unequaled in a conflict of argument, of reason, of intellect. You could read there majesty in response, terrific momentum in movement. In forming the Olympian Jove Phidias might well have chosen his like for an immortal model.

David Daggett presided, honored with high official position, venerable with age, revered throughout the state for judicial eminence, acquirement in learning, unsullied integrity and sterling worth. With dignified air he rose and in few, impressive, well-chosen words, introduced as the orator of the occasion "the Honorable Daniel Webster, the defender of the Constitution of the United States."

Webster rose and acknowledging the honor done him, soon spoke of General Jackson, his character and public policy as President of the United States. He said charges had been made against General Jackson that he was dishonest, illiterate, immoral and unpatriotic. All these he characterized as unfounded and untrue, and affirmed that as a man, in private character he was honest, intelligent, sincere, virtuous and patriotic. He spoke of their social relations as of the most friendly character, and said that after his speech in reply to Hayne, Gen. Jackson came to him and with tears in his eyes, thanked him for that service he had rendered to the country, in defence of the constitution, and union of the States, and of his administration as President. It was a noble and magnanimous tribute of justice to a life-long political foe, such as only a great hearted statesman, with such commanding power like Webster, could give, and it thrilled the audience to the inmost heart. Webster had said that after Gen. Jackson thus thanked him he sent his carriage to convey him wherever he wished to go in the city of Washington, so that the friends of both in the audience, apprised of their friendly relations, were temporarily the more impressed and the more friendly to each other.

Continuing Webster said, regarding the public policy of Gen. Jackson and his claim to be and act as the representative of the people of the United States, they differed *in toto coelo*, that such claim was utterly unwarranted and unauthorized by any rightful theory of our government, that Congress assembled in Senate and House of Representatives, was the representative of the people of the United States, and by the Constitution and uniform procedure made the only proper representative of the people, that the President was clothed with power, as the Executive to execute and enforce the laws enacted by Congress, and any claim as a representative of the people to set aside their enactment, was an invasion of the rights of the Legislative power and usurpation wrongfully grasped by him. The argument was so fair, so clear, so fortified, as to be unanswerable. Thought on thought, reason on reason, blow on blow, in logical sequence, struck with ponderous power, unite in crushing conclusion, no foothold was left for adverse defense. The hostile fort was stormed and taken.

The audience, dismissed, retired in silence, moved by the momentum of facts so stated as to be undeniable, principles so expounded as to be self-evident, arguments so advanced as to force conviction. The impression made was too deep for diversion, too permanent for trifling, too sacred for naught but meditation. No murmur of dissent, no whisper even of friendly greeting broke the silence of that retiring audience. Moving homeward, as if still in the presence of the most majestic personality of the time, the greatest logician of his age, as if still in hearing of his voice, the spell long remained unbroken. Hosmer and I walked almost to College street, when I spoke the first word, saying: "Hosmer, what do you think of that." With deepest emphasis he said, "I will never say another word against Daniel Webster as long as I live, so help me God!" I asked for his reason. He assigned the fair, manly way in which he spoke of Gen. Jackson and the full measure of justice awarded to him—that it was so admirable, so generous, so noble, that he could not speak against him, and again repeated his vow to that effect. My warm-hearted Democratic classmate was converted from a foe to a friend, a testimony to the power of the speaker. I have found no report, and no notice of this speech in the published works and speeches of Daniel Webster, and for that reason have minutely recorded the substance, as I remember it, here and now.

The next forenoon Webster spoke briefly, encouraging words to the Yale students. Afterwards, at Saratoga, I heard his speech at a mass meeting, August 19, 1840.

RELIGION.

In a periodical magazine, years ago, I read an article on the requisites of a perfect religion. Much impressed by the article, chiefly from memory, with my own thoughts, I, in part, try to reproduce it in the form of these three rules:

1. Worship can never reach the highest unless the Being worshipped is perfect.

2. When that Being, in love for the worshipper, descends from the Divine to the human form and limitations of His human worshipper, compassion reaches its utmost, and is a demonstration of a perfect Being.

3. When the human worshipper and the Divinity worshipped are set in such relations, that in a sense God shall be a partaker of human nature, and man of the Divine nature, religion is perfect.

1. The worship of an imperfect being must be imperfect, as in all the idol worship of ancient, classic, or modern heathen times. That a perfect Being can be the only object of perfect worship is an axiom and a self evident truth.

2. The descent of the Divine to the human form and limitations, is evidence of a pity and compassion boundless in beneficence and mercy, worthy of the Divine Being, and satisfying the

highest ideal of the human worshipper. He can conceive no loftier act in his highest thought of the Divine compassion. That such compassion could come and only come from a Divinity perfect in all his attributes, is a truth axiomatic and self evident.

3. Example is better than precept. It is truth, not in theory but act. It is obvious that God could impressively teach men how to live and how to die by an example in human form and with Divine limitations, and according to human experience, He could not otherwise so impressively teach men as by such an example. He who created all forms could assume any form. He who had all power, could limit His power in a certain sense, in its display. He who could impart life to and take it from other forms, could so in a human form to and from Himself, could animate and extinguish and revive life, and more, as a spirit He could impart a spiritual or Divine life to man, thereby uniting in will and aim and desire, the Divine with the human so that the human is merged in the Divine in sweet, universal harmony, each with the other, eternal, indissoluble, enlarging, progressing, uniting, not only each with the other, but with the whole Universe, material and spiritual, created or to be created, knowing no limit in space and no end in time. And all this is self evident, simple truth, so simple as to be axiomatic, and as truth, a mark and rule of a perfect religion. Carefully reading and pondering these three propositions, intelligent thoughtful minds, almost universally would assent and accept them as such.

Not in the form of creeds, verbose, antiquated, distorted, disputed, misunderstood, misrepresented, not even stated in the phraseology of the Bible, they are the great, underlying principles of the Gospel, and when so stated awaken thought, animate interest, force conviction as often the words of the sacred Scriptures fail to do from their very familiarity and frequent repetition. Using so often their form, we forget their meaning, substituting words for spirit.

The God of the Testaments, old and new, is a Being all perfect, knowing no limit in power, purity, wisdom, goodness, truth or in any excellence: a perfect God.

The God of the Gospel "was manifest in the flesh." He "gave His only begotten Son, that whosoever believeth on Him should not perish, but have everlasting life;" and "as many as are led by the Spirit of God, they are the Sons of God." The compassion of God, the tenderness of God, His paternal care, His abounding love, the divinity of Christ Jesus, the love of God in Jesus, as our brother in humanity, the moral tone of the Gospels are all perfect and contain all the requirements of a perfect religion. All other systems are always imperfect, always defective, often debasing, on their face bearing marks of human invention.

The Gospel is a gem without a spot. Its Christ is perfect, its morality perfect, its salvation perfect. Human laws touch acts and outward conduct only and reach no deeper. The Gospel pierces through all disguise and goes down to the thought and intent of the heart. Where human laws and systems fail that takes hold and prohibits the desire or thought of crime, as if that were already done, condemns the conception as if executed. In the boundless bearing and sweep of the Gospel law, no thought, no word, no act is left untouched. There can be no evasion, no omission, no avoidance, no escape. That law is perfect. It is worthy of a God. I cannot believe it had other origin. Give Mohammed's system full swing and you fill the world with sensuality in the *mortal and immortal life*. Do this with Mormonism and you get the same result. Do it with the gross idolatry of India or China and you do it to the degradation of mankind. Do it with Christianity and you transform the world into a garden of peace, of joy, of righteousness. Therein shall grow the unfading flowers of virtue, therein the imperishable trees of a more than human goodness, therein the verdure of perennial grace, therein the immortal garlands, wherewith God shall crown the head of him that overcometh.

YALE COLLEGE CONTINUED.

My diploma, certifying that I graduated an A.B. from Yale College, is signed by Jeremiah Day, President, and Elizur Goodrich, secretary; is attested by the college seal, and dated August 15th, 1838. A diploma likewise signed and sealed, certifying that I took the degree of A.M., is dated August 18, 1841.

Forty-five of our class took appointments for orations, disputes, dissertations and colloquies, awarded as honors for scholarship, in the coming commencement; showing that we were a studious class. My appointment to compose and deliver a third colloquy was 42d in number. Although not exalted it was soothing. The rules required my presence in New Haven, if I delivered my production on the stage, and rather than remain there, I relinquished it for these reasons. The summer was then intensely warm: I had just delivered an oration before the Linonian society, as the farewell parting of our class, and was much worn down. Prof. Goodrich criticised this oration, corrected and cheered me through it, and gave me this word or praise: "*You have earnestness,* that is an element *essential to success.*" My farewell oration was well received, beyond my expectations.

At graduation my age was within two months of twenty-one years. Richard Henry Stoddard wrote "The Departure of Youth!"

> *"There are gains for all our losses,*
> *There are balms for all our pain,*
> *But when youth, the dream, departs,*
> *It takes something from our hearts,*
> *And it never comes again.*
>
> *We are stronger and are better*
> *Under manhood's sterner reign;*
> *Still, we feel that something sweet*
> *Followed youth with flying feet,*
> *And will never come again.*
>
> *Something beautiful has vanished,*
> *And we sigh for it in vain;*
> *We behold it everywhere,*
> *On the earth and in the air,*
> *But it never comes again."*

Solomon said, "My son be admonished: of making books there is no end, and much study is a weariness of the flesh." I was "*admonished,*" and remained in East Hampton after graduating, some eight months, for recreation and culture of the physical machinery, working on the farm, and, in their season, engaged in fishing for menhaden, bass, and off-shore whaling. Menhaden or bunker fishing on shore allowed much respite from work, which was hard only when fish were plenty. Bob Hedges and I were not seine owners, but had half shares in the catchings. Bob was amusing and kept the company in good humor by his drollery. He was unsatisfied about the way of dividing fish, and said they did it thus: "They multiplied by Wick Isaacs, divided by Josiah Dayton's Nigger, Sam Miller and John Dayton took what they wanted, and the shares got the rest, if there was any left." Bass fishing was wet, cold work, tolerable only for the hardiest, toughest men. We had no rubber boots, or oil skinsuits. We fished off shore near the village of East Hampton, drawing nets to shore for bass or bunkers, and went bassing to

Montauk Point for a week or more, making only moderate paying
hauls. After that came whaling. *We killed a whale.* Our boat was
manned by Lewis Gann, captain, myself, Edward Dayton, Henry Chatfield, Jeremiah Huntting, and Chas. B. Loper, harpooner. In another boat
was William Parsons, captain, commonly called "Great Bill," Theron
Filer, George Hand, Hiram Sherrill, Chester Taylor and Giles Haveus, harpooner. Dayton and myself are the only survivors of the two boats'
crews. In my *History of East Hampton,* on page 178, is an account of
this whale killing. When we began to tow the whale to shore two boats
came from Amagansett to help us. Away in the southwest, some ten
miles, three whales were playing. Jeremiah Huntting said to Gann, "Let
the Amagansett boats tow our whales ashore and let us go and kill
those three whales and make a day's work of it." Huntting had the tenderness of a child and the courage of a hero. His sterling worth demands this tribute to his memory.

In my college course I wasted no money on peanuts, confec-
tionery, strong liquors or luxuries, but saved to buy books. Chiefly with
these savings, I bought these histories, Gibbon's *Decline and Fall of
the Roman Empire,* Hume, Smollett, and Miller's *England,* Robertson's
Charles V and Scotland, Ferguson's *Rome,* Josephus' *Plutarch's Lives,*
Russell's *Modern Europe,* Rollin's *Ancient History,* &c.; also Addison's
Spectator, Essays by Foster and others, *Selections of British Poets,* by
Southey and Aiken; The works of Burns, Byron, Goldsmith and Shakespeare, the *Commentaries* of Blackstone, interleaved for notes. With
my school books which were retained, I had the solid nucleus of a
working library. In the winter of 1838 and 9 I read Gibbon through, a
masterly history of nearly all the known world for fifteen hundred
years, dipped a little into the essays, skipped along the poets, memo-
rized parts of Byron and Burns (always delighting in Burns.) I head
Robertson's *Charles Vth,* (Byron called the introduction to *Charles Vth*
a masterpiece.) I read my Blackstone, read Goldsmith, Junius' *Letters,* a
volume of the best English speeches &c.

In May, 1839, I entered the Yale College Law school, studying there
one year. In May, 1840, I studied in the office of David L. Seymour, in
Troy, Rensselaer Co., N.Y., who then was District Attorney for that
county, and in October of that year entered the law office of Hon.
George Miller, of Riverhead, and remained there until March, 1842.
Thereafter studying in the office of Joseph C. Albertson in New York
City, until my admission to the bar of the state. I was examined in the
City Hall in New York, and have a license dated May 13th, 1842, autho-
rizing me to practice in the Supreme Court, as an attorney. It is signed

by Samuel Nelson, afterwards a Justice of the Supreme Court of the United States, and the certificate that I had taken the oath prescribed, as an attorney, is signed by W.P. Hallett, clerk of that court. Singular but true, the law, notwithstanding the license by the Supreme Court, required a license to practice in the Court of Common Pleas, and without examination, I obtained that license, dated May 16th, 1842, signed by Hugh Halsey, chief of the five judges of the Court of Common Pleas, for the county of Suffolk, and Samuel A. Smith, commonly called "Ardent Smith," as clerk of the court, certified that I had taken the prescribed oath. After three years practice as attorney, a license to practice as Counsellor in the Supreme Court could be obtained. My license thereto is dated May 16th, 1845, and signed by Greene C. Bronson, Justice of the Supreme Court, and the certificate that the required oath was taken is signed by W.P. Hallett, clerk. In my 28th year I was an attorney and Counsellor of the Supreme Court in my native state.

LOOKING FOR A NEST.

In August, 1842, I looked for a location to practice law. In this pursuit I visited Poughkeepsie, Albany, Troy, Hoosick Falls, Seneca Falls and other places in this state; went to Buffalo and thence by steamer to Cleveland, Ohio, and thence by canal and stage to Akron, Columbus, Dayton and Cincinnati. In the streets of Cincinnatti, unexpectedly, I met my classmate Thomas M. Key, of Kentucky, nephew, I think, of that Key whom Gen. Sickles shot. He cordially invited me to go with him to his law office, where I found his partner, Alphonzo Taft. Taft had been tutor in Latin to our college class. He was a native of Vermont, full six feet high, large boned, muscular, powerfully built, dark eyed, black haired, strong, mentally and physically, kind hearted, with large endowment of good, common sense; a man easily moved by reason but no more to be driven than a mountain. He became an eminent jurist, Secretary of War in 1876, Attorney General of the United States after that, and minister to Austria and Russia. At his invitation, I took tea with his family. He was father of several sons who have attained distinction, one of whom is William H. Taft, former Governor of the Philippine Islands, loved and revered by their people for his wisdom and philanthropy in which he was like his honored father.

Ohio, later the mother of victor military chieftains, statesmen and presidents, then gave promise of being a growing, populous and powerful state. I decided to return and perhaps reside there. In October, 1842, I went to Cleveland, Ohio, and was there a few weeks and thence went to Newton Falls, in Trumbull Co., staying there through the winter, returning home in March, 1843, and staying there until the 26th day of September of that year, when I removed to Sag Harbor, rented an office and resided there until March 16, 1854, when I removed to Bridge Hampton, still retaining the Sag Harbor law office until May 18, 1893. I outline these movements preparatory to a review and recital of other memories. My personal history and life are of so little account to the outer, active world that conflicting forces impel to silence and disclosure, silence, because my life work has been so small, disclosure, because my experience even if disastrous, may show others the rocks whereon I struck.

And you, Mr. Boughton! Editor of THE EAST HAMPTON STAR! with your winning and beguiling ways, have led me on to this dilemma, where all your readers are looking at me, and I am where the colored minister wished to be when he prayed, "Lord make thy servant conspicuous." Dear, beguiling Editor! I feel like shaking my *metaphorical fist at you!*

In the Yale Law school, Judges David Daggett and Samuel J. Hitchcock were our teachers, men of large acquirement in the science of jurisprudence, of unsullied character and with great tact in explaining, illustrating and enforcing the principles of law and equity. Hitchcock had a way of stating definitions and rules and facts as a foundation and progressing by steps, so clear, so gradual, so converging to a conclusion, intricate, difficult or doubtful, seemingly, that the student traveled with him in light to his decision, as a man follows the steps of a guide, out of a wilderness, into the clearing. In this marvelous quality I have never seen him excelled. I have never regretted that year's study in the Yale Law school. While there the famous Amistad case, was tried, and I attended court through the trial. In my history of East Hampton, on page 156 and onward, the story of that case is told. John Hooker, of Hartford, was in the Yale Law school at that time. He became a distinguished member of the bar, of the State of Connecticut, and for more than thirty years, reporter of cases in its highest courts. His wife was Isabelle Beecher, youngest daughter of Lyman Beecher D.D. At their request I prepared and published in the Sag Harbor *Express*, of January 31st, 1901, a memorial article entitled "Anecdotes, Recollections, Impressions and Traditions of Lyman Beecher D.D."

In Troy, as clerk in the office of David L. Seymour, afterwards member of Congress, I knew Hon. Job Pierson, a native of Bridgehampton, a lawyer of large attainments and practice, sometime surrogate of Rensselaer county, and for two terms member of Congress; Hon. John P.

Cushman, member of Congress, and then circuit judge of the Supreme court; Hon. Martin I. Townsend and others. The Bar of the City of Troy was one of the most distinguished in the cities of our state.

Riverhead was a small village of fifty or sixty dwelling houses, when in October, 1840, I entered the law office of Hon. George Miller as clerk. It was the county seat, the law center, and growing. Miller was a man of few words and many thoughts, a lawyer, comprehending clearly great legal principles, and relying in argument on them, more than the authority of adjudged cases. Standing on some principle, as a foundation, he fought his cases, often to a successful result. Tall, spare, pale, exsanguineous, he looked as if soon to become a disembodied ghost, the incarnation of thought and spirit. Ungifted in utterance, fighting with bodily weakness, he bore little resemblance to the glib, sprightly, self assurance of the typical lawyer. He was Surrogate of the county. He had a strong sense of right and wrong. His conscience was his victorious power. He was an excellent equity lawyer and when convinced he was right, would fight in court until he could fight no longer. There I became acquainted with practice in Surrogate's courts, pettifogged in justices courts and profited by the instruction and example of one of the best lawyers Suffolk county, in all its history, has produced. Miller came to Riverhead in 1826, when it was but a hamlet. He organized, and for years conducted religious services in the Court House previous to the erection of the Congregational church. He built and kept running a school for young ladies, called the Ladies' Seminary. He lectured on Temperance in the early days of the Total Abstinence cause, when it was reviled, opposed, and its advocates persecuted. In school houses and churches, in evil and good report, this man, contending against his many physical infirmities that would have appalled most men, fought the grandest fight for purity of life, elevation of morals, female education, suppression of intemperance, advancement of mankind, that Riverhead ever saw. If in recognition of his work that town and this county should rear the loftiest monument within their bounds to his memory, it would not exceed his exalted worth.

In New York, previous to my admission to the Bar, I saw in the courts their famous lawyers, Daniel Lord, George Wood, Gerard Cutting and others, and heard the famed libel case of James Fenimore Cooper against Horace Greely. Richard Cooper, nephew of the novelist, argued for him, and Governor Seward for Greely, in the Supreme court.

MY FIRST CASE.

I commenced practicing law in Sag Harbor, Sept. 26th, 1843. Samuel L. Gardiner had been residing there as a practicing lawyer, about three years. Samuel S. Gardiner, of Shelter Island, was still in like practice, but soon retired as an acting lawyer. Judges Hugh Halsey and Abraham T. Rose, were in Bridgehampton; Joseph H. Goldsmith was at Peconic; Judge Miller and Sidney L. Griffing at Riverhead; Selah B. Strong at Setauket; Wm. P. Buffett at Smithtown, and Charles A. Floyd at Huntington. In the Town of Southampton were four lawyers, in Riverhead two, and one each in Southold, Shelter Island, Brookhaven, Smithtown and Huntington. Samuel D. Craig for a short time did some business at Quogue, and including him and myself, there were twelve lawyers only in the county. The last court calendar contains a list of 70 lawyers resident in Suffolk county. In 1840 the population of the county was 32,469; the population of the town of Southampton was 6,205, and of East Hampton, 2,076. These two towns contained over one-fourth of all the population of the county, and probably owned one-third of all the wealth and furnished at least that proportion of all the business of the county. The lawyers were not misplaced and excepting those residing in Sag Harbor and Riverhead, resided on their farms and derived a support therefrom. Halsey was almost continuously in public office, as assemblyman, surrogate, judge, senator, state surveyor general. As a whole the Bar of the county were well educated, able, upright men. Halsey, Rose, Buffett and the writer became county judges and surrogates, Strong was afterwards a judge of the Supreme Court, and on the Court of Appeals. My most frequent and formidable adversaries were Gardiner, of Sag Harbor, and Judge Rose. Gardiner was fertile in resource, quick to discover a new decision of Court that overturned previous opinions, persistent and pugnacious in conflict. Rose was in perception intuitive, in expression fluent, in expedients inventive, in argument persuasive, in manner pleasing, in eloquence by far the first in the county. With such competitors I commenced the practice of law, in an office in Major John Hildreth's Brick Building, under the office now occupied by the Sag Harbor *Corrector.*

To a young man beginning professional life, comes the sense of uncertainty, of responsibility, the conflict of hope and fear, alternate confidence and distrust. The careless world lightly inquires, will he succeed or fail? He asks that question with the interest that thrills the heart. I hoped some one would read my sign, "H.P. Hedges, Atty. at Law," and bring me business. Days came and went, ten solitary, dark, despondent days. Saturday afternoon came and had almost gone. I was about to close my office when, with soft, timid steps, a woman came and told the story of her wrongs and sufferings, the pitiful tale of brutal abandonment by her husband—my first client, a woman in tears, poor, forsaken, friendless, an object of pity. I gave her the best counsel. She took from her pocket a little worsted knit purse and I could see through the stitches the gleam of a few silver pieces. She asked what my charge was. I said, "My friend, I feel poor enough but you are the poorer." That Saturday night I slept the sleep of the just. Sunday was a day of serene, exalted, spiritual experience. The air, the earth, the o'er arching Heavens, breathed their harmonies to my listening soul. It is rapture to think that you are at peace with God, and His almighty hand holds yours.

Monday morning clients flocked to my office and for ten days kept me on the keen jump. It was as if the Power that controls the universe had said, "Trust in the Lord, and do good, so shalt thou dwell in the land, and verily thou shalt be fed." This was followed by other like lessons, impressing the great yet self-evident truth that God, who holds all wealth in the hollow of his hand, is the greatest rewarder and pays the highest wages for beneficent service. Men, measuring this life by that of the beasts who perish, degrade themselves. Immortal hope and joy dwells only with immortal life.

The reader asks, did I succeed, and how? I answer: As a free-born American I held and now hold to the right to sell my labor and skill at my own price, free from the dictation and tyranny of any one man, or the union of any number of men. I own myself, my powers of mind and body, subject always to the laws of the land, and this right is not only "inherent," it is "inalienable." I had a right to draw deeds, contracts, wills, for high price, low price, or nothing. I did do it for a low price and got a run of business. I worked hard at low wages, stuck to my office, studied law and persevered. Without the masterly eloquence of Rose, or the wide scholarship of Gardiner, they could beat me in trials before courts and juries at first. The road was long and hard, but grew easier. Office business grew, the confidence of people was gained, funds were placed in my care, and year by year, more funds. Finally, jurors listened to my appeal and I had hopes of getting a verdict, when deserved. All this by hard work, and only that. There is no hill, no mountain so high that the persistent feet of the persevering man may not tread its towering top. Did my ardent advocating total abstinence as a beverage from intoxicants or arguing for prohibition of their sale for that purpose, drive off patronage? No! Men loudly opposed, condemned, threatened, and then wanted me to write their wills and settle their estates. Drinking men have the most confidence in sober men. They know all about it.

May 9th, 1843, Gloriana Osborn and I were married. We could not help it. We were unembittered by divergent aims, unvisited by cankered jealousies, undissolved by colliding interests. John Howard Payne, in a letter dated 14th Aug., 1839, and published in Lipincott's Magazine, had written, "I am told there is a Miss Gloriana Osborn, who is capturing all the world. What a fine name! Gloriana. There is something *regal* about it." Our *"home"* was all that Payne had fancied in his immortal song. It was an ideal marriage. Her spirit fled from earth to the "land of uprightness," on the 1st day of February, 1891. Little as I have achieved, it would have been far less, but for her word of cheer in disaster, of hope in defeat, of sympathy in misfortune, of patience in suffering. This tribute to her memory, beneath her worth, is written with tears, and as if eyes from Heaven were overlooking the record.

> *"Still o'er these scenes my memory wakes,*
> *And fondly broods with miser care,*
> *Time but the impression deeper makes,*
> *As streams their channels deeper wear."*

THE MONTAUK LAWSUIT.

In 1851, and previously, local causes largely affected parties in New York State politics. Temperance organizations advocated prohibition of the sale of intoxicants as a beverage. On the Tariff question Whigs and Democrats differed. On the Slavery question opinions clashed. Within the Whig party the "Silver Greys" were pro-slavery, and the "Free Soilers" opposed to the extension of slavery in the territories. In the Democratic party there was a like cleave line. "The Old Hunkers" were pro-slavery; "The Barn Burners" were free-soilers. Besides there were "Loco Focos," and their adversaries, "Renters" and "Anti Renters." Vast Colonial estates in Albany, Rensselaer, Columbia and other counties granted the Van Rensselaers. Livingstons, Schuylers and others, rented in perpetuity for produce, payable in kind, as wheat, corn, cattle, fowls, eggs, &c, were held by tenants complaining, threatening, resisting and refusing payment, and finally by armed combination and hostile force preventing payment of rent and successfully resisting the authority and agents of courts moving for collection. Anti-rent rule even to bloodshed and murder was the rule in whole counties. The Anti Renters claimed that the price of produce, as wheat, corn &c, had so risen as to make their rent oppressive, exhorbitant, intolerable, and work a forfeiture of improvements, injust and ruinous to them. They often held the balance of power, in close votes deciding elections. The spirit of unrest, and challenge of titles and vested rights roamed over the state, and reached and worked in the town of East Hampton. In my History of East Hampton, on page 111, and on, there is a brief allusion to the *Montauk Lawsuit*, in 1851, of which, as an almost solitary witness, I can more fully tell.

In 1686, at the time of the Dongan Patent, the Montauk tribe of Indians held possession of North Neck, and all Montauk, east of Great Pond. The Patent gave exclusive power of purchase to the Town Trustees. They could purchase for the town, or for the benefit of individuals, and chose to purchase for individuals, who advanced the purchase money, and thence held the equitable interest therein, in proportion to the several sums they paid. The Trustees held the nominal legal title, as a trust estate for their benefit. They held it as guardians, executors, assignees of debtors, hold in trust for the benefit of parties equitably interested, and they so managed it for their interest, discharging their duties in trust for the benefit of the equitable owners, until near 1851. A pamphlet containing copies of the papers and title deeds of Montauk was published and circulated. It was good evidence against any claim of the town to own Montauk in fee simple. It was misread, misunderstood and interpreted to give such title to the town. The anti-rent view raging elsewhere raged here. The firm of Lott, Murphy & Vanderbilt, of Brooklyn, N.Y., was formed by these three great laywers, John A. Lott, Henry C. Murphy and John Vanderbilt. On a statement of facts that the town Trustees had been in absolute possession of the lands of Montauk as owners thereof, purchased under the patent and claiming title from time immemorial, they gave a written opinion, that the *whole title* was in the town. A lawyer consulted by a Scotchman, asked him if he had told the truth. The Scotchman replied, "Yes! I thought *you could put in the lies yourself.*" That opinion, based on a misstatement, confirmed the Town Trustees that the town claim was valid and they proceeded to act thereon, and ignore the rights of the equitable owners, hiring rights of pasturage, fishing, &c, in the name and for the benefit of the town. The equitable owners were always called "Proprietors of Montauk," and for short I will call them *Proprietors*. They submitted all the papers and facts to Daniel Lord, a leader of the bar of the City and State of New York, if not *the* leader, and his opinion was in writing, that the Proprietors were the equitable and beneficial owners, and that the Trustees held a mere nominal title in trust for them, and were liable to account for all funds received, and to removal from Trusteeship, for violating their duty as Trustees. The Proprietors of Montauk exceeded one hundred in number, and a suit in all their names was impracticable. Seven men, John Baker, Samuel B. Gardiner, David H. Huntting and John T. Dayton, of East Hampton, Maltby G. Rose, Wilkes Hedges and Henry P. Hedges, of the town of Southampton, in the name and for the behalf of all the Proprietors, bought an action against the Trustees of the Town of East Hampton to enforce their rights, and thus began the famous *Montauk Lawsuit.*

The title to nearly one fourth of all the territory in the town of East Hampton depended on the result of this action, and it attracted deep interest. The case was tried at the October circuit of the Supreme Court, in 1851. Daniel Lord argued the case for the Proprietors and Charles O'Connor for the Trustees. The judgment of the Court accorded with Lord's opinion. The Trustees were adjudged to have forfeited their trust office, and decreed to render an account, and convey all claim they could have to the proprietors. John P. Rolfe was appointed referee to ascertain the true interests of the Proprietors, and report the same, which he did. The Trustees conveyed by deed accordingly. They might have held in perpetuity had they managed equitably. They lost all by derelection of duty. They were not bad men. The temptation of men holding trust funds in corporations, banks, estates, &c, to speculate and enrich themselves, and repay embezzled monies, is so great as to overcome large numbers, who fall before it. The care of trust estates is a power few persons are strong enough to discharge honestly. A man with another's money in his pocket book is apt to think it his own, and the more apt the weaker he is.

The Proprietors of Montauk, by the conveyance of the Trustees, became the absolute owners in fee simple of Montauk, subject only to the rights of the Montauk Indians. They were tenants in common without any governing power, and required an act of incorporation from the Legislature whereby rules for its management could be prescribed and enforced, the pasturage regulated properly, the timber and wood preserved and cared for, their rights secured and tresspass prevented. In the preparation of the case for trial I had thoroughly searched the records of the town and procured voluminous transcripts, examined all the Montauk papers and deeds, classified and arranged them in a methodical manner, to be introduced in evidence on the trial, and personally presented them to our counsel in their proper order. Daniel Lord told me my work was "so well done that the case tried itself." And now the Proprietors of Montauk generally, wished me to run as a candidate for Member of Assembly, and if elected procure an act for their incorporation.

IN THE LEGISLATURE.

At the age of thirty-four years I was launched on the turbulent sea of Politics, sustained by the Proprietors of Montauk, the Temperance and Free-soil voters, and opposed by their adversaries. The Anti Temperance vote in the strong Whig districts of Sag Harbor, Bridge Hampton and Southampton was so favorable to my competitor, that it was believed he was elected, and at a hilarious meeting of his friends at Bridge Hampton, on Thursday evening of election week, they celebrated his victory over the "flowing bowl." On Friday news came from Shelter Island and the towns of Riverhead and Southold, leaving the election doubtful, with Wading River to hear from. Saturday the returns from Wading River showed that I was elected Member of Assembly by about forty majority. The unexpected majority was due to the large Temperance vote in Shelter Island, Orient, Greenport, Southold, Mattituck, Riverhead and Wading River, and the efficient labors of E.D. Skinner M.D., of Greenport, then a power in Suffolk County politics.

In 1808 a law was passed authorizing the Proprietors of Montauk to meet on a day named, at the Meeting House in East Hampton and organize themselves into a corporation. This law was probably drafted by Nathan Sandford, a native of Bridge Hampton, afterwards Chancellor of this state, and passed by the agency of my grandfather, Deacon David Hedges, the a Member of the Assembly. It gave *each proprietor* a vote, and each owner of an eighth of a share a vote for every eighth he owned, but no one could cast over eight votes. By this law a majority in number although a minority in interest could govern, yet public sentiment in East Hampton opposed this law because it did not give all owners, however small, an equal vote with the larger, however large. Political aspirants fanned the fire of opposition, and it burned so fiercely on the day fixed for incorporating that the meeting of Proprietors in the church was broken up by the noisy clamor of opposition, the church bell rang amid cries of "the Law is dead." My grandfather, who manfully stood for justice, was hooted at in derision and ignominiously burned in effigy at the stake. His sin was that he was in advance of the age. Living witnesses of this event related it to me and acknowledged with contrition their action therein and justified the conduct of my grandfather, over whose character they aided to cast this dark cloud. Standing where my grandfather stood, shall I like him fail?

In the Legislature of 1852, as Member of Assembly, I was a novice, and quietly working therefor, procured the enactment of a law incorporating the Proprietors of Montauk. Unadvised of the views of the Governor, Washington Hunt, regarding it, I called at the Executive Chamber and he heard my explanation of the purpose and scope of the law, and said that he had "thought it some scheme of speculators and intended to veto it, but my statement satisfied him and, he would sign it." After enactment by the Legislature it came so near defeat. The Proprietors organized under this law and equitably improved Montauk, until its sale to Arthur W. Benson, in 1879. They held as tenants in common the title, subject only to the power of the corporation to prescribe rules for its improvement. If the title had been in the corporation, it could have been sold as a whole, probably for a larger sum, but the owners were unwilling to vest title therein. A partition suit was brought, and sale had, in that action. Thus this vast property was lost to the owners and gained by city buyers, at a low price. The same old story, from Brooklyn to Montauk. The mighty arms of the Metropolis reach and grasp vast fortunes, from the Equator to the Poles.

In the Legislature the Temperance question would now down. The committee on the Excise Law, reported a minority for and a majority against a prohibitory, then called the "Maine Law." I thought the reasons against it unsound, the attitude of the anti-prohibitionists arrogant, their exultant scorn insulting. The cause demanded a hearing, my constituents expected it, the fire burned within me. When the report came up for debate I delivered my message like a shot, straight to the mark. The license to sell intoxicants is a monopoly bought by the rich and denied to the poor. The traffic in them is the manufactory of criminals, paupers, idlers and drunkards—a vampire drinking the blood and tears of the people. The reports of the Albany County Penitentiary for the years 1850 and 51 showed therein over 1,000 prisoners, and over nine-tenths of them admitted that intemperance caused the crimes for which they were convicted. I called the attention of the Assembly to the blessings Temperance sentiment had wrought in our own county. Formerly intemperance had reigned. Farms were mortgaged, crime and pauperism abounded, desolation and misery prevailed. The Temperance reformation wrought wonders; mortgaged farms were redeemed, lands better tilled, comforts obtainable, crime and pauperism reduced, drunkenness almost extirpated. In Shelter Island, only three adult persons were unpledged to total abstinence from intoxicants as a beverage, and only twenty dollars raised by tax for the poor, the past year. In Orient, and Rocky Point, now East Marion, there were only five so unpledged. In Greenport and other places like blessings came. My voice resounded through the corridors of the Capitol. The galleries were filled. Senators left their chamber to listen to this assault on the rum traffic. Its advocates looked astounded, Its enemies looked confirmation. At its conclusion Assemblymen said to me they had intended to vote for license, but now would vote against it. Gerrit Smith and E.C. Delavan, radical reformers, said it was the best speech of that session of the Legislature. Charles R. Dayton was that winter in Albany, and is the only living witness I remember who can attest to my statement, and to him I confidently appeal.

In the Broadway Tabernacle, in New York City, the religious and other societies held their May anniversary meetings, and by invitation I spoke before the State Temperance society, as a representative of the Legislature. Lyman Beecher D.D., made the next speech, and Stephen H. Tyng D.D. after him. The subject was near my heart, the vast audience inspiring. Believing the audience expected an account of the steps and progress of temperance legislation in the Assembly, and their attitude therein, I spoke of action in committees, and reports, &c. The audience was uninterested. John Marsh D.D., then presiding, shook his gray head at me, as a signal to stop and that completely confused me. I made then and there the most unacceptable, incohesive, ineffectual speech of my life. It was a most miserable failure before the greatest audience, in the very metropolis of the State and Nation. With regard for truth, I record as well my success in sounding the bugle blast of war, as my failure to sound the sweet tunes of harmony and peace.

Dr. Beecher was in his 77th year and failed to arouse the enthusiasm of the audience, as in the days of his meridian splendor. Dr. Tyng was tactful, resourceful, eloquent and in electric touch with the audience. He moved their hearts, as the breeze evokes music from the strings of the harp. His speech was a consummate triumph, mine an absolute failure.

OFFICIAL AND FARM LIFE.

In the fall of 1852 I bought a farm of one hundred acres in Bridgehampton, without buildings except an old wreck of a house. Elias Halsey formerly owned the house and rented rooms to that noted old scoundrel Stephen Burroughs, who taught school there. It was a miserably poor, run-down farm. The outlay for buildings, fences, fertilizers, stock, tools, seed, hay grain, &c. was five times the cost of the land. Whaling business in Sag Harbor failed. Pent up in my office nearly ten

years, I required more open air life and exercise. It was desirable to
bring up my three sons on a farm. There their life would be healthier
and the family easier maintained. In March, 1853, Daniel S. Edwards
took charge of my farm. He was a practical, hard headed, hard working
farmer, of superior judgment, residing in East Hampton, from whom I
received many valuable suggestions. March 16, 1854, I removed with
my family to Bridgehampton, where my dwelling house was to be
built. My law office in Sag Harbor I attended on stated days. It was a
long hard pull to pay bills incurred in building, fencing, fertilizing,
stocking, &c. When the war struck the Nation in 1861, the farm was
fairly productive.

In the fall of 1861, ten years after my election as member of Assembly, I was elected District Attorney of the county. The salary was
$300 yearly, a small sum for the work. I was forty-four years old, hard-
ened by farm labor, and with great powers of endurance. The office
brought larger practice. I always hated slavery and was with the earliest adherents of the Republican party, when only about 36 Republican
votes were cast in Bridgehampton. I 1864 I was reelected. In 1865, was
elected to the office of County Judge and Surrogate, which office I entered upon Jan. 1, 1866, having before resigned the office of District Attorney to take effect that day. At a salary of twelve hundred dollars I
served the county in that capacity until January 1, 1870. In the election
of 1869, as a candidate for reelection I was defeated by about forty majority, through the relief of Republican voters that I could be re-elected
while they were not voting, but husking corn. Out of office and with a
smaller professional practice, I hammered away on the farm or in the
law office, where most needed, always busy, and toning up for the next
battle. In 1873, I was again elected County Judge and Surrogate, by a
large majority. More than three-fourths of all the votes in the town of
Southampton were cast for me, and in Bridgehampton nine votes only
were polled for my opponent. I have recorded and again here record
my thanks! The term of office now was six years and the salary $2,500.
The population of the county had grown to over 50,000. The wealth
had exceeded that proportional growth. The duties were arduous, the
outlay for clerk hire and traveling expenses exceeded $1,000 yearly.
Large estates came under the case of the Surrogate, contested wills
multiplied, lawyers fought furiously and long with rich pickings. In one
battle over a contested will, involving an estate of half a million, nine
lawyers were engaged. The testimony taken covered 2,000 pages of
written and 1,000 pages of printed matter. I worked as nobody ever
ought to work, and in four summers, from overwork, had five carbun-

cles. I thought the Supervisors of the county ought to make an allowance to me for clerk hire. My application therefor was refused and by some severely criticised. I then thought and think now it was just and equitable, and leave the question to the judgment of those now living. The offices were divided to take effect Jan. 1, 1880, on the expiration of my term. I was the last holder of the combined two.

My last carbuncle was a *sog dollager*. Coming in August, it lasted into February following, sapping my vitality, sealing my courage, undermining my strength. When on Jan. 1, 1880, I closed my official career, at 62 years of age, I was crippled in activity, run down in health, with little legal business, and unfit to do much. All that year I devoted largely to recuperating and by the next January had recovered fairly in health and built up a good law business. When I went out of office I staid out. In the canvass of 1873, coming home from worship on Sabbath afternoon, I found two fishermen wanting me to pay them to leave fishing and vote for me. That was the first and last time I was asked to buy votes. Even now I think of it with a sad loathing hard to express. *Government for sale! Votes for sale! The liberty of the Republic for sale!* Great God! "in whose sight the Heavens are not clean" and "who charged his angels with folly!" Where is this country going? When after this, party leaders demanded that I run for office as a duty to the party, I found even parties were selfish. Recalling to mind that Sabbath visit of those two men, I felt as the boy said, "Mother I don't like castor oil, *it's too rich*." Eminence as a lawyer is an exalted attainment. Official position adds nothing to its lustre. Such a lawyer can seldom afford to hold office and a poor lawyer is often a poor official. President Hadley of Yale has advised professional men against running for office, until provision adequate for family support is made, and his opinion has been severely criticised. I think him to be a man of superior, sound judgment, and his opinion wise. The longer a lawyer holds office the more he loses practice, and when he loses office, has lost both. Turned out of office when his party or its boss has no farther use for him, like an old horse to browse for a living, he is an object of pity if not contempt. If a young man is growing in his professional as a rule it is better to keep growing. Ask not for office from the people. Let them ask you.

There are curious, inquisitive persons in almost all villages very much concerned about the business of others, and often not properly attending to their own. Living or dying, their first question is, *how much money has he got?* They have their rights, and perhaps I ought to answer that question. I will do so by anecdote. There were two brothers, both ministers, in Connecticut, one highly educated and very precise in the phraseology of his conversation, the other with great native genius, as careless as his brother was careful. The careless brother often said, "I *kinder* think," "I *kinder* wish," and was reproved by the precise one for using the word "*kinder*." Writing to his careless brother he asked this question: "Brother how much money have you got? *I kinder want to know*." The answer came: "I have not got so much money but that *I kinder want more*."

SABBATH THOUGHTS.

Great leaders of mankind in all ages have had their friends and foes. Controversy raged around the person, character, mission and teaching of Jesus Christ from the beginning of his ministry, and with diminishing volume until now. As a lawyer sifting evidence. I think his mode of baffling his crafty persecutors demonstrates his superior and supernatural wisdom. When asked "Is it lawful to give tribute to Caesar, or no?" "He said unto them, 'Render therefore unto Caesar the things which be Caesar's, and unto God the things which be God's.'" His answer was perfect as a practical truth. It covered the whole truth. It defeated the intent of his adversaries. They intended to charge him with treason if he had said no, and thereby arraign him before the Roman authority. If he had said yes they would have accused him before the Jewish authorities as an advocate of their enemies, and in either case they would have procured his condemnation. In the question put to him by the Sadducees concerning the woman married successively to seven deceased brethren, inquiring whose wife she should be in the resurrection, how clearly He expressed the conditions of spiritual life, as incapable of marriage, and likened it to that of the Angels in Heaven. How He illumined the revelation of Jehovah to Moses. "I am the God of Abraham and Isaac and Jacob." "God is not the God of the dead but the living." In his questions as to the baptism of John, "Was it from Heaven or of men?" and of the Messiah, "If David call him Lord how is he then his son?" He demonstrated a knowledge of the Heavenly Kingdom, of the spiritual state, of the inner meaning of the scriptures, unknown to his countrymen and to his age, transcending the highest attainment of the human mind. The blazing light of nineteen centuries has shone, and failed to reveal to mankind answers more appropriate, questions more far reaching, truths more profound than the utterances of the Carpenter of Nazareth.

The power of Jesus to overcame [sic] all evil spirits, to heal all diseases has not been emphasized as I think its magnitude demands. In Capernaum "*all they* that had any sick with divers diseases brought them unto Him, and He laid His hands *on every one of them and healed them.*" (Luke, 4, 4) "Great multitudes came unto Him having with them lame, blind, dumb, maimed, and many others and cast them down at Jesus' feet, and He healed them." (Matthew 15, 10.) If these and other miracles of Jesus were false, the falsehood could and would at the time have been exposed. If He did not revive the dead son of the widow at the gate of Nain, if He did not open the eyes of the man born blind, if he did not raise Lazarus from the dead, the affirmation that He did would have met a roar of disproof from his foes that would have come down the ages to our day. If Caesar wrote that he had conquered Gaul when he had not done it, History would have exposed the falsehood. It would have been as easy to expose the falsity of the revival of the widow's son or of Lazarus, or of the opening of the eyes of the man born blind, if the statements were untrue. In all the attributes of Preacher, Lawyer, Doctor the penetration and power of Jesus excel all human elevation and must have been born of Heaven. As a Preacher He saw the spiritual wants of men and the way of restoration as none ever before. As a Lawyer His philosophy of legislation went down beneath all form and ceremony to the intent and thought of the heart. As a Physician no malady but fled at His word, no pain but vanished at His touch. His gift was sight to the blind, hearing to the deaf, speech to the dumb, reanimation to the palsied, purity to loathsome leper, restoration to the lame, revival to the dead. In him God disclosed to the world what He could do for the wants and woes of a suffering world, by the power of His saving word, the touch of His beneficent hand, the flow of his exhaustless love.

At seven years of age I had read the Bible through and got the dollar offered by my father therefor. As a child I believed it. Unfavorable influences effaced early impressions. I lived always believing in God, yet dreading Him whose commands I was disobeying and whose just displeasures I knew I had incurred. In the marvelous outpouring of the Spirit in August, 1831, at East Hampton, during the ministry of the Rev. Joseph D. Condit, one hundred and fourteen members united with the church. This was the era of what was called "the four days meetings." I fought against spiritual impressions, regarding God as a Being whom I feared and did not love. Always attending public worship, always, in a formal way, reading the Bible, gradually growing more deeply impressed with the conviction that it was God's message for the soul of man, in October, 1840, while in Riverhead, and with no marked evidences of any existing spiritual special impressions, this conviction deepened into a power, pervading, persistent, ascendant, alarming. Vainly trying to convert myself, the darkness grew more dense. God seemed far away. The Bible spoke no new word. Days and nights of hopeless agony went and came. One Saturday evening, reading "Abbot's Young Christian," where he illustrates the parable of the Prodigal Son, I came to this: "When he was a great way off his Father *saw him* and ran and fell upon his neck and kissed him." Instantly, as by a flash of lightning out of a dark cloud, I saw myself that poor miserable prodigal, God the ever-living, ever-loving universal Father, pitying, yearning for, welcoming his lost child. Hope was born. "My peace flowed like a river." I slept the sleep of reconciliation. On the morning of the Sabbath my soul was in harmony with the Universe, and with its Creator. The air breathed of His sweetness, the birds sang of His praise, and sun radiated his glory. If I have laid bare my heart, it is for no idle purpose. There is a spiritual endowment in man, a spiritual perception whereby he may commune with the great eternal Spirit, and receives its Heaven-sent message.

> *"So sometimes come to soul and sense*
> *The feeling which is evidence*
> *That very near about us lies*
> *The real of spiritual mysteries.*
> *The sphere of the Supernal Powers*
> *Impinges on this world of ours.*
> *The low and dark horizon lifts,*
> *In light the scenic terror shifts.*
> *The breath of a diviner air*
> *Blows down the answer of a prayer,*
> *That all our sorrow, pain and doubt*
> *A great compassion clasps about,*
> *And law and goodness, love and force*
> *Are wedded fast beyond divorce.*
> *Then duty leaves to love its task,*
> *the beggar self forgets to ask.*
> *With smile of trust and folded hands,*
> *The passive soul in waiting stands*
> *To feel, as flowers the sun and dew,*
> *The one true life its own renew."*

LITERARY LIFE.

Men live some one, some two and some many lives, mechanical, agricultural, maratime, mercantile, financial, military, official, literary, scientific, &c. The elastic activities of the American citizen may reach into many lives. Julius Caesar could dictate at the same time to four amanuenses, holding in mind each subject and continuously employing them in writing letters, messages, orders, &c. My literary work, comparatively insignificant, comprises much of my life. In college I took part in discussing many debatable questions, and among others this: "Did the French Revolution produce the most good or evil?" I studied on this question intensely, and was convinced that the Revolution lifted most oppressive burdens, forced on the common people by an intolerant, grinding aristocracy. It emancipated the soil and its tillers from the bondage of ages. With all its turbulence and carnage, it freed France from the paralysis of despotism. Contrary to the prevailing opinion, I believed its benefits overbalanced the evils, and so wrote. This was my first attempt at historical investigation and an era in my literary life. From thence I date a trend of mind to the study of history and free institutions in the civilized world. The courses of reading advised in college required years to complete. I was guided only partly thereby. Foster's *Essays* are a mine of gold, teaching the reader to think; Addison's *Spectator* is a model of expression, and those I read in college. Holmes' *Annals of the United States* is an authority in history. That and a few other books sum up my college reading. In childhood old almanacs had a charm not now outgrown. Newspapers had attraction until now undiminished. A series of letters in a newspaper was a formative power in all my after life. September 4th, 1839, David Gardiner commenced the publication, in the Sag Harbor *Corrector* of "The Chronicles of East Hampton," which I read with great interest and admiration, devouring and digesting his story of the early history of the town. It was the result of exhausting study, wide research and the intelligent work of years. It was afterwards published in the collections of the Historical Society of the State of New York. In these "Chronicles," I found congenial thought, impelling me to search the town records, trace out and treasure up traditions and legends of past generations, explore the fountains whence sprang our free institutions. David Gardiner never knew that he largely shaped the current of all my after literary life. He never knew that I would practice law to get money and practice antiquity until I spent it, and with increasing delight to this day. I bring this sprig of laurel to honor and perpetuate his memory worthy to endure in coming ages in the heart of every citizen of the town of East Hampton.

In preparing cases for trial a lawyer is often obliged to trace titles to the original source, laws to Colonial or ante-Colonial times, conditions and customs to an antiquarian origin, descendants to a remote ancestor. In the Montauk case the patents of the Town from the Royal Governors, the rights of the Montauk Indians and papers concerning them, the Town Records, Trustees' Records, old title deeds, all required searching scrutiny. In other cases ancient deeds and records were foundations of claim of title. My law practice fostered a predilection for antiquarian research, and my retentive memory held them in mind. My antiquarian inclination became known to many. An invitation was given to deliver an Historical address December 26th, 1849, on the celebration of the 200th Anniversary of the settlement of the town of East Hampton, and on that day I delivered it. This address with additions, historical, genealogical, &c, forming a pamphlet of 100 pages, was printed at the *Corrector* office in Sag Harbor. In August, 1899, I delivered an Historical address on the celebration of the 250th anniversary of the settlement of the same town. It is rare that the same person lives to take prominent part in celebrations, divided by a half century. The contrast between the two ceremonies is not less noticeable. The first was a simple meeting in the time-hallowed church of 1717, with the address, and followed by a dinner at the Inn of Thomas T. Parsons, with no sound of martial music, no show of procession or parade, marked by silent reverent thought, the devout homage of the living to the honored dead. The last commenced in the evening with the Historical address in church, and the next day was continued, in the morning with flag staff raising, gorgeous display of emblem and symbol, exhibition of antique mementos, lengthened processional ceremonies with types of ancient costume, accouterments, arms, vehicles, boats, Indians, horsemen, a grand marshall, and a grand calvacade. In the afternoon, at a mass meeting, from a grand stand, addresses were made by distinguished dignitaries of church and state, not forgetting the affable and honorable William H. Baldwin, Jr., president of the L.I.R.R. Co., who may belong to both or neither. The manners of the two centuries are marked in the two celebrations. They are no less marked in funeral ceremonies. In my early days the dead body was put in a stained white pine coffin. On a bier, on the shoulders of four men it was reverently borne to the grave and buried. Now! I decline to extend remark further than this: The righteous dead would prefer to receive a kind word living to harsh words living and deceitful expressions of regret when dead. I must soon "join" the innumerable caravan, that moves to that mysterious realm, where each shall take his chamber in the silent halls of death." God of my fathers! Then let expressions of sorrow be withheld or be sincere.

The committee of citizens of East Hampton, who invited and by letter requested publication of the address and other historic material in 1849, were Samuel B. Gardiner, David H. Huntting, Jeremiah Miller, Daniel Dayton and John C. Hedges, all departed this life near a score of years past.

In 1840 and for many after years, I spoke often at temperance and political meetings. At different places I delivered a lecture on "The Traits of Boyhood," another on "The Spirit of the Puritans." In 1843, I delivered an oration, on the Fourth of July, in East Hampton, and after that a like one in Orient and two in Bridgehampton, September 15th, 1850. I delivered an address in Sag Harbor on "The Claims of the Sabbath School," and January 15, 1853, another at Islip, before the County Temperance convention, on "The History of the Excise Law in the State of New York," both of which were printed and circulated as tracts. I delivered two addresses before the Suffolk County Agricultural Society, one in 1868, and one in 1883.

I made two historical addresses in Bridgehampton, one a centennial, July 4th, 1876, and one November 10, 1886, at the celebration of the bi-centennial of the church. These were published as "The History of Bridgehampton," and are now on sale. November 15, 1883, at Riverhead, the Bi-centennial Anniversary of the organization of Suffolk county was celebrated. Several addresses were made and published as a History of Suffolk County. My address on the occasion was on the Development of Agriculture in the County. In later years the value of historical records has been recognized and societies for their preservation have multiplied. I was early a member of the Suffolk County Historical Society. October 1st, 1889, at Riverhead, I delivered an address before that society on the Priority of Settlement of the Towns of Southampton and Southold. In 1890, both towns celebrated the Bi-centennial Anniversary of their settlement. The addresses delivered on their celebrations were published. The celebration in Southampton occurred June 10th and my address, quite long, was printed with others. August 27th, Southold celebrated, and there, as representing the towns of East Hampton, Southampton, and the Suffolk County Historical society, I read a paper. There was a celebration in Sag Harbor in 1868 or thereabouts, of the centennial anniversary of the Presbyterian church, which I attended. Wm. H. Gleason delivered an historical address, which was not printed. The early settlement there was a field not much explored. By invitation of the Sag Harbor Historical Society, on the 4th of February, 1896, I delivered an address, since published, and now on sale as "The History of Sag Harbor." For many years I thought to compile a History of East Hampton, which the load of business I carried postponed until it seemed doubtful if life would last for its accomplishment. In 1897, the year when I attained four score, I saw that work done. At great expenditure of money, toil and time these contributions to the history of Southampton, Bridgehampton, East Hampton and Sag Harbor, have been made. That expenditure in professional service would have brought a return of thousands in cash, yet coming generations may reap benefit from my humble labors, and I indulge no regret. Some wag said he had found a remedy for hard times. It was *"ten hours' work every day well rubbed in."* I have been his disciple all my life. In 1899, when I was 82 years old, my classmate, Theodore S. Gold, Secretary of the Board of Agriculture of the State of Connecticut, asked me to prepare an address "On the Sea," to be made before that board. I accepted and at Meriden, Connecticut, December 11th, 1900, delivered the same, which was published with the report of the board for that year. December 11th, 1900, before the same board, at New Haven, I read a paper on "The Duties of Fathers to Sons," likewise so published. Thus ever at work according to my strength, my powers by use the slower decay.

ON READING!

The Yankee habit of asking questions extends naturally to Eastern Long Island by association and inheritance. What shall I read? How shall I read? What shall I skip? What is your experience? To this I remark: In my early days novel reading was by elderly men largely prohibited as worse than a waste of time. Modern opinion sanctions it. I think it best to encourage the young to read romance rather than nothing, because thereby a taste for reading is formed. That thirst will grow into a taste for more substantial knowledge. If it does not, the mind lacks expansive power for great achievement and the failure is small. Until manhood I did not enjoy "Shakespeare." I grew to it. At twenty "Edwards on the Will" was a cloud, at forty a pillar of fire. The world talks much of "self-made men." Every man is "self-made," if he is made to amount to much. A diploma to a college booby does not transform him. In the conflict of actual life mind, disciplined by exertion, exercised by thought, invigorated by combat, elastic by self-education, resourceful by reflection, moves with accelerating momentum. There is a law of growth, not limited to the physical, but pertaining to the mental and moral, progressing through mortal, and, I believe, through immortal life. Can I recommend a course of reading? Yes! But it will be a short one. The ancients had a saying, "Beware of the man of one book." One book mastered is worth a dozen half understood. In days of exhausted energy I have sought to recuperate in reading the comedies, tales and poetry of Goldsmith. The instructive historical romances of Scott, the *"Leather Stocking"* and *"Sea Novels"* of Cooper, the writings of Irving, the poems of Cowper, Milton, Burns, Gray, Scott, Byron, Pope, Tom Moore, Whittier, Longfellow and Lowell. My chief reading has been historical, as a pursuit and an education. Charles A. Dana, former editor of the New York *Sun*, a most accomplished scholar and judge, recommended ten books as indispensable to the American citizen, and in naming I accept his list:

1. The Bible. The greatest statesmen, orators and poets, have drawn from the Bible their maxims of justice, perfection of style, power of persuasion, sublimity of imagery.
2. The Life of Lincoln.
3. The Declaration of Independence.
4. The Constitution of the United States.
5. Bancroft's History of the United States.
6. Irving's Life of Washington.
7. Franklin's Auto-Biography.
8. Shakespeare.
9. Channing's Essay on Napoleon Bonaparte.
10. Gibbon's Decline and Fall of the Roman Empire.

A mastery of these books would form a base on which a vast structure of knowledge could be built, would tend to perfect a style of expression condensed, elevated and appropriate to inform the reader with the principles, history and genius of American Institutions. The common sense and victorious achievement of Franklin and Lincoln are our American heritage. The great Declaration and Constitution are the admiration of souls that pant for freedom the world over. Bancroft and Irving adorn the tree of American life with unfading blossoms of beauty. Channing demonstrated the littleness of martial achievement, compared with the enduring exalted attainment of moral elevation. The grand sweep of Shakespeare's genius covers the horizon of Nature, and the thought and emotion of the universal human heart. Gibbon's *Decline and Fall of the Roman Empire,* the work of twenty years, is practically a history of the world for fifteen centuries, and the key that unlocks the mystery of the fall of Nations in all ages.

VARIED CARES AND BUSINESS LIFE.

A negative life is unfruitful. A spiritual life centered in formalism is a "sounding brass and tinkling cymbal." A true fellowship with the everlasting Church of God, visible and invisible, is a fellowship of active labor. So believing, in the autumn of 1840 I commenced teaching a Bible class, and have continued the work to this date. Every Sabbath after the Sabbath school, I read over the next Sabbath's lesson, fixed the subject in mind, thought of it during the week, read sometimes 1,000 pages to get light on the question and tried to sound its depths. I now look back on over 63 years of that work. October 3d, 1841, I united with the Presbyterian church in East Hampton. January 7th, 1849, I was ordained an elder in the Presbyterian church in Sag Harbor, and I served as such over five years. In 1857 I was ordained an elder in the Presbyterian church in Bridgehampton, and now serve as such. Such service covers some 52 years. From 14 to 86 years of age, I heard on the Sabbath sometimes three sermons, sometimes two and sometimes one; on an average not less than 75 yearly for 72 years making a total of about 5,500 sermons, not including lectures or exhortations. The sermonizing was generally able, instructive, elevating and a great aid in Bible class work. I acknowledge my great debt to the ministers of the everlasting Gospel. The weekly evening prayer meetings which I attended and often led, for over 50 years, would sum up at 2,500. The Sabbath has been no idle day for me for nearly 70 years. In that time there have been lived of Sabbaths ten years, unimproved what a loss! Wisely used what a gain! Even an average scholar, in that time, should make great progress in knowledge Biblical, theological, mental, moral, historical, philosophical. In early life I read the Bible, as one book from Genesis to Revelations, as was then the custom. The genealogical, ceremonial, sacrificial records of the Old Testament, typical, symbolic, prospective, superceded by the teaching of Christ, I regard with lessening interest. For 50 years I have read, commencing January 1st, the New Testament and Psalms, finishing about Sept. 1st, each year. Then I read the Old Testament and finish that in a little over four years. I think that a fair proportion of allotted time devoted to the two. Men may preach learned sermons on the construction of the Ark and Temple, but if they resulted in converting any sinner from the error of his ways, I have not seen it. Why cannot scholars preach the Christ typified instead of the type, the reality and not the dead shadow? Looking back on my Sabbath life, imperfect as it may be, I cannot think it an idle life. In a rough outline of cares and business, varied and responsible the reader may see that which may light him to judge.

I was president of the Sag Harbor Savings Bank from 1868 to 1898, carrying that load thirty years; president of the Sag Harbor and Bulls Head Turnpike Co. from 1852 on for over 40 years, all the while between the two fires. The public wanted improvements, the stockholders wanted dividends, wants antagonizing. I was president of the Hampton Library in Bridgehampton, from its inception in 1876, to the present time, some 28 years. The numerous and responsible trusts devolved on me as Trustee, executor, administrator, guardian, etc., must pass unspecified. The account would fill a volume. There was constant work and care and supervision of the farm required. I led a life of high pressure, until near 80 years of age, which is now the law of my being. In 1857 I was elected a director of the Suffolk Co. Mutual Insurance Co., and have so continued until now. For over thirty years was an agent of that company, doing a large business, until about 1898. Standing in the full glare of publicity, I could not escape criticism, often adverse. It is amusing to notice the sudden change of tone when enterprise turns from apparent success to failure. I was interested in the Sag Harbor cotton mill and finally one of the agents to wind up its disastrous career. When, supposed to succeed, I met co-owners the hilarious inquiry would be, "How is *our* mill getting along?" When failure came the contemptuous inquiry was, "How is *your* darned old mill getting long." "I have *been through the mill.*"

Trained in the school or arduous labor, strict economy, frugal life, early rising, simple diet, I was healthy in youth, vigorous and active in manhood, declining slowly in age. All the while asking for work, which all the time I got. At 75 years of age my father said he never had a headache. At 86 I can say, excepting one hour, for 60 years I have not had it. Regular habits, a strong inherited constitution, continuous activity contributed to perpetuate capacity to labor. Every man ought to make the most of himself. Bees tolerate *no drone in the hive.* Almost with the precision of a machine I could count on the ability to do a day's work the next day. The demands of social life and much visiting detract from the volume of labor a man can or ought to do. This was a danger I early foresaw. If I had executed the plans of social visitation and enjoyment friends marked out for me I could have done not much more. The criticism that I was *unconventional* I have borne and must bear. The claims of duty are more sacred and imperious than those of social enjoyment. The one who shines in social circles often makes that the aim of life and fails to attain what he might have made of himself.

To a young lady about to be married an old maid said, "It is a *solemn thing to be married.*" The reply was, "It is a good deal *solemner not to be.*" February 23d, 1892, Miss Mary G. Hildreth, then in charge of the Hampton Library in Bridgehampton, and I were married. I was 74 years of age and this was noticed, under flaming headlines in the newspapers. It was a choice morsel for gossip. The novelty of discussion and the giggling of girls at length subsided. I reconstructed a new, quiet home, went on with work as before. Twelve years have gone by. No scandal of inharmonious life has ensued. The living cannot live with the dead. My second marriage occurred from no disregard of the memory of the first. That is a sacred, abiding reality, surviving "while life and thought and being last, and immortality endures."

> *"Ah, let us think though none before us*
> *The vanished friends of days no more,*
> *They watch with fond affection o'er us,*
> *And bless us from their heavenly shore.*

TEMPERANCE.

In the spring of 1842 I was studying Law in New York City. Tom Marshall, Member of Congress from Kentucky, came there, and spoke three evenings in the Broadway Tabernacle on Temperance. He had been an inebriate and claimed to be reformed. He was over six feet high, slim built, pale, with dark eyes, long dark hair, gaunt, with a look intellectual and genteel. His reputation as a genius and orator preceded him. In the stump speaking of the then southwest his name was famous. On one occasion his opposing candidate for Congress boasted of his identity with the common people, and stated that his father was a cooper, and apparently carried the crowd with him. Tom Marshall replying said he admitted the claim. His father might have been a cooper and a good one, but if so one thing was certain (pointing to his adversary), *"He put a might poor head on that beer barrel!"* Fertile in resource, quick in retort, happy in fancy, exhuberant in expression, admired and loved by his constituents and friends, Tom Marshall attracted a large audience, and I was one of the many for the three evenings. His voice was shrill and unmelodious, his gestures not graceful, his manner unattractive. It took him nearly all the first night to get hold of his audience and carry them with him. His superior genius at length did it. The second evening argument flowed on argument, thought on thought, flash of illustration on flash, wave of emotion on wave, until he played on the feeling of his hearers, as the master on the organ wakes all notes symbolic of sorrow or joy, of attraction or aversion, of rapture or revulsion. It was a triumph of oratory. The third evening was a scene of the highest, widest, wildest achievement of the speaker. Tom Marshall pictured the degradation of the drunkard, the grandeur of temperance, and swayed the thought of the thousands there as truly as Demosthenes moved the populace of Athens by the momentum of eloquence. Yet this man of towering genius, triumphant oratory, radiant achievement *fell* a shining victim of temperance, and *filled a* drunkard's grave.

I heard John B. Gough speak on the same subject some forty years after. As an actor his power of imitation and personating was unrivalled. With unlimited elasticity, with marvelous quickness, he changed from gladness to gloom, from jest to earnest, adapting instantaneously the gesture, attitude, tone, expression to the character personified. He was singly a living combination of actors, tragic and comic, in a way peculiarly his own. His method was a constant succession of surprises. Hearers listened and could not help it, were charmed and could not help it.

Is the virtue of temperance gaining or losing? The question is too grave for neglect or evasion. A recent issue of the United States Statistical Abstract shows the average consumption of intoxicants in gallons per capita as follows:

FIVE YEARS AVERAGE		MALT LIQUORS	DISTILLED SPIRITS	WINES
1871–1875	galls	6.73	1.59	0.44
1890–1894	"	15.13	1.44	0.43
1985–1899	"	15.34	1.09	0.34
YEARLY AVE.				
1900	"	16.01	1.27	0.40
1901	"	16.20	1.33	0.37
1902	"	17.49	1.86	0.68
1903	"	18.04	1.46	0.48

In distilled spirits there is a decrease of 13-100, in wines an increase of 4-100, yet on an average, in 1903, every man, woman and child consumed nearly half a gallon of wine and a gallon and a half of distilled spirits, probably ten times as much as was required for medical purposes, and therefore ten times as much as was beneficial, and which wrought unmixed evil. In malt liquors, from 1871 to 1903 the consumption rose from 6.73 to 18.04, an increase of over eleven and a half gallons to every inhabitant of the United States. Remember that less than one-fifth of the inhabitants are voters, that minors and women are largely counted out from the drinkers; that comparatively few are habitual tipplers; that one-tenth of the population swig down the most of this average liquor, say 1-10 use up 4-5 of all as a beverage, and you get this result: an army of drinkers, chiefly heads of families and voters, consuming yearly, each on an average, over 158 gallons, and over 3 gallons weekly. They are largely wasters of time, disabled from labor, apprentices to crime, moving to the poorhouse and prison, bringing misery and want on their households, training their children to follow them in the descent to degradation. The drunkard defrauds the state of what he ought to be as a useful citizen. He defrauds his family of what they ought to be as useful members of the community. He sustains the trafficker in intoxicants and the saloon keeper, upholding thereby a useless, dangerous, desolating oligarchy. God of the widow and fatherless, of the friendless and forlorn! Shall no warning blast by thy word be blown? Shall this Moloch of Rum Traffic go on, unheeding the curse of broken hearts, unrelenting at the pangs of injured innocence, unappeased by the blood of victim thousands? Shall his merciless sceptre bear sway, his giant hand hold the keys of power, his iron heel crush the hope of humanity forever?

Admitting the benefits of intoxicants as a medical agent, when required, who does not know that their habitual use as a beverage destroys their efficacy as a remedy? Nay more! Not only destroys but renders other remedies powerless. Fever, lurking in the system saturated with alcohol burns with tenfold heat. Gangrene poisons with more velocity. Amputation fails because arteries, brittle, are tired only to break, and bleed afresh. In the great struggle for the restoration of the Union the Temperance cause was overshadowed. Since then a fraction of the temperance men have nominated and voted for a ticket of exclusively Prohibition candidates. As if no man not a prohibitionist was a suitable candidate for office. That is a mistake. Nine-tenths of the temperance men vote their party ticket. One tenth or less the separate ticket, which is a divisive force in the Temperance ranks, effecting no practical good, electing no one, and weakening the cause. I deplore this disorganizing and ineffectual movement, and the more so because its adherents, in my view misguided, are men of the purest purpose and unsullied life.

My testimony, living or dying, will affirm the blessings of temperance, will condemn the practice of using intoxicants as a beverage. If this be ignominious I am content to bear it. If it would aid in freeing my country from the galling bondage of intemperance let it be engraved in enduring letters on the granite that shall mark my grave.

THE DECLINE OF LIFE.

At 86 years of age I retain comfortably the powers of digestion, recuperative sleep, sight, hearing, locomotion, thought and perception. All these are impaired, and my memory the most. There is some tremor of nerve, but not to prevent writing; slowness of perception, delaying yet not precluding the grip of comprehension; aversion to strife, but not beyond arousal. I can do less than half the manual labor, and more than half the brain work possible in my prime. I have very little rheumatism and no headache. The bodily machine moves slow but it moves regular. God is no hard master. He is satisfied with a half day's work, if that is my limit, as much as with a whole day's work, when I was in my prime. Comforting myself with this thought, I keep right on with my work. Some old people, because they can do but little, will do nothing. And some, fretting about it, shorten life. The law of six day's labor and the Sabbath of rest is clear and imperative to me, as if written in burning letters, on the overarching heaven. Idleness nurtures discontent. Labor cures it. When I quit work, I soon quit life. The inquiring reader may ask the question, What causes prolonged my life? I have seen stated the theory that life is measured by heart pulsations, so many heart beats to a human life. Acceleration there hastens the end. The inebriate and the glutton wear out the heart. The voice of an accusing conscience, the dread of retribution in a coming judgment, the vision of an avenger of a wrong, the horrors of guilt, in fancy self-condemned, exposed, convicted, betrayed. All these haunt and hunt their victim until life is intolerable, death a seeming, though false refuge from contempt. Every pang of remorse, every fearful heartbeat of horror, every throe of agony in view of infamy wears and strains and tears the warp and woof of life. The soul that aims at justice thereby aims at longevity. The mind that lives in peace is complying with an essential condition for long life. When mean eat, and keep on eating, *because it tastes good*, they suffer and may, but seldom do, learn that reason and experience should control appetite. I eat very sparingly, and live on plain, simple food, chiefly vegetable, with fruits in plenty; sleep much longer than in earlier years, and in long days take a nap after dinner. My father drank water freely and had no headache. I drink no tea, little coffee, much milk, and chiefly cold water. In old times medical adversers prescribed rum and prohibited water, a fatal mistake. If the outside of the body requires cleansing by water, the inside, much fouler, requires it more. Removing impurities, the disturbances of inflammation and lurking fever also flee away. My freedom from headache, I think is caused largely by a free use of water.

Hippocrates, Father of Medicine, lived, according to authors, as stated by some to 85, and others to 109 years. His manner was calm, mind active, powers of sight, hearing, memory, observation and locomotion well preserved. He attributed his longevity largely to a simple diet, with full allowance of milk. He ate little at one time and took some nourishment five times a day. I noticed that he was of tranquil mind and seemed always pursuing some enterprise or employment. Years ago I saw Thomas McLean, of Pennsylvania, at my house, who had held a commission as colonel from General Washington. At 90 years of age he was more vigorous than the average man of seventy. He had strongly marked the same manner of tranquillity. I knew Judge John Woodhull, late of Jamesport, in this county, who died in his 102d year. A man of pure life, regular habits, strong love of justice, respected by his fellow men, condemned by them as a Federalist, when they were living, and made executor of their wills when dying, because they would trust none other. His peace of mind was apparent to all observers. Regular habits in labor and rest, without overwork lengthen life. Pure air is an element essential to good health. Temperance is a virtue: Dissipation a vice. In old age the circulation is slow. Much more underclothing and outer clothing is then required. Death is cold, life warm. A patient asked a doctor how to attain long life. He answered, *"I can tell you but you won't do it."* He referred to the simple, spare diet and self denial, which are conditions so hard to observe. He knew however rich, the fare must be that of a poor man. Please remember these few words: 1, Tranquillity, 2 Employment, 3 Regularity, 4 Temperance, 5 Plain Food, 6 Pure air, 7 Suitable clothing.

Old age has its history. I can recall the scenes of childhood, youth, manhood and years extending far beyond the average of human life, events long since transpired. In memory I hear again the accents of voices long unheard. Clinton Academy was part of my early life, and is so now. The old church of 1717, once part of my life, is so now. My schoolmates, dead to the living world, in my remembrance live. The teachers, long fled from mortal life, have left their lessons of truth with me. The ministers of the everlasting Gospel, gone where the light outshines star and sun, still speak to me. Backward I look on life with thanksgiving. Forward dare I look at the failing sight and sense, at gasping breath, dissolving life, the coffin closed, the mounded grave?

To this picture, in closing narrative, I come. How repellent it is thought I well know.

> *"For who to dumb foregetfulness a prey,*
> *This pleasing, anxious being e'er resigned,*
> *Left the warm precincts of the cheerful day,*
> *Nor cast one longing, lingering look behind."*

In his immortal Elegy so wrote Gray, and so men think. So do not I think. Even the most glorious death is likened to the setting sun, yet the setting sun is always rising, radiant emblem of immortal light, symbol of a glorious resurrection, set by Almighty hands in the heavens, as a signal that the darkness of death has its coming eternal morn. A life of growing infirmity, imbecility and suffering perpetuated would be intolerable. To the aged death is the gate of release from this agony of pain and degradation. With unfeigned joy I look for it in God's own good time. And more! Far more! I hope for and expect an immortal life wherein sorrow and suffering are unknown, a life of ever growing powers of mind, of moral grandeur, here unattained and unattainable, beyond all that Poet or Philosopher, Seer or Saint, saw or foretold; beyond the power of human thought to conceive, or human tongue to tell. I look for a new body, spiritual, indestructible, immortal, subject to no infirmities or weariness, like that of the "Angels who excel in strength." All this not for my merits, but because I love God as manifest in the life and death of our Saviour, and the life of justice and righteousness he commended. In the hope that my Biography may forward the reign of righteousness in my country, I come to its close.

SUPPLEMENTAL ARTICLES
(Continued from May 7, 1904)

In the latter part of May, 1905, I was struck down near to the gates of Death, the result of over-exertion, and for nearly six months Jas. B. Terry of East Hampton, a trained nurse, took care of me with an intelligence and fidelity seldom equalled. General opinion decided that I would die. My belief was that I would live. The agony of my malady was not only spasmodic but unrecessing. If told, I would not have believed it possible I could have endured so much and live. For nearly six months it was a fight for life, with dark doubt whether death would not win the battle. A victim of catarrh knows how persistent it is and I had catarrh of the bladder. With little respite it held me in malignant gripe over

three years, and now, contrary to ordinary expectation, and growing infirmity, and great age of 91 years, it is lulled if not subdued.

Have I learned anything by the ministry of suffering? Has its visit
been as an Angel of Light or a minister of darkness, doubt and unbelief?
Nothing can occur without God's permission. Conceding to him all
power, we must concede this. If God did not strike me down He permitted it. Out of my inmost soul I now say He struck me no harder than
I deserved. If Jesus Christ was made perfect through suffering, how
much more we mortals, weaker, frailer, lower, need the lesson and ministry of pain. In the exhuberance of health and strength, we tread the
earth with exultant, self-sufficient step, unmindful of the weakness, the
poverty, the dependence, the calamities of our fellow men. God lets go
His hold that held us up and the agony which was theirs, is our own,
their weakness ours, their poverty, their helplessness, their calamity, as
with an earthquake shock, conviction of their sorrows comes with
ours, their afflictions with ours. Now our eyes, closed before, see the
wants and woes of our fellow men. Our ears are open to hear their
moan of desolation. Our hearts respond in sympathy with their distress. Medical advisers tell us, "Pain is the Sentinel of Danger," I think it
the Pioneer of Salvation. On the bed of sickness and suffering God
makes us learn the lesson of our dependence on Him of our insuffi-
ciency to stand of ourselves, of the tenderness of our Father in Heaven,
of the common brotherhood of all men of all races, of the nothingness
of all sacrifice without the heart, of the emptiness of all form, all ritual,
all sacrament not the expression of the soul. My descent into the dark
valley and shadow so near to the Valley and Shadow of death was exalted and enlarged my spiritual life, clarified my conceptions of the
character of God, brought Him and brought my fellow men nearer to
me than ever before. Humbled I believe, chastened I think, purified I
hope, by the Grace of God I look without dread on death, come when
and how it may, as the Gate of Freedom out from infirmity, imbecility
and decay into a life endless in duration, unfaltering in progression,
unimbittered by disappointment, unendangered by temptation, not
merited, not earned, but the free gift of Him, who "so loved the world,
that he gave his only begotten son that whosoever believeth on Him
should not perish, but have everlasting life." My long illness in extreme
old age I think the most instructive and profitable years of my life. All
that I have in these "memories" written in defence of the "Faith once
delivered to the saints," all that I have argued and urged in support of
the Bible as a Light for man to seek and follow, all that I have affirmed
advocating total abstinence from intoxicants as a beverage, all that I

have written as rules or requirements for longevity, I now here declare; republish and affirm as one almost buried in the earth and revived at the Gate of Death to be a messenger and witness of the earth as God gives me to see the earth; and to declare this with less partisan bias, with more charity for dissenters, who at another standpoint see things with other eyes, hear voices with other ears than mine.

THE MISERY OF INFIDELITY!

The unbeliever in God, in the Bible, in the coming reign of Righteousness, is traveling in doubt, darkness and despair. Anchored on nothing, moving towards nothing, ending nowhere, he is the victim of his own delusion. In a long experience with saint and sinner, believer and unbeliever. I have known no more unhappy men than unbelievers and of them I have known many. The verdict of humanity age after age has been, "Let me die the death of the Righteous and let my last end be like His." This much the common conscience of mankind, bad and good, has recorded of Righteousness. In the enjoyment of exhuberant animal life, the whispers of conscience are often faint, unheard or unheeded. In the decline of the life as infirmities bear heavier, pains grow sharper, conscience cries louder, and the soul sits in judgment on itself, a judgment of condemnation. Hope gone, faith gone, joy gone, light gone, what is left but clouds without a sun, darkness without a ray of light, wretchedness unrelieved and unrelievable. If Righteousness is a dream, if God is a delusion that dream is more inspiring, that delusion more satisfying that unbelief.

THE CHURCH OF GOD
THE HOPE OF THE WORLD.

When I record my conviction that the Church of God is the hope of the world, I mean to include not only the organized denominational church, but all persons who are living a life of Righteousness and benevolence as obedient and loving children of the Universal Heavenly Father. Not undervaluing the organized, I estimate the invisible unorganized spiritual believer as a part of that church and a power for good much greater than in former years. Actual attendance on church services is falling off. To offset that I believe fortified hostile infidelity has lessened and in the main the world is not worse, but better than ever before. While it may be and I think is true that family government is less stringent and faithful than formerly, this reaction from ancient sternness is but a natural and expectant result. The coming promise of Federation of churches, the cessation of sectarian warfare, the alliance of denominations once belligerent, the consolidation of all forces of Righteousness are signs of progress grateful to all lovers of humanity and evidence that the church of God is the hope of the world, while it is true that the church is generally criticised and is imperfect as all human institutions are imperfect. We must remember that God had only poor stuff whereof to make his church. If He had better stuff than we are, He would have a better church.

Since I was struck down in May 1905, changes great in character and vast in extent have surprised the world. The herald who would have foretold that Japan would have overthrown Russia, the most gigantic military and the most despotic political power in all Christendom both on land and sea, would have discredited and disbelieved; the critic who dared charge insurance companies in our own land with extortion in rates of insurance and misappropriation of funds as disclosed, would have been adjudged a slanderer; the censor who asserted the predominance of corruption in the management of railroad and standard oil companies through rebates, watered stock, consolidation and merger into gigantic, unscrupulous trusts, would have been counted a defamer; the politician who predicted the overthrow of absolutism and the introduction of government by representation of the people in Legislative Assembly in Russia, in Turkey, in Persia, in China and almost universally, would have been reckoned a visionary dreamer; the public man who in our own United States declared that conditions required all parties to unite and wage a war on graft in municipal government, on extortion in insurance companies, on robbery by trusts, on frauds by oil companies and railroads, and who predicted that all parties would make these issues, would have been looked on as a lunatic; yet all these unexpected conditions have transpired. The voice of the people crying for rule by the people, for the people, is in no manner to be drowned. It is a roar as loud as ocean's roar, and wide as earth itself. It is as deep, as intense, as fearful as the subterranean fires that blaze from the chimney of the volcano. Its movements is the earthquake's shock. Dynasties fortified, thrones entrenched, crowns guarded, fall before its march. Is its march to be destructive as the whirl wind or beneficent as the breeze of the temperate clime? On the decision of this question hangs the fate of empires and nations. The people of those nations will decide the question.

The abounding preference of the people for peace over war, is the hope and the harbinger of righteousness to coming ages. Japan victorious cries for peace; Russia humbled, thwarted, exhausted, defeated, cries for peace; Germany staggering under the burden of armament on sea and land, cries for peace; England re-echoes the cry of Germany, the United States with the vision of a post civil war of proportions so vast, expenditure so exhausting, slaughter so terrific, desolation so wide, agonizes for peace; the South American Republics, long the home faction of misrule and revolution, raise the repentant cry for peace; the world without dissenting voice, seeks peace as never before, hates war as never before. Thank God that the people are educated to the blessings of peace, as never in all the ages they were before. The time is past when sovereigns of their own pleasure, set their subjects in hostile array as a game to be played, while they unfeelingly looked on. It should gladden the heart of every citizen of this country, that our statesmen have led the way in the radiant progress of international peace and none more ardently, more efficiently, more sincerely, than Theodore Roosevelt. Small men with small ideas, have bitterly criticized what they called his "big stick." When their names have sunk in oblivion, his name will be honored so long as patriots and patriotism live. All human character is imperfect. Even the sun has its spots, yet how gloriously it shines and "there is nothing hid from the heat thereof."

SOCIALISM!

I am writing for no idle and I think no selfish purpose when I name socialism as the subject. For thousands of years mankind lived largely in walled cities and fortified camps. War, robbery, plunder ranged, and armed troops moved to every spot, where hope of soil invited. History must be so read, even the Bible rightly understood must be so read, much more than it is so read. When robbery by arms ceased to be custom, robbery by fraud succeeded and played the game of deceit which it is playing yet, and will do so until "Righteousness shall run down our streets like a river and Judgment like a mighty stream." If I am not mistaken and I hope I am, human selfishness will not surrender until it makes a final stand on socialism, to get something for nothing, the earnings of the worker into the pocket of the idler. The battle will rage in every land and under every form of government, and it will be a fight to the finish. The movement for government by the people is so wide, and has gathered such momentum that I infer it must universally prevail. Then what? Yes what? Just exactly what the people say, and they will say just what their sense of justice and their degree of selfishness moves them to say. Before the surging billows of socialism sweep over our land, full, free and fair, discussion should prepare all patriotic hearts for an enlightened understanding and resolve. At the last presidential election, one of the candidates had previously advocated paying fifty cents worth of silver for a dollars worth of gold and avowed the opinion that government should own and run the railroads, so if not farther he had traveled towards socialism and sixteen states gave him their solid electoral votes. Allowing that they so voted hoping he would not be elected they may so vote again. I know that some socialists interpret the New Testament as enjoining their theory, and even some ministers of the Gospel agree thereto. They base their argument on the community of goods and possessions of believers at the Pentacostal outpouring of the spirit, where by the thousand the church received accessions. If this was not a permanent but merely transient condition of the community of goods as it certainly was, it is no precedent or warrant for any abiding reconstruction of society, on socialistic foundations. In like conditions I do not deny that like devotion to the redemption of the world may demand like sacrifice. Remember the condition came once and has not come again. I have no fears of a reverent and fair reading of the Bible and hope it will be read more universally. Nor do I fear the reading rightly of Acts 3d vs. 41-47 and 4th vs. 31-37.

In the early settlement of towns on eastern Long Island large tracts of land were inclosed [sic] by fences made in proportional tracts improved in the common fields for pasturage, tillage and even garden, as well as the larger crops. This went on for a time as a kind of common improvement until it failed to work fairly and the lands were allotted in severalty. Right here communism was tried and failed over two hundred years gone by. If the Pilgrim Fathers, salt of the earth, founders of states, could not make it work, we may well think it now unworkable. As a rule communities based on the family institution, the family home, the Bible principles have had the cohesive power of perpetuity, based on free love, community of goods, infidelity one or all, lacked that power and explosion and extinction soon consigned them to oblivion.

Pour all individual property, all household goods, all family treasures, trifling in intrinsic value, priceless in ancestral memory, all annuities, the staff of old age, all pensions the poor reward of blood shed, privation endured, lives lost; pour everything dear to the individual and to the family, and dear to none else, into the common stock and you destroy the treasures that affection has consecrated, that love has hallowed, that memory holds sacred.—O, God! For what! For what!! For what!!

The socialist may say I have overdrawn the picture of his theory. He does not mean to invade the rights of home and tear away the individual rights of property to such an extent. But if my farm is not mine and my lands not mine and my little money securities not mine, who can tell what is mine or say where the invasion of personal rights will stop. Necessarily and diplomatically the position of the socialist and his appeals now are soothing as the cooings of a dove. Give him the power and make him judge of his own power and what logical restraint or limit can there be to communism. It owns and must claim all or none. Do my countrymen understand this? Do they know that the sway of socialism is the destruction of personal right to property and its transfer to the community? A new dividing to give to somebody something for nothing! The very beginnings of this proposed division will be like the letting out of many waters. If not repelled now it will be too late then to restrain the surging flood.

TEMPERANCE!

With hope renewed and joy exalted I bail the progress of Temperance moving counties and whole states to the rule of local option and abandonment of the use of intoxicants as a beverage. In my early days the habitual use of strong drink was deeply entrenched in the state and church. This use and sale advocated as ardently by men within as without the church, by officials as private citizens, by a majority of the people, by judges and juries, who ridiculed, sneered at and despised adherents of disuse of intoxicants as a beverage. By experience I know as such an adherent how they were marked, tabooed and as extreme visionaries excluded from influential or official position. The tentacles of the saloon held its victims in a grasp mercenary, merciless, slavish and helpless. The cohesive power of selfishness, profit, appetite, the active aggressive power of the Legions of Alcohol, moving with the momentum of passion hindered, resisted and largely suppressed and unorganized forces of their assailants. Rum ruled regardless of all law except what the interests of its advocates desired. Even now ministers of the everlasting gospel claim that prohibition and local option create hypocrites and work more evil than license. My experience as a lawyer for over three score years convinced me that the hypocrisy of the saloon men on the saloon question found no equal among opponents of license. The rankest perjury I ever saw in all my practice I found in witnesses for the saloon. The most brazen faced hypocrisy I ever found I found there. Who does not know that almost every rum seller trains his patrons to deny the truth whenever he makes a sale of strong drink illegally? Who does not know that right there is a school of hypocrisy of which the world hardly equals. Nine tenths of the actions against the rum seller that are lost, are lost by the perjury and hypocrisy of witnesses who patronize the saloon. The name that drinks moderately or to excess and tries to conceal it, as most men do, is already a hypocrite made so by the drink traffic and not by the abstainer. The objection to my position will be that I have given my opinion but have not sustained it by facts. If space permitted I could fill a volume with facts. I only state one case out of many like ones in my experience. Some sixty years ago I, as attorney for the Overseer of the Poor of the town of Southampton commenced the action against a rum seller for selling without license and to recover the penalty. His clerk as a witness for the prosecution, who did most of the business and made most of the sales swore that he could not remember the name of any particular person to whom he sold strong drink. There was no doubt he sold it not only daily but often and to many persons every day and there was no doubt that he committed perjury and thereby the case was lost to the plaintiffs. Such was the state of public sentiment that it was vain to appeal to courts or juries for justice—perjury won! Advocates of license receive no credit from me on the issue of hypocrisy. I have seen their scholars and teachers and had experience of the depravity of their school. A rum seller sued for a large amount of penalties knowing he would be beaten, offered to discontinue the sale and not sell again on condition that the actions against him were withdrawn and made oath to that effect. The actions were discontinued on the expectation he would keep the faith. The witnesses against him were gotten away and contrary to his oath and the faith reposed in him he again and for years clandestinely and illegally sold as before.

Another rum seller prosecuted in like case and to such an amount as to ruin him financially begged me to get him released on the promise to quit the sale. I said to him, "You will when released sell again." He said, "No! I never will, I hope God will strike me dead if I ever sell again." I then said, "Can I trust you to keep you word." He said, "Yes! you can have my head for a football if I ever sell again." I interceded for him and got him released. As soon as the witnesses against him were gotten away and he dared and in a short time he again sold as before. Is it any wonder after seeing rank perjury, after being thus deceived and betrayed so barely, that I should when charged with hypocrisy as one of the defenders of Temperance, shoot back?

PROGRESSION, MENTAL AND MORAL.

At my age public opinion would count me a conservative and would count wrong. From the beginning of adult life, I have been in law, in public affairs, in theology, a new school man, on the law as touching the choice of judges by appointment of officials or vote of the people on the slavery question, not as an abolitionist but as an advocate of free soil, free speech, and a free press, and in our civil war as an ardent advocate of maintaining the Union by arms, and in most public affairs I have been a progressive, arguing that government should be kept as near the people direct as practicable and that officials should be accountable to the people rather than bosses and I abide in that faith still.

Theologically I was once enchained under the dominant power of the old Testament. Some of my friends and even some ministers are there yet. I got out of the old into the New Testament, many years gone by. The sermon on the Mount, and the first of Hebrews show clearly that regarding polygamy, slavery and the largeness of neighborly love, the New Testament was wider, deeper, higher and antagonized the toleration of evils if not sanctioned hardly condemned by the old. The savagery and barbarism of early ages could not bear the later revelation and some things, "God winked at" see acts 17, 30. The progress of the child to manhood and the enlargement of the powers of manhood are not unlike the progress and enlargement of nations. It was long before I could enjoy and enter into the comprehension of Shakespeare, long before I was emancipated from the bondage of the Old Testament. In my own experience I see a possibility and power of growth and progress unceasing, almost illimitable, and mark this as a sign for hope of the future in the elevation of the individual and by all races and Nations. The History of Man from barbarity to civilization is a history on which optimism may surely rest. A citizen of East Hampton eighty years ago said, "East Hampton folks always travel in the old ruts." That saying is now untrue.

HOLIDAYS!

Habits, manners, customs, change in the progress of time. Our Puritan Fathers observed Thanksgiving Day as an occasion for worship, family gatherings, feasting and outgoing of the heart in friendship and affection. That was their great holiday. Slighter notice was taken of New Year's and Christmas even in my youth. Their observance of Christmas had just been tolerated then with all the romance that youth attached to Santa Claus. Stockings were hung up by the expectant children; few arranged for, expected, or made New Year's or Christmas calls. Holidays were too trifling for maturity and were chiefly for the young. Even the birthday of Washington was not very generally regarded. Next to Thanksgiving the heart of America was in the spirit of the Fourth of July. Somewhere about 1824 or '25, that day was celebrated in East Hampton Church with all the formalities then practiced. I remember the procession with fife and drum, the display of the national flag, the Liberty cap carried next to it in church, the seating of four revolutionary soldiers on the stage. I remember they were Reuben Hedges, a fine looking man, grand in his ruffled bosom shirt, who was said to have been one of Washington's Life Guards; Benjamin Miller, Leek—I think Benjamin—and John Gann, venerable for age, majestic in presence, hallowed in memory as champions of freedom, imposing relics of that army, who were faithful to the last in their country's cause. Who could look and not notice? Who could think and not remember? Judge Jonathan S. Conkling was then vigorous although near the decline of life, a man of large attainments, strong original intellect, long legislative experience, large and powerful physique, commanding presence, and there and then delivered the Fourth of July oration. In this celebration East Hampton did her best, and her best is rarely exceeded elsewhere. With an audience crammed to the utmost, with every eye and ear open, with attention alert, with all hearts intense in the spirit of the day, who could fail to sing his best the ode composed by Miss Cornelia Huntington for the occasion? Who could fail to deliver the message of Liberty to her waiting sons? That ode I read every 4th day of July and recall the old time celebration, so sincere, so heartfelt, so patriotic! Like martial music the opening lines fire the blood.

> *"Thus had the spirits of the dead,*
> *Whose blood in Freedom's Cause was shed,*
> *Exulted, could their lips have shared*
> *The banquet which their hands prepared."*

The lofty spirit of patriotism that animated the celebration in my early days has degenerated. The remembrance of the days when blood and life and fortune were laid as a sacrifice on the Altar of Independence seems forgotten. The moderns celebrate largely by trying to climb a greased pole or catching a greased pig. Vulgarity usurps the place of patriotism, low amusement banishes the most elevated sentiment. By request I have just been writing up the history of Bridgehampton and of Sag Harbor in the Revolution. Our fathers to a man were true to their country's cause in her hour of greatest need. All that the conquered may suffer from the barbarity of the victor they bore and more, all that the misguided and rapacious of their own country-men charged or robbed they bore with a constancy never overcome by the consciousness of injustice done. More than seven years Long Island was bound under the iron heel of martial law. If the harvest ripened or the flocks increased the Americans robbed them because they said the British would thereby be fed if they did not, and the British said the same. Friend and foe alike plundered, and the people were ground between the upper and neither millstone. The Revolutionary page of eastern Long Island is unsullied and is worthy of the loftiest monument and unperishable memory. How other holidays have in later years cheered the wearied toiler, enlivened old and young, rested the careworn man of business, renovated the statesman, renewed the intellectual elasticity of the student, harmonized the whole structure of society, the present age well knows. Thank God for holidays, and thanks! everlasting thanks! for the Holy days of the Sabbath, emblem of the Eternal Rest.

TIME.

Human life on earth is measured by time. All men know this and yet how few live as if they knew it. Examining myself and observing others, I cannot fail to see that wasted opportunities, unimproved privileges, unperformed duties are almost universal errors. What we have done and what we might have done are measures wide apart. As age lengthens the review of our career is inevitable and in but few cases nothing but self condemnation results. The looking back brings regret, often remorse. That everyone should so live, rest, eat, work, as to tone up his body and mind to the best he can do is self-evident. All food over that required to supply wastage of the system is a load of damage, and hindrance to efficient action. All sleep other than required to restore elasticity to the material and spiritual being is so much dross infused to the detriment of normal action. Even in early life I found that eight hours sound sleep was all the amount required to tone me up to do my best and for many years this eight hours was generally a period of unbroken forgetfulness, ending in complete restoration, and I did not exceed that limit. Sunday snoozing and Sunday stuffing do much to stupify the mental and moral elevation of the idlers who thus indulge. Our forefathers who founded these old towns where we live, by precept and example, commended the improvement of time as something for which they must account and believed misimprovement called for condemnation. Their children do well to cherish and follow their examples.

CLOSING.

Visitors, speakers, writers, prolong visits, addresses, writings, often beyond the mark of propriety. Books, even the best, submitted to hydraulic pressure leave but brief remnants of extracts of abiding value. Long winded arguments can be compressed into brief compass. Long prayers wear out first favorable impressions. Long visits dispel first pleasures. A hundred years ago the leader of the five o'clock meeting in the Hook School House called one to pray. Nathaniel Dominy, great grandfather to the present oldest Nathaniel, said, "No! I don't want him to pray, he prays too long, call on such a one," (naming him). Reminding myself of the infirmities of man and desiring to avoid prolixity, with all good wishes to the readers of these "Memories," I now close.

CHAPTER XVI

THE STORY OF BRIDGEHAMPTON, LONG ISLAND, 1660-1910

Delivered at the Court-House in Riverhead in 1910 at the age of 93

ADDRESS OF HON. HENRY P. HEDGES

ON THE FIRST PAGE of the first volume of *The Records of the Town of Southampton* is recorded a paper entitled "The Disposal of the Vessel." It is dated March 10, 1639, was signed by twelve men called therein "undertakers," who afterwards admitted eight others associates and signers. The vessel was a sloop costing eighty pounds and was owned in shares and bought by the signers for the use of a plantation, and by them sold to Daniel Howe its captain and one of their company, who agreed not to sell it without consent of a majority of the company. These men were Freeholders, residents in Lynn, Massachusetts. This paper stated that the vessel was to go on an "expedition to settle a plantation to be owned in shares like the vessel," and was to be ready at Lynn three times each year in the first, fourth and eighth month to take passengers and transport freight, a half ton for each undertaker free to the plantation. Rules for owning and governing the plantation were prescribed. The establishment of a church there was looked for. The document has marks of profound thought and wide experience worthy of the founders of a commonwealth, and of a place as a statesman-like paper. In prospective Southampton thus began and by men who were in dead earnest. As we proceed it must be remembered that this was in the time of old style the year beginning March 25. As agent for the Earl of Sterling James Farrett, by patent dated April 17, 1640, conveyed to Daniel Howe, Job Sayre, George Wilbe and William Harker and their associates, the right "to sitt down upon Long Island aforesaid,

335

there to possess, improve and enjoy, eight miles square of land, or as much as shall contain the said quantity." "And they are to make their choice to sit down upon as best suiteth them." The quit rent was to be fixed by John Winthrop, and the inhabitants at their leisure were required to purchase of the Indians having "lawful right" to said land (see *Southampton Town Records* Vol 1 p 9.)

This paper was signed and sealed by Farrett as a deed, was witnessed by Theophilus Eaton, governor of New Haven, and John Davenport, minister there, and therefore we know that it was executed there and that the authorities there knew its contents and that it was a deed in terms covering "all Long Island" and so covering that it denied and barred any claim these authorities had to any part of Long Island or to Southold recognized by them. Not only did they recognize it as a deed but John Winthrop who by indorsement thereto fixed the amount of quit rent to be paid to the Earl of Sterling, understood that to be the deed of the coming settlements. The location could be fixed by verbal agreement and then the deed without a writing or with it was by a flash of lightning conveyed the premises located. By another record it will appear that an expedition to settle a plantation on Long Island had started from Lynn, obtained this deed from Farrett at New Haven and gone to Cow Bay or near there in Queens County and been expelled therefrom, in an attempt to make a settlement, by the Dutch authorities.

THE EXPEDITION TO SETTLE A PLANTATION.

In the yacht Prince William with a party of 25 Dutch soldiers under orders from the Dutch Governor at Fort Amsterdam, these six men were arrested viz: Job Sayre, George Wilbe, John Farrington, Philip and Nathaniel Kirtland and William Harker. All signers of and named among the undertakers. All owners of land in Lynn, and taken as prisoners to Fort Amsterdam. On examination they testified in substance that Howe and Farrett cut down the arms of the state and that these two had gone with the sloop that landed them (at Cow Bay) to Red Hill, meaning New Haven, with their commission, meaning probably their conveyance of land. That they left, on their arrest, two men, a woman and child to take care of their goods. That they "had built a small house and were building another not finished." That they came "to plant and build dwellings." That "it was intended that 20 families should come and if the land was good they expected a great many people." These men were arrested May 15, 1640, and discharged May 19, 1640, these being the Dutch dates. The English dates are 1639 and are wrong as we know, because this discharge was on Saturday, May 19, and May 19, 1639 was Thursday. Like errors occur often in transcribing records before and even after the adoption of the new style in 1652. These men were not discharged until they had signed a paper stating their coming to settle on the "Territory of the States General without knowing the same, being deceived by Mr. Farrett, Scotchman," and a promise "to remove from the territory immediately" vid. *Colonial Hist. of N.Y.* Vol. 2 p. 146 etc. These argonauts of Southampton thus deceived and betrayed, arrested and released, forerunners of the company who were to occupy by settlement the ground which they had prepared, were proceeding under authority procured from the agent and attorney of the Earl of Sterling. After the signing of this paper we trace their expedition by means of another paper dated June 12, 1639, meaning 1640, by which Farrett conveyed to Edward Howell, Daniel Howe, Job Sayre, and their associates all land "lying and being bounded between Peaconneck and the Easternmost Point of Long Island with the whole breadth of said Island from sea to sea with all land and premises contained in said limits, except those lands already granted by me to any person***"in consideration of a barge line, besides they being drove off by the Dutch from the place where they were by me planted, to their great damage, and with a competent sum of money in hand paid before the ensealing and delivery of these presents, all amounting to four hundred pounds sterling." Peconic was an Indian settlement at the head of Peconic Bay. The Lynn Company now could locate on any point of all eastern Long Island, excepting only where Farrett had previously conveyed "to any person." Farrett by agreement with the Earl of Sterling had a right to choose 12,000 acres as compensation for his services as agent, and had chosen Robbins Island and Shelter Island. It is claimed that he had conveyed by deed dated August 15, 1640, 150 acres to a Richard Jackson, carpenter, who built a house thereon in Southold and afterward sold to Witherby or Wetherby, who on October 22, 1640, sold the same to Stephen Goodyear of New Haven. Vid. Address C.B. Moore at Southold celebration in August 1890 p 127.

It is also claimed that Matthew Sunderland or Suiderland had leased or obtained right to land in the territory of Southold from Farrett. There is no evidence that these persons were preparing to found a town and much to negative such a supposition.

We can further trace this expedition to settle Southampton by an instrument dated July 7, 1639, meaning 1640, by which the eight miles square were located by boundaries on the west at a place entitled the name of the place "where the Indians draw over their canoes, out of the North Bay over to the south side of the Island," (being Canoe Place) and on the east "to the easterly end of an island or neck of land over against the island known as Mr. Farrett's Island" being Shelter Island.

This instrument was signed by Farrett and conveyed to Edward Howell, John Gosmer, Edmund Farrington, Daniel Howe, Thomas Halsey, Edward Needham, Allen Breed, Thomas Sayre, Henry Walton, George Wells or Welby, Wm. Harker and Job Sayre. August 20, 1640, the Earl of Sterling confirmed this instrument of July 7, 1640.

The instrument of July 7, was witnessed by Thomas Dexter and Richard Walker, both of Lynn, and large land owners there. Dexter was the first purchaser of the famed Nahant. That proves that the instrument was executed at Lynn and that the expedition to locate a plantation had, previous to that, examined the territory between Canoe Place and the eastern bounds of Southampton, and north and south "from sea to sea" and decided on at as a settlement, and more, they had arranged for the purchase of the territory from the Indians and probably made the first payment to them of 16 coats, named in their deed of December 13, 1640, of the First Town Purchase and had done all this before a messenger could start from Southampton to carry the news to Lynn and thereafter get this document drawn and executed. From June 12th to July 7th is only 25 days in which the territory must be explored by land and sea, bounds fixed, the result reported by voyage to Lynn, and all this, if the parties were on the ground doing it, would require as much as 25 days, and probably more, proving that this expedition must have been in Southampton by, if not before, June 12th as tradition reports. The option covered the whole breadth of the Island from "sea to sea" and excluded the settlement of any other town. Southold claims priority of settlement on these grounds: 1 Southold is older by purchase of the Indians; 2 by renting, purchase and improvement of lands; 3 by union in civic government; 4 by its organized church. (See Whitaker's *History of Southold* page 41).

It is claimed that on the 18th of June, 1639, Matthew Sunderland leased of James Farrett lands in the town of Southold and on September 4, 1639, took a receipt for rent paid thereon; a second time September 9, 1640. See Whitaker's *History of Southold,* p. 36. The Southold records show receipts for rent of land at Cow Bay but none for land in Southold. If it were proved that Jackson and Sunderland made individual settlements, Southold would and does thereby defeat her own claim to priority because Lyon Gardiner's Indian deed is dated May 30, 1639. (See Letchford's *Note book,* p 129) And he came to his Island before any other Englishman settled on Long Island. That would give priority to the town of East Hampton wherein lies Gardiner's Island. September 20, 1640, Sunderland's bill of exchange to Thomas Robinson states his residence as at New Port, Rhode Island. (See Letchford's *Note book* p 283) There is no evidence that Sunderland or Jackson ever settled or designed to settle and found a town in Southold or that they were looking after any interest except their own as individuals. Nothing appears showing that they resided there but much that their residence was elsewhere.

The Southold claimant still says: you have not proved and cannot prove that this expedition expelled from Cow Bay went to Southampton and there founded that town. I answer:They were sent for that purpose and must be presumed to have performed that duty, until some evidence is shown overcoming that presumption of which there is none. Roger M. Sherman son of the famous Roger of Connecticut, it is said, prosecuted an offender who pleaded "not guilty." And Roger said to the rural court, "He has pleaded 'not guilty' now let him prove it," and had the court with him. If Southampton's case is to be so tried, remember every motive, selfish and unselfish impelled these men to pursue the purpose of the expedition. To build houses and plant corn and prepare to feed and shelter the coming copartners, wives and children in the next winter and who actually did come with, so far as appears, no complaint of neglect against their preceding associates. Had there been such base default of duty the whole country would have rung with clamorous condemnation of their crime to their shame and lasting contempt. Southampton cannot permit her founders to suffer so unjustly.

Southampton is the first town on these grounds: 1 Its founders bought the vessel for the use of the Plantation by Englishmen. 2 It formed the first constitution for settling and governing such a town on Long Island. 3 It made the first exploration to examine and locate a town eight miles square or its equivalent thereon. 4 It has the first deed for the English title to a territory large enough to form a town there. 5 Even after the expulsion at Cow Bay, that deed of option for the eight miles excluded any other purchase prior thereto on all eastern Long Island in the territory of Southold. 6 It expended the sum of 400 pounds sterling in establishing a town before any other founders of an English town, so far as appears, spent a cent. 7 It located the eight miles square and had a company formed to settle on it and at work planting and building houses thereon, real settlers, before any other town there. Its records show that it governed itself internally as a town from the start and independent of any other colony in the choice of its officers and magistrates and making of laws, and are the earliest town records by years to be found in any English town on Long Island. It is worthy of the name of such a town by the disasters and expulsion of its founders, by their vast expenditure of treasure, toil, hardship and all its long and glorious history.

John Winthrop, Governor of Massachusetts, residing at Boston near Lynn, was known by all the Lynn parties who trusted him and well knew them. As a witness his testimony would be reliable. In his journal under date 1640, 4th month he records notice of this expedition expelled by the Dutch and states: "Upon this the Lynn men finding themselves too weak and having no encouragement to expect aid from the English deserted that place and took another at the eastern end of the same island and being now about forty families they proceeded in their plantation." Remember "this expedition of Lynn men" expelled "took another place at the east end of the same island." Can any record coeval more clearly prove the expedition went to Southampton? Winthrop's endorsement of the quit rent to be paid to the Earl of Sterling on the option deed of April 17, 1640, proves that the parties thereto understood that to be the deed relied on.

Many years ago I thoroughly examined this question and arrived at the conclusion since held, that Southampton was the first English town settled on Long Island.

George R. Howell was of the same opinion. See his pamphlet on that subject published in 1882, and his history of Southampton published in 1887.

Wm. Wallace Tooker is of the same opinion. See his article published in the Sag Harbor Express April 2, 1893.

William S. Pelletreau is of the same opinion. These three eminent antiquarians after exhaustive examination all concur in this conclusion.

In an address I delivered before the Suffolk County Historical Society in October 1889, and in another address in 1890, at the 250th anniversary of the Town of Southampton, I advanced the same conclusion. The Southold celebration in August 1890 was a memorable event and at its meeting on the second day of the celebration the Hon. James H. Tuthill presided. He was presiding and present at the delivery of the address first named and present at the Southampton celebration next named, and at the Southold celebration in introducing me as speaker said, as recorded in printed proceedings p 93: "The next speaker represents the town of Southampton which has about as much history as we have with five minutes more or less."*

THE INDIAN TITLE.

By deed dated December 13th, 1640 the Shinnecock Indians conveyed to the Undertakers that part of Southampton, extending from Canoe

Place, East; to the West bounds of the town of Easthampton, in consideration of "Sixteen coats already received and also four score bushels of Indian corn to be paid upon lawful demand by the last of September 1641, and upon further consideration "that the said English shall defend us, the said Indians, from the unjust violence of any Indians that shall illegally assail us."

By deed dated August 16th 1703, the Indians conveyed to the Trustees of the town of Southampton, in consideration of 20 pounds, the territory of Southampton which they had before sold and conveyed to them or others and the town paid them twice for the same land.

The first deed was witnessed by Abraham Pierson, minister and father of that Abraham who became the first President of Yale College, and also by six other men. The second deed was signed by 3 sachems and 32 other Indians and acknowledged before Justice John Wheeler of Easthampton. The names of Pierson and Wheeler are proof that these deeds were fairly obtained without fraud.

From the founding of the town of Southampton to this day in their relations and business with the Indians, no blot mars the banner of Southampton. In a recent romance entitled "Lords of the Soil," the founders of the towns on Eastern Long Island are represented as obtaining conveyances of their land from the Indians by the use of strong drink called "fire water." This is not only romance; it is utterly false, and disproved by the facts. Southampton at the first besought by the Indians, agreed to defend them from the illegal assaults of the hostile Indians and kept her covenant. East Hampton sheltered the Montauk remnant saved from almost entire extermination by the Narraghansetts. But for the humanity of the Eastern towns the Narraghansetts would have annihilated all the Indian tribes on Eastern Long Island. Even now the Shinnecock tribe occupy their Neck, worth a thousand times more than when the English began to clear the forest. The State has often made appropriations to maintain a school there and the tribe besought the Presbytery of Long Island for aid and rests under its sheltering wing. Give old Southampton her due—she asks no more.

THE UNITED COLONIES OF NEW ENGLAND.

May 29th 1643 the colonies of Massachusetts, Plymouth, Connecticut and New Haven with the plantations in combination with them adopted Articles of Confederation for their mutual welfare and protection. This Confederation was called "The United Colonies of New England." May 30th 1645, the town of Southampton was received in combination with the colony of Connecticut and thereby this town came in combination with the four "United Colonies of New England" and bound for their defence and they in like manner bound for her defence. The colony of Connecticut admitted to vote those outside of the Church and New Haven excluded all from voting not within the church. The Rev. Abraham Pierson their minister desired to combine with New Haven and because the majority decided for Connecticut he with many others removed from Southampton. Largeness and liberality of soul cost Southampton much in her earliest days in the loss of their first minister, a man of towering ability and pure spirit and has in all her history cost much. She was, thank God, guilty of thinking ahead of her age.

THE ENGLISH TITLE.

England conquered and absorbed the Dutch settlements in the province of New York in 1664. The Duke of York then claimed title to all Long Island and by this Governor Nichols demanded that all the Eastern towns take title by patent forthwith from him or they would be deemed to have forfeited their rights to their land and dealt with as trespassers. Protest was disregarded, resistance hopeless. At great expense the town obtained a new patent and paid quit rent to this new claimant and extortioner, which was for the second time a payment to purchase the English title. In 1675 another English Governor even more unprincipled and rapacious than the first, contended that Nichols patent did not cover the town territory and again for the third time they paid for another patent from Governor Andross. Still unsatisfied another Governor, made under like pretences a demand and they obtained from Governor Dongan a patent dated December 6th 1686, which was the fourth purchase and payment for their title to the towns territory. By their conduct Kings forfeited the regard and respect of our forefathers. Their contempt we inherit.

THE TOWN SELF-GOVERNED 1640-1664.

From the settlement of the town in 1640 to the conquest of New York from the Dutch by the English in 1664; almost a generation had gone. The founders born in old England, emigrating from New England, bound to her by ties of kindred, blood and purpose, allied for mutual defence, alike in spiritual vision, alike in aspiration for liberty; alike as pioneers in enterprise and daring; alike in the power and practice of self Government, were to all intents a part of New England. Severed therefrom they yearned the old union and associations in vain. They hated to become vassals of the Duke of York and from 1664 to 1775, for a hundred years on their altar the fire of freedom burned unquenched. In that long conflict Bridgehampton nobly bore her part. The champions of liberty and people's rights in no part of this town or county maintained their cause more heroically than the sons of Bridgehampton. The Piersons, Henry, the speaker of Assembly, and his son David, member of Assembly, sturdily stood for popular rights against the arbitrary and oppressive claims of the royal governors, and that for nearly twenty years. No honor of knighthood; no embellishment of armorial bearings can worthily tell the story of their high souled devoted patriotism.

THE TERRITORY OF BRIDGE HAMPTON.

From the flag staff to the Water Mill, the west bounds of Bridgehampton, is a little over three and a half miles and to its east bounds is a little short of two and a half miles, from the ocean to the middle line, probably its proper north line, is say four and a half miles and its whole area is about 27 square miles. The forest covers about four and a half square miles, the waters about two and a half square miles. Mecox Bay is estimated at 1,200 acres, Mill Pond at 60, Kelly's Pond at 40, Sagg Pond at 100. This is the judgment of a practical surveyor and the estimate of water in Mecox Bay assigned to Bridgehampton seems large. Still deducting all waters and forest it leaves for Bridgehampton's cultivated area 15 square miles and 9,600 acres of fertile land rarely excelled. A magnificent heritage bequeathed by the foresight of the founders of the town and village to their sons. Kelly's Pond and Mill Pond are like emerald gems set in her crown. The expanse of bay of living waters, Mill creek, Hay Ground creek, Swan and Sams creek reach their arms far inland. And farther yet Sagg and Poxabogue and Crooked Pond with gushing springs and pure streams revive life in forest and fertile field, contribute that moisture to the clouds that drop fatness. The waters are growing less and the land increasing. Hacker's Hole is plowed and gone. The potash is lessening. I think the dry land may equal 10,000 acres. More than all the enchantment of ocean inspired to greatness of soul, largeness of thought, pureness of purpose and spiritual ideals. Its magnitude spoke to the onlooker of his weakness. Its roar of wrath upbraided mans presumption. Its low dirge moan warned the wicked to forsake his way, measureless, mysterious, mighty ocean, it spoke to our fathers as it speaks to us in notes impressive and unforgotten. Its breeze was reviving, its charm enduring. Its presence in all ages begot in the dwellers on its shores adventurous endeavor and enterprise. The Greek felt its impelling power and for a thousand years held the sway of empire. The Roman heard and answered to its call and held in his compelling hand the destiny of far reaching domains. The British Isles had but just gained supremacy on the ocean when our forefathers founded Southampton. Their descendants in all generations living on its shores, have moved to the music of its majestic and mysterious call.

SAGAPONACK ALLOTTED.

The first land allotted in Sagaponack was in 1653, and was all south of Bridge Lane and Daniels Lane.* This laying out covered nearly all the land from the East Hampton bounds to Sagg Pond, and the fact that no mention is made of any resident, any dwelling house or any individual land within the bounds creates a presumption that there was none and negatives the theory that there was then any settlement. The first houses were on Bridge Lane and a wigwam and whaling station, probably near the east bounds of the allotment and possibly another near to Sagaponack may have been there. (see Town Records vol. 1 p. 98) Even the dwelling of Josiah Stanborough there in 1661, may have been a temporary rent. All the records fail to prove a settlement until about 1660 and even then that of Stanborough only. The land would be improved at first for pasture and the whaling stations first occupied would soon call for permanent residents and thus the settlements would grow. In my early days at the whaling station was a wigwam with boats near by and a stage pole raised high on which when a whale was sighted the watchman climbed and made a weft, swinging his jacket to call the crew to the shore and man the boats.* As early as 1671 Indians agree to whale at Sagaponack for Anthony Ludlam and Arthur Howell, showing there then two whaling stations. (See T R. p. 57 Vol. 2.)

MECOX AND SAGAPONACK GROW.

We know with little certainty the progress of settlement of the neighbors of Sagaponack and Mecox. The territory near the ocean was first cleared of the forest and the fields in its vicinity tilled and dwellings there reared. The location of the first church built about 1696, near the west side of Sagaponack Pond would probably be north of the then center of population to allow for the coming growth of the people. The site of the second church just east of the Esterbrook corner in 1737, would for the same reason be north of the like center. In 1842 when the present church was built the forest had been practically cleared and the clearing work closed and that site would be near the center geographically, as it is, and also of the population. These three churches stand nearly three quarters of a mile northwesterly of each other and so standing mark the divergence of the centers of Bridgehampton.

In 1686 the census of Southampton town shows the inhabitants to be christian males 389, negro men slaves 40, christian females 349, women slaves 46, total 738, Indians 153.

Howell's *History* p. 31, states that all after No 270, were inhabitants of Sagabonac and Mecox which I think is correct, and if so Bridgehampton then numbered 119 males and 103 females. Total of the two is white inhabitants 222, being a little over one-third of all in the town. There were reported two merchants and 76 soldiers and troopers in the town.

July 4, 1776 John Gelston made affidavit to a census of the people east of the Water Mill and reported it to be: males 687, females 745, total 1,432. Deducting Noyac, Sag Harbor and North Haven estimated at 212, leaves for Bridgehampton 1,220.

July 22, 1776, Hugh Gelston reported west of the Water Mill, total inhabitants 1,349, making for the whole town 1,781. That would give east of the Water Mill over that west thereof 83. In 1790 this towns population was 3,408, and was the largest in Suffolk County. In 1870 the census of this town was 6,135. That of Bridgehampton then was 1,334, that of Southampton village 943, Shinnecock, 97, Sag Harbor 1,723. The census of 1910 reports the inhabitants of the town of Southampton at 11,240.

SEATING THE CHURCH AND
TAX TO MAINTAIN IT.

The church societies in eastern Long Island were organized as congregational churches, after the New England model. The salary of the minister was paid by tax assessed, levied and collected as the town taxes were and if unpaid the chattels of the delinquent might be distrained and sold by the collector to pay the rate. The pews were free except that men were appointed to seat the attendants according to age, social or official position. The pulpit was raised at least as high as on a level with the gallery, and entered by stairs leading to it, over it was the sounding board and underneath and in the rear of the sacrament table sat the elders and deacons. In front of the table overlooking the congregation sat the magistrates. The men were seated on one side of the church and the women on the other side, the wives ranking as their husbands and the elders in the front seats, and so on down to the youngest. Even in my early days the salary was collected and paid as stated, and for over a hundred years the seats were free. In Bridgehampton church when the pews were sold to pay the ministers salary there was much opposition. One man declared he would not again go in that church and there is a tradition that he never did.

WHALING.

In 1700 the founders of the town had died. Henry Pierson was living at Sagg with five sons: David, Theophilus, John and Abraham and Josiah, two minors. Capt. Elnathan Topping was there with sons Elnathan, Steven and Sylvanus, Abraham Howell, also, brother in law of Henry Pierson. Theophilus Howell was there, a man of ability, often supervisor of the town. In Mecox was Anthony Ludlow and his son, Anthony, John Cook, son of Ellis, Lemuel and Elisha, sons of Arthur Howell, Abraham, son of Abraham Howell, Doctor Theophilus, son of Major John Howell. In each of these two places two whale boat crews could muster. And Indians often formed part of such crews. They were self-possessed and efficient and would go down fighting. Canoes first used in whaling had been superseded by the evolution of the whale boat, which was sharp at each end to override the breaking waves, lower mid ships to bring the oar near the water and as a model for a sea boat unexcelled. Six men manned the boat. The harpooner was foremost. The captain steered until the whale was struck and then he took the harpooners place to kill the whale and the harpooner steered. In my early manhood, the wigwams were standing on the beach banks in Amagansett, East Hampton and Wainscott and probably in Sagg and Mecox, in which watch was kept looking out for a whale. When one was sighted, the watch mounted the stage pole, swinging his coat as a signal and made what was called a "weft," to call the crew to man the boats. If the whale came nearer, he wefted harder. The alarm went like the cry of fire. All were excited, even school was let out. It is no vain imagination to suppose that in 1700, a whale was sighted off Sagaponack and chased by all the four boats of that and the Mecox station, that the Indian harpooner in Capt. Theophilus Howell's boat made fast to the whale and the Captain killed it after a long and bloody fight and all the four boats joined and towed the whale to the Sagaponack shore. We know that a whale was killed by that Captain and towed on that shore about that date. That whale had a memorable and a lasting history, which we now relate. In the night, a strong easterly wind and tide floated the whale some forty miles west, and by request of Theophilus Howell, owner, who had killed the whale and had a license from the Governor therefor, he to pay the twentieth part, Richard Floyd and his two sons cut up and tried out into oil, the blubber and were prosecuted for the tax on the whale. Nine men were subpoened as witnesses to go to New York to testify against him and among others, Samuel Mulford and his two sons, most of whom knew nothing of the case. Great expense needlessly made to innocent parties and the willful extortion of fees exacted that would be a shame, even in the most shameless days of modern corruption. Mulford was the man who went to England from East Hampton and temporarily obtained from the King freedom for whalers from the imposition of the tax on oil. A tax on an enterprise that should never be exacted because it took from the ocean the wealth there hidden, increased that of the community, and benefited all and injured none. In equity a premium instead of a tax would be well merited. The reader will find the whole story told in the *Documentary History of New York*. Vol 2 pages 376 and on.

BRIDGEHAMPTON GOES FOR INDEPENDENCE.

For twenty years Henry Pierson and David his son in the Assembly of Colonial New York contended for the rights of the people in a representative Legislature free from arbitrary power of despotic unprincipled royal governers. For twenty years Samuel Mulford consecutively fought the same glorious battle, Eastern Long Island was true from first to last in contention for popular rights. The heroes of liberty there mustered were outspoken and true in all the Colonial history of New York. Suffolk County counted as preeminently the star of Freedom, in every age from its first settlement up to the Revolution and was among the first to proclaim for independence in 1776. The training of her sons impelled to enlist for the great declaration and one of them was its signer. No descendant of Suffolk County ancestry need fear for her record or her fame in her colonial or revolutionary days.

BRIDGEHAMPTON IN THE REVOLUTION.

The causes that impelled the colonies to confederation and revolution are recorded in the great declaration and in history. Long Island had grievances long suffered and unfelt by inhabitants of the interior. The imposition of a tax on oil oppressed her whaling industry.

The Press Gang roved through her territory and compelled her young sailor men to serve in the British Navy just as it impressed men in the British Isles. It tore them from peaceful homes and dependent families and without preparation or warning took them on long voyages in armed vessels to far off lands. When a battleship appeared on our coast, it spread terror to our homes, young men fled to the woods to escape impressment. More fuel fed the fires of freedom on eastern Long Island than in most other localities on this continent. In Southampton every man capable of bearing arms and between the age of 16 and 60 signed the "Association" document to resist the British, dated April 25, 1775. No Torys name dishonors the record of Bridgehampton. From first to last in the great Revolution, her heart beat time to liberty and her voice was the re-echo of Lexington and Bunker Hill.

The second regiment of Suffolk County, February 10, 1776 consisted of 760 officers and privates of whom East Hampton furnished two companies, Bridgehampton and Sag Harbor jointly two, and Southampton three. I think Bridgehampton furnished at least the equivalent of three and probably more. The census of 1776 so indicates (see Howell's *History of Southampton,* p. 68-9). The organization of the militia changed so often it is hard to trace it. August 21, 1775, the 2nd battalion of Suffolk at the east had these officers (as given by Onderdonk p. 20): David Mulford 1st Col., Jonathan Hedges 2nd Col., Uriah Rogers 1st Major, George Herrick 2nd Major, John Gelston Adj., Phineas Howell 2nd Adj. The officers of the Bridgehampton companies were: 3d Co. Capt., David Pierson; 1st Lieut., Daniel Hedges; 2nd Lieut., David Sayre; En., Theophilus Pierson. 9th Co. Capt., John Sandford; 1st Lieut., Edward Topping; 2nd Lieut. Philip Howell; En., John Hildreth. 6th Co., partly Bridgehampton, Capt., Wm. Rigers; 1st Lieut., Jesse Halsey; 2nd Lieut., Henry Halsey; En., Nathan Rogers. The minute men were selected out of the militia to be ready to march immediately on orders and the artillery company were selected in the same way and both armed, organized and officered. Capt. David Pierson's company in Col. Josiah Smith's regiment numbered 11 officers and 42 privates (see Onderdonk p. 26). At a later date, probably just before the battle of Long Island, Col. Josiah Smith's regiment was reconstructed and out of twelve companies the officers were Capt. Zephaniah Rogers; 1st Lieut., Edward Topping; 2nd Lieut., Paul Jones; Sergts., Hugh Gelston, Tim Halsey, David Lupton; Corporals, Jehial Howell, Jonah Cook. Formerly I believed Col. Josiah Smith's regiment was not in the battle of Long Island. Later investigation shows that it was engaged therein. After the battle of Long Island which occurred August 27, 1776, the whole Island was subject to British control under martial law, executed by an infuriated soldiery of an obstinate and then insane King. For over seven years, practically abandoned by their countrymen, they were insulted, robbed, swindled, plundered, cheated, assaulted and beaten by irresponsible victors.*

Their sons had fled to the continent. The aged, infirm, sick, immature, defenceless and unprotected remained. A high souled race will dare to resist wrong if hope of success, however desperate, lights the way. That hope gone and nothing but abject submission left, the strongest spirit can only suffer and that suffering is the bitterest trial. A historian of Long Island (Prime p. 63 quoting Wood) writes of the British exactions: "They compelled them to do all kinds of personal services, to work at their forts, to go with teams on foraging parties, and to transport their cannon, ammunition, provision and baggage from place to place as they changed their quarters and to go and come on the order of every petty officer who had charge of the most trifling business." *** The people "had no property they could call their own of a lovable kind. The officers seized and occupied the best rooms in the houses of the inhabitants. They compelled them to furnish blankets and fuel for the soldiers and hay and grain for their horses. They took away their cattle, sheep, hogs and poultry and seized without ceremony and without compensation whatever they desired to gratify their wishes." Very large quantities of produce, hay and grain taken by the British, they gave their promise would be paid for at headquarters in New York city and the claims, therefore were sent there in expectation of payment, and payment was delayed until November 25, 1783 when New York City was evacuated and the British fleet sailed with bills never paid.

By an act of the legislature of the State of New York passed May 6, 1784, a tax of $100,000 was imposed on the Southern district and $37,000 of which was assigned to Long Island as a compensation to the other parts of the state for not having been in a condition to take an active part in the war against the enemy. What had been their misfortune was interpreted as a crime. It is difficult to find in the whole course of human legislation a grosser violation of public law and inevitable principles of justice.

THE WAR OF 1812.

The British fleet in Gardiner's Bay blocked the entrance to Long Island Sound, as in the Revolution. The garrison at Sag Harbor took many men from Bridgehampton. When news came that the British fleet was in Gardiner's Bay Gen. Abraham Rose requested those assembled for worship on the Sabbath to remain after service, and from the church door addressed them urging that they volunteer in defence of their country to which the patriotic response was unanimous. In that garrison from here were Captain David Hedges, Levi Howell and a commission and both were afterwards colonels. Rufus Rose was surgeon, Wm. L. Jones, musician, Jared Hedges a soldier, Rodney Parker a privateersman. Ellis Squires, Elisha Halsey and David Topping are reported as in the garrison.

BRIDGE HAMPTON IN THE CIVIL WAR.

The record of Bridgehampton in the war for the restoration of the Union is magnificent. The resolve of the people for union was overwhelming. The list of her sons who fought for the flag shows ninety four. Col. Edwin Rose, a graduate of the West Point school was for a time, until disabled by failing health, Col. of the 81st N.Y. Volunteers. He had been long a Justice of the Peace, sometimes Supervisor of the town and member of Assembly in 1848-9. An examination of the record would show that this village furnished officers sufficient to supply a regiment. Bridgehampton's contributions to relieve the sick, wounded and disabled soldiers in the war, were munificent. Of the men from here in the war 19 were killed in battle or died in service or from cause incurred therein.

LAWSUITS.

The Pioneer self-reliant is a dominating individual, resolute in defending his rights; slow to abandon a position once taken; persevering in conflict once begun. This inheritance from the fathers for generations descended to their sons. Their noted law suits between noted personalities illustrate these traits of character. Go back about 100 years and you find on record a famous case entitled "Pierson agst Post." The facts connected with it were these; Jesse Pierson, son of Capt. David, coming from Amagansett, saw a fox run and hide down an unused well near Peters Pond and killed and took the fox. Lodowick Post and a company with him were in pursuit and chasing the fox and saw Jesse with it and claimed it as theirs, while Jesse persisted in his claim. Capt. Pierson said his son Jesse should have the fox and Capt. Post said the same of his son Lodowick and hence the law suit contested and appealed to the highest court in the State which decided that Post had not got the possession of the fox when Pierson killed it and that he had no property in it as against Pierson until he had reduced it into his own possession. This became the leading case often cited because it established; and I think, for the first time, by the court of last resort in the State, that to give an individual right in wild animals, the claimant must capture them. To the public the decision was worth its cost. To the parties who each expended over a thousand pounds, the fox cost very dear.

Some sixty years have gone since the action called the Sagg Mill case was tried at Riverhead before a supreme court or circuit court judge, involving principles that affected substantial interest in titles to land and engrossing curiosity of the whole community. Hiram Sandford and others bought a windmill at Bullshead and for their convenience and that of their neighbors, removed and set it on an old mill site in the highway at Sagg, opposite the homestead of Paul Topping, where Elisha O. Hedges now resides. Topping brought action of ejectment to recover the mill as a fixture on his property, claiming title to the land as subject only to the travel right of the people. The mill owners claimed that all the land in highways were subject only to the same right of travel, the property of the proprietors of the town, who still had title therein. They urged in defence that the church of 1737 near Esterbrooks corner was partly in the highway. That the highways were grazed by cattle and sheep kept by a shepherd, as was a custom in very early days. The plaintiff lawyers claimed that in the original allotments of land the lots were bounded by highways and that the same boundaries were given in conveyance by deed generally and the legal effect thereof was to convey the title to the center of the highway, subject only to the right of travel. The court ruled for the contention of the plaintiff and that for all time settled the question that no obstruction could be legally put opposite the owner of land next the highway.

EDUCATION.

Bridgehamptoners born of English blood whose founders emigrated from Massachusetts, would be false to her traditions if she failed to educate her sons. Away back in Revolutionary days, Joseph Gibbs, called "old master Gibbs" taught school in Sagg. In 1775 he resided in Sag Harbor on premises next north of the house of Lemuel Reeves, later owned by Henry A. Reeves, his son. Ministers Woolworth and Francis taught a select school to scholars studying the classics and higher mathematics. Later citizens of Bridgehampton bought land near the house of Samuel L. Halsey, decd., and west thereof, built a school house thereon where for many years a select school was taught. Later still in 1859 an Academy was built whose history has been written by Mrs. Emily C. Hedges and published in the Bridgehampton News of April 19th, 1910. Eighty years ago Bridgehampton abounded in school teachers. Three teachers from there kept school in my early boyhood at Wainscott: John Cooper, Josiah White and Thomas Rose my instructors.

LEGISLATORS AND LAWYERS.

In the Sagg cemetery lie the bodies of five members of Assembly. Henry Pierson, at one time speaker of the House; his son David; Deacon David Hedges; Doctor Nathaniel Topping and David Pierson, son of Jesse and grandson of Capt. David. In the cemetery near the Presbyterian Church repose the bodies of Abraham T. Rose and Hugh Halsey, both lawyers and judges of the County Court; both presidential electors. The body of Gen. Abraham Rose was buried in the Hay Ground cemetery. He was an elector and voted for President Harrison in 1840. Halsey voted for Polk in 1844 and Abraham T. Rose for Gen. Taylor in 1848. The New York civil list mistakenly credits Gen. Rose to St. Lawrence County instead of Suffolk. Jeremiah Halsey, brother of Hugh, left here in Revolutionary days and became a noted lawyer in Stonington, Connecticut. Job Pierson went from Sagg nearly a century ago and became Surrogate of Rensselaer County, N.Y., member of Congress and eminent lawyer. Robert E. Topping of Sagg became in New York City an honored member of the bar and lawyer of good repute. The legislators and lawyers of Bridgehampton, of whom Nathan Sandford as chancellor of this State and senator of the United States was perhaps most distinguished, have been men of honor and a credit to our village and our country.*

DOCTORS.

There is a mention in the town record of a doctor Terbell, I think, but only once, whom I cannot place. In the census of 1776, Doctor Benj. Chapin, Henry White, and Stephen Halsey are named. Samuel H. Rose was then not of age to be an M.D. Chapin fled to Connecticut after the battle of Long Island. Halsey and Rose were surgeons in the Revolutionary army and when the war closed removed to Bridgehampton and for many years practiced their profession. Rufus Rose, brother of Samuel, and younger, practiced medicine here many years, residing at Hay Ground where his body was buried. He was surgeon in the garrison at Sag Harbor in the war of 1812. Dr. Nathaniel Topping of Sagg has been named as a legislator. In the cemetery adjoining the Presbyterian church were buried the bodies of Stephen Halsey and Samuel H. Rose doctors, and also of the same profession as that of Charles E. Halsey, son of Judge Hugh, who was surgeon in the Civil War, and that of Levi D. Wright, M.D., practitioner nearly fifty years, and his son, Nathan H.; also of John L. Gardiner, M.D., like practitioner over half a century, and his father, David Gardiner M.D., and James Rogers M.D., and Samuel H. Rose M.D., son of Hon. A.T. Rose, David Arson Hedges, M.D. son of David and grandson of Capt. David, ten doctors in this one cemetery.

MINISTERS.

The story of the ministers of Bridgehampton has heretofore been recorded in the history. The long and arduous labors of Ebenezer White for over half a century; the devotion of James Brown; the learning and logic of Aaron Woolworth; the spiritual exaltation of Amzi Francis; the philosophic expositions of Cornelius H. Edgar; the pathetic appeals of David M. Miller, loved and early lost, all live on the historic page. William H. Lester went from Bridgehampton more than a half century past and now lives in West Alexandria, venerable for age, star of spiritual light revered, beloved, and blessing to a far away Church. Of them all it may truly be said:

> *"He lives in morning's wave of splendor*
> *He lives in evening's pensive gloom,*
> *He lives in memories sweet and tender.*
> *Where roses burn, where violets dream;*
> *His image fills all sacred places—-*
> *A shape that time can never dim;*
> *In life he hallowed all the graces,*
> *And dead, all graces hallow him.*

THE METHODIST CHURCH.

The first Methodist Church in Bridgehampton built in 1820, stood just north of the corner of Rev. Amzi Francis land, and was sold July 3rd, 1833, and became the study of Mr. Francis when removed. That year a new and more commodious church was built on a lot between the premises of the late David Hallock and John Hull, decd., who purchased the church site and in 1870 the same church was removed to its present site. St.Ann's Episcopal Church now stands on the John Hull premises, a part of which formed a part of the former site of the Methodist Church.

A picture of the conditions of the common people; how they lived, what was their food and clothing, what their thoughts, their manners, their education, their character, almost ninety years ago, may be interesting and instructive. The pioneer must be hardy, self-reliant, inventive, patient, quick to think and act. His resolutions must be adamant, his forethought incessant; his industry untiring. A weakling is no pioneer. Our forefathers were the pioneers and their descendants strong in their personality; aggressive in training; persistent in opinion; undaunted in danger; unyielding in opposing oppression, made of the stuff that founded States. They could contend in lawsuits among themselves as individuals. When their rights as a community were invaded they united in resistance as one man. These grand old heroes lived as the common people in the most plain and frugal way. Their food was modestly prepared from corn as samp, hominy, hasty pudding, Indian loaf, and Johnny cake. They ate rye bread and seldom, except on extra occasions, wheat bread. Their clothing was from the wool and flax they raised, spun, wove and knit. Their hats in summer were straw they braided in winter the caps they wore were made of the furs of the animals they shot. Their shoes and boots were made at home of the hides of cattle they raised. The harness the farmer used he made himself. The yoke of his oxen he worked out except the ring and bolt that held it. To this generation it would be an astonishing lesson to learn how self supporting his grand father was, and how little he bought and sold.

In physical stamina, sharp eyesight, strong teeth, heart and lung power, this generation is inferior, although more highly organized, more advanced in literary and scientific acquirement and social adjustment.

TEMPERANCE AND MORAL.

Intemperance and war are the giant demoralizers of nations. When Woolworth in 1787 was ordained over the church in Bridgehampton its membership had dwindled to 33, in all of which there were only 11 males, (see Primes History p. 207) although the state of morals was not lower there than elsewhere and the Sabbath was observed not less than in other places. Philanthropists throughout Suffolk County ardently sought reformation, by the institution of societies in the county and villages about 1811. Bridgehampton in 1817, March 31, organized such a society. Stephen Halsey, M.D., was moderator and Levi Hedges was chosen president, Stephen Halsey vice president, Dr. Samuel H. Rose treasurer, Stephen Rose secretary, Abraham Topping, Caleb Pierson, Jesse Woodruff and Jacob Halsey, standing committee; sub committee, to solicit additional members. A copy of these proceedings and of the constitution of the society were found in the desk of Deacon Stephen Rose by his daughter Maria. The constitution is a marvel of forcible, laconic and classic expressions worthy of Woolworth and Beecher whose marks seem to be read therein.

The friends of temperance and morality are often discouraged by adverse public sentiment. Historical review of the past general excess in strong drink, when the whole community, young and old, laity and clergy, habitually indulged, would prove that reformation has progressed. It would prove more, it would prove that the effort to moderate and regulate drinking is a failure. My long life and experience enable me to attest as a witness that drunkenness in the past far exceeded that of the present. That centuries of attempt to regulate and moderate do not regulate. That total abstinence from intoxicants as a beverage is the only safe ground. All this false cry of "prohibition don't prohibit" is as an epigram, a self evident lie. An abstainer does abstain. A Prohibitionist does prohibit himself. A drinker drinks and is no abstainer and no prohibitionist. He can say that of himself and he cannot say it of me or of any other than of one like himself.

THE LAST WORD

of an address should be no trivial thought. When the founders of this town went down to their graves, all that they had done for self was buried with the sod that covered their bodies. All that they had done to benefit and bless their fellow men lived in the lives of their descendants and could never die. By the same immutable, universal law, when we go down all that we have done for self will be shut down by the coffin lid to rise no more. All that we have done to establish right and destroy wrong, to promote virtue and prohibit vice, to exalt freedom and crush the tyrant, to enlarge joy and lessen woe, to extend intelligence and expel superstition will live an eternal life surviving all changes, all disaster, all storm. To be good and do good is the ideal revealed of Him who is over the universe, the King eternal, immortal, invisible.

NOTES

---

*See Page 335

In a memorandum of July 7, 1639 it was agreed upon between James Farrett, agent and Edward Howell, John Gosmer, Edmund Farrington, Daniel Howe, Thomas Halsey, Edward Needham, Allen Breed, Thomas Sayre, Henry Walton, George Wells, (Welby) William Harker, Job Sayre. That whereupon it is agreed upon in a covenant passed between us touching the extent of a plantation in Long Island that the aforesaid Edward Howell and his co-partners shall enjoy eight miles square of land or so much as the said eight miles shall contain and that now lie in the bounds being laid out and agreed upon. It is to begin at a place westward from Shinnecock entitled the name of the place where the Indians draw over their canoes out of the North Bay over to the South Side of the Island and from there to run along that neck of land eastward the whole breadth between the bays aforesaid to the easterly end of an island or neck of land lying over against the Island commonly known by the name of Mr. Farrett's Island. (Shelter Island) To enjoy all and every part thereof according and as expressed in our agreement elsewhere with that island or neck lying over against Mr. Farrett's Island (meaning North Haven) formerly expressed.

James Farrett,

Thomas Dexter and Richard Walker, Witnesses.

These witnesses were both residents and large land holders in Lynn, Massachusetts. (Vid. *History of Lynn* by Newhall p. 172) and Dexter was the purchaser of Nahant.

---

*See Page 340

Bayles *History of Suffolk County* states: "after their expulsion from Cow Bay, some time during the month of June, they commenced the settlement of Southampton," page 305. Of Southold he says: "The first settlement of town was made in September 1640" p. 360.

Munsells *History of Suffolk County* reads: "There can no longer be any doubt that Southampton was settled in June, 1640, see Article Southold p 9. And the deeds Farrett to Jackson and Jackson to Weatherbee are spoken of as misdated in 1639 and should be 1640.

Abiel Holmes, father of Oliver Wendell Holmes, an accurate Historian wrote the "Annals of America" and therein noted the expulsion from Cow Bay and states "the adventurers now removed to the east end of the island," Vol. 1, p. 258 and quotes as authority Winthrops *Journal.*

Ogilbys *History of America* was printed in London in 1671 when living men knew the facts, on page 61 it states "About the year 1640 by a fresh supply of people that settled on Long Island was there erected the twenty-third town called Southampton, by the Indians Agawam, which gives a priority as a town in number over Southold and the same priority is given in Edward Johnson's "Wonder Working Providence" (see chapter 18 of the planting of Long Island). And in Lechfords "Plain Dealing or News from New England" p. 101, a like record.

In Brodheads *History of New York,* the careful and capable Historian writes of the expulsion as leading "to the immediate settlement of the town of Southampton" Vol. 1 p. 300.

The vessel was bought "for the use of the plantation" and made three voyages there in the 1st. 4th. and 8th. months. The expulsion voyage counted nothing, three voyages must be made in 1640 and at least two before the December voyage. It is probable the vessel was too small to convey all the emigrants at once and that some came on the voyages before that in December. Such a presumption seems fair and fits all the conditions and all contemporary records of the settlement of the town.

Irrelevant testimony, side issues, different tests of settlement by Historians, confusion of dates by reason of change from old to new style, and other causes have multiplied such confusion on the question of priority of the settlement of the towns of Southampton and Southold, that a clearing of these matters would lengthen this address into a monotonous and dreary length that would be intolerable. And yet a note clarifying the subject would not only be admissible but valuable and therefore this explanation. The actual occupation by settlers and owners of lands of a town is a settlement of a town then and thereafter continued and just that was the way the settlement of Southampton began by the men of the Lynn expedition in June, 1640, who were acting in the name and by authority of all the original proprietors and founders of the town. Their act was the act of all and their settlement began the settlement of all of the town. By the terms of their deed they could settle anywhere on Long Island and by the same terms no others could begin to settle until after they had located their eight miles square. We start now in no fog. There might be a purchase from the Indians, and even a church organized elsewhere, before a settlement or occupation of land, which the purchaser might buy not to settle but to sell. Now Southold organized her church in New Haven with settlers not in Southold but in New Haven where the church was. Southampton organized her church in Lynn, and, before that, had settled in Southampton, occupying her territory and therefore these were the first settlers.

Silas Wood dates the settlement of Long Island Towns from the date of purchase of the Indians (see Woods *History of Long Island* page 13.)

Prime dates the settlement from the organizations of the church (see Primes *History of Long Island* p. 64.) Both historians differ, both give priority to Southold and both are wrong and both confusing.

Benjamin F. Thompson's *History,* 1st edition, gave priority to Southold, one vol. *History.* In his 2nd edition, 2 vols. he gave no such priority, yet the Southold claimant cites his 1st vol. as authority and made unauthorized more confusion. In his 2nd. edition he cited Winthrops *Journal* and therefore witnessed the priority of Southampton. (see vol 1 p. 32.) In a *History of Long Island* published in 1905 by the Lewis publishing Co., begun by Ross and completed in 3 vols. by Wm. S. Pelletreau, Southampton is stated to be settled by the men of the expedition on or about June 12, 1640 (see page 287 Vol. 2.) giving priority to Southampton.

Farretts deed to Jackson, a carpenter, is dated August 15, 1640. Four months afterward Jackson conveyed to Witherbee and Witherbee to Goodyear by deed dated October 22, 1640. So that between August 15th and October 22nd, in 68 days, a house was built and the house and land had been sold three times and last to a merchant and probable speculator in New Haven, and so far as appears not one of these parties ever intended to settle in Southold and yet this is claimed as evidence of a priority of Southold before a Southampton settlement. Nor did the authorities in New Haven acknowledge the rights of the grantees of Sunderland and Jackson as prior to their grant and right so far as is shown, but rather the reverse.

The constable who at that time was the chief officer in the early *History of Long Island* towns, was not chosen by the freemen of Southold but appointed by the New Haven authorities. See Atwaters *History of New Haven* p. 179.

More than twenty years ago I examined this question and was then convinced that Southampton had priority of settlement. All after examination has confirmed that conviction.

The New Haven authorities with a firm grip held their deed to the territory of Southold and did not release it to the Southold equitable owners for some nine years. They wished to bring that colony under their form of government by the church members excluding all others. A majority of the people there desired to combine with the colony of Connecticut as finally they did after a contest like that in Southampton. The historians and antiquarians of Southold have lamented the loss of a supposed first volume of their records as irreparable. As they were kept in subjection by the New Haven authorities who appointed their constable, their only officer and as the people were not allowed in their first years to choose any officials there could be no records of town meetings and little to record except the maps or plots of land drawn and allotted and they probably were kept in loose paper rolls. Neither Howell, Pelletreau, Tooker nor myself believe there ever was a lost volume of their early records because they had no town meeting proceedings to record and as far as appears no requirement for such a supposed lost book—Some of these rolls or maps may have been worn out, defaced or lost and that seems to be all that could be lost.

---

*See Page 344

The line between East Hampton and Southampton Town runs from the ocean North, and on the West sides of the homestead formerly of my father and later of Herman Strong to the country road and then jogs East some 40 rods and then runs straight just West of the foot of Sag Harbor dock which is in East Hampton. The jog can be explained thus: When the Sagaponac allottment was made in 1653, East Hampton had encroached on Southampton territory by allotments to individuals and West of the true line about 100 rods at the ocean and up to and North of Daniels Lane and probably more or less to the country road. When I first remember, 86 years ago, Jesse Strong owned 6 acres West of the line and South of Daniels Lane, West of him James Strong owned a 6 acre lot, next to that my father owned a lot called "Chatfields Close" of 24 acres and south of that Bethuel and James Edwards owned lots and had access thereto by a road fenced. Then North of Daniels Lane and opposite "Chatfields Close" my father owned a lot of 14 acres called "Leeks Lot" and East of that and West of said line Elishas Lot of 11 acres, now John Hands corner lot, and North of that a lot of 10 acres called the Barn Lot, and North of that John S. Osborn owned a lot of 10 acres on the corner of the line highway and "Hedge's Lane", as the rough plot of all these lots shows. All these were encroachments over the Southampton line, and as Chatfield and Lee were East Hampton men the encroachment seems both proved and confirmed, and explains the contention about the line, and the jog at the country road was an equivalent for the jog at the South of it, given up to the East Hampton men to whom, by mistake, it was allotted, and it explains all the entries in the *Southampton Town Records* of the trial at Hartford against Chatfield, and the Indians testimony as to the line of Shinnecock Tribe. See *Town Records* Vol. 1, Pages 98, 114. Vol. 2. Pages 3 and 4, 134, 135, 136, 182, 187, 212, 194.

The boundary line between the Towns of East and South Hampton was in dispute from 1660 until its final settlement in 1695. Originally it was a straight line as is proved by the decision of the court in Hartford in May 1661, recorded in the *Colonial records of Connecticut* on page 367, which reads thus:"It is agreed between Capt. Topping, Mr. Halsey, Mr. Stanborough and John Cooper, in behalf of all of Southampton unsatisfied about their bounds, and Mr. Baker, and Mr. Mulford in behalf of ye town of East Hampton, that the bounds between the two Plantations shall forever be and remain at the stake set down by Capt. Howe an hundred pole Eastward from a little pond, the said state being two miles or thereabouts from the East side of a great pond commonly called Sagaponack and so to run from the South Sea to the stake and so over the Island by a straight line to ye Eastward end of Hog Neck. According to the true, intent and purpose of what is expressed in the grant and deed subscribed and allowed by Mr. James Farrett, agent for the Right Noble Earl of Sterling. It is further to be understood that what agreement is here made doth no way intrench upon any of the rights, privileges or immunities conferred upon Southampton by their patent purchased of the aforesaid James Farrett &c.

When in 1663 the Sagaponac allottment was made the Town of East Hampton had previously alloted as part of their territory land west of the true line to persons of their town as far as about 100 rods and up to the little pond mentioned in the decision of the court at Hartford. The encroaching allotments of East Hampton probably somewhat cleared and fenced and improved were enhanced in value thereby. It would be unneighborly and unjust to take them from East Hampton and get for nothing this enhanced value. Therefor they were left as they were. The Sagaponac allotment began near where the encroachments ended at lot No. 1. (24 acres to the wigwam and pond near the extent of the town bounds toward East Hampton and to be laid out to them yt they shall belong to (see Southampton Town Records Vol. I, Page 98.) Lot No. 3 of 7 acres was on the East side of Sagaponac Pond, which is, I think, Fairfield Pond. From the west side of that pond to the east side of Sagaponac Pond was 22 allotments and about 240 to 250 rods, and including lots from No. 4 to 25. I think the little pond near the extent of the Eastern Town bound is a little pond in the lot of Bethuel and James Edwards, near the ocean where the cows pastured and drank in my early days, about 100 rods west of the line between the towns. The 6 acre lots of Jesse and James Strong were west of the line and west of them were the lots of Bethuel and James Edwards and the Chatfields Close of Zephaniah Hedges. All these were encroachments South of Daniels Lane. North of that Lane were encroachments of the lots of Zephaniah Hedges, in my youth called Leeks Lot, Elishas Lot, Barn Lot and the lot of John S. Osborn, bounded north by Hedges Lane, and probably there were encroachments still farther north. Chatfield's close was probably the close of an ancestor of Lawyer H.H. Chatfield, of Bridgehampton, and Leeks lot the close of a Leek. These were names of East Hampton men and unknown in Southampton. In the settlement of the line between the towns, June 25, 1695, although the line south of the country road was unchanged there was a jog eastward 35 poles allowed to Southampton in compensation of the encroachments which were made and retained in the ownership of the East Hampton men within Southampton bounds. See Southampton Records Vol. 2. p 134, 5 and 6. This is the explanation of the jog in the line at the country road and of the many entries in the Town records about it.

The Indian tribes had exact boundary lines. One tribe could convey only its own territory. In the controversy between Southold which claimed meadows South of Peconic Bay, claimed also by Southampton, the latter won because they had the Shinnecock Title in whose territory were these meadows. See *Southampton Town record* Vol. 2 p. 110, 111, 112. The testimony of Indians as to the line and bounds of the towns noted often in the town records is thus explained. That part of Sag Harbor lying in East Hampton bounds went by the Indian name of Wegwaganuck or Wigwaganuck. At the foot of Sleight's Hill was an Indian village called Wequae-wan-auke meaning "land or place at the end of the hill." Tradition says that Indian wigwams stood near Round Pond long after East and Southampton were settled. The boundary line of the Montauk and Shinnecock tribes was the boundary of the East and Southampton towns. The Indians of the village at Sag Harbor knew their bounds and where Daniel Howe should place his stake near the ocean. Their testimony did not agree with that of the Indian and squaw sent by the Shinnecock Sachem to the Town meeting June 19, 1657, who testified that the Shinnecock Indians bounds "went to Georgica or Wainscott at the least or there-abouts" See *Southampton Records* Vol 1, p 114.

---

*See Page 349

Following is a list of Refugees from Bridgehampton who fled to Connecticut before and chiefly after the battle of Long Island, August 26, 1776. Daniel Albertson, Hezekiah Bower, Stonington and East Haddam; Dr. Benjamin Chapin, E. Haddam; Margaret Chapin, Benjamin Chappel, Silas Cooper, Stonington; Jonathan Cook, Saybrook; Major Silas Cook, Jeremiah Gardiner, Maltby Gelston, E. Haddam; David Gelston, John Gelston, William Gelston, Thomas Gelston, Daniel Haines, David Haines, Elias Halsey, Henry Halsey, killed at New London and named on the Groton monument; Jeremiah Halsey, lawyer, Stonington; John Halsey, Josiah Halsey, Phebe Halsey, widow; Theophilus Halsey, Timothy Halsey, William Halsey, David Hand, Gideon Hand, Widow Hedges, Daniel Hedges, Co. Jonathan Hedges, Jonathan Hedges, Jr., Steven Hedges, Joshua Hildreth, Stonington; Daniel Hopping, Daniel Howell, Saybrook; David Howell, Edward Howell, Saybrook, Hartford and Colebrook; Elias Howell, Ezekial Howell, Joshua Howell, Isaac Howell, Philip Howell, Recompence Howell, Ryall Howell, Walter Howell, and son; Matthew Jagger, Anthony Ludlow, Stonington, William Ludlow, Duncan McCCullum, Daniel Moore, Henry Moore, Hannah Moore, Andrew Morehouse, William Nicholson, Silas Norris, Silas Jessup, Capt. David Pierson, E. Haddam; Elias Pierson, E. Haddam; Lemuel Pierson, E. Haddam; Lemuel Pierson, Jr., E. Haddam; Lemuel Pierson 3d, E. Haddam; Matthew Pierson, E. Haddam; Sylvanus Pierson, Stonington; Theophilus Pierson, Zebulon Pierson, Zachariah Pierson, Elias Post, Saybrook; Jeremiah Post, Saybrook; Nathan Post, Saybrook; Widow Rogers, Sarah Rogers, Capt. Jeremiah Rogers, Killingworth; Jarvis Rogers, John Rogers, Jonathan Rogers, Joshua Rogers, New London; Nathaniel Rogers, Capt. Zachariah Rogers; Capt. William Rogers, Abraham Rose, Ezekiel Sandford, E. Haddam; Abraham Sayre, Benjamin Sayre, Benjamin Sayre, Jr., E. Haddam; David Sayre, Stonington and East Haddam; James Sayre, Lewis Stanborough, Daniel Topping, Charles Topping, Stonington, Henry Topping, Stonington; Joseph Topping, Saybrook and Middletown; Paul Topping, Stonington; Capt. Stephen Topping, Saybrook; Capt. Thomas Topping, Saybrook; Edward Wick, Guilford; Daniel Woodruff, E. Haddam; Dr. Henry White, Stonington; Benjamin White, David White, John White, Silas White.

List of Bridgehampton refugees who served in the army on Long

Island and after that served in the army in Connecticut: Henry Brown, James Foster, David Hand, Jr., Jonathan Hand, Joseph Hand, Abraham Pierson, Jonathan Russell, David Sandford, John Sandford, probably Capt.; David Smith, Christopher Vail twice on the pension list.

---

*See Page 352

Paternal ties seem to forbid the author of this address to make mention of one who was accomplished, bright, genial and endeared to the people of Bridge Hampton. Edwin Hedges, son of Judge Henry P. Hedges, was born Feb. 12, 1847, graduated from Yale College in the class of 1869. He married Miss Emily, daughter of Richard Cook, was engaged in the practice of law with every prospect of a long, happy and useful life when stricken by a fatal malady, he came to an untimely death on May 8, 1881, mourned by a devoted wife, loving parents and a host of friends. It can be truly said, he was a man of strict integrity, the soul of honor and left the good heritage of a character without a stain. This gentle tribute is here offered to the memory of one with whom I was associated in youth and early manhood, and whom I can proudly claim as a friend.   G. CLARENCE TOPPING.

---

*See Article "Temperance and Moral" p 355

The constitution of the moral society in Bridgehampton was as follows: When impiety and vice prevail to an alarming degree, it highly becomes those who regard the welfare of the community to make all reasonable and provident exertions to arrest their progress and promote reformation.

Impressed with this conviction we the subscribers, inhabitants of the parish of Bridgehampton, have unanimously agreed to form ourselves into a society to be denominated the Bridgehampton Moral Society, for the suppression of vice and the promotion of virtue. In doing this we rely on the blessing of God for success and hope for the encouragement and co-operation of our fellow citizens.

And that no mistake may arise relative to the particular vices against which we mean to bear special testimony we unanimously agree that both in our own conduct and that of our families we will pay a sacred regard to the following things.

I. That we will avoid slander and not wantonly defame the character of our neighbors but be tender of the reputation and good name of all with whom we are connected.

II. That we will at all times by our example and on proper occasions by friendly admonition discountenance profane language of every description.

III. That we will always be upon our guard in the use of ardent spirits, will not make a common practice of using them in our social visits and will in all prudent ways use our influence to prevent the excessive use of them in others; in short we resolve to direct our exertions against the horrible vice of intemperance believing it to be of all others the most fruitful source of vice and calamity.

IV. We also engage to pay a conscientious regard to the holy Sabbath not only avoiding those things which are contrary to the Divine Law but by performing the appropriate duties of the day and to use our influence to prevent the profanation of it by others.

V. We promise to aid and encourage the civil magistrate in administering the laws of the state against immoralities.

And to assist us in carrying the objects of this Institution into effect we unanimously agree to the following "Articles of Association."

I. The society shall meet semi-annually at such place as they may appoint and oftener as occasion may require at the call of the president any 15 of whom shall constitute a quorum to do business.

II. The officers of the society shall be a president, vice president, secretary and treasurer who shall be chosen at every annual meeting.

III. At every stated meeting four persons shall be chosen who with the above mentioned officers shall constitute a committee to manage the concerns of the society.

IV. It shall be the duty of the committee to meet on the first Thursday of April ensuing and afterward quarterly and oftener if necessary, to exert themselves in every prudent and lawful way to suppress vice in general and especially those flagrant immoralities which have been specified above and to report their proceedings to the society at every stated meeting and the society engage to support them in all the regular measures which they may adopt and prosecute.

V. The committee shall have power to appoint such subcommittees as may be necessary to effect the designs of the institution either from their own body or from the society at large.

VI. The committee shall supply all vacancies which may happen in their board as in their sub-committees.

VII. There shall be a standing sub-committee of three persons to solicit from the friends of virtue and order, additional members.

VIII. Any person of fair moral character may become a member of this society by subscribing to this constitution. The society shall have power at any regular meeting to dismiss any member whose conduct is manifestly unfriendly to the design of the Institution. And any member wishing to withdraw from the society may do so by signifying his desire to the society.

IX. The expenses of the society shall be defrayed by the voluntary contributions of its members.

X. The secretary shall register the names of all the members and conduct the correspondence of the society and of the committee and keep a fair record of their respective proceedings.

XI. The society shall by their committee make a report of their state proceedings to the "Suffolk County Moral Society" at their annual meetings in May.

XII. These articles shall be subject to revision and may be altered at any stated meeting of the society by a vote of two thirds of the members present.

At a meeting of a respectable number of persons held by adjournment to form a Moral Society in Bridgehampton on the evening of March 31st 1817, Stephen Halsey, moderator, Levi Hedges, Clerk. A constitution was presented; amended and unanimously adopted and is as follows:

The meeting then proceeded to the choice of officers as follows: Deacon David Hedges, President; Stephen Halsey, Esq. Vice President; Dr. Samuel H. Rose, Treasurer; Stephen Rose, Secretary; Abraham Topping, Caleb Pierson, Jesse Woodruff and Jacob Halsey, committee. William Pierson, Lewis Sandford and Silas Corwith, standing sub-committee to solicit additional members. Resolved that the above proceedings, signed by the Moderator and Clerk, be published in the Suffolk County Recorder.

Stephen Halsey, Moderator,
Levi Hedges, Clerk

Selected Bibliography

―⌐∾∾∾―

THIS SECTION ORIGINATED IN 1998 with The 350th Anniversary Lecture Series of the Town of East Hampton. Dorothy King, former East Hampton Town Historian, and Tom Twomey, President of The East Hampton Library and current Town Historian, added other books to the list to provide the reader with a comprehensive bibliography on East End and Long Island history. In addition, note the list of books favored by Henry Hedges in "The Controversy Concerning The Settlement of Southampton and Southold" contained herein.

Many of the items set forth in the bibliography, can be found in The Long Island Collection at The East Hampton Library. Although virtually all of these books are out of print, many—but not all—of them can be found from time to time by the collector in rare book stores or on the Internet.

However, readers are welcome to use these books and materials for research purposes at The Long Island Collection. In these comfortable surroundings, professional and amateur historians, family genealogists, writers and journalists can use these items, without cost, to their heart's content. Librarian Diana Dayton stands by to assist with your research. Please stop by for a visit at 159 Main Street, East Hampton, or call 324-0222 for further information.

Abbott, Wilbur C. *Colonel John Scott of Long Island, 1634(?)-1696*. New Haven, Connecticut: Yale University Press, 1918.

Adams, James Truslow. *History of the Town of Southampton*. Bridgehampton, New York: Hampton Press, 1918.

―――*Memorials of Old Bridgehampton*. Bridgehampton, New York, by the author, 1916.

Andrews, Charles M. *The Colonial Period of American History.* 4 vols. New Haven, Connecticut: Yale University Press, 1934-1938.

Atwater, Edward. History of the Colony of New Haven to its Absorption into Connecticut. 2 vols. Connecticut: Journal Publishing Company, 1902.

Bailyn, Bernard. *The New England Merchants in the Seventeenth Century.* Cambridge, Massachusetts: Harvard University Press, 1955.

Bayles, Richard. *Historical and Descriptive Sketches of Suffolk County, and Its Towns, Villages, Hamlets, Scenery, Institutions and Important Enterprises; with a Historical Outline of Long Island, from Its First Settlement.* Port Jefferson, New York: Richard M. Bayles, 1874, 1873.

Becker, Lloyd. "Two Local Studies by Jeannette Edwards Rattray." *Street Magazine* II, no. 2 (1976): 39-42.

Beecher, Lyman. *Autobiography.* 2 vols. Edited by Barbara M. Cross. Cambridge, Massachusetts: Belknap Press of Harvard University Press, 1864, [c1961].

———.*A Sermon, Containing a General History of the Town of East Hampton.* Sag Harbor, New York: Alden Spooner, 1806.

Berbrich, Joan D. *Three Voices from Paumanok.* Port Washington, New York: Ira J. Friedman, Inc., 1969.

Black, Robert C. *The Younger John Winthrop.* New York: Columbia University Press, 1966.

Boughton, E. S., ed. *Historic East Hampton, Long Island; the Celebration of Its Two Hundred and Fiftieth Anniversary.* East Hampton, New York: E. S. Boughton, 1899.

Boxer, C. R. *The Dutch Seaborne Empire, 1600-1800.* New York: Knopf, 1965.

Breen, T. H. *Imagining the Past: East Hampton Histories.* Reading, Massachusetts: Addison-Wesley, 1989.

———. *Puritans and Adventurers: Change and Persistence in Early America.* New York: Oxford University Press, 1980.

Bridenbaugh, Carl. *The Colonial Craftsman.* Chicago: University of Chicago Press, 1950.

Brodhead, John Romeyn. *History of the State of New York.* 2 vols. New York: Harper & Bros., 1853-1871.

Cave, Alfred A. *The Pequot War.* Amherst, Massachusetts: University of Massachusetts Press, 1996.

Ceci, Lynn. "The Effect of European Contact and Trade on the Settlement Pattern of Indians in Coastal New York, 1524-1665: The Archaeological and Documentary Evidence." Ph.D. diss., University of New York, 1977.

Clemente, Vince, ed. "John Hall Wheelock." *Paumanok Rising.* Port Jefferson, New York: Street Press, 1981, 81-113.

———."John Hall Wheelock: Poet of Death and Honeysuckle." *Long Pond Review* (Jan. 1976). 10-18.

———."Walt Whitmen in the Hamptons." *Street Magazine* II, no. 1 (1975).

Clowes, Ernest S. *The Hurricane of 1938 on Eastern Long Island*. Bridge-hampton, New York: Hampton Press, 1939.

Cole, John N. *Away All Boats*. New York: Henry Holt and Company, 1994.

————.*Fishing Came First*. New York: Lyons & Burford, Pub., 1989.

————.*Striper*. Boston: Little, Brown and Company, 1978.

Daniels, Bruce Colin. *The Connecticut Town: Growth and Development, 1635-1790*. Middletown, Connecticut: Wesleyan University Press, 1979.

deKay, Charles. "East Hampton the Restful." *The New York Times Illustrated Magazine*. 30 October 1898: 40-43.

————."Summer Homes at East Hampton, L.I." *The Architectural Record*, XII. no.1 (Jan. 1903).21-29.

Demos, John. *Entertaining Satan: Witchcraft and the Culture of Early New England*. New York: Oxford University Press, 1982.

Dunn, Richard S. *Puritans and Yankees: the Winthrop Dynasty of New England, 1630-1717*. New York: Norton, 1962.

Duvall, Ralph G. and Jean L. Schladermundt. *History of Shelter Island, 1652-1932; with a Supplement 1932-1952*. Second Edition. Shelter Island Heights, New York, n.p., 1952.

East Hampton, New York (Town). *Journal of the Trustees of the Freeholders and Commonalty of the Town of East Hampton, 1725-1960*. 10 vols. [East Hampton:Town of East Hampton, 1926-1976].

East Hampton, New York (Town). *Records of the Town of East Hampton, Long Island, Suffolk Co., New York, with Other Historic Documents of Ancient Value*. vols. 1 and 3. Sag Harbor, New York: J. H. Hunt, Printer, 1887-1905.

Edwards, Everett Joshua and Jeannette Edwards Rattray. *"Whale Off!": The Story of American Shore Whaling*. New York: Frederick A. Stokes Company, 1932.

En Plein Air: the Art Colonies at East Hampton and Old Lyme, 1880-1930. East Hampton, New York: Guild Hall Museum, 1989.

Fernow, Berthold, (ed.). *The Records of New Amsterdam from 1653 to 1674 Anno Domini*. 7 vols. New York: Knickerbocker Press, 1897.

Flint, Martha. *Early Long Island: A Colonial Study*. New York: G. P. Putnam's Sons, 1896.

Fiske, John. *The Dutch and Quaker Colonies in America*. 2 vols. Boston: Houghton, Mifflin, 1902.

Force, Peter. *American Archives, Fourth Series: Containing a Documentary History of the English Colonies in North America, from the King's Message to Parliament, of March 7, 1774, to the Declaration of Independence by the United States*. 11 vols.Washington, D.C.: M. St. Clair Clarke and Peter Force, 1837-1853.

Foster, Stephen. *Their Solitary Way, the Puritan Social Ethic in the First Century of Settlement in New England*. New Haven, Connecticut: Yale University Press, 1971.

Fryxell, Fritiof. *Thomas Moran, Explorer in Search of Beauty*. East Hampton, N.Y.: East Hampton Free Library, 1958.

Furman, Gabriel. *Antiquities of Long Island*. New York: J.W. Bouton, 1874.

Gabriel, Ralph Henry. *The Evolution of Long Island: a Story of Land and Sea*. Port Washington, New York: I. J. Friedman, 1960, 1921.

Gardiner, Curtiss Crane. *Lion Gardiner and His Descendants*. St. Louis: A. Whipple, 1890.

Gardiner, David. *Chronicles of the Town of East Hampton, County of Suffolk, New York*. New York: [Bowne Printers], [1840, 1871].

Gardiner, John Lyon. *Gardiners of Gardiner's Island*. East Hampton, New York: Star Press, 1927.

Gardiner, Lion. "Leift Lion Gardiner, His Relation of the Pequot Warres". Chap. in *Collections of the Massachusetts Historical Society*, Vol. 3, 3rd, Series, 131-160. Cambridge, 1833.

Gardiner, Sara Diodati. *Early Memories of Gardiner's Island; (The Isle of Wight, New York)*. East Hampton, New York: East Hampton Star, 1947.

Gaynor, James M. and Nancy L. Hagedorn. *Tools: Working Wood in Eighteenth-century America*. Williamsburg, Va.: Colonial Williamsburg Foundation, 1993.

Godbeer, Richard. *The Devil's Dominion: Magic and Religion in Early New England*. New York: Cambridge University Press, 1992.

Goodman, Charlotte Margolis. *The Savage Heart*. Austin: University of Texas Press, 1990.

Hauptman, Laurence M. and James D. Wherry, eds. *The Pequots in Southern New England: The Fall and Rise of an American Indian Nation*. Norman: University of Oklahoma Press, 1990.

Heatley, Jeff, ed. *Bully!: Colonel Theodore Roosevelt, The Rough Riders & Camp Wikoff, Montauk Point, New York 1898, a Newspaper Chronicle with Roosevelt's Letters*. Montauk, New York: Montauk Historical Society; Pushcart Press, 1998.

Hedges, Henry Parsons. *A History of the Town of East-Hampton, New York: Including an Address Delivered at the Celebration of the Bi-Centennial Anniversary of Its Settlement in 1849, Introductions to the Four Printed Volumes of Its Records, with Other Historic Material, an Appendix and Genealogical Notes*. Sag Harbor, New York: John H. Hunt, Printer, 1897.

Heyman, Christine Leigh. *Commerce and Culture: The Maritime Communities of Colonial Massachusetts, 1690-1750*. New York: Norton, 1984.

Howell, George Rogers. *The Early History of Southampton, L.I., New York*. Albany: Weed, Parsons & Company, 1987.

Hummel, Charles F. "The Business of Woodworking, 1700-1840." Chap. in *Tools and Technologies: America's Wooden Age*. eds. Paul Kebabian and William Lipke, 1979.

⸺*With Hammer in Hand: The Dominy Craftsmen of East Hampton, New York*. Charlottesville, Virginia: University Press of Virginia, 1968.

Huntington, Cornelia. *Odes and Poems and Fragmentary Verses*. New York:A. Huntington, 1891.

————.*Sea-Spray:A Long Island Village*. New York: Derby & Jackson, 1857.

Innes, John H. *New Amsterdam and Its People; Studies, Social and Topographical, of the Town under Dutch and Early English Rule*. 2 vols. 1909. Reprint, Port Washington, New York, I. J. Friedman, [1969].

Innes, Stephen. *Creating the Commonwealth: The Economic Culture of Puritan New England*. New York:W.W. Norton, 1995.

Jameson, J. Franklin, ed. *Narratives of New Netherland, 1609-1664*. 1909. Reprint, n.p., Barnes & Noble, [1959].

Jennings, Francis. *The Invasion of America: Indians, Colonialism, and the Cant of Conquest*. New York: Norton, 1976, 1975.

Jones, Mary Jeanne Anderson. *Congregational Commonwealth Connecticut, 1636-1662*. Middletown, Connecticut:Wesleyan University Press, 1968.

Karlsen, Carol F. *The Devil in the Shape of a Woman:Witchcraft in Colonial New England*. New York: Norton, 1987.

Kelsey, Carleton. *Amagansett, a Pictorial History, 1680-1940*. Amagansett, New York:Amagansett Historical Association, 1986.

Kennedy, John Harold. *Thomas Dongan, Governor of New York (1682-1688)*. New York:AMS Press, 1974.

Kupperman, Karen Ordahl. *Providence Island, 1630-1641:The Other Puritan Colony*. Cambridge, Massachusetts: Cambridge University Press, 1993.

Lancaster, Clay, Robert A. M. Stern. *East Hampton's Heritage*. Second Edition. East Hampton, New York: Ladies Village Improvement Society, 1996.

Lockridge, Kenneth A. *A New England Town: The First Hundred Years: Dedham, Massachusetts, 1636-1737*. New York: Norton, 1985.

Long, Robert, ed. *Long Island Poets*. Sag Harbor, New York:The Permanent Press, 1986.

Love, William DeLoss. *The Colonial History of Hartford; Gathered from Original Sources*. [Chester, Connecticut]: Centinel Hill Press, [1974].

————.*Samson Occom and the Christian Indians of New England*. Boston: Pilgrim Press, 1899. Syracuse, New York: Syracuse University Press, 1998.

Marhoefer, Barbara. *Witches, Whales, Petticoats & Sails:Adventures and Misadventures from Three Centuries of Long Island History*. Port Washington, New York:Associated Faculty Press, 1983.

Martin, John Frederick. *Profits in the Wilderness: Entrepreneurship and the Founding of New England Towns in the Seventeenth Century*. Chapel Hill, N.C.: North Carolina Press for the Institute of Early American History and Culture,Williamsburgh,Virginia, 1991.

Mather, Frederick G. *The Refugees of 1776 from Long Island to Connecticut*. Albany: J. B. Lyon Company, 1913.

Matthiessen, Peter. *Men's Lives.* New York: Vintage Books, 1988, 1986.

Mayo, Lucinda A. "'One of Ours': The World of Jeannette Edwards Rattray." In *Long Island Women: Activists and Innovators.* ed. Natalie A. Naylor and Maureen O. Murphy. New York: Empire State Books, 1998.

McGrath, Franklin, ed. *The History of the 127th New York Volunteers, "Monitors," in the War for the Preservation of the Union—September 8th, 1862, June 30th, 1865.* n.p.: ca. 1898.

McIntyre, Ruth A. *William Pynchon; Merchant and Colonizer, 1590-1662.* n.p.: Connecticut. Valley Historical Museum, 1961.

Miller, Mary Esther Mulford. *An East Hampton Childhood.* East Hampton: Star Press, 1938.

Miller, Perry. *Errand into the Wilderness.* Cambridge, Massachusetts: Belknap Press of Harvard University Press, 1956.

———.*Nature's Nation.* Cambridge, Massachusetts: Belknap Press of Harvard University Press, 1967.

———.*The New England Mind: from Colony to Province.* Cambridge, Massachusetts: Harvard University Press, 1953.

Miller, Perry and Thomas H. Johnson, eds. *The Puritans: A Source book of Writings.* 2 vols. New York: Harper & Row, 1963.

Mowrer, Lilian T. *The Indomitable John Scott: Citizen of Long Island, 162?-1704.* New York: Farrar, 1960.

Munsell, W. W., ed. *History of Suffolk County, New York, with Illustrations, Portraits and Sketches of Prominent Families and Individuals.* New York: W. W. Munsell & Company, 1882.

New York Historical Society. *Collections of the New-York Historical Society for the Year 1809.* New York: I. Riley, 1811.

Niles, Nath. *Samson Occum. The Mohegan Indian Teacher, Preacher and Poet, with a Short Sketch of His Life.* Madison, New Jersey: [Privately printed anonymously], 1888.

Nylander, Jane C. *Our Own Snug Fireside: Images of the New England Home, 1760-1860.* New York: Knopf, 1993.

O'Callaghan, E. B., ed. *Documents Relative to the Colonial History of the State of New York.* 11 vols. Albany: Weed, Parsons and Company, 1853-1861.

———.*History of New Netherland; or, New York under the Dutch.* New York: D. Appleton, 1848.

Occum, Samson. "Account of the Montauks." In *Collections of the Massachusetts Historical Society.* 106-111. Boston: The Massachusetts Historical Society, vol. X, 1809.

Onderdonk, Henry. *Revolutionary Incidents of Suffolk and Kings Counties: With an Account of the Battle of Long Island, and the British Prisons and Prison Ships of New York.* New York: Leavitt, 1849.

Osgood, Herbert L. *The American Colonies in the Seventeenth Century.* 3 vols. Glouchester, Massachusetts: P. Smith, [1904], 1957.

Palfrey, John Gorman. *History of New England.* 5 vols. Boston: Little, Brown & Company, 1858-1890.

Pena, Elizabeth S. *Wampum Production in New Netherland and Colonial New York: The Historical and Archaeological Context*. Boston: Boston University, 1990.

Pennypacker, Morton. *General Washington's Spies on Long Island and in New York*. 2 vols. Brooklyn: The Long Island Historical Society. East Hampton, New York: East Hampton Free Library, 1939, 1948.

Phelan, Thomas Patrick. *Thomas Dongan, Colonial Governor of New York, 1683-1688*. n.p, 1933.

Pisano, Ronald G. *Long Island Landscape Painting*. 2 vols. Boston: Little, Brown, 1985, 1990.

Prince, Henry W. *Civil War Letters & Diary of Henry W. Prince, 1862-1865*, compiled by Helen Wright Prince. Riverhead, New York: Suffolk County Historical Society, 1979.

Quick, Dorothy. "Long Island Poet." *The Long Island Forum* 3, no. 8 (Aug. 1949): 165-66 and 168.

Rattray, Everett T. *The Adventures of Jeremiah Dimon*. Wainscott, New York: Pushcart Press, 1985.

————. *The South Fork, the Land and the People of Eastern Long Island*. New York: Random House, 1979.

Rattray, Jeannette Edwards. *East Hampton History, Including Genealogies of Early Families*. Garden City: Country Life Press, 1953.

————. *Montauk: Three Centuries of Romance, Sport and Adventure*. East Hampton: The Star Press, 1938.

————. *Ship Ashore!: A Record of Maritime Disasters Off Montauk and Eastern Long Island*. New York: Coward-McCann, 1955, 1962.

————. *Up and Down Main Street: An Informal History of East Hampton and Its Old Houses*. East Hampton: East Hampton Star, 1968.

Ritchie, Robert. *Captain Kidd and the War Against the Pirates*. Cambridge, Massachusetts, 1986

————. *The Duke's Province: A Study of New York Politics and Society, 1664-1691*. Chapel Hill: University of North Carolina Press, 1977.

Roosevelt, Theodore. *The Rough Riders*. New York: Scribner, 1902; reprint, Da Capo Press, 1990.

Seabury, Samuel. *Two Hundred and Seventy-five Years of East Hampton, Long Island, New York: A Historical Sketch*. East Hampton, New York: privately printed, 1926.

Seyfried, Vincent F. *The Long Island Rail Road: a Comprehensive History*. 7 vol. Garden City, N.Y.: Seyfried., 1961.

Shammas, Carole. *The Pre-industrial Consumer in England and America*. New York: Oxford University Press, 1990.

Sleight, Harry D. *Sag Harbor in Earlier Days*. Bridgehampton, New York: Hampton Press, 1930.

Stone, Gaynell. "Long Island As America: A New Look at the First Inhabitants." *Long Island Historical Journal* 1, no. 2 (Spring 1988): 159-169.

————. "Long Island Before the Europeans." In *Between Ocean and Empire: An Illustrated History of Long Island*. ed. Robert MacKay, Geoffrey L. Rossano, and Carol A.Traynor, 10-29. Northridge, Calif.: Windsor Publications, 1985.

―――. *The History & Archaeology of the Montauk*. 2d ed., rev. Stony Brook, New York: Suffolk County Archaeological Association, 1993.

―――. ed. *The Montauk Native Americans of Eastern Long Island*. East Hampton, New York: Guild Hall, 1991.

―――. ed. *The Shinnecock Indians: A Culture History*. Stony Brook, New York: Suffolk County Archaeological Association, 1983.

Stone, Gaynell and Nancy Bonvillain, eds. *Languages and Lore of the Long Island Indians*. Stony Brook, New York: Suffolk County Archaeological Association, 1980.

Strong, John A. *The Algonquian Peoples of Long Island from Earliest Times to 1700*. Interlaken, New York: Empire State Books, 1997.

Taylor, Robert Joseph. *Colonial Connecticut: A History*. Millwood, New York: KTO Press, 1979.

Thompson, Benjamin F. *History of Long Island from Its Discovery and Settlement to the Present Time*. Third Edition. New York: Robert H. Dodd, 1918.

Tooker, William Wallace. *Early Sag-Harbor Printers and Their Imprints*. Evanston, Ill., 1943.

Trelease, Allen W. *Indian Affairs in Colonial New York: The Seventeenth Century*. Ithaca, New York: Cornell University Press, 1960. Reprint, Lincoln, Nebr.: University of Nebraska Press, 1997.

Underhill, Lois Beachy. *The Woman Who Ran for President: The Many Lives of Victoria Woodhull*. Bridgehampton, New York: Bridge Works Pub.; distributed by, Lanham, Md.: National Book Network, 1995.

Van der Zee, Henri and Barbara van der Zee. *A Sweet and Alien Land: The Story of Dutch New York*. New York: Viking Press, 1978.

Van Rensselaer, Schuyler, Mrs. *History of the City of New York in the Seventeenth Century*. N.Y.: Macmillan, 1909.

Van Wyck, Frederick. *Select Patents of New York Towns*. Boston: A.A. Beauchamp, 1938.

Waard, C. de, jr., ed. *De Zeeuwsche Expeditie Naar de West onder Cornelis Evertsen den Jonge, 1672-1674, Nieuw Nederland een jaar onder Nederlandsch Bestuur.* ës-Gravenhage, M. Nijhoff, 1928.

Weeden, William B. *Economic and Social History of New England, 1620-1789*: 2 vols. n.p.: Houghton, Mifflin & Company, 1890. Reprint. N. Y. Hillary House Publishers, 1963.

Wheelock, John Hall. *Afternoon: Amagansett* Beach. New York: Dandelion Press, 1978.

―――. *The Gardener and Other Poems*. New York: Charles Scribner's Sons, 1961.

―――. *Poems Old and New.* New York: Charles Scribner's Sons, 1956.

―――. *This Blessed Earth*. New York: Charles Scribner's Sons, 1978.

―――. *What Is Poetry?* New York: Charles Scribner's Sons, 1963.

————.ed. *Editor to Author: The Letters of Maxwell E. Perkins.* New York: Charles Scribner's Sons, 1950.

Wheelock, John Hall, New York, letter to Mrs. [N. Sherrill] Foster, East Hampton, 6 Feb. 1976. [X FG 86], Long Island Collection, East Hampton Library, East Hampton, New York.

Whitaker, Epher. *History of Southold, Long Island, Its First Century.* Southold, New York: by the author, 1881.

Whitman, Walt. "From Montauk Point." *Complete Poetry and Selected Prose*, ed. James E. Miller, Jr. Boston: Houghton Mifflin Company, 1959.

————.*Leaves of Grass.* New York: W.W. Norton & Company, Inc., 1973.

Winthrop, John. *The Journal of John Winthrop, 1630-1649.* ed. Richard S. Dunn and Laetitia Yeandle. Abridged ed. Cambridge, Mass: Belknap Press of Harvard University Press, 1996.

Wood, Silas. *A Sketch of the First Settlement of the Several Towns on Long Island with Their Political Condition to the End of the American Revolution.* Brooklyn: Alden Spooner, 1828.

Woodward, Nancy Hyden. *East Hampton: A Town and Its People 1648-1992.* East Hampton, New York: Fireplace Press 1995

Zaykowski, Dorothy. *Sag Harbor: The Story of an American Beauty.* Sag Harbor, New York: Sag Harbor Historical Society, 1991.

Ziel, Ron and George H. Foster. *Steel Rails to the Sunrise.* New York: Hawthorn Books, 1965.

Index